HEALTH AS A HUMAN RIGHT

Does human rights law work? This book engages in this heated debate through a detailed analysis of thirty years of the right to health – perhaps the most complex human right – in Brazil. Are Brazilians better off three decades after the enactment of the right to health in the 1988 Constitution? Has the flurry of litigation experienced in Brazil helped or harmed the majority of the population? This book offers an in-depth analysis of these complex and controversial questions grounded on a wealth of empirical data. The book covers the history of the recognition of health as a human right in the 1988 Constitution through the Sanitary Movement's campaign and the subsequent three decades of what Ferraz calls the politics and judicialisation of health. It challenges positions of both optimists and sceptics of human rights law and will be of interest to those looking for a more nuanced analysis.

OCTÁVIO LUIZ MOTTA FERRAZ is a Reader in Transnational Law at King's College London, where he co-directs the Transnational Law Institute, and a Senior Global Fellow at Fundação Getúlio Vargas in São Paulo. He holds an LLB and MPhil in Law (University of São Paulo), an MA in Medical Ethics and Law (King's College London), where he won the Benjamin Geijsen prize and a PhD in Law (University College London), which he did under a Graduate School Scholarship. Previously, he was a senior research officer to the UN Special Rapporteur for the right to health, an Associate Professor at Warwick Law School and practiced law in São Paulo, Brazil, mostly in the fields of corporate public law and medical law. He is still a member of the Brazilian Bar and contributes regularly to the Brazilian press. He has worked as a consultant to the World Bank and NGOs on human rights, the rule of law and development issues.

CAMBRIDGE STUDIES IN LAW AND SOCIETY

Founded in 1997, Cambridge Studies in Law and Society is a hub for leading scholarship in socio-legal studies. Located at the intersection of law, the humanities and the social sciences, it publishes empirically innovative and theoretically sophisticated work on law's manifestations in everyday life: from discourses to practices and from institutions to cultures. The series editors have long-standing expertise in the interdisciplinary study of law and welcome contributions that place legal phenomena in national, comparative or international perspective. Series authors come from a range of disciplines, including anthropology, history, law, literature, political science and sociology.

A list of books in the series can be found at the back of this book.

HEALTH AS A HUMAN RIGHT

The Politics and Judicialisation of Health in Brazil

OCTÁVIO LUIZ MOTTA FERRAZ
King's College London

CAMBRIDGE
UNIVERSITY PRESS

CAMBRIDGE
UNIVERSITY PRESS

Shaftesbury Road, Cambridge CB2 8EA, United Kingdom

One Liberty Plaza, 20th Floor, New York, NY 10006, USA

477 Williamstown Road, Port Melbourne, VIC 3207, Australia

314–321, 3rd Floor, Plot 3, Splendor Forum, Jasola District Centre, New Delhi – 110025, India

103 Penang Road, #05–06/07, Visioncrest Commercial, Singapore 238467

Cambridge University Press is part of Cambridge University Press & Assessment, a department of the University of Cambridge.

We share the University's mission to contribute to society through the pursuit of education, learning and research at the highest international levels of excellence.

www.cambridge.org
Information on this title: www.cambridge.org/9781108729017

DOI: 10.1017/9781108678605

First published 2021
First paperback edition 2025

A catalogue record for this publication is available from the British Library

Library of Congress Cataloging-in-Publication data
Names: Ferraz, Octávio Luiz Motta, 1971– author.
Title: Health as a human right : the politics and judicialization of health in Brazil / Octávio Luiz Motta Ferraz.
Description: 1. | New York : Cambridge University Press, 2021. | Series: Cambridge studies in law and society | Includes bibliographical references and index.
Identifiers: LCCN 2020010198 (print) | LCCN 2020010199 (ebook) | ISBN 9781108483643 (hardback) | ISBN 9781108729017 (paperback) | ISBN 9781108678605 (ebook)
Subjects: LCSH: Right to health–Brazil. | Human rights–Brazil. | Medical care–Law and legislation–Brazil. | International law and human rights. | Public health laws, International. | Political questions and judicial power–Brazil.
Classification: LCC KHD3023.5 .F47 2021 (print) | LCC KHD3023.5 (ebook) | DDC 344.8104/1–dc23
LC record available at https://lccn.loc.gov/2020010198
LC ebook record available at https://lccn.loc.gov/2020010199

ISBN 978-1-108-48364-3 Hardback
ISBN 978-1-108-72901-7 Paperback

to Franziska, Joe, Bia and Kefa

CONTENTS

FIGURES

MAP

TABLES

PREFACE

The idea of a human right to health goes back at least to the constitution of the World Health Organization of 1946 and is now firmly established both in international and domestic laws. The International Covenant on Economic, Social and Cultural Rights, whose Article 12 recognises a 'right of everyone to the enjoyment of the highest attainable standard of health', has been ratified by 166 countries. An increasingly larger number of constitutions and other domestic laws also recognise the right to health in some form or another.[1] But does the right to health matter?

When we look at the reality of health conditions around the world, it remains appalling for a large proportion of individuals. According to the latest data from the yearly *World Health Statistics 2020*, 800 women still die every day of complications during pregnancy or childbirth, a rate of 211 per 100,000 live births, more than fifty times the rate in the most developed countries in the world. Approximately 144 million children under the age of five suffered from stunting in the world in 2019. Of the 38 million people living with HIV, 33 per cent (13 million) had no access to antiretroviral treatment (690,000 died in 2019 alone). Further, 400,000 people died of malaria, the vast majority of whom were children under the age of five, and 1.4 million people died of tuberculosis, a treatable and curable disease.[2]

Are we to conclude from this saddening state of affairs that the human right to health has been of little or no significance? Is the right to health

[1] G. Backman et al., 'Health Systems and the Right to Health: An Assessment of 194 Countries', (2008) 372 *Lancet*, 2047–2085; E. D. Kinney, B. A. Clark, 'The Right to Health: Institutional Effects of Constitutional Provisions on Health Outcomes', (2004) 37(2) *Cornell International Law Journal*, 285–355.

[2] For all data cited in this paragraph with the exception of data on HIV-AIDS, see World Health Organization, *World Health Statistics 2020*, available at https://apps.who.int/iris/bitstream/handle/10665/332070/9789240005105-eng.pdf?ua=1. For data on HIV-AIDS, see World Health Organization, 'HIV/AIDS data and statistics', available at www.who.int/hiv/data/en/. Both accessed 23 July 2020.

just another 'phantom right' that is 'systematically marginalised' alongside other social and economic rights?[3]

The effectiveness of human rights law, and law in general as a tool of progressive social change, has always been the subject of controversy. Highly visible and persistent gaps, such as the one just mentioned, between the ideal normative world of human rights law and the real world of human rights deficits has provided continuous fuel for this discussion. No one seems to seriously dispute the existence of such a discrepancy, but there is enormous variation of opinion in how it should be interpreted. Some see it as clear evidence of the failure of law, whereas others, pointing to empirical data showing actual decreases in that gap in some areas, view it in a more positive light, that is, as evidence that human rights law, despite limitations, actually works.

The debate is not academic. Human rights law is one among other potential means of advancing the moral values of dignity, freedom and equality that underpin the *moral* idea of human rights. Knowing if and how human rights law is effective is therefore immensely important for one's choice of strategies for advancing those values, especially as time and resources are not unlimited. As Kathryn Sikkink has aptly and concisely put it, 'we need to determine what works and what doesn't work', in order to 'stop doing what doesn't work and do more of what does'.[4]

This book aims to contribute to this debate through a more detailed and focused analysis than is often seen in the literature. Although it may be possible to draw some interesting insights about the effectiveness of human rights law *in general*, these insights will be necessarily limited due to inevitable and crucial variations that *specific human rights* are likely to manifest in *local contexts*. Human rights law forbidding torture, for instance, will likely have different effects in Honduras and in the United Kingdom, or in the Philippines and in Canada. Peculiar characteristics not only of the legal systems in these countries, but also of how they interact with many other political, social, economic and cultural factors will most certainly lead to different outcomes. The same is true, I suggest, of any right in the human rights law system. Thus, although the recent interest in the effectiveness of human rights law in general is

[3] P. Alston, 'Phantom Rights: The Systemic Marginalization of Economic and Social Rights', Open Global Rights, 6 August 2016.

[4] K. Sikkink, *Evidence for Hope: Making Human Rights Work in the 21st Century* (Princeton: Princeton University Press, 2017), 227.

welcome, it is important to conduct more fine-grained analysis of specific rights in local contexts if we really want to reach more robust and useful conclusions.[5]

It is in that spirit that I have delved into what is perhaps one of the most complex rights of the human rights law system, the *right to health*, and in one of the countries that has embraced that right most avidly from an early stage, Brazil. As Brazil has now undergone three decades of experience of a constitutionally recognised right to health, reinforced by the ratification of several international law treaties that include that right, it provides us with a very good case study to probe its effectiveness. Are Brazilians better off in the actual enjoyment of their moral right to health three decades after its legal recognition in the Constitution of 1988? If so, can we attribute any role in such improvements to the legal recognition of health as a human right?

The Brazilian experience is particularly interesting and relevant for testing effectiveness as it is one of the first and few countries outside the developed world to have expressly committed, through constitutional and ordinary law, to provide the whole of its large population (currently 210 million people) with health-related actions and services funded by general taxation as a 'right of everyone and a duty of the state' (art. 196 of the 1988 Constitution). It is also one of the countries where litigation grounded on the right to health (the so-called judicialisation of health) seems to have occurred more intensely, with hundreds of thousands of lawsuits having reached the Brazilian courts since the mid-1990s.

The balance of these first three decades of legal recognition of health as a human right in Brazil has been so far mixed and complex, but overall positive, or so I argue in this book. International and domestic human rights law have certainly helped to improve the profile of health in society's and government's agenda of priorities and, as a consequence, the actual health conditions of the Brazilian population. But there is still a long way to go and no guarantee that the right to health can provide the required fuel for the long journey ahead or that it is sufficiently resilient to withstand the pushbacks that are always lurking around and have increased in recent years. As I also argue, the constitutionalisation of the right to health has produced negative unintended consequences that need to be urgently addressed, namely, the appearance and growth of a type of litigation that does not advance the right to health on any plausible

[5] To cite Sikkink again: 'We must look at human rights issue by issue since it is impossible to make accurate general statements about all human rights.' Ibid., 51.

interpretation of that right, but rather distorts health policies and enhances health inequities.

The lessons that can be drawn from three decades of the right to health in Brazil are therefore neither entirely positive nor wholly negative, as many tend to claim in our age of heightened polarisation. My hope is that this book's detailed study and arguments may help to improve our understanding of the complex role of health as a human right, as well as human rights in general, in the advancement of people's well-being.

***

I started to think about the idea of health as a human right in the late 1980s due to a combination of biographical factors. During the day, I was pursuing a law degree at the University of São Paulo in the first cohort of students to study for the whole degree under the new Constitution of 1988, the 'Citizen Constitution', so nicknamed for its lavish chapter on human rights (or fundamental rights as they are called in the Constitution). Among these rights, there was of course the right to health, recognised in Articles 6 and 196 of the text. In the evening, back at my family home, my father Fernando would often complain about the significant lack of resources under which he had to carry out his work in the public hospital of the Federal University of São Paulo. As a neurosurgeon working under the newly created National Health System (SUS), he would often tell us about operations cancelled at the last minute, with the patient already in the operation theatre, for lack of some essential surgical material, medication or equipment abundantly available in the private system. He would also complain about materials of inferior quality breaking in the middle of operations, making his work much harder and putting the lives of his patients at risk. Employees of our middle-class residential block (cleaners, porters) and soon of the whole neighbourhood would often knock on our door to see if my father could help them or some relative to be admitted to his overly subscribed public hospital. Surely, I thought then, the law, that is, the new Constitution, can be used by lawyers to do something about all these cases! But I don't recall my father ever mentioning a single case of litigation in those five early years of the Constitution when I was still doing my law degree.

Things have obviously changed dramatically since then. The public health system, though still underfunded and inefficient, has improved significantly. Litigation grounded on the right to health has become a common practice. According to the latest numbers that I present and discuss in this book, more than 100,000 cases are now reaching the courts every year to claim that right. Whether and how these two relate to each other is a matter of fierce controversy that I discuss at length in this book. I regret that my father is not around any longer to witness and contribute to (as I am sure he would) my effort to shed light on this complex and controversial issue. But I feel lucky to have had him as a close interlocutor in those important formative initial years of my thinking about health as a human right.

I was also lucky enough to have encountered, often serendipitously, a large number of knowledgeable and generous people during my decade-long studies that culminated with this book. My early collaboration with pharmacologist and health economist Fabiola Sulpino Vieira, which resulted in our joint article 'The Right to Health, Scarce Resources, and Equity: Inherent Risks in the Predominant Legal Interpretation' (2009) – my very first on the topic – provided me with a solid foundation on which I built all my later work. I am grateful to Fabiola for initiating me in the complexities of public health systems and saving me from the arrogant mistakes I was bound to make had I remained isolated in the ivory tower of the legal world. I am also grateful to her for providing always timely and insightful advice on literature and data during the writing of this book.

Alicia Yamin, after reading my piece with Fabiola, gave me the first opportunity to develop my initial research further and make my findings available to a broad international audience. Her invitation, together with Siri Gloppen, for me to become a part of what I call in this book the Harvard–Bergen project – culminating with the book *Litigating Health Rights: Can Courts Bring More Justice to Health?* (2011), in which I author the Brazil chapter – was a crucial step on the path towards this book. The discussions we had during that project in Buenos Aires, Cambridge (MA) and Bergen were the ideal environment for me to test and develop my ideas. I am deeply grateful to Siri and Alicia for that opportunity, as it was during that project that I met some of the people who would become important interlocutors and collaborators and whose influence can be easily identified in the pages of this book. It was then that I met Roberto Gargarella, Varun Gauri, Dan Brinks, Bruce Wilson, Paola Bergallo, Oscar Parra-Vera, Camila Gianella, Ottar Mœstad, Lise Rakner, Ole Frithjof Norheim, Cesar Rodríguez-Garavito and Malcom Langford, all of whom, during the last decade, have proven invaluable interlocutors (and often critics), without whom my ideas would not have received the probing criticism that is so vital in any academic endeavour.

Another international network from which I benefited immensely in the development of my views was the International Social and Economic Rights Project (iSERP), led by Lucy Williams and Karl Klare from Northeastern University. I am grateful to them and all the participants for invaluable discussions in workshops in Italy and India.

Closer to home (both of them), I am indebted to several people who have contributed in different ways to the final product the readers now have in their hands. In Brazil, I have had the privilege of presenting and discussing many of the ideas, arguments and data of this book on several formal and informal occasions, with Conrado Hubner Mendes, Diogo Rosenthal Coutinho, Virgílio Afonso da Silva, Jean Paul Veiga da Rocha, Marcos Paulo Veríssimo, Oscar Vilhena Vieira, Ronaldo Porto Macedo, Diego Werneck Arguelles, Natália Pires, Fernanda Terrazas, Caio Mario Pereira Neto, Marta Arretche, Marcelo Medeiros, Teori Zavascki, Mario Schapiro, Marta Machado, Ana Luiza Chieffi, Ana Paula de Barcellos and Luciana Gross Cunha. I am particularly grateful to Marta Arretche and Marcos Paulo de Lucca Silveira for helping me organise the workshop 'Thirty Years of the Right to Health in Brazil' at the University of São Paulo in September 2018, where I learned a lot from all the participants: Lígia Bahia, Mário César Scheffer, Luis Eugenio Portela Fernandes de Souza, Carlos Octavio Ocké-Reis, Vera Lúcia Edais Pepe, Ana Luiza Chieffi, Fabiola Sulpino Vieira, Daniel Wang, Eduardo Levcovitz, Celia Maria de Almeida and Lenir Santos. For generous help with data and conversations with those who work on the front line of the Brazilian health and judicial systems, I am grateful to Alethele de Oliveira Santos, Paula Sue Facundo de Siqueira, Alberto Beltrame, Reynaldo Mapelli Jr, Luiz Duarte de Oliveira, João Pedro Gebran Neto, Gabriela Moreira de Azevedo Soares, Erik Jennings Simões and Maria Célia Delduque. For first-hand accounts by claimants who found themselves litigating the right to health on behalf of their children in rather challenging situations, I thank Lindamar Lima and Luiz Eduardo Serafim. For an invaluable opportunity to spend one week in the Secretariat of Health of the State of Bahia with access to data and staff dealing with litigation in 2015, I am grateful to Magnus Lindelow and David Oliveira de Souza from the World Bank, as well as Zaida de Melo from the Secretariat.

In the United Kingdom, I have had the incredible luck to live and work very near two leading academics on the topic of my book. I am grateful to Jeff King for several years of continuous conversations on the topic and, in particular, for his careful reading of and insightful comments on an earlier draft of what became Chapter 9 of the book. His early support of my, then, less widespread and less well-received critical view of judicialisation was an important source of encouragement. To Daniel Wang, once my research assistant and now a rising star in the field, I also owe years of conversations and comments on Chapters 5 and 9 of the book. Before moving to King's College, at Warwick University, I benefited immensely from discussions and comments from Victor Tadros, James Harrison, Matthew Clayton, Andrew Williams (the philosopher), Andrew Williams (the lawyer), Ed Page, George Meszaros, William O'Brian, Sharifah Sekalala and Abby Kendrick. For incisive comments on some of the arguments of the book presented in the London Bioethics Colloquium in 2018, I am grateful to Jonathan Montgomery, Annette Rid, John Tasioulas, James Wilson, Benedict Rumboldt and Sridhar Venkatapuram. For help with references I am grateful to Felipe Tirado. At Cambridge University Press, I thank Tom Randall, Gemma Smith and Jane Bowbrick for steering the editorial process so smoothly and Trent Hancock for superb copyediting.

Last but not least, I am grateful to several people who provided me with the environmental, material and emotional support without which this project could not have been completed. Marilia Boim, Louise Ronnest, Naima Bock, Ondrej Novotny and Sacha Lacey provided me with delicious soups and coffee at the 119 Cafe in Lower Clapton (East London), where large sections of this book were written. My mother Nancy provided essential childcare help and useful conversations in London as well as – alongside my siblings Fernanda, Carola and Fausto and their beautiful families in São Paulo and, with Dalva in Ibiúna – a warm environment during my stays in Brazil where some parts of this book were researched and written. My older children, Joe and Bia, perhaps without realising, gave me the perfect excuse to switch off from the book for a few hours and recharge my batteries in their priceless company. To my wife, Franziska, for looking after our son Kefa, Zuza, our home and our holidays – in short, for holding the fort so well during my long periods of absence while writing this book – I owe the greatest debt of all.

***

Note on the cover image: Choosing the cover image of my book was not an easy task. Long searches during the writing were fruitless until I came across the magnificent book *Mais Médicos*, by the accomplished Brazilian photographer Araquém Alcântara. Araquém travelled across Brazil to photograph the now extinct federal government programme Mais Médicos (More Doctors), which took primary care to the farthest and poorest corners of Brazil, often for the first time in history. The picture on the cover shows Cuban doctor Abel del Toro Pereza caring for a girl's broken arm inside the clinic-boat, which used to visit her village, Novo Airão, at the heart of the Amazon, once every three months. I am deeply honoured by Araquém's enthusiastic acceptance to associate his dazing picture with my work. It depicts perfectly, in my view, the ambivalence evoked by health as a human right that I describe in this book.

1

Introduction

Does the Right to Health Matter?

> Health is a right of all and a duty of the state . . .
>
> Article 196, Brazilian Constitution of 1988

What is the point of recognising health as a human right in the constitution? Does it make any difference to the actual health of the people these rights are supposed to benefit? If so, through what precise mechanisms? Can they be improved? It is of course a truism that writing things on a piece of paper, even if we call it a constitution, does not automatically change things on the ground. But whether it does change anything, and if so by how much, and how, are difficult and contentious matters over which debate has raged for a long time.

This book aims to contribute to this debate through a comprehensive and detailed investigation of these questions in the context of Brazil, perhaps the largest country in the world to expressly guarantee the right to health as a constitutional human right. Article 196 of the Brazilian Constitution of 1988 states, solemnly, that 'Health is a right of everyone and a duty of the state'. But what has this actually meant to the approximately 210 million people who live in Brazil? Has it improved the historically frail health conditions of the majority of the Brazilian population?

For a country not particularly known for taking human rights very seriously, one may be tempted to assume that the constitutionalisation of the right to health has changed little on the ground. Such a conclusion would be in line, moreover, with two widespread narratives on the status of social rights across the world.

One more radically sceptical view sees social rights as by and large incapable of producing significant social change; the other sees these rights as currently neglected by governments yet capable of being made effective by lawyers and judges through strong legal accountability, in particular, through litigation. The former questions the whole project of social transformation through rights; the latter believes in the project yet sees it as effective only when its purported guardians (lawyers and judges) take an assertive stance, forcing the recalcitrant political branches of the state into compliance.[1]

My analysis of three decades of the right to health in Brazil reveals a very different picture from both of these narratives. As this book argues, the inclusion of the right to health in the Brazilian 1988 Constitution has been far from futile. On the contrary, it has played an important role in the considerable improvements of the population's health conditions witnessed during the same period and, in this process, has helped to reduce health inequalities. Yet, as this book also shows, most of these positive effects had little (if anything) to do with the work of lawyers and judges through litigation. They were rather the result of social policies formulated and implemented by legislative and executive bodies, either out of a sense of constitutional duty or through pressure from civil society. Litigation in the field of health, in contrast, has on balance produced regressive effects, a conclusion I had already reached in my earlier work and have confirmed here based on more extensive empirical evidence. It has by and large diverted an increasingly larger amount of

[1] As representatives of the first sceptical view I have in mind are opinions such as those of Cass Sunstein, though his arguments seemed to be restricted to eastern European countries transitioning from communist regimes, C. Sunstein, 'Against Positive Rights: Why Social and Economic Rights *Don't* Belong in the New Constitutions of Post-Communist Europe', (1993) 2(1) *E. Eur. Const. Rev.*, 35–38, at 37; S. Moyn, *Not Enough: Human Rights in an Unequal World* (Cambridge, MA: Harvard University Press, 2018) and, for a shorter version, his piece 'Human Rights and the Age of Inequality', where he claims that 'the chief tools of the human rights movement … are simply not fit for use in the socio-economic domain', www.opendemocracy.net/en/openglobalrights-openpage/human-rights-and-age-of-inequality/, accessed 18 June 2019. For an excellent comprehensive review of the sceptical literature, see C. Rodríguez-Garavito, S. L. McAdams, *A Human Rights Crisis? Unpacking the Debate on the Future of the Human Rights Field*, available at https://papers.ssrn.com/sol3/papers.cfm?abstract_id=2919703, accessed 17 July 2019. The second type of view is common among supporters of social rights in the legal community, such as Phillip Alston, seeing 'a situation in which the majority of states avoids proper recognition of these rights and fails also to hold anyone to account when they are routinely ignored … even in countries whose constitutions deem economic and social rights to be justiciable the courts resist or reject proposals to implement them'. P. Alston, 'Phantom Rights: The Systemic Marginalization of Economic and Social Rights', Open Global Rights, 6 August 2016, www.openglobalrights.org/phantom-rights-systemic-marginalization-of-economic-and-social-rights/, accessed 17 June 2019. See also David Bilchitz, arguing that social rights are 'systematically marginalized across the world, *more honoured in the breach than in the observance*', D. Bilchitz, *Poverty and Fundamental Rights: The Justification and Enforcement of Socioeconomic Rights* (Oxford University Press, 2007), at 1, and Sandra Fredman, calling social rights 'the Cinderella of the … human rights corpus'. S. Fredman, *Human Rights Transformed, Positive Rights and Positive Duties* (Oxford: Oxford University Press, 2008), at 2.

the already severely limited health budget to health treatments of dubious effectiveness and priority (mostly expensive new medicines) to a minority of people who are capable to litigate.

Why do my conclusions diverge so much from those popular narratives on social rights? Is the right to health in Brazil an outlier? Am I perhaps too generous in my assessment of government compliance with the right to health in Brazil and too harsh on courts? Readers of this book will be able to judge for themselves, but I suspect that the discrepancy between my conclusions and those popular narratives has more to do with differences in the analytical framework that we apply to the question.

In my view, the effectiveness of human rights law is in great part an empirical question and, as such, requires the analysis of wide-ranging empirical data.[2] How are we to know if the right to health, or any other right for that matter, has made a difference in the lives of the people that these rights are supposed to benefit if we do not look at the facts of the real world where they live? It also requires, for the proper understanding and analysis of that data, engagement with the corresponding social policy literature of the area of the particular right in question. How can we assess if the state has complied or not with its constitutional duties without discussing the policies it has implemented (and failed to implement) in the relevant area?

Yet most of the legal commentary on these rights often proceeds without any reference, let alone systematic analysis, of empirical data and social policies. Most discussions within the legal literature relies almost exclusively on legal materials, such as international treaties, constitutions, legal doctrine and adjudicative bodies (mostly courts) decisions.[3] This may explain not only why so many legal commentators have

[2] I say 'in great part' because it is also, of course, a normative and theoretical one, in the sense that what human rights law actually require in terms of the precise content of the duties they generate is often a matter of reasonable disagreement among people. See, for a good discussion, M. M. Feeley, 'The Concept of Laws in Social Science: A Critique and Notes on an Expanded View', (1976) 10 *Law & Soc'y Rev.*, at 501.

[3] For notable exceptions, see D. S. Law, M. Versteeg, 'The Evolution and Ideology of Global Constitutionalism', (2011) 99 *California Law Review*, at 101; J. King, *Judging Social Rights*, 1st ed. (Cambridge: Cambridge University Press, 2012). For a similar argument, see R. Hirschl, E. Rosevear, 'Constitutional Law Meets Comparative Politics: Socio-Economic Rights and Political Realities', in Campbell, T., Ewing, K. D. and Tomkins, A. (eds.), *The Legal Protection of Human Rights: Sceptical Essays* (Oxford: Oxford University Press, 2011), at 208, arguing that: 'To truly "rescue" socio- economic rights, a more realist approach is required, one that goes beyond idealist normative accounts or

an overly pessimistic view of the political branches of the state but also why they put so much faith in lawyers and courts (through litigation) as crucial tools for making rights effective.

My conclusions in this book rely on analysis of extensive empirical data on the performance of executive and legislative bodies, as well as courts, related to the right to health in the past three decades. I look at the trajectory of several important health indicators during this period and at the leading policies formulated and implemented by the legislature and health administrators. As regards the performance of courts, I look at the number of health cases adjudicated, their geographical distribution across the country, the socioeconomic profile of claimants and the object of litigation and their impact on the health budget. In order to assess the performance of both courts and the political bodies in advancing the right to health, I engage with the expert literature on public health policy.

If this empirical and interdisciplinary approach is correct and my analysis of the Brazilian case is sound, those of us interested in improving further the right to health, in Brazil and elsewhere where similar conditions obtain, are well advised to look away from courts and focus our limited resources on the political sphere.

1.1 Outline of the Book

The Right to Health in Politics

In Part I (Chapters 2–4), 'The Politics of the Right to Health', I focus on the performance of the political branches in advancing the right to health, that is, on the legislative and executive initiatives related to that right that may have had an impact on the health conditions of the population.

This is a topic largely neglected by the literature, which tends to focus almost exclusively on litigation when it discusses the impact of the right to health. Yet courts are by no means the only – nor usually the primary, or most important as this book will show – arena in which the right to health (and other rights) produces impact.[4] The right to health can also

insular constitutional discourse to understand these rights as part of a larger matrix of public policy, economics, and politics.'

[4] My own previous work has also been mostly focused on courts. This book is therefore an effort to expand the focus and carry out a more comprehensive analysis. For interesting studies but mostly focused on courts, see A. Yamin, S. Gloppen (eds.), *Litigating Health*

influence *directly* the adoption of policies by the legislature and executive, that is, without any input from lawyers and courts. If we focus exclusively on courts, we miss therefore a large and important area where a lot, if not most, of the action on the right to health is.[5]

The very recognition of the right to health in the Brazilian Constitution of 1988 is perhaps the best example of legislative activity to advance the right to health. As we will see in Chapter 2, it was the upshot of an unrelenting and ultimately successful campaign of the so-called Sanitary Movement, a political group of public health activists from academia, government and civil society whose purpose was to entrench, in the new post-authoritarian constitution, their long-standing moral and political claim that the state has a duty to protect and promote the health of its citizens. It counted, as far as I could establish, no lawyer or judge among its members. No one in the movement seems to have thought either, at the time, of litigation as an important or even complementary tool in their fight to guarantee the right to health of the Brazilian population.[6]

Securing a place in the new Constitution for health as a fundamental human right was, thus, a *political* strategy, a way of empowering the members of the Sanitary Movement and society more generally to keep fighting, politically, that is, in their demands for legislative and executive health policies aimed at improving the health conditions of the population. The very wording of the constitutional clause that the movement managed to approve in the constituent assembly reflects this primarily political character of the right to health.

Rights: Can Courts Bring More Justice to Health? (Cambridge, MA: Harvard University Press, 2011); R. Gargarella, P. Domingo, T. Roux, *Courts and Social Transformation: A New Institutional Voice for the Poor?* (Aldershot: Ashgate, 2009); V. Gauri, D. M. Brinks (eds.), *Courting Social Justice: Judicial Enforcement of Social and Economic Rights in the Developing World* (Cambridge: Cambridge University Press, 2008).

5 For a good, yet more theoretical critique of this court-centric tendency, see G. Webber, P. Yowell, R. Ekins et al., *Legislated Rights: Securing Human Rights through Legislation* (Cambridge: Cambridge University Press, 2018).

6 This is perhaps explained by the fact that courts then, at the twilight of the military regime, were not exactly bastions of rights. A sustained attempt to improve that aspect of the rule of law was made also through the new Constitution but the record is so far mixed. See, for an insightful account, O. V. Vilhena, *A Batalha dos Poderes, Da transição democrática ao mal-estar constitucional* (São Paulo: Cia das Letras, 2018).

> Article 196. Health is a right of all and a duty of the state and shall be guaranteed by means of *social and economic policies* aimed at reducing the risk of illness and other hazards and at the universal and egalitarian access to actions and services for its promotion, protection and recovery.[7] (my emphasis)

Chapter 2, 'Health Becomes a Right', recounts in some detail the fascinating story of the largely successful campaign of the Sanitary Movement to have health recognised as a right in the new Constitution. But there was no guarantee, of course, as there never is, that anything would change after the Constitution. It was certainly possible that neither the legislature nor the executive would pay much attention to the constitutional clause just cited. Chapters 3 and 4 carry out an assessment of the changes spurred by the Constitution and of their magnitude, that is, what has been achieved and what remains to be done. Chapter 3, 'The Constitution Works', discusses the significant improvements of the health conditions of the Brazilian population in the past three decades and argues that the inclusion of the right to health in the Constitution has played an important role in those improvements. It shows how a national health system funded through taxes and accessible to all (the 'Sistema Único de Saúde', the SUS) was created where previously only employment-linked medical insurance, private services and a limited network of public and charitable hospitals operated. The creation of SUS, which was expressly mandated by Article 198 of the Constitution, expanded access to health actions and services to tens of millions of Brazilians, from primary care to complex surgical procedures, from immunisation programmes to access to a comprehensive list of medicines. These policies, which I argue would not have been adopted (at least not with the same intensity and urgency) without the strong backing of the right to health in the Constitution, have helped to improve health and reduce some of the historically high health inequalities prevalent in the Brazilian population, as some key indicators such as infant mortality and child mortality show (see Figure 1.1). It provides strong evidence, I argue, of the positive impact of the constitutionalisation of the right to health and of the importance of legislative and executive bodies as key protagonists in advancing that right.

Yet all these important initiatives have clearly not yet been able to deliver the ambitious constitutional aim of guaranteeing equitable access

[7] My direct translation from the Portuguese: 'Art. 196. A saúde é direito de todos e dever do Estado, garantido mediante políticas sociais e econômicas que visem à redução do risco de doença e de outros agravos e ao acesso universal e igualitário às ações e serviços para sua promoção, proteção e recuperação.'

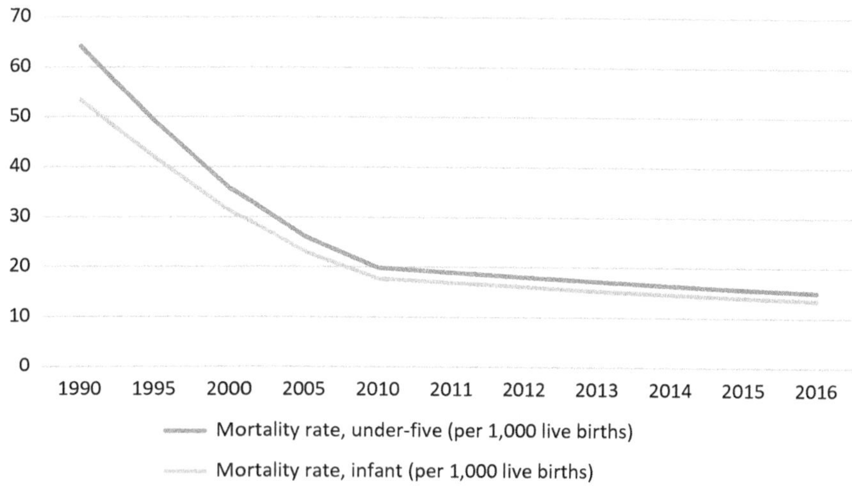

Figure 1.1 Infant and child mortality in Brazil.
Source: United Nations Development Programme, Human Development Reports

to a comprehensive package of health actions and services universally, that is, to the whole of the Brazilian population. Chapter 4, 'Two Brazils', is dedicated to an in-depth analysis of the long road ahead towards that aim. Most significant in the view of public health experts has been the failure of the Brazilian state, so far, to reduce to acceptable levels the inequalities in health that have been a shameful historical mark of Brazil and one of the main impetuses for the Sanitary Movement's right to health campaign. One of the greatest obstacles, as we will see, is the persistent insufficiency of resources devoted to public health by successive Brazilian legislatures and governments and their unequal distribution among the population, which helps to explain why some regions of Brazil still display health indicators, such as life expectancy, infant and maternal mortality, most commonly found in the poorest countries (see Figure 1.2).

The conclusions of Part I are therefore mixed. On the one hand, legislative and executive action to advance the right to health has clearly had a non-trivial positive impact in the improvement of the health conditions of the Brazilian population. The right to health has certainly not been futile, nor a 'phantom right', completely marginalised and neglected by Brazilian politics as the popular narratives on social rights mentioned earlier would lead us to expect. On the other hand, there is still a lot to be done and some persistent political obstacles, such as underfunding and unequal distribution of health resources, which clearly prevent (or slow down) the full realisation of the right to health.

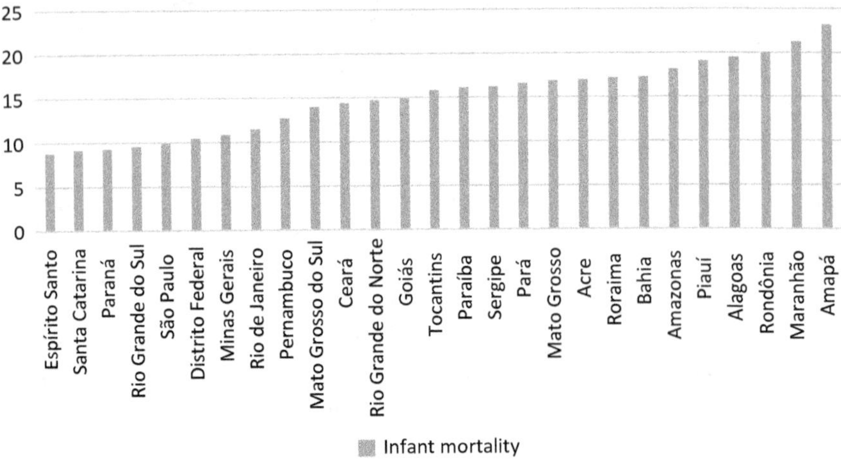

Figure 1.2 Infant mortality in Brazil by state.
Source: IBGE

Can lawyers and courts come to the rescue? This is the main topic of Part II of the book, 'The Judicialisation of Health in Brazil'.

The Right to Health in the Courts

Although no one seems to advocate that litigation is the primary means of guaranteeing the right to health, that is, above legislation and executive action, the strong focus of the legal literature on litigation reflects a widespread belief that lawyers and courts are very important actors in that enterprise. The idea is that, once health and other interests are recognised as legal rights, individuals can resort to a stronger form of accountability, that is, judicial enforcement, when the state fails to guarantee the right to health enshrined in the constitution. Alicia Yamin captures that well in the following passage:

> perhaps what a rights-based approach to health uniquely adds to other work in medicine and public health focused on social justice lies precisely in the definition of relationships between rights-holders and duty-bearers, which permits the creation of a framework for and mechanisms of accountability, including effective recourse in the event of violations.[8]

[8] A. Yamin, 'Will We Take Suffering Seriously? Reflections on What Applying a Human Rights Framework to Health Means and Why We Should Care', (2008) 10(1) *Health and Human Rights*, 45–63, at 49.

This seems in principle correct, but one should guard against the strong tendency among lawyers, as mentioned earlier, of overestimating the delinquency of the political branches while underestimating the willingness and capacity of judges, through litigation, to make things better. This is in great part a result, as I said earlier, of lack of analysis of empirical data and engagement with social policy literature. The best way to proceed, in my view, is to scrutinise the impact of all branches of the state based on their *actual performance* and not *on idealised roles.* Part I of this book does that in relation to the political branches and finds the delinquency narrative to be far removed from the reality on the ground. Part II focuses on the performance of legal actors through litigation and also encounters important problems in the popular narrative of litigation as an effective accountability tool to advance the right to health.

Part II is divided into four chapters. Chapter 5, 'The Judicialisation of Health in Numbers', provides as comprehensive a picture as possible of some of the main characteristics of the right to health litigation in Brazil. What is the scale of the judicialisation of health in Brazil? How is it geographically distributed in such a large and diverse country? What kinds of health interventions are mostly claimed in the courts? Who are its main actors? How much does it cost the public coffers? With the strengthening not only of legal rights but also of legal remedies and the justice system as a whole in the 1988 Constitution, resort to the courts through litigation has been growing steadily in the past three decades in all areas of life in Brazil.[9] The area of health rights, although not one of the first to be judicialised, nor one of the leading areas in terms of volume of cases (labour law–related suits are by far the champions of judicialisation in Brazil), have experienced significant and growing litigation. According to the latest available data, the aggregate number of cases between 2014 and 2019 ranges between 702,739 (the most conservative estimate) and 1,293,625 (the least conservative estimate), an average of between 117,123 and 215,604 a year.[10] Its costs are also mounting quickly and have now reached sizeable proportions of the health budget. From 2009 to 2016, the aggregate costs of health litigation against all spheres of government (municipalities, states and the federal government) are estimated to have grown 126 per cent, from around R$2 billion in 2009

[9] L. W. Vianna et al., *A judicialização da política e das relações sociais no Brasil* (Rio de Janeiro: Revan, 1999).

[10] See Chapter 5 for full references and the method of calculating these figures.

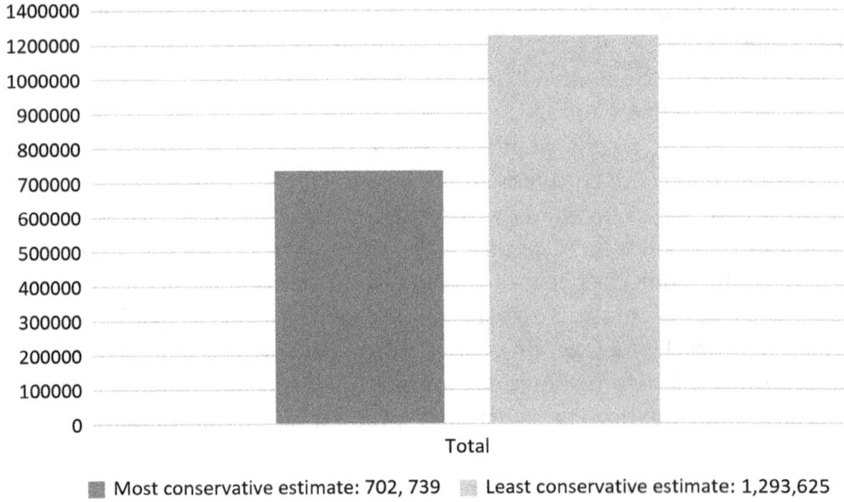

Figure 1.3 Number of health lawsuits, 2014 to 2019.
Source: Own formulation with data from CNJ

(US$1.545 billion), approximately 0.4 per cent of the total health budget then to R$7 billion in 2016 (roughly US$3.5 billion), approximately 3 per cent of the total health budget.[11]

The picture that emerges from Chapter 5 is not yet fine-grained enough, but it is sufficient to give us a good general idea and to dispel some common misconceptions about health litigation in Brazil. Despite the large *absolute* number of claims, the *relative* numbers are not that high, given Brazil's large population (circa 210 million people). We are talking, thus, of approximately 0.1 per cent of the population reaching the, courts every year to litigate the right to health, but likely fewer as part of those claims are likely from repeat litigants. Moreover, health litigation is not evenly dispersed across the whole country, but rather is highly concentrated in some states – about 80 per cent of health litigation originates in the seven (out of twenty-seven) states of the South and Southeast, see Figures 5.3 and 5.4 in Chapter 5 – and further

[11] See Chapter 5, Section 5.5 for full references. I have used exchange rates at purchase power parity to calculate those figures in US dollars.

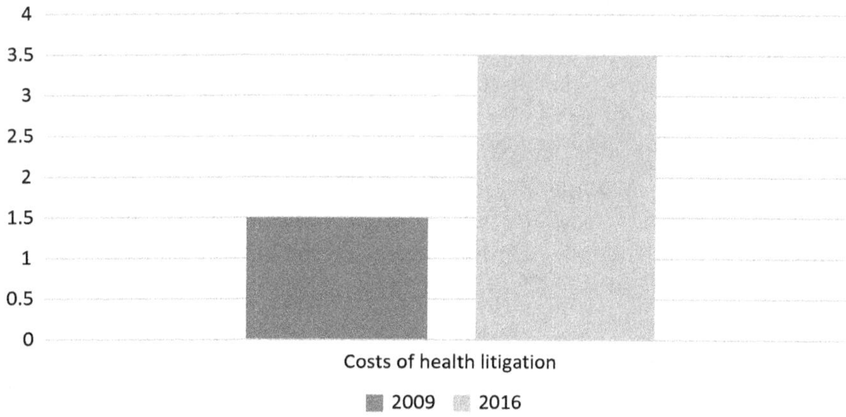

Figure 1.4 Public expenditure with health litigation, in US$, billions.
Source: Own formulation with data from the Ministry of Health

concentration takes place in some municipalities within states and even in some districts within municipalities (see Chapter 7).

It is perhaps exaggerated, thus, to talk of a health litigation 'explosion', as I myself have done in the past, let alone an 'epidemic'. It is not a homogenous *national phenomenon*, a '*Brazilian* thing', like soccer, carnival, coffee or capoeira. Though it has indeed spread across all regions of the country (see Map 1.1), it has *not* percolated through all municipalities, districts and households. What seems particularly 'Brazilian' about health litigation is thus precisely the opposite, that is, its highly unequal distribution across the population and high concentration in some places.[12] It would therefore be more appropriate to talk of pockets of high-intensity health litigation or, to keep with the health metaphor, an 'outbreak' of litigation in some well-defined areas.

What can explain such concentration of health litigation in some pockets of the country? What is the 'vector' carrying health litigation that seems to be present in some places but not in others? In the spirit of Jon Snow, the pioneer in epidemiology who traced the source of a cholera outbreak in 1854 in Soho, London, by jotting dots and crosses on a map and working out that most cholera victims (the dots) lived near an

[12] P. Lotufo, 'Coffee, Samba, Football and . . . Inequalities: Reflections on Mortality in São Paulo, Brazil', (2001) 119(3) *São Paulo Medical Journal*, at 4–6.

infected well (the crosses), I took out the vast map of Brazil to gauge if there was anything particularly striking about the areas where litigation converges. The most glaring factor leaping off the page is a strong correlation between litigation and levels of socioeconomic development (see Map 1.1). The more developed an area is, the higher the number of lawsuits per capita tends to be. No similar correlation can be found between litigation and health need or deficiencies in the health system. On the contrary, the most deprived areas of the country, located in the North and Northeast (see Chapter 4), are precisely those with little or no litigation whatsoever.

This correlation between level of development and prevalence of litigation at the state level does not yet give us enough information to

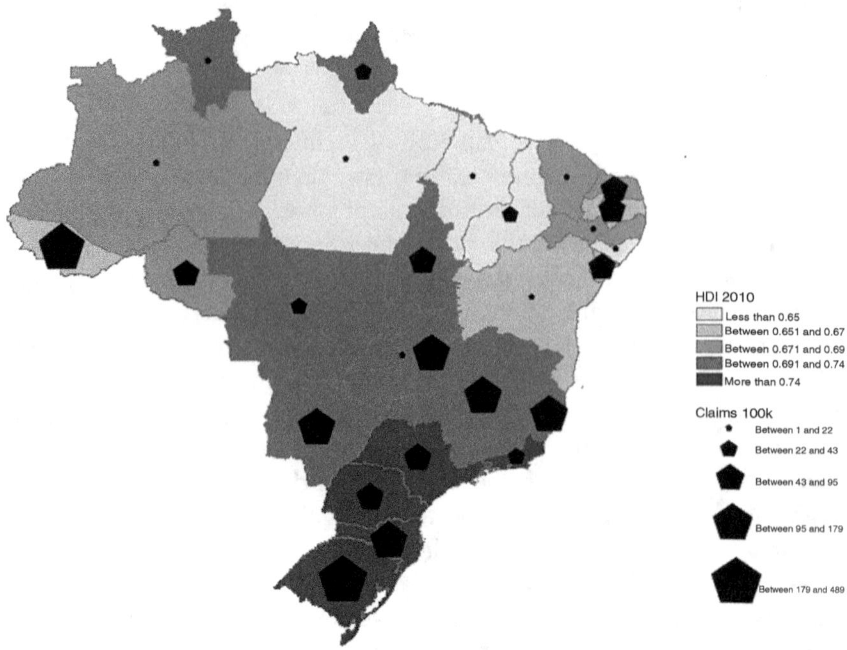

Map 1.1 Geographical distribution of litigation across Brazilian states, number of claims per 100,000 population and HDI.
Source: Own Formulation with Data from CNJ[13]

[13] This map was conceived and executed with the invaluable assistance of Ana de Menezes Silva.

draw robust conclusions about the drivers and impact of litigation in advancing the right to health. But it does provide us with a plausible hypothesis for its drivers and an initial sense of its likely impact. Brazil's persistent high level of socioeconomic inequalities, discussed in some detail in Chapter 4, seems to determine not only health outcomes but also ability to litigate. Better- off individuals are not only likely to have better health conditions but also to be more capable of using litigation to advance their health interests. If this is true, the impact of health litigation is likely regressive. We should thus be sceptical about the possibility of litigation to perform the idealised accountability role mentioned earlier. If litigation was indeed working as an effective remedy to the purported failures of the political bodies to guarantee the right to health, we would expect to see more of it in the poorer states, that is, where the health conditions of the population are comparatively much worse (as discussed in Part I of the book).

I pursue this hypothesis in greater detail in the remainder of Part II (Chapters 6–8), refining the initial picture that emerged from Chapter 5. In Chapter 6, 'How the Haves Come Out Ahead in Health Litigation', I employ a well-established framework developed in the political sciences and socio-legal scholarship, the 'opportunity structure for legal mobilisation', to gauge the drivers of health litigation in Brazil. The 'opportunity structure', in brief terms, is constituted by a set of conditions whose presence is crucial to open the traditionally narrow channels of litigation to the potential litigant. Its components include not only a friendly judiciary but also rights awareness and, most crucially, access to legal representation and financial resources to initiate and sustain litigation.

The available data shows, perhaps unsurprisingly, that severe inequalities in opportunity structures for legal mobilisation still prevail in Brazil. Although courts are rather open to right to health claims, in particular, individualised ones, litigation is neither a realistic nor an attractive option for most Brazilians. On the contrary, for most Brazilians and, in particular, the most disadvantaged, an adverse combination of insufficient resources, rights ignorance and difficulties accessing legal representation puts litigation well out of reach. This helps to explain to a great extent the relatively low amount of health litigation as a percentage of the population (less than 0.1 per cent as mentioned earlier) and their high concentration in some more developed pockets of the country, suggesting that *capacity to litigate* is a more important driver of health litigation in Brazil than failures of the political bodies to guarantee the right to health.[14] The 'haves', that is, the minority able to independently afford the expensive services of private lawyers, whom I estimate, rather loosely, to be around 7 per cent of the population (the so-called class A of income, around 13 million people) certainly are way ahead in health litigation. The rest of the population, more than 190 million people, face severe difficulties due to deficiencies in their opportunity structure for legal mobilisation (lack of rights awareness, financial resources, difficulties in accessing legal representation). These difficulties vary, of course, depending on the personal circumstances of each individual that affect more or less each of the elements of her opportunity structure. The 40 per cent most disadvantaged, a vast mass of around 86 million Brazilians, are virtually excluded from even dreaming of litigation, given their almost non-existent opportunity structure. The remaining 'intermediary classes' likely experience an improvement in their opportunity structure the higher their socioeconomic condition, in particular, as relates to education, income and place of residence (i.e., proximity to the severely limited state lawyers' services), but most still face important obstacles to access justice, as Chapter 6 shows.

Chapter 7, 'Islands of Rights Revolutions?', tests the hypothesis further by analysing the increasingly detailed, if still limited, empirical data on the socioeconomic profile of health litigants. The idea is to build a more precise picture of the litigants behind the claims, that is, the *direct* beneficiaries of health litigation. The picture that emerges reinforces the conclusions of Chapter 6. A large proportion of claims, varying in different states but always sizeable, feature litigants that have a much higher average socioeconomic status than the rest of the population. These claims are very often represented by private lawyers and tend to focus on state-of-the-art curative medical treatment, mostly medicines, that private health insurance providers tend not to cover. Another sizeable proportion of claims are brought to court by public defenders and public prosecutors representing mostly individual litigants (and less often collective interests). The socioeconomic profile of the beneficiaries of these claims is harder to gauge. Unlike private lawyers, whose access is

[14] Even if, implausibly, all 200,000 cases a year featured a poor person as a litigant, we would still be talking about only a very small percentage of the poor using health litigation: 2 per cent, if we take the World Bank's extreme poverty threshold (10.1 million poor); 0.75 per cent, according to the national threshold (26.5 million poor); and 0.23 per cent, according to the bottom 40 per cent threshold (86.3 million poor), http://povertydata.worldbank.org/poverty/country/BRA, accessed 30 March 2019.

severely limited as mentioned above to around 7 per cent of the population, public defenders are *in principle* available to almost everyone else in the country, as the income threshold to qualify for their services is relatively high in light of the country's income profile. (Almost 90 per cent of the population could in principle qualify.) Public prosecutors' remit is even larger, as the scope of their mandate to protect individual and collective health interests is virtually unlimited. What we see, thus, is that within this vast potential constituency of almost 190 million people, the relatively small numbers that are able to reach the courts through state lawyers and small claims courts are also often comparatively better off than the rest of the population. Very few individuals from the lowest income groups are able to overcome the significant opportunity structure barriers discussed at length in Chapter 6.

My conclusion, thus, is that health litigation, though in principle available to everyone, is highly skewed towards those with a better opportunity structure for legal mobilisation. These tend to be by and large the relatively better off within the Brazilian population, living in the most developed states, municipalities and districts and who are aware of their rights, capable to initiate and sustain litigation either independently (through private lawyers) or through the severely limited services of public defenders and public prosecutors.

Chapter 8, 'Unequal Justice: What Is Litigated, Why, and Who Really Benefits?', the concluding chapter of Part II, deals with an important remaining issue (the so-called *indirect effects* of litigation) without which the analysis of health litigation in Brazil would not be complete. The argument from indirect effects runs more or less like this: even if health litigation features mostly – or even exclusively – better off individuals as claimants, it can still constitute an important tool of state accountability and potentially benefit the most disadvantaged *if* (i) it involves health actions and services that the state ought to provide but doesn't; and (ii) it leads to broad policy changes that end up benefiting everyone, including the poor. The paradigmatic example in Brazil – even if not undisputed as discussed in Chapter 8 – seems to be the HIV-AIDS-related litigation of the mid-1990s when judicialisation by better off claimants (alongside other political strategies) seems to have induced broader policy changes that ended up benefiting a larger constituency than the litigants themselves, including some of the poor.

As important as knowing *who* litigates, thus, is to know *what* is litigated and *if* it leads to policy change. Chapter 8 discusses these issues in detail and finds that both accountability and indirect effects are very limited in the Brazilian context and often outright negative. Here are, in brief, the main reasons. Firstly, health litigation concentrates significantly on secondary and tertiary health care, that is, curative treatment (in particular, on *medicines and hospital treatment*, see Section 5.1 in Chapter 5) and not on primary care and public health measures, such as basic sanitation, the Family Health Strategy, access to essential vaccination, etc. – which are arguably the chief responsibilities of the health system and the highest priorities of the most disadvantaged (see Chapters 3 and 4). Secondly, even in the narrow field of access to medicines, litigation, claims and costs concentrate significantly on certain non-basic, off-list and off-label medicines that cannot be regarded, again, as unquestionably part of the state's duty nor as high priorities for the most disadvantaged. Some of these drugs have been expressly excluded from the health system for several recognised valid reasons, for example, lack of effectiveness, excessive costs, existence of reasonable alternatives in the system, etc. (see Section 8.4 in Chapter 8).

There is a significant mismatch, thus, between what is mostly litigated in health claims and what the health system ought arguably to provide within its limited resources in light of the health needs and priorities of the Brazilian population. There are of course exceptions to this pattern, in particular, cases of genuine failure of the health system to provide medicines and to carry out operations that are included in its own lists. There is also a chronic shortage of hospital beds, in particular, in intensive care units, that generate some litigation. But these do not represent the bulk of litigation, neither in terms of volume, nor in terms of costs, as Chapter 8 explains in detail.

This finding is somewhat expected given the persistently large inequalities among the population in health needs and litigation capacity (i.e., opportunity structure for legal mobilisation). Why would the better off, who have a better opportunity structure, litigate for basic primary care, public health interventions, essential medicines, etc. that they already have easy access to without the help of the courts? To use Daniel Brinks' and Varun Gauri's insightful concept, without a 'shared policy space' between better off litigants and disadvantaged non-litigants indirect effects cannot eventuate.[15]

***

[15] D. Brinks, V. Gauri, 'The Law's Majestic Equality? The Distributive Impact of Litigating Social and Economic Rights', Policy Research Working Paper 5999 (2012), at 15.

Right to health litigation has given rise to a highly polarised debate in Brazil and elsewhere between fierce supporters and detractors of the practice. For supporters, health litigation is a positive development and has a simple explanation: the Brazilian state persistently violates its constitutional duty to guarantee the right to health. Litigation is therefore seen as a necessary, legitimate and effective response to this constitutional delinquency of the political branches.[16] It is legal accountability working at its best; a genuine 'right to health revolution' to borrow the evocative phrase of Charles Epp.[17] For detractors, it is rather a disruptive and iniquitous tool used mostly by economic elites. It diverts precious scarce resources from the public health system, preventing the state from doing more for the poorest. Rather than progressive legal accountability, it is rights opportunism at its worst.[18]

As it is often the case in highly polarised debates, not much attention is paid to the empirical and complex realities on the ground. The arguments are fought with little or no input from data on what health litigation actually does, whom it actually serves and how it relates to the wide-ranging activities of the legislative and executive bodies.[19] Parts I and II of this book try to carry out a more well-informed analysis. As Parts I and II show, the truth is much closer to the view of critics of judicialisation, but is more complex than often portrayed in some of their more radical formulations. The analysis offered here will hopefully not only contribute towards a better understanding of the issue but also help us to think about more effective evidence-based strategies to improve the right to health.

[16] Brazilian legal culture seems in this field remarkably close to the American one and what Stuart A. Scheingold calls the 'myth of rights' in his seminal book *The Politics of Rights: Lawyers, Public Policy, and Political Change*, 2nd ed. (Ann Arbor: University of Michigan Press, 2004), at 85. As Scheingold puts it: 'Litigation is, in this view, an effective tool because it provides access to the substantial political power of courts . . .. Litigation is pictured as an effective way to redress the mistakes and deal with the shortcomings of American politics that result in denial of rights and neglect of constitutional values. Litigation, in short, is said to provide for more or less direct delivery of constitutional promises.'

[17] C. R. Epp, *After the Rights Revolution: Lawyers, Activists and Supreme Court in Comparative Perspective* (Chicago: University of Chicago Press, 1998).

[18] For a summary of this polarised debate, see O. L. M. Ferraz, 'Moving the Debate Forward in Right to Health Litigation', (2016) 18(2) *Health and Human Rights*, 265–268; J. Biehl, M. P. Socal, J. J. Amon, 'On the Heterogeneity and Politics of the Judicialization of Health in Brazil', (2016) 18(2) *Health and Human Rights*, 269–271.

[19] O. L. M. Ferraz, 'Where's the Evidence? Moving from Ideology to Data in Economic and Social Rights', OpenGlobalRights, 27 January 2015, available at: www.openglobalrights .org/wheres-evidence-moving-from-ideology-to-data-in-economic/, accessed 8 July 2020.

1.2 Any Role for Courts?

If my arguments in Part I and II are correct, Brazil provides an interesting and complex illustration of the effectiveness (and ineffectiveness) of recognising health as a human right in the Constitution. On one hand, it seems clear that constitutionalisation has worked. It has prompted legislative and executive bodies to create a comprehensive public health system, funded by the state and open to everyone, which invests a reasonably large amount of resources on a myriad of actions and policies that have undoubtedly improved the health conditions of the Brazilian population. Not a mean feat by any standards. On the other hand, that system has suffered from chronic underfunding since its birth, which, coupled with problems such as unequal distribution of its limited budget, managerial inefficiency, political interference and corruption, makes it stop way short of fulfilling the constitutional promise.

It is tempting under such circumstances, especially for a human rights lawyer, to see litigation as the natural and easy solution to the problem. The chapters of Part II of the book show why we should resist that temptation. But that does not mean that we should therefore discard any role for the courts in the protection of the right to health. As I argue in the final chapter of the book, (Chapter 9, 'To Interfere or Not to Interfere: The Courts' Dilemma'), litigation can, under certain conditions, entail positive results. But we need to approach litigation with caution and realism, harnessing its limited potential without succumbing to its pitfalls.

Courts in Brazil (and elsewhere where similar conditions obtain)[20] should be able to play a more positive role than they have so far in health litigation. What they must do, first and most urgently, is be aware of the actual reality they are dealing with when they adjudicate the health

[20] For similar scenarios in Latin America, see O. Maestad, L. Rakner, O. L. M. Ferraz, 'Assessing the Impact of Health Rights Litigation: A Comparative Study of Argentina, Colombia, Costa Rica, India and South Africa', in Yamin, A. and Gloppen, S. (eds.), *Litigating Health Rights: Can Courts Bring More Justice to Health?* (Cambridge, MA: Harvard University Press, 2011), chapter 11 and the individual chapters on Costa Rica, Argentina and, to some extent, Colombia in the same book. See also the special section of Health and Human Rights, O. L. M. Ferraz, 'Health in the Courts of Latin America', (2018) 20(1) *Health and Human Rights*, 67–77, in particular, the articles on Uruguay: L. B. Pizzarossa, K. Perehudoff, J. C. Forte, 'How the Uruguayan Judiciary Shapes Access to High-Priced Medicines: A Critique through the Right to Health Lens', (June 2018) 20(1) *Health and Human Rights*, 93–105, and on Costa Rica: O. R. Loaiza, S. Morales, O. Norheim, B. Wilson, 'Revisiting Health Rights Litigation and Access to Medications in Costa Rica: Preliminary Evidence from the Cochrane Collaboration Reform', (2018) 20(1) *Health and Human Rights*, 79–91.

claims that reach their benches. They should abandon the popular but simplistic and empirically ungrounded narrative that the state simply neglects the right to health of Brazilian citizens and that anyone who litigates is automatically a victim of a rights' violation. They should also abandon the related flawed interpretation of the right to health as an *unlimited individual entitlement* to all health interventions that a citizen may need, whatever the costs, so long as it is recommended by the claimant's medical doctor. This 'right to everything', as I call it in this book, would bankrupt any health system in the world, however rich, efficient and non-corrupt. In the severely underfunded conditions of the Brazilian system, interpreting the right to health in this way is even more imprudent, not to say utterly irresponsible. The only way in which this 'right to everything' can be sustainable is if it is restricted only to the minority who can litigate, which is actually the case in Brazil as shown in Part II, yet represents of course the very denial of the idea of a universal right to health. Abandoning these simplistic understandings that lead to the Orwellian scenario I describe in Part II of this book, in which some citizens are 'more equal' than others as regards the right to health, is the first step towards a more progressive and effective judicial involvement in the implementation of the right to health.

The right to health, like any other human right, is held simultaneously and on equal terms by all citizens. This is what is meant by the concepts of universality and equality expressly mentioned in Article 196 of the Brazilian Constitution cited earlier, which simply reflect the concept of universal human rights. The corresponding duty of the state is thus neither to provide everyone with all health interventions they may need (which would be simply unfeasible) nor to provide only those who can reach the courts with any interventions they request (the current inequitable scenario). The duty of the state is a much more complex one: to provide equitable access to a necessarily limited package of health actions and services affordable within available resources. (I call it the 'right to equitable access' in this book.)

Once this is understood, the appropriate task for courts becomes clearer but also much more complex. It is of course much easier to order the state to provide 'everything'. It requires no criteria, no analysis, no knowledge of the public health system, no moral dilemmas. To properly review the duty of the state to provide everyone with an equitable package of health actions and services is a thoroughly different, infinitely more complex task. Many have claimed, persuasively, that it is not a task that courts are institutionally well-equipped to perform. It would involve judicial interference with some of the most complex and disputed challenges of modern welfare democracies, ranging from broad decisions on the rate and progressivity of the tax system, to the amount of the state budget to be devoted to each government department (including Health) and how much should be allocated to each of the myriad parts of any health system (doctors, nurses, hospitals, equipment, materials, etc.) to cater to the numerous health needs of the population.[21]

The task is so complex and devoid of clear-cut, 'right answers', that it is hard to see how the judiciary could stake any legitimate claim to strongly interfere with the substance of such decisions. As I argue in Chapter 9, the decisions of the political and technical institutions and officials of reasonably well-functioning democracies, that is, parliament, the executive, health departments and other official specialised bodies (e.g., the Sanitary Vigilance Agency; the Commission on the Incorporation of Health Technology, etc.) should enjoy a strong prima facie presumption against judicial interference. Only in very genuinely exceptional cases, for example, when beset by clear irrationality or blatant discrimination, should in my view the judiciary consider strong interference; they should perhaps even make cautious use of the minimum core approach (in the way I discuss in Chapter 9), yet still think very cautiously about the potential negative unintended consequences of the order it contemplates to issue. As Neil Komesar aptly notes, 'tasks that strain the abilities of an institution may wisely be assigned to it anyway if the alternatives are even worse'.[22]

Beyond such cases, courts should limit themselves to what I call 'less interfering forms of adjudication' of social rights, that is, a review of the fairness of the decision-making process based on criteria such as transparency, non-discrimination, participation and rationality.

The approach I am defending in this book is certainly more deferential than many courts are used to exercising in the protection of rights. It should not mean, however, a return to (what feels now like a prehistoric) era of non-justiciable social rights, largely regarded as rendering social rights toothless. As I argue in Chapter 9, less interfering forms of review of the decision-making process of representative institutions, if performed well, can help improve both the quality and the fairness of that

[21] For a classic volume, see A. Coulter, C. Ham, *The Global Challenge of Healthcare Rationing* (Buckingham: Open University Press, 2000).

[22] N. K. Komesar, *Imperfect Alternatives: Choosing Institutions in Law, Economics, and Public Policy* (Chicago: University of Chicago Press, 1994), at 6.

process, which is by no means an irrelevant contribution for courts to make in democratic regimes. In order to do it well and effectively, however, courts must stop pontificating about correct answers (which are simply not provided by the constitutional text in most social rights cases) and become more interested in understanding the intricacies of the work of legislatures and administrators in the allocation of the scarce resources of the health budget and in the design and implementation of health policies.

1.3 Conclusion

This book argues, against the current wave of pessimism about rights that seems to have engulfed so many, that rights *can* work, at least some rights and in some contexts. The right to health recognised in the Constitution of Brazil, now thirty years old, provides a good example.

It has not worked seamlessly and perfectly (however one defines it), of course not. This is not how rights work. As political scientist Kathryn Sikkink reminds us, 'where it has occurred, human rights progress has been the result of activism and struggle, and such progress is not at all inevitable, but rather contingent on continued commitment and effort'.[23] The detailed analysis of thirty years of the right to health in Brazil carried out in this book can hopefully shed some light on how rights work and how further progress can be achieved.

[23] K. Sikkink, *Evidence for Hope, Making Human Rights Work in the Twenty-first Century* (Princeton: Princeton University Press, 2017), at 19.

PART I

The Politics of the Right to Health

2

Health Becomes a Right in Brazil

> Never doubt that a small group of thoughtful, committed citizens can change the world. Indeed, it's the only thing that ever has.
>
> Margaret Mead

> Health and Democracy. (Saúde e Democracia.)
>
> Slogan of the Sanitary Movement

The inclusion of health as a fundamental right in the Brazilian 1988 Constitution was not the work of human rights lawyers and judges. Nor was it a mere transplantation of Article 12 of the UN International Covenant on Economic, Social and Cultural Rights or other international norms, as may perhaps be assumed by those unfamiliar with the Brazilian context. It was the upshot of a long, intense and well-organised political movement, composed mostly of public health experts from both academia and practice (the 'Sanitary Movement', as I refer to it in this book).[1] With the support of some trade unions, politicians from several parties and a part of civil society, its collectivist conception of health as a public good (*saúde coletiva*) managed to overcome fierce opposition and become entrenched in the 1988 Constitution as a fundamental right.

This chapter recounts in some detail the fascinating story of this improbable political victory. That story is not only interesting in itself,

[1] The movement is referred to in the literature in different ways, including Movimento Sanitarista (Sanitaristic Movement), Movimento da Reforma Sanitária (Movement of Sanitary Reform) and Partido Sanitário (Sanitary Party). I use Sanitary Movement (Movimento Sanitário) for its simplicity. For a classic account of the history of the movement, see S. Escorel, *Reviravolta na saúde: Origem e articulação do movimento sanitário* (Rio de Janeiro: Editora FIOCRUZ, 1999). The term 'sanitary reform' seems to have been inspired by a similar experience in Italy: J. A. Oliveira, 'Reformas e reformismos: Para uma teoria política da reforma sanitária (ou, reflexões sobre a reforma sanitária de uma perspectiva popular)', in Costa, N. R. et al., (eds.), *Demandas populares, políticas públicas e saúde* (Petrópolis: Vozes, 1989), at 19.

it provides invaluable insight for the understanding of the way the right to health can and does often work through politics – that is, through legislators, executive bodies and civil society – an issue often overlooked in the legal literature, whose focus tends to be on lawyers, judges and litigation.

2.1 Health, Democracy and Inequality

It is impossible to dissociate the history of health as a human right in Brazil from the process of redemocratisation that started in the late 1970s and the strong social justice component that infused that process. As the 'economic miracle' (a period of exceptional economic growth during the military dictatorship)[2] started to wane and then turned into economic crisis, it became clearer that poverty had not been solved by the 'trickle-down' strategy of that period.[3] As the authoritarian regime (1964–1985) drew closer to its end, the yearning not only for political freedom but also social and economic justice grew, galvanising various actors including trade unions, opposition parties and social movements around several different specific themes, such as land reform, workers' rights, education and housing.[4] As explained by Sonia Fleury, a leading Brazilian social policy expert: 'The construction of a democratic institutional order supposed a rearrangement of social policies in response to society's demands for greater social inclusion and equality.'[5]

The Sanitary Movement was part and parcel of that broader context. The slogan 'health and democracy' encapsulates its strong political message. As Sérgio Arouca, a leading member of the movement, forcefully put it during his opening address to the 8th National Health Conference

[2] The 'economic miracle' was a period of high growth, averaging around 10 per cent, that lasted from the late 1960s to the mid-1970s; see A. Fishlow, 'Brazil's Economic Miracle', (1973) 29(11)*The World Today*, 474–481.

[3] R. P. Barros, R. Henriques, R. Mendonça, 'Desigualdade e Pobreza no Brasil: Retrato de uma realidade inaceitável' ('Inequality and Poverty in Brazil: Portrait of an Unacceptable Reality'), (2000) 15(42) *Revista Brasileira de Ciências Sociais*, 123–142.

[4] The 'constituent moment' fomented new social movements, especially on urban issues, such as residents' associations. For an example of the participation of such movements during the constituent assembly, see the speeches of Senator Geovani Borges (PFL-AP) (27 August 1987, Livro Vol. 8, p. 4980), Brasil. Congresso. Câmara dos Deputados. Separatas e discursos, pareceres e projetos. 48.a Legislatura, 1.a Sessão Legislativa, no. 59.

[5] S. Fleury, 'Brazilian Sanitary Reform: Dilemmas between the Instituting and the Institutionalized', (2009) 14(3)*Ciência & Saúde Coletiva*, at 745.

of 1986 (a seminal step in the constitutionalisation of the right to health, as we shall see later):

> Wealth grew in Brazil but the number of hungry people also grew. Wealth grew but the misery of a large majority of the population also grew. Wealth grew but marginalisation also grew . . .. This is not bearable . . .. 'Health and democracy'! Behind this phrase the understanding is that it would be impossible to improve the well-being of the population until the economic model that concentrates income and the authoritarian political model remained in existence.[6]

These social, economic and political dimensions of the historical context are crucial to the understanding of the project of the Sanitary Movement that culminated with the legal recognition of health as a human right in the 1988 Constitution. Public health experts, such as Arouca and many other active participants in the movement, were acutely aware that the problem with health was not simply a shortage and mismanagement of health services (hospitals, equipment and medicines) but also, and mainly, the significant deprivation of large sections of the population from access to the social determinants of health (education, food, income, safe working conditions, etc.).

The aim of the Sanitary Movement was thus not simply to improve the then insufficient and failing public health system (a consensus at the time)[7] but to transform the very idea of health from the mere treatment of diseases into a broader concept of physical and mental well-being inextricably dependent on other social, economic and political factors.[8] As we shall see in Section 2.4, this is strongly reflected in the textual formulation of the right to health that ended up in Articles 196–200 of the Constitution.

[6] S. Arouca, Speech at the 8th National Health Conference, Brasilia, 1986, available on video at https://pensesus.fiocruz.br/sa%C3%BAde-%C3%A9-democracia, accessed 28 May 2019. My translation from the original in Portuguese.

[7] See N. R. Costa, 'Inovação Política, Distributivismo e Crise: A Política de Saúde nos Anos 80 e 90', (1996) 39(3) *Dados*, 479–511 for the crisis of the health system, and also for the interesting debate about whether the military period, at least in the health-care sector, actually helped towards universalism and equity, discussing the argument of J. Malloy, *A Política de Previdência Social no Brasil* (Rio de Janeiro: Graal, 1985).

[8] Such an idea was of course influenced by international discussions promoted by the WHO and other international bodies, most prominently in the Alma Ata Conference and its Declaration of 1978, sponsored in collaboration by the WHO and UNICEF. See Declaration of Alma-Ata, International Conference on Primary Health Care, Alma-Ata, USSR, 6–12 September 1978, www.who.int/publications/almaata_declaration_en.pdf?ua=1.

2.2 The Constitutional Moment and the Sanitary Movement

Democratisation and, in particular, the decision to enact a new constitution, presented a particularly favourable political environment for new ideas about social reform such as those proposed by the Sanitary Movement. To quote Fleury again, 'all this democratic effervescence was channelled to the National Constituent Assembly'.[9] Health, as already noted, was only one among several political movements trying to make the most of that opening.[10] It was also one of the most well-organised ones. Though the movement became perhaps more prominent during the constituent assembly, which took place between February 1987 and September 1988, it was not a specific-purpose campaign formed simply to include health as a right in the new constitution. It was actually much older and had a much broader and perennial goal – that is, to improve health in Brazil through reforms of not only the public health system but also the economic and political ones.[11]

As one of its most active members, Eleutério Rodriguez Neto, reminds us in his fascinating first-hand account of that period, the fact that it already had a reasonably well-established institutional existence allowed the health movement 'to reach the National Constituent Assembly with the most complete, discussed and legitimised proposal'.[12]

[9] Fleury, 'Brazilian Sanitary Reform', at 745. In her own words: 'The construction of a democratic institutional order supposed a rearrangement of social policies in response to society's demands for greater social inclusion and equality. Projected for the social policies system as a whole, this demand for inclusion and reduction of inequalities acquired the concrete connotations of affirmation of social rights as a part of citizenship.'

[10] Although the military regime ended officially in 1985 with indirect elections for president, small spaces for political movements began to develop as early as the mid-1970s during what came to be known as the *abertura política* (political opening) or *distensão* (distension). Elections for the Senate (1974, 1976 and 1978); relaxation of censorship (1975 and 1979); the Amnesty Law of 1979; the return of multiple parties and the end of the highly repressive Institutional Act no. 5 (1979) are examples of what some refer to as the 'gradual and slow opening'. See L. C. Bresser-Pereira, 'Os limites da "abertura" e a sociedade civil', (1983) 23(4) *Revista de Administração de Empresas*, 5–14. See also C. H. A. Paiva, L. A. Teixeira, 'Health Reform and the Creation of the Sistema Único de Saúde: Notes on Contexts and Authors', (2014) 21(1) *História, Ciência, Saúde-Manguinhos*, 15–36.

[11] See Escorel, *Reviravolta na saúde*, and also the webpage of the Oswaldo Cruz Foundation, https://pensesus.fiocruz.br/reforma-sanitaria, for comprehensive resources on the sanitary reform.

[12] E. Rodriguez Neto, *Saúde: Promessas e limites da constituição* (Rio de Janeiro: Fiocruz, 2003), at 51.

As a self-proclaimed movement with a distinct political identity, it dated back to the 1970s, when an interesting development started to occur, namely, the gradual 'infiltration' of a group of public health experts with progressive, left-leaning ideas, in key technical posts in the bureaucracy of the military dictatorship.[13] This group formed one of the early 'seeds' of the Sanitary Movement, starting to introduce small incremental changes in the public system, such as the Piass, Programa de Interiorização de Ações de Saúde e Saneamento (Programme of Interiorisation of Health and Sanitation Actions), in 1976, aimed at expanding basic services and actions to the poor hinterlands of the country[14] and the companion Ppreps, Programa de Preparação Estratégica de Pessoal de Saúde (Programme of Strategic Training of Human Resources in Health), aimed at developing the human resources required to implement those actions and services.[15]

In the same year, the creation in São Paulo of Cebes, the Brazilian Centre for Health Studies (Centro Brasileiro de Estudos de Saúde), a think tank, and its journal *Saúde em Debate* (*Debating Health*) would give further grounding in civil society to the nascent movement.[16] That grounding was strengthened a couple of years later with the creation of Abrasco, Associação Brasileira de Pós-graduação em Saúde Coletiva (the Brazilian Association of Post-graduation in Collective Health), in September of 1979, congregating post-graduate courses that adopted the innovative view of health advocated by the Sanitary Movement.[17]

[13] I put infiltration in inverted commas as I have no evidence that this was a deliberate and well-organised, conspiracy-type action by progressive public health professionals. It seems to have been more of a haphazard development. According to Paiva and Teixeira, 'the aim of improving care and reducing expenditure on resources tended to require technical and scientific personnel who were not always immediately available in the government agencies. This shortage of skills, in the view of Escorel (1999), provided the opportunity for access by a group of medical professionals with innovative ideas to positions in the government technical bureaucracy. Many of these were of a progressive nature, and this group gradually formed a movement for the reform of the health system, as part of the opposition to the regime'. Paiva, Teixeira, 'Health Reform and the Creation of the Sistema Único de Saúde', at 7.

[14] Ibid.

[15] Ibid.

[16] Escorel, *Reviravolta na saúde.*

[17] Ibid.; Rodriguez Neto, *Saúde*; J. S. Paim, 'A Reforma Sanitária Brasileira e o Sistema Único de Saúde: Dialogando com hipóteses concorrentes', (2008) 18(4) *Physis Revista de Saúde Coletiva*, 625–644. Its name changed to simply Associação Brasileira de Saúde Coletiva (Brazilian Association of Collective Health) in 2011. See www.abrasco.org.br/site/sobreaabrasco/, accessed 28 May 2019.

By the end of the 1970s, therefore, one could already talk of a Sanitary Movement that was reasonably well-organised and consolidated, with a strong grounding both in academia and, somewhat paradoxically, in the bureaucracy of the conservative military government. These developments paved the way for the First Symposium of National Health Policy in October 1979, taking place in the Brazilian National Congress, to discuss a paper produced in partnership by Cebes and researchers of the IMS, Instituto de Medicina Social (Institute of Social Medicine) of the State University of Rio de Janeiro, where the main proposals of the Sanitary Movement were summarised.[18]

It is here that we find, perhaps for the first time in an formal document in Brazil, the idea of *health as a universal right*, alongside several other principles and ideas that came to be adopted in the Constitution, such as the intersectoral character of the social determinants of health; the role of the state as regulator of the health market; decentralisation, regionalisation and hierarchisation of the health system; popular participation and democratic control.[19] These ideas would be further developed and consolidated at the historic 8th National Health Conference in 1986, already cited earlier in this chapter, sometimes referred to as a 'pre-constituent assembly'.[20]

[18] See H. Cordeiro, 'O Instituto de Medicina Social e a luta pela Reforma Sanitária: Contribuição à História do SUS' ('The Institute of Social Medicine and the Health Reform Struggle: A Contribution to the History of the Unified National Health System in Brazil'), (2004) 14(2) *Physis: Revista de Saúde Coletiva*, 343–362. The document had as a basis a paper written by Hésio Cordeiro, José Luiz Fiori and Reinaldo Guimarães, 'A questão democrática na Área da Saúde' ('The Democratic Question in the Field of Health'). In one of its most assertive passages, it argues: 'Politics that replaces the voice of the population with the wisdom of the technocrats and the pressures of the various business sectors; health policy that accompanies in its outline the socio-economic position of the government – privatizing, business oriented and concentrated in income, marginalizing about 70% of the population of the material and cultural benefits of economic growth .... Politics of health, in short, that forgets the real needs of the population and is guided exclusively by the interests of the minority constituted and confirmed by the owners of medical companies and managers of the health industry in general.' Available at http://cebes.org.br/2015/10/a-questao-democratica-na-area-da-saude/, accessed 19 June 2019. It became the handbook (*cartilha*) of the sanitary movement; see Rodriguez Neto, *Saúde*, at 35.

[19] Cordeiro, 'O Instituto de Medicina Social', at 346.

[20] See the final report in Portuguese, 'Relatório Final da 8ª Conferência Nacional de Saúde', Brasília, 17–21 March 1986, available at http://bvsms.saude.gov.br/bvs/publicacoes/8_conferencia_nacional_saude_relatorio_final.pdf. According to Rodriguez Neto: 'The VIII National Health Conference can be considered the most significative event in the construction process of the platform and strategies of the movement for the

By the time the National Constituent Assembly started its operation on 1 February 1987, this coalition of public health academics and public health professionals that came to be known as the Sanitary Movement had therefore at least one decade of reasonably well-organised existence and was able to exert significant influence in the wording of the constitutional text. The political strength of the movement was such that it was sometimes referred to as the 'Partido Sanitário' (Sanitary Party) during the assembly's works.

It wasn't just the timing of the constituent assembly that was favourable to the Sanitary Movement. The broader political context was also helpful for at least two reasons. First, the idea that the health system needed reform was maturing rapidly in Brazil with the increasing financial crisis of the social insurance system in the late 1970s (to which health belonged) and its incapacity to provide access to health services to large sections of the Brazilian population.[21] A plausible argument defended by the movement was that one important reason for this crisis was the high cost of services provided by private companies, whose participation in the system had grown during the military regime. A credible solution accepted already during the final years of military period was, thus, to diminish private participation and enhance public delivery of services through what came to be known as 'integrated health actions' ('Ações Integradas de Saúde' – AIS), which aimed at greater integration of the municipal, state and federal levels of the public network. Secondly, the movement's focus on health as a collective good of public relevance was in line with broader international trends. It was part of the international effort started in the 1960s and consolidated in the 1980s to transform the then-prevalent model of health from a curative, illness focused, hospital-centric and high technology–based one into a preventive model, focussed on primary care and the social determinants of health.[22] The Conference

democratisation of health in all its history.' (Rodriguez Neto, *Saúde*, at 49). The conference involved more than 4,000 participants from all social and political sectors. Of the 1,000 delegates, 50 per cent were representatives of organised civil society. See also M. S. C. Oliveira, "Participação, Saúde e Direito na Assembléia Constituinte: Um Resgate do Debate," www.publicadireito.com.br/conpedi/manaus/arquivos/anais/XIVCongresso/093.pdf, accessed 19 June 2019. It is interesting to note that a few days before it started, the private health sector withdrew from the conference; see Arouca, Speech at the 8th National Health Conference.

21 T. M. Lima, 'O direito à saúde revisitado: Entre os ideais da Constituição de 1988 e o drama jurídico atual', (2014) 51(202) *Revista de Informação Legislativa*, at 183–184.

22 Paiva, Teixeira, 'Health Reform and the Creation of the Sistema Único de Saúde', at 19.

of Alma-Ata in 1978 and its goal of health for all by 2000 is perhaps the most prominent expression of this international consensus in that period.[23]

The time seemed ripe, thus, for the ideas of the Sanitary Movement to percolate through the constituent assembly and find its way into the constitutional text. Yet it would be wrong to conclude that its impressive victory was an easy and smooth one. Nor was it fully comprehensive. Sections 2.3 and 2.4 recount in some detail, first, the monumental and politically volatile process of formulation, debate and approval of the new constitution (Section 2.3) and then the strong opposition mounted by conservative groups against the proposals of the Sanitary Movement, its improbable overall victory and the scars left by those battles in the final constitutional text (Section 2.4).

2.3 The 'Citizen Constitution'

Calls for a new constitution had been made since 1971, thus, not long after the coup d'état that brought the military to power in Brazil in March 1964.[24] But the campaign for redemocratisation (of which a new constitution was an integral part), became more intense only in the late-1970s, in reaction to an upsurge in authoritarian measures by the military government retreating from the slow opening ('*distensão*') started in the mid-1970s.[25] Some of its main protagonists were the OAB, Ordem dos Advogados do Brasil (Brazilian Bar Association), the CNBB, Conferência

[23] It is noteworthy that no reference to international human rights law is made in the Sanitary Movement's documents, as far as I could establish, despite the fact that the UN International Covenant on Economic, Social and Cultural Rights was adopted in 1966 and came into force in 1976.

[24] These first calls were made in the city of Recife, state of Pernambuco, by the political party MDB, Movimento Democrático Brasileiro (Brazilian Democratic Movement) during a seminar (II Seminário de Estudos e Debates da Realidade Brasileira) that ensued in the 'Letter of Recife' ('Carta de Recife'); see Centro de Pesquisa e Documentação de História Contemporânea do Brasil (CPDOC), Fundação Getúlio Vargas, Entry Assembléia Nacional Constituinte 1987–1988 (CPDOC-FGV), www.fgv.br/cpdoc/acervo/dicionarios/verbete-tematico/assembleia-nacional-constituinte-de-1987-88, accessed 28 May 2019.

[25] This upsurge was itself a reaction to the gains obtained by the opposition in elections after the 'opening' and was named the April package ('Pacote de Abril'). The package closed the Congress, imposed restrictive campaigning rules for the elections of 1978, created the infamous figure of indirect elected senators (*senadores biônicos*) for a third of the Senate, altered the composition of the Electoral College, extended the presidential mandate to six years and reduced to simple majority the quorum for constitutional amendments. Ibid.

Nacional dos Bispos do Brasil (National Conference of Bishops of Brazil), the SBPC, Sociedade Brasileira para o Progresso da Ciência (Brazilian Society for the Progress of Science) and the only opposition party at the time, the MDB, Movimento Democrático Brasileiro (Brazilian Democratic Movement).

In the indirect elections at the end of General Ernesto Geisel's presidential mandate in 1978, the candidate of the opposition, General Euler Monteiro, promised to call a constituent assembly if he won. The election was, of course, won by the candidate of the military regime, General João Figueiredo, yet, at that time, the dictatorship had lost so much strength that Figueiredo famously announced in his inauguration speech that 'it was his unswerving aim to make of this country a democracy'.[26] Two important openings followed quickly in 1979 that gave impetus to the project of a new constitution, namely, the Amnesty Law, which allowed back into the country and into politics several of the main opponents of the regime, and the Multi-party Law, which revoked the ban on new parties beyond the only two official ones allowed throughout the military dictatorship (the pro-military Arena and the opposition MDB).[27] Yet the new constitution would need to wait almost another decade, becoming a reality only after the final defeat of the military regime by the opposition front in the presidential (still indirect then) elections of 1984.[28]

The next battle was over whether the constituent assembly should be 'free and sovereign' (i.e., directly elected by the people) and 'exclusive' (i.e., with the exclusive remit to formulate the new constitution and then be disbanded), as most progressives and radicals wanted,[29] or if it should

[26] My translation from Portuguese: 'Reafirmo: é meu propósito inabalável – dentro daqueles princípios – fazer deste País uma democracia.' General João Batista Figueiredo, Inauguration Speech, 15 March 1979, Biblioteca da Presidência da República, available at www.biblioteca.presidencia.gov.br/presidencia/ex-presidentes/jb-figueiredo/discursos/discursos-de-posse/discurso-de-posse, accessed 29 May 2019.

[27] CPDOC-FGV. It is interesting to note that to the redemocratisation argument for a new constitution a technical, and therefore more neutral one was also often invoked. So many changes had been made to the constitution during the military regime that it looked like a 'ragbag'.

[28] The constitutional amendment for direct elections for president was defeated in 1982 yet, with the weakening of the military regime and growing infighting among its supporting base, the opposition managed to win the 1984 indirect elections with the moderate candidates Tancredo Neves (president) and Jose Sarney (vice-president) running under the Aliança Democrática (Democratic Alliance), a coalition between the MDB and the PFL, a dissident party of the pro-military party PDS.

[29] For a classic manifestation in favour of an exclusive constituent assembly, see the open letter of Goffredo Telles Júnior, professor of the University of São Paulo Law School, on

be a 'congressional constituent' (i.e., entrusted to the regular National Congress) to be elected in the forthcoming 1986 elections with the exception of the senators already elected in 1982 for eight years (one-third of the seats), the position preferred by conservatives. In the end, the latter prevailed[30] and the 559 members of the National Congress, who would be at the same time ordinary and constituent legislators (487 representatives in the lower chamber (deputados) and 72 senators, including 23 elected in 1982), started their work on the new constitution in February 1987.[31]

Two important factors have likely influenced the make-up of the constituent assembly. Firstly, the election for congress was held at the same time as elections for governors in the then twenty-three Brazilian states, likely distracting the attention of the electorate from the important

behalf of Plenário Pró-Participação Popular na Constituinte (Plenary for the Popular Participation in the Constituent Assembly), titled 'Carta dos Brasileiros ao Presidente da República e ao Congresso Nacional' ('Letter to Brazilians, to the President of the Republic and to the National Congress'), of 8 August 1987, arguing: 'Let us start from the essential. We start from the statement that the Constituent Power is not Legislative Power. As a consequence, we argue that Legislative Power cannot be promoted into Constituent Power. In other words: the National Congress cannot be converted into a National Constituent Assembly. That would be arbitrary and illegitimate.' My translation from the Portuguese, available at: www.goffredotellesjr.adv.br/site/pagina.php?id_pg=30, accessed 19 June 2019.

30 Emenda Constitucional (Constitutional Amendment) no. 26, approved on 25 November 1985, mandating the establishment of the constituent assembly on 1 February 1987. For Brazilian constitutional lawyer José Afonso da Silva, Emenda Constitucional no. 26 was not a genuine constitutional amendment, but rather a 'revolutionary act, as it put into question the existing constitutional order'. J. A. Silva, *Poder Constituinte e Poder Popular (Estudos sobre a Constituição)* (São Paulo: Malheiros Editores, 2002), at 78.

31 Many believe, wrongly, that the so-called *senadores biônicos* (cyborg senators) indirectly elected in 1978 following Emenda Constitucional (Constitutional Amendment) no. 8, of 14 April 1977, participated in the constituent assembly and therefore reduced its legitimacy. These cyborg senators all finished their mandates in 1986 and thus before the constituent assembly started. Emenda Constitucional no. 15, of 19 November 1980, re-established direct elections for senators. I am indebted to Virgilio Afonso da Silva for preventing me from repeating this mistake. See V. A. da Silva, *The Constitution of Brazil: A Contextual Analysis* (Oxford: Hart Publishing, 2019). Whether the participation of the one-third of senators elected in 1982 was legitimate was a different question, also fiercely disputed. See the challenge ('*questão de ordem*') raised in the second session in 2 February 1987, by representative for São Paulo Plínio Arruda Sampaio (PT), rejected by José Carlos Moreira Alves (then president of the Supremo Tribunal Federal) and by the Plenary by 394 to 124 votes and 17 abstentions. See Assembléia Nacional Constituinte. Diário da Assembléia Nacional Constituinte. Ata da 2ª Sessão (2 February 1987). Brasília: Centro Gráfico do Senado Federal, 1987–1988, p. 9–13. Cf. C. Michiles et al., *Cidadão Constituinte: A saga das emendas populares* (Rio de Janeiro: Paz e Terra, 1989), at 32.

constituent role they were exercising. Secondly, the president then in charge, conservative José Sarney, had just implemented a wide-ranging policy (*pacote econômico*, economic package) to address a severe economic crisis (including a populist 'prices' freeze' across the economy). At the time of the election, the policy was working well and Sarney's popularity was very high. (The policy would derail badly and be abandoned just after the elections.)[32] The predictable but still astonishing outcome of those 1986 elections was that the party of the president (PMDB) won the elections for governors in twenty-two out of the then twenty-three states and, together with its allied centre-right party (PFL), won a staggering majority of 77 per cent of the seats in the lower house and of 81 per cent in the senate, never to be repeated again in Brazilian history.

These circumstances of the elections contributed towards a more conservative National Congress (and, as a consequence, National Constituent Assembly) than social movements and other progressive forces were hoping for.[33] Such make-up would inevitably result in fierce disputes throughout the work of the assembly between those who had

[32] In a tragic development, president-elect Tancredo Neves, the less conservative, though still so, member of the coalition that won the elections against the militaries' candidate (Paulo Maluf from PDS), died of a hospital infection before his inauguration. The presidency was thus occupied by his vice-president, José Sarney, who had collaborated closely with the military dictatorship but opportunistically jumped ship to the opposition alliance when it became clear that he would not be the military's chosen candidate. See entry Alianca Democratica, CPDOC-FGV, www.fgv.br/cpdoc/acervo/dicionarios/verbete-tematico/alianca-democratica, accessed 19 June 2019. Sarney's economic plan ended so badly that Brazil declared a moratorium on its international debt in January 1987.

[33] The actual distribution of the 559 elected members belonging to 13 different parties was as follows: Partido do Movimento Democrático Brasileiro (PMDB) – 303; Partido da Frente Liberal (PFL) – 135; Partido Democrático Social (PDS) – 38; Partido Democrático Trabalhista (PDT) – 26; Partido Trabalhista Brasileiro (PTB) – 18; Partido dos Trabalhadores (PT) – 16; Partido Liberal (PL) – 7; Partido Democrata Cristão (PDC) – 6; Partido Comunista Brasileiro (PCB) – 3; Partido Comunista do Brasil (PCdoB) – 3; Partido Socialista Brasileiro (PSB) – 2; Partido Social Cristão (PSC) – 1 and Partido Municipalista Brasileiro (PMB) – 1. See CPDOC-FGV, note 24. These results added up to a majority of more conservative members, according to Adriano Pilatti. He divides the members of the constituent assembly into a minority progressive bloc formed by the parties of the 'left' (PCB, PC do B, PDT, PSB, PT and, from June 1988, the PSDB – a dissidence from the PMDB) and a majority conservative bloc composed of the following parties: PDS, PFL, PL, PDC, PTB. In one of those Brazilian peculiarities difficult to explain to international audiences, the PMDB, the party with the largest number of congress members (303), and of the President José Sarney, was divided into a progressive wing and a conservative wing, respectively allied to the corresponding bloc. From November 1987, the conservative bloc started to call themselves the 'Centrão' (Big

fought for a new constitution in the hope to change things and those who might have done quite fine without one,[34] starting from the determination of the crucial rules of the operation of the assembly itself (the procedural rules).[35] In the end, the approved procedural rules turned out to be much more favourable to the aims of the progressive group than one could expect from the political make-up of the assembly. And so did the final text of the Constitution, as we will see below, in no small part due to some of these procedural rules. The most important was perhaps the possibility of so-called *Emendas Populares* (Popular Amendments), which allowed for amendment proposals from the public to the text of the Constitution as long as they were supported by a relatively low threshold of signatures (30,000 electors) and had the support from three organisations from civil society.[36]

The enhanced possibility of popular participation through *Emendas Populares* and also public hearings (*audiências públicas*) constituted a powerful counterbalance to the conservative make-up of the assembly. One hundred twenty-two popular amendments were presented (eighty-three of them formally valid) and several proposals contained in such

Centre). Cf. A. Pilatti, *A Constituinte de 1987–1988: Progressistas, Conservadores, Ordem Econômica e Regras do Jogo* (Rio de Janeiro: Editora Lumen Juris, 2008), at 3–4.

34 Some believe that for the conservative group, the ideal was a brief constitutional reform that got rid only of the most truculent aspects of the dictatorial regime and that President Sarney's expectation was precisely that when he commissioned a constitutional bill to the group led by Afonso Arinos. He would be completely disappointed with the rather progressive result. See O. V. Vilhena, *A Batalha dos Poderes* (São Paulo: Cia das Letras, 2019) and P. A. Sampaio., 'Para Além da Ambiguidade: Uma Reflexão Histórica sobre a CF/1988', in Cardoso Junior, J. C. (ed.), *A Constituição brasileira de 1988 revisitada: Recuperação histórica e desafios atuais das políticas públicas nas áreas econômica e social* (Brasília: IPEA, 2009), at 41.

35 The RIANC, Regimento Interno da Assembléia Nacional Constituinte (Procedural Rules of the National Constituent Assembly) was finished only at the end of March, delayed by tensions and conflicts between the conservative and progressive blocs. See Pilatti, *A Constituinte de 1987–1988*, at 28. For the full text in Portuguese, see www2.camara.leg.br/atividade-legislativa/legislacao/Constituicoes_Brasileiras/constituicao-cidada/publicacoes/regimento-interno-da-assembleia-nacional.

36 Michiles et al., *Cidadão Constituinte*. According to Michiles, happy coincidences also made the procedural rules more porous to the inclusion of progressive norms in the constitutional text than they might have otherwise been. One of them was the participation of senator Mario Covas, a high vote getter (PMDB and then PSDB, São Paulo), in a TV debate in São Paulo on popular participation in the constituent assembly just before the works started where innovative progressive ideas made an impression on him. Ibid., at 58. In the end, Fernando Henrique Cardoso, who was the rapporteur of the RIANC, decided to include Covas' proposal, which was however strongly criticised by many parliamentarians.

amendments made it to the final text of the Constitution, including, as we shall see below, several involving health. As the president of the constituent assembly Ulysses Guimarães put it in the same speech where he coined the famous phrase 'the Citizen Constitution':

> There is . . . a representative and oxygenated breath of people, of the street, of the square, of the favela, of the factory, of the workers, of cooks, of needy minors, of Indians, squatters, businessmen, students, retirees, civil and military servants, attesting the contemporaneity and social authenticity of the text that now comes into force.[37]

But the disputes over the final constitutional text were fierce all along and became more dramatic towards the end, as the economic crisis became more acute and social problems, including security, worsened.[38] The centre-right coalition of members (Centrão [Big Centre])[39] also realised, late in the day, that it would have difficulties stopping what they perceived as an overly 'leftist' text, including too many social rights and some prohibitions of private investment in some areas (e.g., oil) and tried to organise a counter-attack. President José Sarney, their man in

[37] My translation from the Portuguese: 'Há, portanto, representativo e oxigenado sopro de gente, de rua, de praça, de favela, de fábrica, de trabalhadores, de cozinheiros, de menores carentes, de índios, de posseiros, de empresários, de estudantes, de aposentados, de servidores civis e militares, atestando a contemporaneidade e autenticidade social do texto que ora passa a vigorar.' Extract from the speech of Ulysses Guimarães, in the promulgation of the Brazilian Constitution on 5 October 1988. Contituent Assembly's Journal Exhibition, 'A Participação Popular nos 25 anos da Constituição Cidadã', Brasília, from 29 October to 8 November 2013, www.senado.leg.br/noticias/especiais/constituicao25anos/exposicao-senado-galeria/Jornal-Constituinte.pdf.

[38] President José Sarney started to blame them on the slowness of the constituent assembly. To compound the problem, the municipal elections of 1988 started to become closer, which diminished the quorum in Congress, as members often travel back to their constituencies more often for campaigning. This, according to some, provided an important advantage to the progressive bloc. Being more assiduous in Brasília than the conservatives, they could negotiate the approval of some of their proposals in exchange for not stopping the work of the assembly for lack of quorum. Sampaio, 'Para Além da Ambiguidade', at 45.

[39] Constituent Parliamentarian Vilson Souza (PMDB-SC) provides a good and concise description of 'Centrão': 'Formed mainly by parliamentarians linked to the military dictatorship (Arena and PDS) and representing the private interests of the dominant oligarchy, maintained by the ideological cement of conservatism, by physiology, patronage and all sorts of corruption, despite their parliamentary majority, they are a minority in the population, since in the last elections they received less than 30% of the votes of the national electorate.' See Senado Federal, Anais da Assembléia Nacional Constituinte, 27 January 1988, p. 339, available at: www.senado.leg.br/publicacoes/anais/constituinte/N011.pdf, accessed 23 June 2019.

government, went as far as doing an official broadcast to the nation at the end of July (something reserved only for exceptional urgent statements) to criticise the text of the proposed constitution and warn that it would lead to a 'brutal explosion of public expenses' and 'make the country ungovernable'.[40] That provoked the immediate response of Ulysses Guimarães, the assembly's president, who persuaded a majority of his peers to approve the text on an urgent vote the following day and delivered an inflamed speech in favour of the Constitution that was also broadcast nationally in the evening news, stating that 'ungovernable was the misery' in which so many Brazilians still lived.[41]

At the end of the assembly's colossal work, riven by fierce political disputes and consistent attempts by the majority conservative bloc to water down the most progressive clauses to the very end, the final text of the Constitution was much more progressive than one would have expected from the composition of the assembly.[42] Among its 315 articles (245 permanent ones and 70 transitional provisions), it contained a large list of human rights, including many social and economic ones and very progressive clauses such as those related to the social function of private property (Art. 5, XXIII), the progressiveness of urban property taxation (Arts. 156, Paragraph 1 and 182, Paragraph 4), land reform (Art. 184) etc. But it also reaffirmed, unambiguously, that private property and free market competition (Art. 170, II and IV) were the basis of the economic system. This led one of the most active members of the progressive bloc of the constituent assembly, Plínio de Arruda Sampaio, to conclude that 'the main characteristic of the 1988 Constitution is ambiguity'. As he added:

40 See 'Sarney diz na TV que Carta deixa país ingovernável', *Folha de S. Paulo* (newspaper), 27 July 1988, https://www2.senado.leg.br/bdsf/bitstream/handle/id/120240/1988_26%20a%2031%20de%20Julho_032.pdf?sequence=3 last, accessed 5.6. June 20292019. He repeated the statement on the 20th twentieth anniversary of the Constitution in 2008 in an interview. https://www.conjur.com.br/2008-set-14/constituicao_88_tornou_pais_ingovernavel_sarney, accessed 20 June 2019.

41 See 'Para Ulysses, ingovernável é a miséria', *O Estado de S. Paulo* (newspaper), 28 July 1988, www2.senado.leg.br/bdsf/bitstream/handle/id/120465/1988_26%20a%2031%20de%20Julho_064.pdf?sequence=1, accessed 20 June 2019.

42 For an interesting first-hand account of the importance of popular pressure and the 'war' waged by the progressive bloc to approve their proposals, see Sampaio, 'Para Além da Ambiguidade' at 44. For him, the success was due to the combination of three different factors: 'the perplexity of bourgeois leaders, the unexpected popular participation, and the competence of the tiny left-wing group of parliamentarians'. One of the tactics of civil society, which crowded Congress during the works of the assembly, was to make large banners with the pictures of members who voted against popular amendments with the title: 'Traitors of the People'.

> This ambiguity is expressed, on one hand, by the reinforcement of the bourgeois order, with the constitutionalisation of the right to property, free enterprise, inheritance and free competition – the foundational institutes of the capitalist regime; and on the other hand, through ordering this bourgeoisie to guarantee the existence of a free, just and solidary society, capable of guaranteeing national sovereignty, of eradicating poverty and reducing social and regional inequalities. It is thus a social democratic charter with nationalistic tonalities.[43]

The Constitution was promulgated on 5 October 1988, having been approved by a vast majority of 474 votes (only 15 voted against it, all of them from the PT [Workers' Party]).

2.4 The Right to Health Survives the Constituent Assembly

The constituent assembly process followed four successive phases: twenty-four sub-commissions, eight thematic commissions, one systematisation commission and the plenary.[44] Health was entrusted to the Sub-Commission of Health, Social Security and the Environment (Health Sub-Commission) in the constituent assembly.[45] Its remit was to listen to and debate with civil society in public hearings to consider their demands and proposals, produce a report and then draft a preliminary bill (*Anteprojeto*) to be sent to the thematic Commission on the Social Order.[46] The Health Sub-Commission was chaired by representative José

[43] Sampaio, 'Para Além da Ambiguidade', at 40.

[44] The assembly worked from February 1987 to September 1988. It was presided over by representative Ulysses Guimarães (PMDB, São Paulo). Every member of the constituent assembly sat in at least one commission as a permanent member and in another as a substitute. The Systematisation Commission (Comissão de Sistematização) had proportional representation, being composed of forty-nine members indicated by the leaders of each party, whose job was to put the eight different texts produced in each of the thematic commissions together into a single bill. This bill was sent to the plenary for vote in two rounds. The power of the rapporteur was significant as he was entrusted with making changes to the text according to assembly members' contributions. Some attribute the length of the final text of the Brazilian Constitution to the lack of trust among the groups involved; others to the mode of operation in so many thinly populated subcommittees. For a great source for all stages of the formation of the Constitution's text, see Senado Federal, A Gênese do Texto da Constituição de 1988, available at www.senado.leg.br/publicacoes/GeneseConstituicao/.

[45] The work of the sub-commissions was done in a relatively short period of time, between the 7 April and 25 May 1987. During this phase, the level of activity (including public participation) was impressive, with 182 public hearings taking place and a staggering 11,989 proposals and 6,417 amendments to the constitutional text.

[46] Rodriguez Neto, *Saúde*, at 59.

Elias Murad of the PTB, Partido Trabalhista Brasileiro (Brazilian Labour Party) and had as rapporteur representative Carlos Mosconi, from the PMDB, Partido do Movimento da Democracia Brasileira (Brazilian Democratic Movement Party), both medical doctors.[47] Like all sub-commissions, it was composed by forty-two members (twenty-one permanent and twenty-one substitutes). At the beginning of the process, few had much knowledge or specific interest in the health system, but the public hearings played an important pedagogic role with presentations from all main representative civil society entities of that sector and government officials.

Rodriguez Neto divides the proposals presented at the sub-commission into three main groups: those in defence of the Sanitary Movement's ideas, those representing the interests of private medicine and those put forward by different federal government departments (namely, the Ministry of Health and the Ministry of Social Security).[48]

The Sanitary Movement, being the most well-organised in comparison to the others, was the only one to present a written draft for the constitutional text to the sub-commission; whereas the other two groups presented only ideas and arguments verbally at that stage.[49] As a result, and with the increasing education and intellectual co-optation of members of the Health Sub-Commission to the theses of the movement, the report approved and sent to the Social Order Commission included almost all of their proposals.[50] This early work was likely determinant to the progressive tone of the final text of the Health chapter of the Constitution, as this initial phase was crucial to including clauses that could later be publicly defended through pressure on members of the thematic and systematisation commissions and the plenary.[51]

47 And both representatives of the state of Minas Gerais, although Carlos Mosconi was originally from São Paulo. For their short biographies as parliamentarian representatives, see www.fgv.br/cpdoc/acervo/dicionarios/verbete-biografico/murad-jose-elias and www.fgv.br/CPDOC/BUSCA/dicionarios/verbete-biografico/carlos-eduardo-venturelli-mosconi.

48 Rodriguez Neto, *Saúde*, at 61. At that time, an internal dispute was raging between these two departments about which one should keep health in its portfolio, Ibid., at 62–63.

49 Ibid.

50 For the full text, see Senado Federal, Assembléia Nacional Constituinte, Ata das Comissões, Anexo à Ata da 24.a Reunião da Subcomissão de Saúde, Seguridade e do Meio Ambiente, 25 May 1987, at 326.

51 This phase was especially important as, unusually in the history of Brazil's previous constitutions, the constituent assembly started its work without a draft bill. See the speech of constituent Afonso Arinos in Congress, on 24 April 1987, whose draft bill was

But the path was not that smooth, nor totally successful. The subcommission's draft text of the Health chapter would face fierce opposition in all subsequent phases of the assembly, especially from members and organisations defending the interests of private hospitals and private health insurance companies. The more radical idea of completely eliminating private medicine from the Brazilian health system, defended by some in the Sanitary Movement, did not take off, not even in the subcommission, which included an article in its draft Health chapter expressly authorising the private health system to operate, though vaguely subordinating it to the principles of the national health policy.[52] The interests of private health and others not entirely satisfied with other parts of the movement's proposal would succeed in further changing the constitutional text in the subsequent phases of the assembly.

Already in the second phase, that is, at the Social Order Commission, two important components of the initial proposal fell off the draft text: the duty of the state to allocate a minimum of 10 per cent of the GDP to health and the prohibition of advertising of medicines, treatments, tobacco and alcoholic drinks.[53]

discarded by President Sarney as we saw earlier. See Senado Federal, Assembléia Nacional Constituinte, Ata das Comissões, Ata da Reunião de Instalação da Comissão de Sistematização, at 8.

52 The text read: 'Art. 6. The free exercise of the liberal activity in health and the organisation of private health services are guaranteed, according to the ethical and technical precepts determined by the Law and the principles that guide the national health policy.' And, 'Art. 4, § 1. The private sector of health services can collaborate in the provision of health assistance to the population, under the conditions established in a public law contract, with preference and special treatment of non-profit entities.' For an interesting exchange between representatives of private medicine and constituent members in favour of strong public control of health, see Senado Federal, Assembléia Nacional Constituinte, Ata das Comissões, 9.a Reunião da Subcomissão de Saúde, Seguridade e do Meio Ambiente, Realizada dia 23 de abril de 1987, p. 98, in particular, the exchanges between parliamentarian Eduardo Jorge and representatives of private health insurance and private hospitals.

53 Art. 3., § 2 read: 'National expenditures on health shall not be less than ten per cent of the Gross Domestic Product. Art. 8. Commercial advertising of drugs, forms of treatment, tobacco and alcoholic beverages is prohibited.' That happened notwithstanding the fact that the rapporteur of the Social Order Commission, representative Almir Gabriel from the PMDB of Pará, was also a doctor closely linked to the movement. A watered-down version of Article 8 was included in the final text of the Constitution in the Social Communication chapter: 'Art. 220, § 4: Paragraph 4. The commercial advertisement of tobacco, alcoholic beverages, pesticides, medicines and therapies shall be subject to legal restrictions, in accordance with item II of the previous paragraph, and shall contain, whenever necessary, a warning about the harm arising from its use.'

In the third phase, at the Systematisation Commission, though by definition just a systematisation phase of the draft bills already approved in the sub-commissions and thematic commissions, amendments by members of the assembly and the *Emendas Populares* were debated and voted upon and had the potential, thus, of substantially changing the draft that came from the Social Order Commission.[54] In discussions of the Health chapter, activity during this phase was very intense. There were six popular amendments and another six different proposals by assembly members, a government minister and the Sanitary Movement.[55] At that stage, most of the work of Sanitary Movement at the previous thematic commissions risked being lost as the rapporteur, Bernardo Cabral, decided to reduce significantly the text of the Health chapter to only three concise articles.[56]

Pressure from parliamentarians aligned with the movement's proposals and from civil society managed to restore most of the original text but were not successful in their attempt to enhance it with further progressive clauses, such as the detailed specification that the right to health was strongly dependent on the following social determinants, which should themselves be recognised as fundamental rights: 'access to land and to the means of production' and 'dignified conditions of work, sanitation, housing, food, education, transport and leisure'.[57] The

[54] One can imagine the complexity of organising the materials generated in this phase under a single constitution. It happened gradually and of course not without a lot of disputes. By 26 June, the first formal amalgamation was completed by rapporteur Bernardo Cabral and had no less than 501 articles. The work was so overwhelming that five adjunct rapporteurs had to be appointed to help in the job of turning the document into a coherent single piece to be voted by Congress. They were Adolfo de Oliveira (PL-RJ), Antônio Carlos Konder Reis (PDS-SC), Fernando Henrique Cardoso (PMDB-PSDB-SP), Nélson Jobim (PMDB-RS) and Wilson Marins (PMDB-MS).

[55] The *Emendas Populares* were presented by the following groups: the Health Plenary (aligned with the Sanitary Movement), professional entities of the state of Mato Grosso do Sul, Brazilian Institute of Natural Medicine, National Federation of Associations of Alternative Medicine, Psychology Commission for the Constituent, and representing private health interests the FBH (National Federation of Hospitals), the Abramge (Brazilian Association of Group Medicine) and Fenaess (National Federation of Health Facilities and Services). According to Rodriguez Neto, the five separate amendments whose ideas converged with the Sanitary Movement's should have been merged to give them more strength. Rodriguez Neto, *Saúde*, at 72.

[56] See, for all textual changes at all phases, Senado Federal, 2013, A Gênese do Texto da Constituição de 1988, Volume I – Quadros, www.senado.leg.br/publicacoes/GeneseConstituicao/pdf/genese-cf-1988-1.pdf#cap1r.

[57] Popular Amendment no. 50 presented by the Federal Medical Council, the Brazilian Nutrition Federation and the Union of Nurses of the Federal District. The relatively low

attempt to establish a state monopoly in the importation of pharmaceutical chemical components and a state duty to invest a minimum of 13 per cent of tax revenues in health, gradually reaching a standard of 10 per cent of GDP also failed. But the movement was nonetheless satisfied with the final result as it preserved most of its main proposals.[58]

The next and final battle would take place in the plenary, when the full constitution's bill was finally debated and voted by all members. As we saw in Section 2.3, this was when the conservative bloc (the Centrão), with the support of President José Sarney and business lobbies, tried more strongly to reverse the progressive clauses of the Constitution's bill. Against them was a procedural rule that prevented 'wholesale' changes to the text of the Systematisation Commission. Changes would need to be done 'piecemeal', with separate proposals and votes for each clause of the Constitution, which would require the mobilisation of 280 members each time, not an easy feat despite Centrão's large number of parliamentarians.[59] To circumvent that obstacle, the Centrão presented a proposal for change of the constituent assembly's procedural rules itself, allowing for so-called global substitute amendments, that is, proposals for complete replacement of the text of the Systematisation Commission.[60] After succeeding in this strategy, it presented its own draft bill of the

number of signatures collected (55,117) was a sign, some claim, of a certain distance between the leaders of the Sanitary Movement and the general public and grassroots associations. Rodriguez Neto, *Saúde*, at 71. For comparison, note that amendments on land reform, public education, workers' rights and children's rights all got close to or above one million signatures. Altogether, Popular Amendments on all issues received 11.2 million signatures across Brazil. See 'Emendas populares obtêm mais de 11,2 milhões de assinaturas', www2.senado.leg.br/bdsf/bitstream/handle/id/129656/Agosto%201987%20-%200484.pdf?sequence=1, accessed 20 June 2019.

58 Popular Amendment no. 71 presented by the groups in favour of private medicine to constitutionalise 'pluralism' of service providers and a right of individuals to choose among them also failed. For all Popular Amendments presented during the assembly see Assembléia Nacional Constituinte, vol. 258, Emendas Populares, Centro Gráfico do Senado Federal, January 1988, www.camara.gov.br/internet/constituicao20anos/DocumentosAvulsos/vol-258.pdf, accessed 18 June 2019.

59 See Centro de Pesquisa e Documentação de História Contemporânea do Brasil (CPDOC), Fundação Getúlio Vargas, Entry Centrao, at www.fgv.br/CPDOC/BUSCA/dicionarios/verbete-tematico/centrao and Camara dos Deputados, 25 Anos da Constituição de 1988, Momentos Marcantes da Constituinte, at www2.camara.leg.br/atividade-legislativa/plenario/discursos/escrevendohistoria/25-anos-da-constituicao-de-1988/momentos-marcantes-da-constituinte, accessed 23 June 2019.

60 Art. 59 RIANC, Regimento Interno da Assembléia Nacional Constituinte (Procedural Rules of the National onstituent Assembly).

Constitution, which, if approved, would erase many of the progressive clauses vigorously fought for in the first three phases of the assembly.

In the Social Security chapter, Centrão's proposal was described as 'a declaration of war against society, a desperate instrument of a class that wants to keep power to direct state action to their own interests'.[61] As regards the specific chapter on health, their proposal was more subtle. It started by recognising health as a right of all and a duty of the state, exactly as proposed by the Sanitary Movement. The devil was in the details of how such a right would be implemented. Whereas the movement's proposal stated unambiguously that the right to health is 'guaranteed' by universal and egalitarian access to public policies aimed at 'eliminating or reducing' health risks, Centrão referred to a milder 'facilitation' by the state of such policies and mentioned only 'reduction' of health risks (not elimination). Its proposal also allowed much more fragmentation in the public system, with greater autonomy for states and municipalities, which went against one of the main planks of the Sanitary Movement's proposal, and which was the creation of a genuinely 'unified' system that brought together all spheres of government (federal, state and municipal), the only way in their view to combat pronounced regional inequalities.[62]

In the end, Centrão's ability to impose its proposals proved much lower than its large numbers suggested. Its members were much less united than had first appeared and popular pressure against their last-minute move was intense.[63] As representative Florestan Fernandes (PT-SP) commented at the time, 'Brazilian society is not approving what "Centrão" is doing; it is reacting and this means something very important. It means that democracy is growing where it is essential that it grows: in civil society.'[64] Some of these reactions from the public seem to have had a particularly strong impact, such as the shower of money on

[61] Representative Vilson Souza (PMDB-SC), Senado Federal, Anais da Assembléia Nacional Constituinte, 27 January 1988, p. 6.600, available at: www.senado.leg.br/publicacoes/anais/constituinte/N011.pdf, accessed 23 June 2019.

[62] See the analysis by Rodriguez Neto of Centrão's proposal, *Saúde*, at 79. It is interesting to note how the fragmentation strategy was also tried by opponents of the British National Health System when it was being proposed by the post-war Labour Government in the late 1940s. See BBC, Birth of the National Health Service, www.bbc.co.uk/programmes/p018vq3l.

[63] In the field of health, one of its most important members, Carlos Sant'Anna, was actually in favour of the Sanitary Movement's proposal. See Rodriguez Neto, Saúde, at 82.

[64] Speech of 6 February 1988, Senado Federal, Anais da Assembléia Nacional Constituinte, vol. 2, 7025.

Centrão members' heads from the Congress' public galleries and the simulation of Centrão's burial in front of the National Congress by trade union leaders.[65]

When the Constitution was finally promulgated on 5 October 1988, the text of the Health chapter was much closer to the Sanitary Movement's ideal proposal than anyone else's. The headline of *Visão Magazine*, a mainstream weakly of the time, gives a good if rather exaggerated indication. 'Constituent: the end of private medicine.'[66] In reality, the movement's more radical aims of eliminating or significantly reducing the participation of private providers in the public system was not achieved, as we saw, far from it. In a strategic concession, private providers were in the end admitted on a 'complementary' basis (Article 199), yet without access to public subsidies, and to this date have a significant presence in the health system, as we will see in Chapter 4. But the universal, egalitarian, state-funded right to health gained a place in the final text of the Constitution, reflecting almost entirely the ideas of the Sanitary Movement.[67] As the final text read:

> Article 196. Health is a right of all and a duty of the state and shall be guaranteed by means of social and economic policies aimed at reducing

[65] See M. Guran (ed.), *O Processo Constituinte 1987–1988: Documentação fotográfica. A Nova Constituição.* (Brasília: AGIL, 1988), at 102 and 108.

[66] Rodriguez Neto, *Saúde*, at 84.

[67] See Paim, 'A Reforma Sanitária Brasileira e o Sistema Único de Saúde', at 632: The movement succeeded 'in inscribing a substantive part of its bill in the Constitution of the Republic and in the infra-constitutional legislation, even though it faced difficulties in the process of implementing what it had promised'. It is interesting to note that, as progressive as they may seem, the Sanitary Movement's proposals were not progressive enough for the trade union movement, whose members wanted the complete elimination of private initiative from health. At the other end of the spectrum, health businesses thought those proposals were way too radical. See I. Falleiros, J. C. F. Lima, G. Matta et al., 'A Constituinte e o Sistema Único de Saúde', in Ponte, C. F. and Falleiros, I. (eds.), *Na corda bamba de sombrinha: A saúde no fio da história* (Rio de Janeiro: Fiocruz, 2010), at 242. The speech of representative Arnaldo Faria de Sá (PTB-SP), of 18 June 1987, illustrates well the businesses' position: 'If the state is unable to perform even basic health actions, or even eliminate mosquitoes that transmit disease, much less will it be able to perform medical and hospital services as the sanitarists want. In any case, if the project is approved as originally proposed, its price, once again, will be paid by the taxpayer. The nationalization will require that the tax burden on Brazilians will be doubled.' Senado Federal, Anais da Assembléia Nacional Constituinte, vol. 5, p. 2755. See also the speech of representative Inocêncio Oliveira (PFL-PE): 'to characterise health actions as being of public nature is to make the private sector unfeasible and, therefore, to make the entire health sector unfeasible in Brazil'. Senado Federal, Anais da Assembléia Nacional Constituinte, 23 July 1987, vol. 6, p. 3531.

the risk of illness and other hazards and at the universal and egalitarian access to actions and services for its promotion, protection and recovery.

Article 197. Health actions and services are of public importance, and it is incumbent upon the Government to provide, in accordance with the law, for their regulation, supervision and control, and they shall be carried out directly or by third parties and also by individuals or private legal entities.

Article 198. Health actions and public services integrate a regionalized and hierarchical network and constitute a single system . . .

Paragraph 1. The unified health system shall be financed, as set forth in article 195, with funds from the social welfare budget of the union, the states, the federal district and the municipalities, as well as from other sources.

Article 199. Health assistance is open to private enterprise.

Paragraph 1. Private institutions may participate in a complementary manner in the unified health system, in accordance with the directives established by the latter, by means of public law contracts or agreements, preference being given to philanthropic and non-profit entities.[68]

2.5 Text and Reality: Did the Constitution Work?

It is a truism that legislative change does not automatically translate into social change. 'Law in books' and 'law in action' inevitably diverge, often widely. It would be therefore naive to expect that the promulgation of the 'Citizen Constitution' in 1988, as progressive as its final text may have turned out, would radically transform, in a short period of time, one of the most unequal countries in the world. Given Brazil's challenging historical legacy – almost four centuries of slavery, strong concentration of power in the hands of small economic and political elites, weak democratic tradition – the most likely development to be expected would have been inertia and outright blockage of the implementation of the transformative clauses of the Constitution.

And this is, to a great extent, what actually happened, to varying degrees, with many of the most progressive clauses. To cite a classic example, Paragraph 3 of Article 192 of the Constitution, which limited the interests that banks could charge to 12 per cent a year, was never implemented through ordinary legislation as mandated by the Constitution and ended up being revoked in 2003 through

[68] These are only the main provisions. For the full text in English, see Constitution of the Federative Republic of Brazil, 3rd ed., Biblioteca Digital da Câmara dos Deputados, 2010, http://bd.camara.leg.br/bd/handle/bdcamara/36019#.

Constitutional Amendment 40.[69] Another example was the blockage, led by the Supreme Court itself, of municipalities that attempted to introduce progressivity in urban property taxes based on Articles 156 and 182 of the Constitution (until Constitutional Amendment 29 of 2000 reinforced the original constitutional norm).[70] As we saw earlier, the Executive at the time was occupied by a president who voiced loudly his opposition to the 'Social Order' chapter of the new constitution, saying that the country would become 'ungovernable' if all the promises of that chapter were actually implemented. The Congress, on which many of the constitutional provisions depended to become effective (the technique of leaving vague constitutional clauses to be specified by infra-constitutional legislation was adopted prodigally) was populated by a majority of conservative members. This unfavourable situation (at least from a progressive perspective) did not change much with the elections of 1989, the first after the military period in which the president was elected through direct popular vote, and the first with the participation of the illiterate in almost one hundred years.[71] The left, led by Luiz Inácio da Silva ('Lula'), did reasonably well in the presidential elections, but lost in the end by a 6 per cent margin to a populist candidate on the right of the political spectrum, Fernando Collor de Mello (from a small party created less than five years earlier that had not managed to elect a single candidate to the constituent assembly).[72] In Congress, where elections were held a year later in 1990, progressive parties captured less than a

[69] See Supremo Tribunal Federal, A Constituição e o Supremo, www.stf.jus.br/portal/constituicao/artigobd.asp?item=%201777, accessed 23 June 2019.

[70] See Supremo Tribunal Federal, Aplicação das Súmulas no STF, www.stf.jus.br/portal/jurisprudencia/menuSumarioSumulas.asp?sumula=1521, accessed 23 June 2019.

[71] The illiterate were allowed to vote in Brazil throughout the period of the colony (which lasted from 1500 to 1822) and empire (1822 to 1889), but were legally disenfranchised in 1891, with Law Saraiva, whose initial project was written by then young lawyer Ruy Barbosa, who would become a leading figure in Brazilian politics. In 1985, when they recovered the right to vote in municipal elections, they were nineteen million people, around 25 per cent of the population. See R. Westin, 'Por 100 anos, analfabeto foi proibido de votar no Brasil' ('For one hundred years the illiterate was forbidden to vote in Brazil'), at 4 November 2016, Senate news, www12.senado.leg.br/noticias/materias/2016/11/04/por-100-anos-analfabeto-foi-proibido-de-votar-no-brasil, accessed 1 May 2019.

[72] Lula would become president twelve years later, in the elections of 2002, and be re-elected in 2006. For Fernando Collor de Mello, see Centro de Pesquisa e Documentação de História Contemporânea do Brasil (CPDOC), Fundação Getúlio Vargas, Entry Partido da Reconstrucao Nacional (PRN) www.fgv.br/cpdoc/acervo/dicionarios/verbete-tematico/partido-da-reconstrucao-nacional-prn.

quarter of the seats (Lula's PT won only thirty-five seats, less than 7 per cent of the total).[73]

Moreover, just as the Constitution started its life in the late 1980s, Brazil faced a serious economic and financial crisis, making it rather difficult, even with strong political will (not the case, as we have just seen) for the resources required for the implementation of the Social Order chapter to be found. The economy contracted by 3.1 per cent in 1990, after an already long period of low or negative rates dubbed the 'lost decade'.[74] Inflation exploded, reaching an annual rate of 1,764 per cent in 1989 and then 2,477 per cent in 1993, its historical record. In 1987, Brazil had to default on its huge international debt with private creditors (R$121 billion), leading to difficult and protracted negotiations involving the IMF.[75] All of that happened, it is important to recall, as neo-liberal thinking was peaking across the world with its fierce opposition to state social expenditure and state-run services. Its spread in Latin America was particularly strong through the adoption of policies that were part of what became known as the Washington Consensus.[76]

[73] See L. M. Rodrigues, *Partidos, Ideologia e Composição Social: Um Estudo das Bancadas Partidárias na Câmara dos Deputados* (Rio de Janeiro: Centro Edelstein de Pesquisas Sociais, 2009), available at http://observatory-elites.org/wp-content/uploads/2011/11/RODRIGUES-L.-M.-Partidos-ideologia-e-composicao-social.pdf, accessed 1 May 2019.

[74] See M. M. Valença, 'The Lost Decade and the Brazilian Government's Response in the 1990s', (1998) 33(1) *The Journal of Developing Areas*, 1–52. For growth data, see The World Bank, https://data.worldbank.org/indicator/ny.gdp.mktp.kd.zg?end=2017&locations=br&start=2017&view=bar.

[75] See P. R. Almeida, 'O Brasil e o FMI desde Bretton Woods: 70 Anos de História', (2014) 10(2) *Revista Direito GV*, 469–496, at 482. See also CPDOC-FGV, entry External Debt, www.fgv.br/CPDOC/BUSCA/dicionarios/verbete-tematico/divida-externa-2, accessed 1 May 2019.

[76] See J. Williamson, 'What Washington Means by Policy Reform', in J. Williamson (ed.), *Latin American Adjustment: How Much Has Happened?*, available at https://piie.com/commentary/speeches-papers/what-washington-means-policy-reform. A Short History of the Washington Consensus, available at https://piie.com/publications/papers/williamson0904-2.pdf. As Williamson, who coined the phrase, explains, what he called the Washington Consensus was 'a list of ten policies that I thought more or less everyone in Washington would agree were needed more or less everywhere in Latin America', among which were fiscal discipline, trade liberalisation, privatisation, liberalisation of foreign direct investment, reordering of public expenditure priorities from 'nonmerit subsidies to basic health and education', but not, according to him, many of the main ideas of neoliberalism, monetarism, supply-side economics, and minimal government, [which] had by then been discarded as impractical or undesirable fads', at 2. In his view, thus, when 'the term is being used as a pseudonym for market fundamentalism . . .. That is a caricature. We have no business to be propagating caricatures', at 13–14.

It seems fair to say, thus, that the economic and political climate in the aftermath of the promulgation of the Constitution of 1988 was far from favourable for the actual implementation of its egalitarian redistributive clauses, including the right to health. Under such adverse conditions, any improvement would be surprising. Yet, as we shall see in Chapter 3, the fact is that the constitutional transformative promises in the field of health have not remained symbolic, in fact, far from that.

3

The Constitution Works

Obey the law![1]

IX National Health Conference, 1992

Mr Rapporteur, we know that one of the greatest difficulties in drawing up a constitution is precisely to give effect to the provisions which are registered there. Otherwise our Constitution will only become a simple formal declaration of rights that will never be implemented in the course of its existence.[2]

Representative Lysâneas Maciel, Constituent Assembly, 1987

It is not difficult to see that the constitutional guarantee of a comprehensive, universal and egalitarian health system is far from being fulfilled in Brazil. Because the ambition of proponents of the right to health was very high (revolutionary, really) and the political and economic obstacles rather daunting, it would be extraordinary if, in the space of three decades, the constitutional promise had been fully redeemed, becoming a well-established and secured reality in the lives of the whole Brazilian population. As Carlos Paiva and Luiz Teixeira have aptly noted:

> The difficulties of putting into practice radical policies, which clashed with the economic interests of highly organized groups, were added to

[1] '*Cumpra-se a lei!*' was the slogan of the IX National Health Conference, which was postponed until 1992 given the political difficulties of the early 1990s to advance the progressive agenda of the Constitution; see M. R. Bertolozzi, R. M. Greco, 'Health Politics in Brasil: Historical Review and Perspectives', (1996) 30(3) *Revista da Escola de Enfermagem da USP*, 380–398.

[2] Senado Federal, Anais da Assembléia Nacional Constituinte, 5.a Reunião Extraordinária da Comissão de Sistematização, 29 June 1987, 163–164, www.senado.leg.br/publicacoes/anais/asp/CT_Abertura.asp, accessed 23 June 2019. Interestingly, his proposed solution was the creation of a Tribunal of Constitutional Guarantees (Tribunal de Garantias Constitucionais).

> the complexity of the challenge represented by the implementation of a unified health system in a country with enormous regional disparities.[3]

What is indeed actually surprising, in my view, is that the right to health has achieved quite a lot in such a short period of time. As this chapter shows, significant health improvements were experienced by a large proportion of the Brazilian population in the last three decades, in particular, among the poor, and these have been strongly influenced, I argue, by the inclusion of health as a human right in the 1988 Constitution. Without the constitutional entrenchment of that powerful political tool, it is rather doubtful that those seeking health reform would have been able to implement their ideals through the concrete institutional and policy changes that, as we will see, have had a significant impact on the health of the population.

The main argument of this chapter, thus, is that the Constitution has worked reasonably well in light of what could have been expected and that the Constitution remains important to prevent backslide (a real risk under present political conditions) and to support further progressive measures in the future. The lessons of how progress has occurred in the past three decades through what I call the 'politics of the right to health' are, in my view, important ones. They start to show something that will become increasingly clear as the book progresses: the most promising route for change in Brazil (but I suspect this is valid for many other democracies) is through *politics*, not *lawyers* and *courts*. This contradicts two opposite but equally problematic views quite prevalent in the literature on the effectiveness of social rights, already mentioned in Chapter 1. One, overly pessimistic, sees social rights as hopelessly futile to produce social change; the other, overly legalistic, sees them as currently neglected by politicians yet capable of being saved by lawyers and judges. Both seem to underestimate the *political* force of social rights, overlooking significant improvements achieved in the past three decades through the mainstream political tools of legislation and administrative action and with little input from (and often despite the unhelpful activity of) legal professionals.

[3] C. H. A. Paiva, L. A. Teixeira, 'Health Reform and the Creation of the Sistema Único de Saúde: Notes on Contexts and Authors'), (2014) 21(1) *História, Ciência, Saúde-Manguinhos*, 15–36.

3.1 Social Improvement Since the Constitution

Let us start with an overview of the progress in population well-being that took place in the period of the Constitution's life, that is, the past three decades. The Human Development Index (HDI), released every year since 1990 by the United Nations Development Programme (UNDP), provides a good starting point. It assesses long-term progress in three basic dimensions of human development: 'a long and healthy life, access to knowledge and a decent standard of living'.[4] It goes from 0 (worst possible rate) to 1 (the best) and is currently subdivided into the following brackets: very high (above 0.8), high (between 0.7 and 0.799), medium (between 0.555 and 0.699) and low (0.544 and below).

Brazil's HDI value for 2017, the latest available, was 0.759, putting it in the high human development category. Between 1990 and 2017, Brazil's HDI value increased by 24.3 per cent, rising from 0.611 (medium) to 0.759 (high) (see Figure 3.1). The largest increase took place in the health component of the index, as life expectancy at birth improved by 10.4 years, going from 65.3 years in 1990 to 75.7 in 2017. The other components improved too: mean years of schooling by 4 years, more than doubling from 3.8 to 7.8 and expected years of schooling by 3.2 years (from 12.2 to 15.4). Brazil's income as measured by GNI per capita increased by about 29 per cent between 1990 and 2017.[5]

One could wonder, of course, how impressive these numbers actually are in comparison to what happened in the rest of the world, where improvements also took place in most countries. It is interesting to note, thus, that Brazil's current HDI is above the average HDI of countries in

[4] According to the UNDP: 'A long and healthy life is measured by life expectancy. Knowledge level is measured by mean years of education among the adult population, which is the average number of years of education received in a life-time by people aged 25 years and older; and access to learning and knowledge by expected years of schooling for children of school-entry age, which is the total number of years of schooling a child of school-entry age can expect to receive if prevailing patterns of age-specific enrolment rates stay the same throughout the child's life. Standard of living is measured by Gross National Income (GNI) per capita expressed in constant 2011 international dollars converted using purchasing power parity (PPP) conversion rates.' See Human Development Indices and Indicators: 2018 Statistical Update, Briefing Note for Countries on the 2018 Statistical Update, Brazil, United Nations Development Programme, available at http://hdr.undp.org/sites/all/themes/hdr_theme/country-notes/BRA.pdf, accessed 3 May 2019. See also, for further details on how the HDI is calculated, the Technical Notes, available at http://hdr.undp.org/sites/default/files/hdr2018_technical_notes.pdf.

[5] All data available from United Nations Development Programme, Human Development Reports, available at http://hdr.undp.org/en, accessed 21 June 2019.

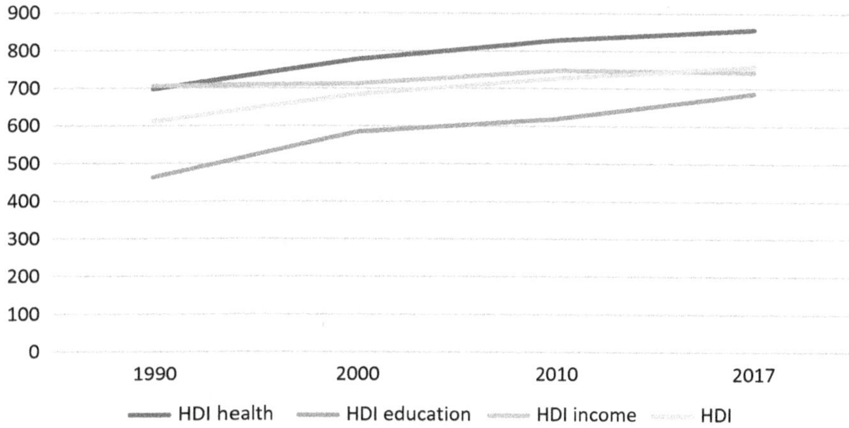

Figure 3.1 Brazil HDI progress.
Source: United Nations Development Programme, Human Development Reports

the high human development group (0.757) and above the average HDI of countries in Latin America and the Caribbean (0.758). Moreover, from 1990 to 2017, it grew at an average annual rate of 0.81 per cent, which is higher than the average world annual rate (0.73 per cent) and the Latin American and Caribbean region (0.71 per cent).[6] It seems clear, thus, that although Brazil is still below where it could (and, in my view, should) be given its wealth (see Chapter 4), there are signs that it did improve significantly in the past three decades and also at a higher rate than global and regional trends.

It is also true, I hasten to add, that the HDI expresses an average and that Brazil's levels of inequality are still so high that these gains have not been felt by those at the bottom of society as much as would have been desirable, as we will see in more detail in Chapter 4. But the most disadvantaged have nonetheless experienced important improvements in their well-being, particularly in health, as we will see in this chapter through more specific indicators than the HDI.

But let us start with the reduction in poverty experienced by the Brazilian population in the past three decades. Extreme poverty, as

[6] United Nations Development Programme, Human Development Reports, table 2, Human Development Index Trends, 1990–2017, available at http://hdr.undp.org/en/composite/trends, accessed 3 May 2019.

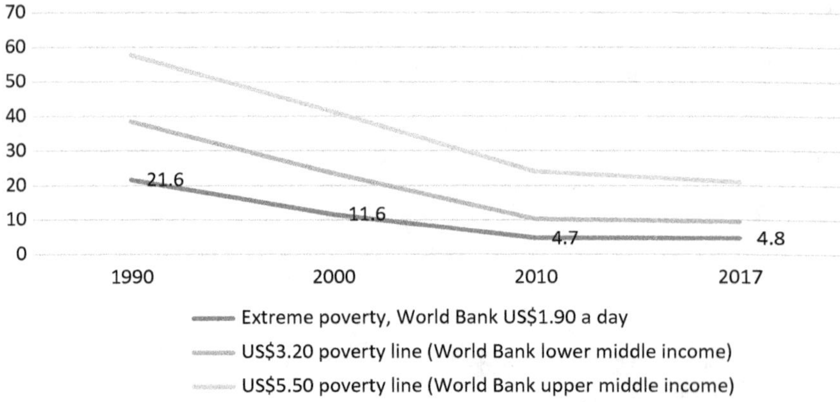

Figure 3.2 Poverty reduction since the Constitution, in % of population.
Source: World Bank Poverty & Equity Data Portal[7]

measured by the controversial yet still useful one dollar a day threshold (currently $1.90) of the World Bank, sunk from 21.6 per cent of the population in 1990 to 4.8 per cent in 2017. When we use other, higher thresholds, improvement has also been significant, falling from 38.5 per cent to 9.6 per cent on the $3.30 a day threshold used for lower middle-income countries and from 57.8 per cent to 21 per cent on the $5.50 a day threshold used by the World Bank for upper middle-income countries (see Figure 3.2).

Improvements in the field of health have also been rather significant in the past three decades. I mentioned earlier that life expectancy went up by 10.4 years since 1990. This was, in great part, the direct result of significant improvements in health and decreases in premature death for all age groups.

In children's health, progress has been perhaps the most significant, with infant and child mortality and morbidity decreasing from very high levels to much (not yet ideal, of course) lower ones (see Figure 3.3). Leading causes of premature mortality changed substantially, such as diarrhoeal diseases, which moved from the first leading cause of premature death in 1990 to the thirteenth in 2005 and then the thirty-sixth position in 2015.[8]

[7] http://povertydata.worldbank.org/poverty/country/BRA, accessed 22 May 2019.

[8] E. B. França et al., 'Cause-Specific Mortality for 249 Causes in Brazil and States during 1990–2015: A Systematic Analysis for the Global Burden of Disease Study 2015', (2017) 15(1) *Population Health Metrics*, at 39.

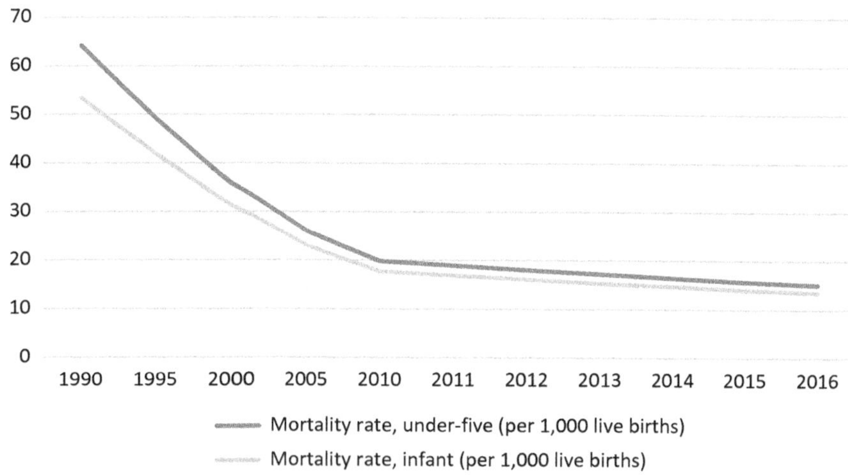

Figure 3.3 Infant and child mortality in Brazil.
Source: United Nations Development Programme, Human Development Reports

Adult mortality and morbidity have also improved, as Figure 3.4 shows, reducing the so-called total age-standardised years of life lost (YLL) in the period from 1990 to 2015 and bringing the burden of premature deaths closer to expected rates given Brazil's Socio-demographic Index (SDI).[9]

These improvements did not occur with the same intensity everywhere in the country (as we will see in Chapter 4), nor for all age groups, but they did occur almost universally.[10] What public health experts call the

[9] In 1990, ischemic heart disease (IHD), stroke, diarrhoea, neonatal preterm birth complications, road injury and violence had ratios higher than the expected, while in 2015, only violence was higher overall and in all states, according to the SDI. França et al., 'Cause-Specific Mortality for 249 Causes in Brazil'. The SDI is a summary measure of a geography's socio-demographic development based on average income per person, educational attainment and total fertility rate (TFR), developed by the Institute for Health Metrics and Evaluation (IHME), which helps to compare countries' health achievements.

[10] At the state level, the decrease varied from 34.9 per cent in the Federal District to 6.7 per cent in Amapá. The notable and sad exception was among males between 15 and 49 years of age, whose risk of death increased between 1990 and 2015 in 12 out of 27 states, in great part driven by gun violence. See França et al., 'Cause-Specific Mortality for 249 Causes in Brazil'.

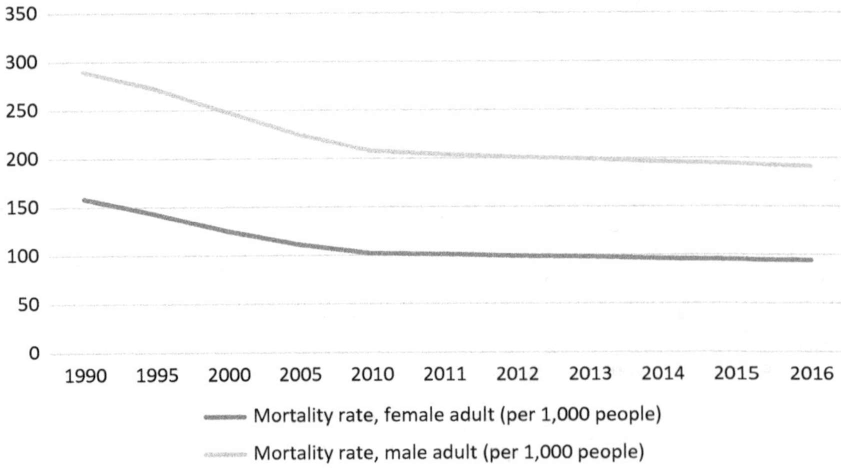

Figure 3.4 Adult mortality in Brazil.
Source: United Nations Development Programme, Human Development Reports

'total age-standardised mortality rate'[11] decreased 28.7 per cent since 1990, from 1102.2 to 786.2 per 100,000 people for both sexes.[12]

***

The expected mismatch between the ambitious promises of the Constitution and the reality on the ground, between the so-called law in the books and the law in action, has, of course, not disappeared in the three decades since the enactment of the 1988 Constitution. It would be unreasonable to expect it to have done so. But it is very difficult to argue that nothing, or not much, has changed. Unless one is willing and able to completely refute the data (more to come in Section 3.2), it is hard to deny that the social progress experienced in Brazil in the past three decades has not been trivial.[13]

[11] As explained by the WHO, 'The age-standardised mortality rate is a weighted average of the age-specific mortality rates per 100,000 persons, where the weights are the proportions of persons in the corresponding age groups of the WHO standard population.' See WHO, Age-Standardized Death Rates per 100,000 by Cause, available at www.who.int/whosis/whostat2006AgeStandardizedDeathRates.pdf, accessed 23 June 2019.

[12] França et al., 'Cause-Specific Mortality for 249 Causes in Brazil'.

[13] Those who fail to see any progress in human rights in general and social rights in particular seem to either overlook the data or adopt what Kathryn Sikkink calls

How significant these improvements have been and how much more could have been achieved are, of course, debatable and controversial issues, which I will return to in Chapter 4.[14] My aim here is simply to show that, against all the challenges discussed in Chapter 2, the Constitution has indeed worked, and not trivially, particularly in the field of health.[15]

But how can we be sure that these improvements have been the work of the Constitution? This is a fair question that many are likely to be impatiently raising by now. At this stage, the classic 'correlation is not causation' point is probably in the mind of many readers. Let me clarify, thus, that my argument is not that the constitutionalisation of the right to health in 1988 is the exclusive or even the main determining factor of all health improvements witnessed in the past three decades. Of course not. As we have seen, during the same period, Brazil also experienced significant economic growth, some reduction in economic inequality through increases in the minimum wage, expansion of education and social security as a whole and many other political, socioeconomic and cultural changes that have all certainly had an important impact in the improvement of the health and well-being of the Brazilian population. My argument, rather, is that without the right to health firmly entrenched in the Constitution, it is difficult to fully explain the myriad concrete

'comparison to the ideal' rather than empirical comparison, as I am doing here. See her excellent book, *Evidence for Hope: Making Human Rights Work in the Twenty-first Century* (Princeton: Princeton University Press, 2017). As she explains (p. 32): 'My understanding of comparison to the ideal is related to maximalist theories of justice [i.e., what perfect justice would look like in an ideal world], while empirical comparisons are connected to the optimum approach, or alternative within the realm of the possible.'

14 For two quite different views by leading Brazilian scholars, see M. Arretche, 'Democracia e redução da desigualdade econômica no Brasil: A inclusão dos outsiders', (2018) 33 *Revista Brasileira de Ciências Sociais*, at 96; L. Lavinas, *The Takeover of Social Policy by Financialization: The Brazilian Paradox* (New York: Palgrave Macmillan, 2017).

15 As Jairnilson Paim and colleagues recall: 'The implementation of a universal health system in Brazil began in an unfavourable political and economic climate, which promoted a neoliberal rather than a universal approach – a perspective that was reinforced by international organisations that argued against publicly financed national health systems or advocated for intermediate stages to achieving it.' J. S. Paim et al., 'The Brazilian Health System: History, Advances, and Challenges', (2011) 377(9779) *The Lancet*, 1778–1797. See also Massuda and colleagues: The 'initial expansion of SUS was limited by weak technical capacity of the federal government and lower levels of administration, inadequate financing stemming from economic instability and postmilitary right-wing governments opposed to social sector investments'. A. Massuda et al., 'The Brazilian Health System at Crossroads: Progress, Crisis and Resilience', (2018) 3(4) *BMJ Global Health*, available at: doi:10.1136/bmjgh-2018-000829.

institutional and policy changes that materialised in the past three decades and, which, as experts agree, made an important contribution to population health.[16] It is, of course, impossible to know now with total certainty if such policies would have been adopted anyway without the right to health in the Constitution, that is, had the Sanitary Movement lost the battle recounted in Chapter 2. Judging by the perennial fight of the movement to keep the right to health alive and to fully implement its ideas, it seems plausible to assume that without Article 196 their campaign and achievements would have been at the very least much weaker.[17]

This conclusion derives further support from the fact that the most impactful policies were either expressly mandated by the Constitution itself, such as the creation of the national health system (in Article 198), or strongly supported by the principles of universality and egalitarian access expressly entrenched in the Constitution. Moreover, the new idea of health as a constitutional (legal) human right pervades all official documents, speeches and campaigns related to health after the Constitution and often attract the criticism of those who would rather not have that right (or any social right) in the Constitution.[18]

[16] Experts in public health raise several potential determinants for the health improvements experienced in Brazil: 'The achievements in mortality levels over the last decades could be related to Brazil's economic and social progress, and to the use of more effective medical technologies and public health interventions.' See França et al., 'Cause-Specific Mortality for 249 Causes in Brazil'. See also A. Santosa et al., 'The Development and Experience of Epidemiological Transition Theory over Four Decades: A Systematic Review', (2014) 15(7) *Global Health Action*, available at: doi: 10.3402/gha.v7.23574; F. Marinho et al., 'Burden of Disease in Brazil, 1990–2016: A Systematic Subnational Analysis for the Global Burden of Disease Study 2016', (2018) 392(10143) *The Lancet*, 760–775. See also, for an interesting argument that the right to health matters based on large quantitative global analysis, M. M. Kavanagh, 'The Right to Health: Institutional Effects of Constitutional Provisions on Health Outcomes', (2016) 51 *St Comp Int Dev*, 328–364.

[17] For an interesting argument of other more subtle ways in which redistribution can be achieved without the implementation of formal law but rather through *forbearance*; see A. Holland, *Forbearance As Redistribution: The Politics of Informal Welfare in Latin America*, Cambridge Studies in Comparative Politics (Cambridge: Cambridge University Press, 2017). But her analysis seems more fitting to the fields of housing and employment opportunities, on which she focuses, and to countries where, as she clarifies, formal welfare provision is low. In the case of health, in particular, in Brazil, her interesting concept of forbearance (the intentional and revocable nonenforcement of the law) seems less useful.

[18] On the webpage of the Ministry of Health, one finds reference to the right to health already in the first paragraph of the explanation of the public health system: 'The Unified Health System (SUS) is one of the largest and most complex public health systems in the

The remainder of the chapter develops this argument in further detail and with support from additional empirical data.

3.2 The SUS: 'Largest Social Inclusion Policy in Brazil'[19]

The SUS, Sistema Único de Saúde (Unified Health System), is the name of the public health system mandated by Article 198 of the Constitution to be the principal instrument to implement the right to health guaranteed in Article 196 (see Chapter 2 for the text).[20] Three decades after its creation, it is easier to focus on its serious problems than on its achievements and the radical transformation it represented from the previous reality on the ground.

As we saw in Chapter 2, the ultimate objectives of the Sanitary Movement were to improve the pitiful health conditions of the vast majority of the population and reduce the pronounced health inequalities that prevailed. The means to achieve these goals were not only to improve and extend health assistance services but also, and most importantly, to shift the health system's excessive focus on secondary and tertiary curative care (i.e., on hospitals, high tech equipment, medicines) towards primary care, public health measures and the so-called social

world, ranging from simple care for the assessment of blood pressure, through Basic Care, to organ transplantation, guaranteeing integral, universal access and free for the entire population of the country. With its creation, SUS provided universal access to the public health system without discrimination. Comprehensive health care, and not only care, has become a right of all Brazilians, from gestation to the end of life, focusing on health with quality of life, aiming at prevention and health promotion.' See Ministry of Health, Sistema Único de Saúde (SUS): estrutura, princípios e como funciona, www.saude.gov.br/sistema-unico-de-saude, accessed 23 June 2019. In the Consolidations of the Norms of the Public Health System (Consolidação das normas sobre as políticas nacionais de saúde do Sistema Único de Saúde), which is composed of 104 pieces of regulation, a search of the term '*direito*' ('right') returns 96 matches, a search of the term '*direitos humanos*' ('human rights') returns 18, a search of the term '*direito à saúde*' ('right to health') returns 7 matches, http://bvsms.saude.gov.br/bvs/saudelegis/gm/2017/MatrizesConsolidacao/Matriz-2-Politicas.html#, accessed 30 May 2019.

19 Opening sentence of public health expert Eugênio Vilaça Mendes in an interview given to Barbara Bretanha from daily newspaper *O Estado de S. Paulo* on 18 July 2014, https://saude.estadao.com.br/noticias/geral,sus-e-a-maior-politica-de-inclusao-social-na-saude,1530727, accessed 1 May 2019. Some claim that SUS is actually the largest social inclusion policy in the world. See C. R. Pierantoni, 'Vinte anos do sistema de saúde brasileiro: o Sistema Único de Saúde', (2008) 18(4) *Physis: Revista de Saúde Coletiva*, 617–624.

20 The actual word in Portuguese is '*único*', which translates literally as 'unique'. I prefer 'unified' in English as it better expresses its actual contextual meaning (see n. 21).

determinants of health (education, nutrition, income, working conditions, etc.). The political strategy was to have health recognised as a human right (and a corresponding duty of the state) in the new Constitution; the main institutional apparatus imagined to implement that idea and pursue those goals was the creation of a comprehensive, universal and egalitarian public health system funded by the state through taxes.

The first practical hurdle was the unification of public health and medical assistance.[21] Before the Constitution, public health was under the remit of the Ministry of Health and dealt mostly with preventive and collective measures, such as the control of endemic diseases, research, production and provision of vaccines and sanitary vigilance.[22] The bulk of medical assistance was under the remit of the Ministry of Social Insurance (Previdência Social), financed by contributions to the pension system and accessible only to those formal workers who contributed to the system, around thirty million people (20 per cent of the population then).[23] Because that contributory administrative logic and funding arrangement was completely rejected by the victorious conception adopted in the new Constitution, which turned health into a universal right funded by taxation (i.e., unconditional on any contributions), the Ministry of Health ended up incorporating the organ of the Social Insurance Ministry[24] that delivered medical assistance, the INAMPS,

[21] This is what explains the somewhat curious word 'unique' in the name of the Brazilian public health system. The unification of public health and medical assistance had been under debate since at least the creation of the Ministry of Health in 1953 through Law 1.920 (before that the Ministry of Health was part of the Ministry of Education and Health, which, in turn, was part of the Ministry of Justice and Home Affairs until 1930). See A. L. G. S. Lima, M. M. S. Pinto, 'Fontes para a história dos cinquenta anos do Ministério da Saúde' ('Sources for a History of the Brazilian Ministry of Health's Fifty Years'), (2003) 10(3) *História, Ciências, Saúde*, 1037–1051.

[22] Medical assistance was provided only residually in a scarce and scattered network of public hospitals, focused mostly on tuberculosis and psychiatry, to those unable to pay, that is, the 'medical indigent'. See Bertolozzi, Greco, 'Health Politics in Brasil', at 380–398.

[23] Before the Constitution was enacted, the link between contribution and medical assistance started to be dismantled through a series of resolutions by the then president of INAMPS, Hesio Cordeiro, a former president of Abrasco and leading member of the Sanitary Movement. Under the guise of 'bureaucratic simplification', he eliminated the need for patients to show identity cards to prove they contributed to the system when accessing INAMPS' hospitals (Resolution INAMPS n.98, of 18 October 1985) and integrated health actions (*ações integradas de saúde*) (Resolution INAMPS no. 138, 1986). See Chapter 2, Section 2.2.

[24] Decree 99.060, of 7 March 1990. I use Social Insurance rather than Social Security as the logic then was predominantly that of insurance, that is, based mostly on contributions.

Instituto Nacional de Assistência Médica da Previdência Social (National Institute for Medical Assistance of the Social Insurance Ministry), which would be extinguished three years later.[25]

The mere universalisation of medical assistance under the SUS,[26] now formally accessible to everyone in the country irrespective of economic and employment status, is perhaps the clearest piece of evidence that the transformative promises of the Constitution of 1988 did not remain symbolic. To call it the 'largest policy of social inclusion' ever implemented in Brazil is not hyperbolic. It eliminated the segregation then in existence between those who could access medical assistance through either private medicine or the state contributory social insurance system and the rest who could not (except for limited urgent services provided by a relatively small network of public and charitable services to the neediest, classified with the stigmatising label of 'sanitary indigent').[27]

It is hard to put an exact figure on how many people actually benefited from this simple but radical change in the health system – from formal segregation and exclusion to formal unification and universalisation – but it is known that it was in the range of tens of millions. In formal terms, the system went from serving 30 million employees and their families to the whole population, then 150 million people. Some argue that around 50 million people benefited immediately.[28]

But the provision of medical assistance was only a part, it is important to reemphasise, of the reforming project that the Sanitary Movement fought to entrench in the Constitution. The movement aimed also at a shift of emphasis from secondary and tertiary care towards primary care and public health measures, which the Constitution expressly lists as one

[25] Law no. 8.689, of 27 July 1993.

[26] The actual creation happened through Law 8.080 and 8.142, both from 1990, the so-called organic law of health. According to Art. 59 of the Transitional Constitutional Dispositions (Ato das Disposições Constitucionais Transitórias), the executive should send a bill to Parliament with a proposal of how to organise the Social Security System, of which Health was a part. President José Sarney took almost ten months to send the Health Bill to Parliament, only after sustained pressure from legislators and civil society. The Bill (Projeto de Lei Ordinária 3110) was sent to the House of Representatives on 1 August 1989 and took a little more than a year to pass through Congress. See E. Rodriguez Neto, *Saúde: Promessas e limites da constituição* (Rio de Janeiro: Fiocruz, 2003)

[27] Mendes, 'Vinte e cinco anos do Sistema Único de Saúde'.

[28] G. Carvalho, 'Financiamento da saúde pública no Brasil no pós-constitucional de 88' ('Financing of Public Health in Brazil for the Post-Constitutional 88'), (2008) 2(1) *Tempus – Actas de Saúde Coletiva*, 39–51, at 42.

of the main directives of the public system when discharging its duties: namely, to 'prioritise preventive activities' (Article 198, section II).[29] This has been pursued, gradually, with the creation or expansion and improvement of programmes of vaccination, health education, primary care attention and control of endemic diseases, which had a material positive influence on the lives of tens of millions of Brazilians. The following discussion provides more detail of specific policies adopted through the SUS with undoubted positive impact on the population's health.

Expansion of Primary Care. Reversing the curative, hospital centred model prevailing before the Constitution and still influential at present was (and remains) one of the main aims envisaged in the idea of the right to health (Article 198, II). Given the extraordinary obstacles, the significant expansion of primary care experienced in Brazil in the past decades seems to represent one of the greatest achievements influenced by the Constitution. The leading policy in this realm is the ESF, Estratégia Saúde da Familia (Family Health Strategy) and the related human resources' policy that created the figure of the Agente Comunitário da Saúde (Communitary Health Agent). The Family Health Programme works through multi-professional teams including doctors, nurses and other health-related technicians, including the Agente Comunitário, specifically trained to operate as the focus of the ESF. These teams provide primary care and health education through visits to people's homes, thus expanding significantly access to these services, in particular, to the poorest groups of the Brazilian population who live further from public hospitals and health units and who have historically been deprived of health attention.

The programme was implemented originally in 1993, expanding gradually and then significantly from the 2000s onwards.[30] From 2000 to 2016, its coverage expanded from 13.2 million to 120.2 million people (from 7.8 per cent to 58.5 per cent of the population), reaching to a

[29] Some of the initiatives, moreover, need to be taken outside the remit of the Ministry of Health, such as the provision of clean water, which was under the remit of the Ministry of Social Development during the important programme Water for All. This ministry has been turned recently into the Ministry of Citizenship, available at: http://dssbr.org/site/experiencias/programa-um-milhao-de-cisternas-leva-agua-e-melhora-qualidade-de-vida-da-populacao-do-semiarido-brasileiro/.

[30] Ministério da Saúde, Secretaria de Políticas de Saúde, Departamento de Atenção Básica, 'Programa Saúde da Família', *Rev. Saúde Pública* (2000) 34(3), 316–319, available at: doi.org/10.1590/S0034-89102000000300018.

greater or lesser extent all states in Brazil and almost all municipalities (5,570) through, currently, 42,355 teams.[31]

To find the resources and to organise access to primary care to more than a 100 million people is no mean feat. The entrenchment of the right to health in the Constitution and the emphasis on preventive measures (Art. 198, II) has represented an important supporting political tool. Moreover, as the expansion of these services were deliberately targeted on the poorest, they helped to diminish inequalities in access among the population, another important constitutional principle.[32] The Family Health Strategy teams concentrate on the municipalities of the states of the Northeast (80 per cent of coverage) and some of the North (79.7 per cent), which are, as we will see in more detail in Chapter 4, the least developed regions of Brazil (compare to the coverage in the South, 66.5 per cent; Centre-West, 60.9 per cent; Southeast, 53.1 per cent).[33] This progressive, that is, pro-poor distribution is not to be taken for granted. Most resources in Brazil, including health resources, are skewed towards the most developed regions of the South and Southeast.

In terms of more specific health gains, studies have shown that the Family Health Strategy has had a significant positive impact in children's health, such as a reduction of hospitalisation of under-five-year-olds for dehydration and pneumonia, underweight births and infant mortality due to acute respiratory infections.[34] There are also studies showing

[31] For the number of teams and municipalities, see http://dados.gov.br/dataset/psf_equipes, accessed 29 May 2019. See also Massuda et al., 'The Brazilian Health System at Crossroads'; R. G. Neves et al., 'Tendência temporal da cobertura da Estratégia Saúde da Família no Brasil, Regiões e Unidades da Federação, 2006–2016' ('Time Trend of Family Health Strategy Coverage in Brazil, Its Regions and Federative Units, 2006–2016'), (2018) 27(3) *Epidemiologia e Serviços de Saúde*, available at: doi.org/10.5123/s1679-49742018000300008.

[32] J. Macinko et al., 'Evaluation of the Impact of the Family Health Program on Infant Mortality in Brazil, 1990–2002', (2006) 60(1) *Journal of Epidemiol Community Health*, 13–19.

[33] Neves et al., 'Tendência temporal'.

[34] As Barreto and colleagues explain: 'Childhood mortality from LRI [lower respiratory infections] was reduced as a result of an increase in wider access to health care, nationwide availability of antibiotics and vaccination policies. Moreover, the universal availability of influenza vaccines since 1999 and the further introduction of polysaccharide pneumococcal vaccines for children (and in recent years for adults), and a herd protection effect from universal vaccination in children could also have led to a morbidity and mortality reduction in adult pneumococcal pneumonia .... The huge decrease of mortality risks from diarrheal diseases in 2015 was associated with access to improved sanitation and to primary health care. Access to treated water supply in urban areas and the "Million Cistern Program" in rural areas has reduced the transmission of bacteria and

improved control of cardiovascular risk factors, such as high blood pressure and diabetes, reduction of general mortality by cardiovascular and cerebrovascular causes[35] and reduction of hospitalisation rates for ambulatory-care–sensitive conditions. It has also been found, interestingly, that access to the programme for a continuous period of eight years improves employment, diminishes the natality rate and increases frequency of school attendance in children from ten to seventeen, showing the strong and positive interdependence of social policies and corresponding social rights.[36]

Expansion of Vaccination Programmes. Another crucial area of population health in which there is consensus that significant improvement has been made is vaccination. Before the 1990s, a large proportion of children had no access to some of the most important vaccines, such as the triple DPT and measles. By the year 2000, these vaccines had been virtually universalised and despite some recent deterioration in vaccination rates, they remain very high for both, and at any rate, a world apart from where they were in the 'pre-constitutional past' (See Figure 3.5).[37]

protozoan spread by fecal-oral transmission. The introduction of rotavirus vaccination for infants in 2006 contributed to the decline observed in under-5 diarrhea-related mortality and hospitalisations.' See M. L. Barreto et al., 'Effect of City-Wide Sanitation Programme on Reduction in Rate of Childhood Diarrhoea in Northeast Brazil: Assessment by Two Cohort Studies', (2007) 370(9599) *Lancet*, 1622–1628; See also D. Rasella et al., 'Reducing Childhood Mortality from Diarrhea and Lower Respiratory Tract Infections in Brazil', (2010) 126(3) *Pediatrics*, available at: doi.org/10.1542/peds.2009-3197; J. E. Fonseca et al., 'Reducing Occurrence of Giardia Duodenalis in Children Living in Semiarid Regions: Impact of a Large Scale Rainwater Harvesting Initiative', (2014) 8(6) *PLoS Negl Trop Dis*, available at: doi.org/10.1371/journal.pntd.0002943; G. M. Carmo et al., 'Decline in Diarrhea Mortality and Admissions after Routine Childhood Rotavirus Immunization in Brazil: A Time-Series Analysis', (2011) 8(4) *PLoS Med*, available at: doi:10.1371/journal.pmed.1001024; and J. Macinko et al., 'Brazil's Family Health Strategy – Delivering Community-Based Primary Care in a Universal Health System', (2015) 372(23) *New England Journal of Medicine*, 2177–2181.

35 D. Rasella et al., 'Impact of Primary Health Care on Mortality from Heart and Cerebrovascular Diseases in Brazil: A Nationwide Analysis of Longitudinal Data', (2014) 349 *BMJ*, available at: doi.org/10.1136/bmj.g4014.

36 M. E. Alfradique et al., 'Ambulatory Care Sensitive Hospitalizations: Elaboration of Brazilian List As a Tool for Measuring Health System Performance (Project ICSAP – Brazil)', (2009) 25(6) *Cad Saúde Pública*, 1337–1349. See also I. Dourado et al., 'Trends in Primary Health Care–Sensitive Conditions in Brazil: The Role of the Family Health Program', (2011) 49(6) *Med Care*, 577–584; M. L. Bastos, 'The Impact of the Brazilian Family Health on Selected Primary Care Sensitive Conditions: A Systematic Review', (2017) 12 *PLoS One*, available at: doi.org/10.1371/journal.pone.0182336.

37 It is concerning, of course, that measles is experiencing a resurgence around the world and that Brazil is among the countries that inspire more concern. See M. Alvim, 'Sarampo

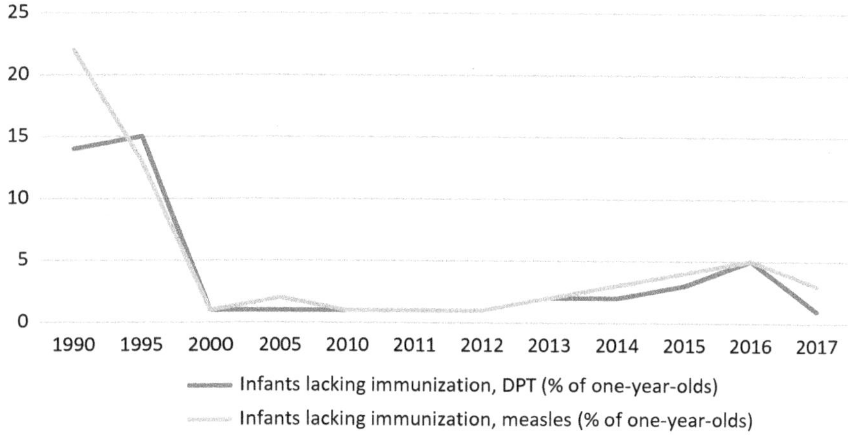

Figure 3.5 Selected immunisation rates in Brazil.
Source: UN Human Development Programme, Human Development Reports

The vaccination programme of the SUS includes also BCG, Haemophilus Influenzae Type b, Influenza, Hepatitis B, Oral Poliomyelitis (VOP), Measles, Mumps and Rubella (MMR), Oral Human Rotavirus (RR), Tetravalent DPT-HepB and Influenza AH1N1.[38]

Maternal Health. Improvements in maternal care in the past three decades include an important rise in several indicators of antenatal care (see Figure 3.6): in 1986, 26 per cent of women gave birth without any antenatal care whatsoever, whereas by 2007, only 1.3 per cent did (virtual universalisation). Pregnant women that had six or more visits of antenatal care went from 75.9 per cent in 1996 to 80.9 per cent in 2007,[39] and those who started antenatal care in the first three months of pregnancy went from 66 per cent (1996) to 83.6 per cent (2007). In 1996, 41.5 per cent of women did not receive one dose of tetanus toxoid vaccine during pregnancy; in 2007, that rate had almost halved to 23.1 per cent. Institutional delivery went from 80.5 per cent (1986) to 98.4 per cent

no Brasil tem avanço preocupante, alerta Unicef', BBC website, 28 February 2019, www.bbc.com/portuguese/geral-47410826, accessed 29 May 2019. Brazil's success in measles vaccination had led to the fall of deaths of children below 5 from 11,000 in 1982 to 61 in 1997 and total eradication in 2000.

[38] Paim et al., 'The Brazilian Health System', at 1782.

[39] C. G. Victora et al., 'Maternal and Child Health in Brazil: Progress and Challenges', (2011) 377 *Lancet*, 1863–1876.

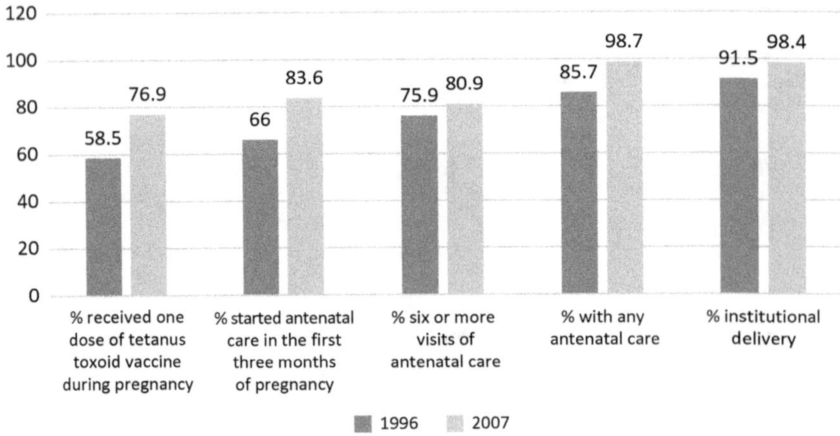

Figure 3.6 Maternal health improvements.
Source: Own formulation with data from Victora et al. (see n. 40)

(2007), again virtual universalisation. These improvements had an impact on maternal mortality, which decreased but remains too high for Brazil's level of development, as we will see in Chapter 4.[40]

Public Health Actions, Education and Campaigns. Educating the population and incentivising it to change unhealthy behaviour is a crucial part of any efficient public health system. Some such policies in the SUS have had significant positive impact. One of the most prominent was the anti-tobacco policy, which achieved a reduction of smoking of about 50 per cent (smoking prevalence reduced to 10.8 per cent in Brazilian capitals), with an estimate of 420,000 deaths averted from 1990 to 2010.[41] That was achieved with a combination of tobacco control via raised taxes and prices, a ban on smoking in public places, prohibition of advertising and publicity campaigns warning against the risks of smoking, including

[40] França et al., 'Cause-Specific Mortality for 249 Causes in Brazil', at 14.

[41] D. Levy et al., 'The Brazil SimSmoke Policy Simulation Model: The Effect of Strong Tobacco Control Policies on Smoking Prevalence and Smoking-Attributable Deaths in a Middle Income Nation', (2012) 9(11) *PLoS Med.*, doi:10.1371/journal.pmed.1001336. See also Brasil, Ministério da Saúde, Secretaria de Vigilância em Saúde, Vigitel Brazil 2014: Protective and Risk Factors for Chronic Diseases by Telephone Survey, Ministério da Saúde, Secretaria de Vigilância em Saúde (Brasília: Ministério da Saúde, 2015), available at, http://bvsms.saude.gov.br/bvs/publicacoes/vigitel_brasil_2014.pdf, accessed 23 June 2019.

in cigarette packages.[42] Similar policies to address alcohol and obesity problems have not had much success.[43] Another successful policy focusing strongly on health education resulted in exclusive breastfeeding rates in children under four months increasing from 4 per cent to 48 per cent from the mid-1980s to the mid-2000s.[44]

Secondary and Tertiary Care. In 2017, according to the Activities Report of the Ministry of Health of 2018, almost 2.5 billion procedures of medium and high complexity were carried out by the SUS across Brazil, consuming R$45 billion.[45] Almost 300 million medical consultations were carried out,[46] and 1.8 million elective surgeries were performed.[47] These involved all sorts of specialties, including rather sophisticated ones such as cardiac surgery in children and organ transplantation. Even if such gigantic numbers should be expected in a large country like Brazil, the point is that these are all funded by the state under its duty to provide universal and egalitarian health actions and services to the population, that is, the right to health, something that did not happen before the Constitution was enacted.

Moreover, and contrary to the usual assumption of those unfamiliar with the system, in particular, the judges who adjudicate right to health cases (see Part II), the quality of the services provided is not poor.[48] Some of its programmes have achieved international recognition, such as the National System of Immunization already mentioned earlier (Sistema Nacional de Imunizações), the Programme for the Control of HIV/Aids (Programa de Controle de HIV/Aids) and the National System for Organ Transplantation (Sistema Nacional de Transplantes de Órgãos), perhaps the largest public transplantation system in the world. The latter spent R$987 million in procedures and another R$398 million in

[42] Tax increases are now under threat by a bill in Parliament supported by the former Minister of Justice, Sérgio Moro, under the alleged implausible justification of combating counterfeit cigarettes. See D. Wang. 'A fumaça do retrocesso', *F. de São Paulo* (newspaper), 6 April 2019.

[43] Interview with José Gomes Temporão, Medicina em Debate, Lobby na Saúde - Uma conversa com o ex-ministro José Gomes Temporão, 2009.

[44] Victora et al., 'Maternal and Child Health in Brazil'.

[45] Ministério da Saúde (2018), Secretaria de Atenção à Saúde, Relatório de Gestão, 2017, at 225.

[46] Ibid., at 234.

[47] Ibid., at 236.

[48] As we will see in Chapter 8, the widespread assumption among the judiciary is that the public health system is inefficient, corrupt and of poor quality, although it is rather unlikely that any judge ever uses it (all judges have private health insurance), and factual data is rarely cited to support the assumption.

immunosuppressant drugs in 2017[49] to conduct more than 25,000 transplants, including 380 heart transplants, 112 lung transplants, 2,107 liver transplants, 5,930 kidney transplants, 15,171 eye (cornea) transplants, 2,388 bone marrow transplants, requiring 5,264 air transports of organs to enable the procedures.[50]

Other areas where important efforts have been made despite severe resource limitations are psychiatric care, dental care, counselling for sexually transmitted diseases and mobile emergency care. The latter is another important new service provided by the SUS, launched in 2003 and gradually spreading to 1,150 municipalities (55 per cent of the population) in 2010 and now covering 170 million inhabitants (82.17 per cent) across 3,532 municipalities.[51]

Infrastructure. In terms of infrastructure, the public health system facilities have grown faster than the population, enhancing significantly their per capita availability (see Figure 3.7). Moreover, with the exception of MRI scans and ultrasound devices, the public system increased the proportion of facilities and equipment it possesses in comparison with the private sector (see Figure 3.8), although it still relies significantly on the latter to provide services, which causes important administrative issues as we will see in Chapter 4.

Investment in Health. None of the expansions and improvements described above could have happened, of course, without investment of more resources in health. As we shall see in Chapter 4, underfunding is still one of the most important challenges to the right to health in Brazil. But expenditure on health by the state increased both in absolute and relative terms. At the end of the 1980s, just before the Constitution was adopted, public expenditure on health was around US$88 per capita (between 2.4 and 2.8 per cent of GDP).[52] According to the latest available

[49] Ministério da Saúde, Relatório de Gestão, 2017, at 117–118.

[50] Ibid., at 126–128. The National System for Organ Transplantation was established through Law 9.434/97, of 4 February 1997, so-called *Lei do Transplante*, currently regulated by Decree no. 9.175, of 18 October 2017.

[51] Ibid., at 335. See also Paim et al., 'The Brazilian Health System'. See also C. V. Machado, 'Mobile Emergency Care Service: Analysis of Brazilian Policy', (2011) 45(3) *Rev Saúde Pública*, 519–528, reporting that it may have improved the quality of pre-hospital care for acute coronary syndrome and stroke patients.

[52] Bertolozzi, Greco, 'Health Politics in Brasil'. See also P. L. B. Silva, A. C. Medici, 'Considerações sobre o Gasto em Saúde no Brasil: Dilemas até o Final do Século', (1988) 1(4) *Cadernos de Saúde Pública*, 88–105, estimating that in 1986 total health expenditure in Brazil was US$10 billion (Cz$343.2 billion), or 3.9 per cent of GDP. Of those, 38 per cent were private. Public expenditure was thus 2.4 per cent. See also Bertolozzi, Greco, 'Health Politics in Brasil', at 394.

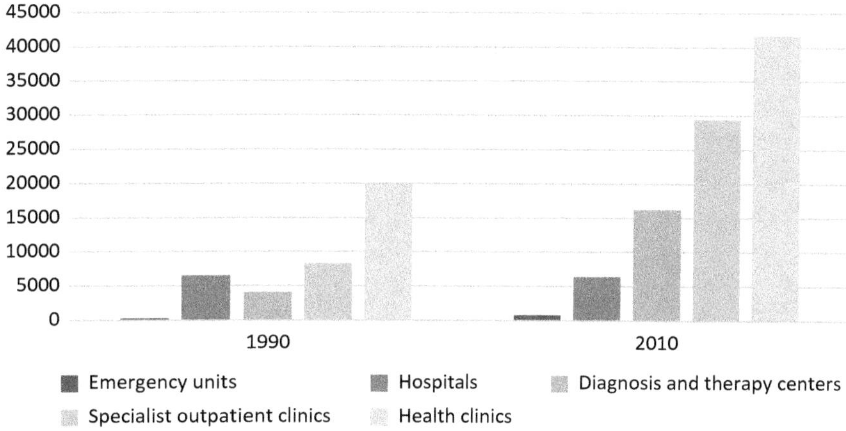

Figure 3.7 Public Health System infrastructure.
Source: Own formulation with data from Paim et al., 2011

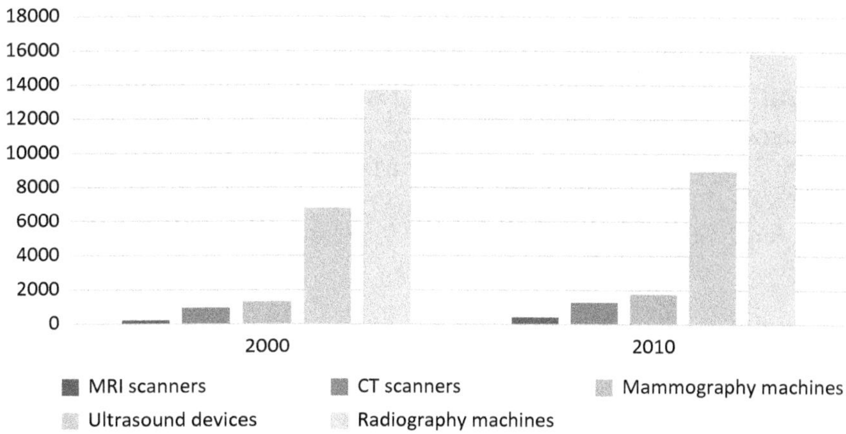

Figure 3.8 Public Health System equipment.
Source: Own formulation with data from Paim et al., 2011

data from the WHO, it is now US$594 per capita, 3.8 per cent of GDP (2015).[53] The largest growth occurred after 2000, with the adoption of

[53] As noted in a World Bank report assessing the first two decades of the SUS, 'spending on health has increased significantly since the early 1980s, growing 224 percent in real terms between the first half of the 1980s and 2010 (and 111 percent increase in per capita

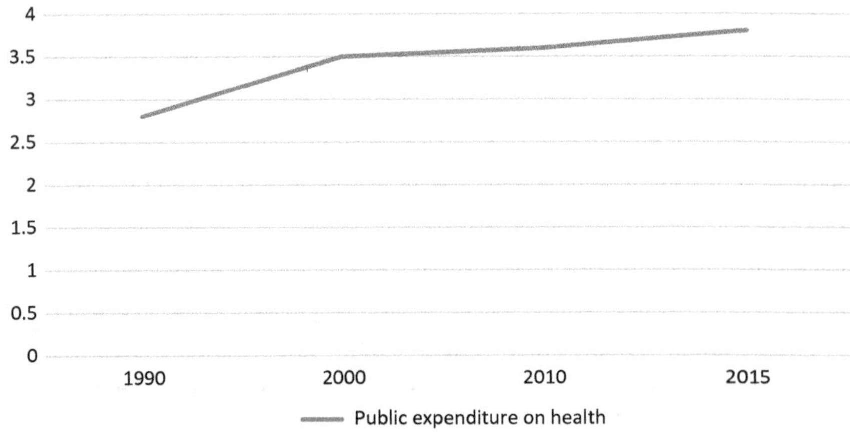

Figure 3.9 Public expenditure on health as a % of GDP.
Sources: WHO Global Health Observatory data repository and Bertollozi, 1996

Constitutional Amendment 29, which finally fixed a minimum mandatory investment on health of 12 per cent of tax revenues for states, 15 per cent of tax revenues for municipalities and a prohibition to spend less than the previous year for the federal government.[54] The increase in funding was substantive, if still insufficient, as discussed in Chapter 4: 112 per cent in absolute terms and 89 per cent in per capita terms between 2000 and 2010 (see Figures 3.9 and 3.10).[55]

terms', (p. 3). It is also noted in the study that 'disparities in government spending across states and municipalities have fallen significantly'. M. Gragnolati et al., *Twenty Years of Health System Reform in Brazil: An Assessment of the Sistem Único de Saúde* (Washington, DC: World Bank, 2013). According to Vieira and Benevides, federal expenditure rose 149 per cent between 1993 and 2015. F. S. Vieira, R. P. S. Benevides, 'O Direito à Saúde no Brasil em Tempos de Crise Econômica, Ajuste Fiscal e Reforma Implícita do Estado' ('The Right to Health in Times of Economic Crisis, Austerity and the Implicit Reform of the State'), (2016) 10(3) *Revista de Estudos e Pesquisas sobre as Américas*, at 12.

[54] See Chapter 4, Sections 4.4 and 4.5, for a detailed discussion of the continuous struggle for resources that characterises the campaign for improvement of the public health system.

[55] S. F. Piola et al., 'The Effects of Constitutional Amendment 29 on the Regional Allocation of Public Funds for the National Health Service in Brazil', (2016) 21(2) *Ciência & Saúde Coletiva*, 411–421, at 419.

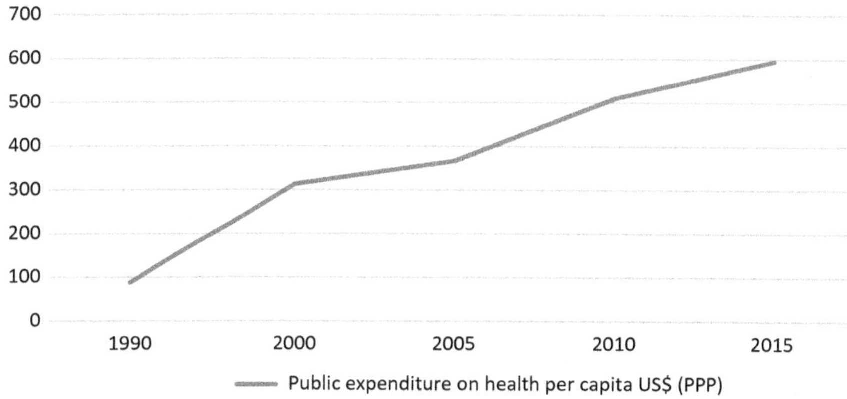

Figure 3.10 Public expenditure on health per capita in US$ (PPP).
Sources: WHO Global Health Observatory data repository and Bertollozi, 1996[56]

***

This section has shown how a myriad of health policies adopted through legislative and executive action over the past thirty years within the SUS, the public health system mandated by Article 198 of the Constitution, are at least partly responsible for the non-trivial advances in the health conditions of the Brazilian population experienced in the past thirty years. Part II of the book will show that the performance of the judicial branch through health litigation has been comparatively much weaker, if not negative. In other words, politics has been by far a more effective means of advancing the right to health than litigation. One may wonder, however, if these progressive health policies are not more contingently linked to the rise of various left-leaning governments who took health care seriously than to the inclusion of the right to health in the 1988 Constitution.[57] As I have already mentioned, it is difficult to disentangle and test all potential variables that may have had an effect on health improvements.[58] It is of course plausible that more left-leaning governments would implement more progressive health policies, and there is some evidence of that in the timing of the scaling up of some of the

[56] WHO Global Health Observatory data repository, available at: http://apps.who.int/gho/data/node.main.HEALTHFINANCING?lang=en.

[57] I am grateful to the editors of the series for pressing this point.

[58] See Holland, *Forbearance As Redistribution*, highlighting the difficulties of measuring both enforcement and political motives.

policies discussed in this section. But there is also evidence of advances during the centre-right governments that preceded the Workers Party period in power (2002–2016). The Family Health Strategy, for instance, arguably the policy with the greatest impact on population health, started as far back as 1993 as we saw. The universalisation of immunisation programmes was achieved by the year 2000 (see Figure 3.5). Increases in funding for the public system, as we also saw, occurred throughout the period and intensified after Constitutional Amendment 29, approved in 2000, that is, two years before the Workers Party acceded to power.[59] Another interesting question is how the right to health is going to withstand the more extreme conservative government that acceded to power in 2018, but it is too early to know.[60]

3.3 Conclusion

The data presented in this chapter shows that the recognition of health as a human right in the Brazilian 1988 Constitution has not remained an empty promise as many feared and was perhaps a plausible expectation to have back then.[61] The inclusion of the right to health in the

[59] As studies have shown, often as a criticism to the Workers' Party, there was not much difference in terms of financing between the two parties that dominated Brazilian politics since 1994 and until 2016. See A. Soares and N. R. Santos, 'Financiamento do Sistema Único de Saúde nos governos FHC, Lula e Dilma', (2014) 38(100) *Saúde em Debate*, 18–25.

[60] See 'Brazil Enters the Bolsonaro Zone' (editorial), (2019) 7(2), available at: www.thelancet.com/pdfs/journals/langlo/PIIS2214-109X(19)30002-6.pdf, accessed 20 March 2019. 'Bolsonaro did little in his inauguration speech to encourage those of us concerned with health and equity. Indeed, his speech was the first since the end of the military dictatorship in 1985 not to mention the need to address poverty and inequality. Many working in the public health field in Brazil are thus extremely worried.'

[61] As the constituent Lysâneas Maciel put it – 'Mr Rapporteur, we know that one of the greatest difficulties in drawing up a constitution is precisely to give effect to the provisions which are registered there. Otherwise our Constitution will only become a simple formal declaration of rights that will never be implemented in the course of its existence or will lack effectiveness .... The Constitutions are made of beautiful principles that are never executed: "Everyone is equal before the law, regardless of color, race, religion, etc." "All power emanates from the people and in their name will be exercised." This is another lie in this country. Or, "The minimum wage is sufficient to guarantee the subsistence of the worker, etc." These beautiful declarations of law have never been implemented, some of them are almost forty years old. As an example we have that one that says that "workers will have a share in the profits of the company" which has never been regulated (the soul of the techniques that legislators use to postpone this right is to refer it to the ordinary law, so that this regulation never occurs).' Senado Federal, Anais da Assembléia Nacional

constitutional text has made a significant difference to millions of people in the Brazilian population. Previously, non-existent or very limited programmes of vaccination, primary care services, public health education and secondary and tertiary services have been created and/or expanded, covering a large proportion of the population. These all operate under the umbrella of a comprehensive national health service, the SUS, funded by taxation and free at the point of delivery, as expressly mandated in Article 198 of the Constitution as one of the main tools for the implementation of the right to health. Although other factors have of course also played a contributory role, it is hard to deny that the public health system created by the 1988 Constitution has been decisive in the significant health improvements described in this chapter.

Public health experts who have studied the Brazilian system in detail have reached the same conclusion. When the system celebrated its twentieth anniversary, Michele Gragnolati, Magnus Lindelow and Bernard Couttolenc from the World Bank reached the following conclusion:

> Over the last 20 years, Brazil has seen impressive improvements in health outcomes, with dramatic reductions in child and infant mortality and increases in life expectancy. Equally important, geographic and socio-economic disparities in outcomes have become far less pronounced.

Constituinte, 5.a Reunião Extraordinária da Comissão de Sistematização, 29 June 1987, at 163–164. For an account of the difficulties of implementing the Constitution due to the victory of Fernando Collor de Mello against Lula in the elections of 1989, see J. C. D. Noronha et al., 'AIS-SUDS-SUS: Os caminhos do direito à saúde', in Guimarães, R. and Tavares, R. (eds.), *Saúde e sociedade no Brasil – anos 80* (Rio de Janeiro: Relume do Mará, 1994), 73–111; P. M. Buss, 'A IX Conferência Nacional de Saúde', (1991) 7(3) *Cadernos de Saúde Pública*, 297–300; Bertolozzi, Greco, 'Health Politics in Brasil', recounting how the IX National Health Conference was postponed till 1992 and how its slogan was '*Cumpra-se a lei!*' (The Law must be observed!) and how those first years were extremely difficult for the project. See also 'O Financiamento da Saúde', Conselho Nacional de Secretários de Saúde (Brasília: CONASS, 2007): 'The Constitution of 1988 was formulated in a context quite different from the current one. In a frame of euphoria due to the return to democratic rules, it seemed that a universal, integral and free health system could be financed by traditional sources (payroll and contributions from the Treasury) and by the new social contributions created at that time (turnover, lotteries, profits of companies). New events, however, would contribute to undermining health financing, including persistent inflation until the Real Plan (1994), the low growth of the economy, which continues to date, the elimination of payroll as a source of health financing (1993); the legal manouvres (later overcome) to procrastinate the payment of Cofins; the growth of pension expenditures leading pensions to absorb increasing portions of the Social Security Budget.', at 25.

> There are good reasons to believe that changes in the SUS have played an important role. The rapid expansion of primary care has contributed to changing patterns of utilization, with a growing share of contacts taking place in health centers and other primary care facilities. There has also been an overall growth in utilization of health services and a reduction in the share of households reporting problems in accessing health care for financial reasons. In short, the SUS reforms have achieved at least partially the goals of universal and equitable access to health care.[62]

When SUS completed twenty-five years, public health expert Mauricio Barreto, from the Federal University of Bahia, and colleagues reaffirmed the conclusion: 'The SUS has guaranteed access to free health care for the population over the last 25 years. Overall, UHC [universal health coverage] has increased at all levels of care, with some important positive trends toward equity.'[63] A recent multi-authored comprehensive study of the main causes of death and their changes in Brazil from 1990 to 2015 helps us to understand better the magnitude of the change:

> The results of this study indicate that a widespread reduction on mortality levels occurred in Brazil, with huge progress among children and an important increase in life expectancy. Major shifts in mortality rates have taken place among GBD [global burden of diseases] Level 1 cause groups [communicable, maternal, neonatal, and nutritional disorders]. In 1990, almost a quarter of all deaths were due to diarrhea, lower respiratory infections, tuberculosis, meningitis, vaccine preventable diseases, and nutritional and neonatal disorders, and were responsible for the majority of premature deaths. In more recent years, the age profile of mortality has shifted to older ages as NCDs [non-communicable diseases] are responsible for most deaths in the country. This occurred even though risks of death for the majority of non-communicable diseases decreased over the period.[64]

The right to health in Brazil provides a good illustration, thus, of the power that legal rights can have as transformative tools, contrary to what many rights' sceptics argue. But it also contradicts a widespread view among rights' supporters who see these rights as completely neglected by the political branches of the state and, as a consequence, in need of strong

[62] Gragnolati et al., *Twenty Years of Health System Reform in Brazil*, at 10.

[63] M. L. Barreto et al., 'Monitoring and Evaluating Progress towards Universal Health Coverage in Brazil', (2014) 11(9) *PLoS Med*, available at: doi.org/10.1371/journal.pmed.1001692.

[64] França et al., 'Cause-Specific Mortality for 249 Causes in Brazil'.

judicial enforcement mechanisms to have any teeth.[65] All major initiatives described in this chapter have been the work of legislators and administrators (often influenced, of course, by civil society and other factors). Unless, implausibly, the right to health in Brazil is an absolute outlier, social rights are neither futile to produce social change nor utterly neglected by politicians (and in urgent need of rescuing by lawyers and judges) as often heard in social rights debates. Both positions seem to underestimate the political force of social rights.

As I mentioned several times during this chapter, the politics of the right to health is still far from delivering the ambitious universalistic and egalitarian aims of the Constitution. Chapter 4 offers a detailed analysis of what still needs to be addressed, that is, how far the Brazilian state is still falling short of fulfilling the right to health. Whether (and how) lawyers and courts can contribute towards addressing these shortfalls are questions I discuss at length in Parts II and III of this book.

[65] See discussion in Chapter 1 and the following references for examples of such views: S. Moyn, *Not Enough. Human Rights in an Unequal World* (Cambridge, MA: Harvard University Press, 2018); P. Alston, 'Phantom Rights: The Systemic Marginalization of Economic and Social Rights', www.openglobalrights.org/phantom-rights-systemic-marginalization-of-economic-and-social-rights/, accessed 17 June 2019; D. Bilchitz, *Poverty and Fundamental Rights: The Justification and Enforcement of Socioeconomic Rights* (Oxford: Oxford University Press, 2007); S. Fredman, *Human Rights Transformed, Positive Rights and Positive Duties* (Oxford: Oxford University Press, 2008). For an excellent comprehensive review of the sceptical literature, see C. Rodríguez-Garavito, S. L. McAdams, *A Human Rights Crisis? Unpacking the Debate on the Future of the Human Rights Field*, available at https://papers.ssrn.com/sol3/papers.cfm?abstract_id=2919703, accessed 17 July 2019.

4

Two Brazils

How Inequality Limits the Right to Health

> Meagre health and many ants are the banes of Brazil . . .
>
> Mario de Andrade[1]

> Brazil has made great strides towards the advanced level of social conditions and programmes that are responsible for the good health enjoyed by many European countries. But one striking characteristic holds Brazil back: the benefits of social progress are not enjoyed equally.
>
> Michael Marmot[2]

When the Brazilian Commission on the Social Determinants of Health was launched in 2006,[3] two of its leading commissioners, public health experts Paulo Buss and Alberto Pellegrini, wrote a short comment for the Brazilian public health journal *Cadernos de Saúde Pública*. Its stark title left no doubt about how they saw the situation then, almost twenty years after the constitutionalisation of the right to health: 'Health Inequities in Brazil: our gravest disease'.[4]

The Commission released its report two years later, presenting a wealth of data that seemed to substantiate the inauspicious diagnosis. As it stated at the beginning of the report:

> Despite important advances in average health indicators in the last years, Brazil is still among the countries with highest health inequities, that is,

[1] M. de Andrade, *Macunaíma, o Herói sem Nenhum Caráter*, (São Paulo: 2017).

[2] M. Marmot, 'Brazil: Rapid Progress and the Challenge of Inequality', (2016) 15 *International Journal for Equity in Health*, at 177.

[3] WHO, Social Determinants of Health, Brazil, www.who.int/social_determinants/thecommission/countrywork/within/brazil/en/, accessed 23 June 2019.

[4] P. M. Buss, A. P. Filho, 'Iniqüidades em saúde no Brasil, nossa mais grave doença: Comentários sobre o documento de referência e os trabalhos da Comissão Nacional sobre Determinantes Sociais da Saúde', (2006) 22(9) *Cad. Saúde Pública*, 2005–2008.

> health inequalities among populational groups that, as well as significant and systematic, are also preventable, unjust and unnecessary.[5]

As we will see in this chapter, despite the important progress discussed in Chapter 3, health inequalities in Brazil remain resiliently high. Access to health action and services has improved for everyone but is still very unequal among different socioeconomic groups in the population. Whether it is Brazil's 'gravest disease' or not is perhaps debatable, but not completely hyperbolic.

More certain is that such high levels of inequality sit very uneasily with the right to health as envisaged by those who fought to include it in the 1988 Constitution, that is, a right to social and economic policies and to universal and equitable access to an appropriate package of health actions and services aimed at the improvement of everyone's health. The significant progress highlighted in Chapter 3 should of course be celebrated but needs to be put into this less auspicious context. That will help us to understand better not only the magnitude of those positive changes but also the important obstacles that lie ahead if further and more permanent progress is to be achieved. It will also enable us to approach more productively one of the main questions of Parts II and III: does judicialisation help or hinder the effort to reduce health inequalities?

4.1 Brazil's Health Inequalities

As we saw in Chapter 3, improvements in population health in Brazil since the Constitution were far from trivial, as shown most vividly by the overall decline in mortality rates among (almost) all population groups (ages and sexes), which resulted in an increase of life expectancy from 64.5 in 1988 to 75.7 in 2017. Yet, as with all averages, they mask variation and, in Brazil, these tend to be significant due to the pronounced income and other socioeconomic inequalities that prevail. As the British

[5] Ibid., at 20. As they continued: 'These health inequities are the product of great inequalities among the several socioeconomic strata of the Brazilian population. According to UNDP 2007 Report, with 2005 data, Brazil is the eleventh most unequal country in the world in terms of income distribution, behind only six African and four Latin American countries.' My translation from Portuguese.

epidemiologist Michael Marmot aptly notes after praising Brazil's impressive progress, these stark inequalities (Brazil's 'striking characteristic') holds the country back.[6]

Moreover, as Brazil has been going through the so-called epidemiologic transition (a shift from communicable to non-communicable diseases), the increase in longevity masks an increase in inequalities in disability and in access to treatment of non-communicable chronic diseases. A recent set of papers on health inequalities in Brazil edited by James Macinko and Célia Szwarcwald for the *International Journal for Equity in Health* ('A Panorama of Health Inequities in Brazil', 2016), provides a good overview. They found important inequalities in life expectancy (including healthy life expectancy), access to care for the elderly, access to mental health care, access to exams and tests, access to doctors and dentists and utilisation of health services.[7] Several other recent studies reveal a resilient picture of inequalities in many health areas across the main regions of Brazil, its states, municipalities and even districts, tracking closely socioeconomic inequalities.

The indicators in Table 4.1 provide a good picture of the health inequalities that still exist across the five main regions of Brazil.[8]

These average inequalities observed among the large regions are even more pronounced when we disaggregate the data further into income strata and within states, municipalities and even districts within municipalities. Infant mortality, for instance, varies from below 10/1,000 in all states of the South and two of the Southeast (Espírito Santo and São Paulo) to above 20/1,000 in Maranhão (Northeast) and Amapá and

[6] Marmot, 'Brazil'.

[7] J. Macinko, C. Szwarcwald, 'A Panorama of Health Inequities in Brazil', (2016) 15 *International Journal for Equity in Health*, available at www.biomedcentral.com/collections/HIB.

[8] Brazil is divided into five political-geographical large regions (North, Northeast, Southeast, South and Centre-West). As a general rule, the North and the Northeast are the most deprived, the South and the Southeast the most developed, and the Centre-West lags a little behind the South and Southeast. In terms of the UN Human Development Index (HDI), out of the 27 federal units (26 states and one federal district), all 4 states of the South and 3 states of the Southeast have high HDI, varying between 0.731 (Minas Gerais) and 0.783 (São Paulo). At the opposite end, all 9 states of the Northeast have medium HDI, varying from Alagoas, the lowest (0.631) to Rio Grande do Norte, the highest (0.684). To put these data into context, Alagoas HDI is similar to India's, whereas São Paulo's is closer to Portugal's.

Table 4.1 *Selected health indicators: Brazil and regions*

	North	Northeast	Southeast	Centre-West	South	Brazil
Infant mortality (per 1,000)	17.6	16.7	10.4	14.4	9.4	13.3
Life expectancy	71.5	72.2	76.6	74.4	76.9	74.8
Maternal mortality (per 100,000)	76.0	75.3	54.3	65.9	43.7	62.0
% Adults who consulted a doctor in the last 12 months	66.4	69.7	79.5	73.8	78.6	75.4
Number of doctors per 1,000 population	0.9	1.09	2.51	1.76	2.06	1.86

Source: Szwarcwald et al., 2016, IBGE, 2016[9] and IBGE, 2015[10]

Rondônia (North) (see Figure 4.1).[11] Maternal mortality is as high as 116.5/100,000 in Maranhão and as low as 30.9/100,000 in Santa Catarina (see Figure 4.2).[12] Even in the more developed states of the South and Southeast, averages hide important inequalities. A recent study of infant mortality in the state of Minas Gerais found 'high levels of infant mortality in the poorest regions' of that state, concluding that 'the almost complete universalisation of services of the last two decades is still far from universalising quality'.[13] A study of the city of Rio de Janeiro, where inequalities are obvious to the naked eye due to the large shanty towns

[9] Instituto Brasileiro de Geografia e Estatística (IBGE), 2016, Tabela 3834, Taxa de Mortalidade Infantil, https://sidra.ibge.gov.br/tabela/3834#resultado, accessed 23 June 2019.

[10] IBGE, 2015, Indicador 3.1.1 – Razão de mortalidade materna, available at: https://indicadoresods.ibge.gov.br/objetivo3/indicador311, accessed 23 June 2019.

[11] IBGE, 2016, Tabela 3834.

[12] IBGE, 2015, Indicador 3.1.1.

[13] R. Faria, P. Santana, 'Variações espaciais e desigualdades regionais no indicador de mortalidade infantil do estado de Minas Gerais, Brasil', (2016) 25(3) *Saúde soc.*, 736–749, at 747.

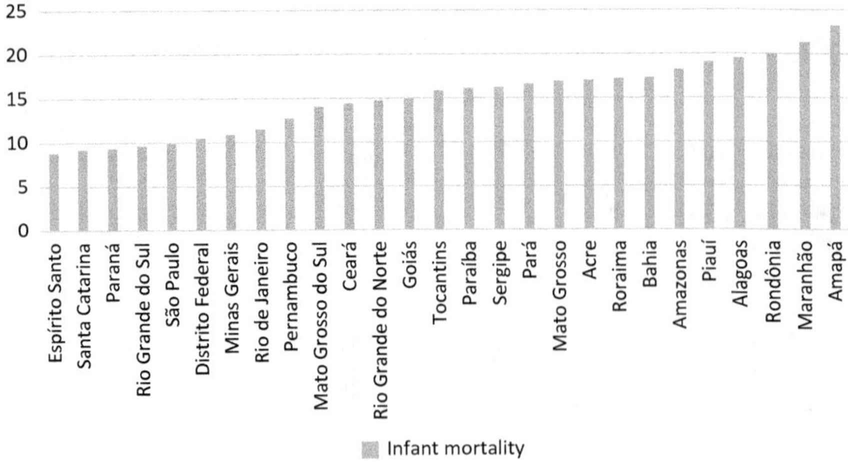

Figure 4.1 Infant mortality in Brazil, all states.
Source: IBGE

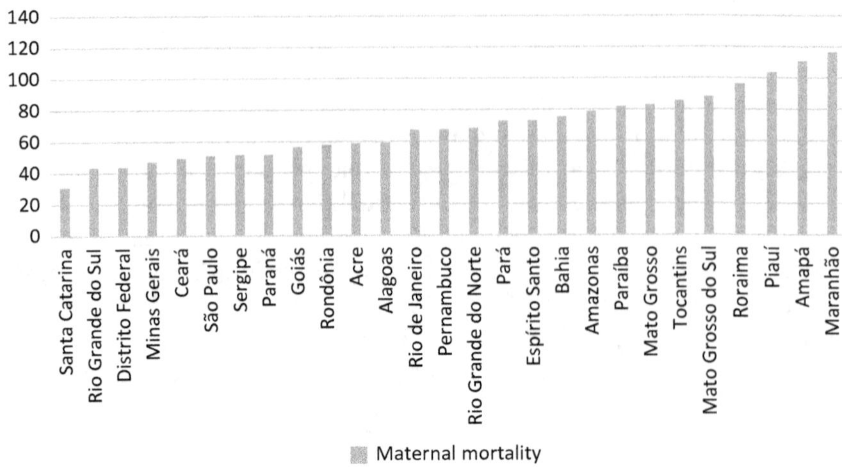

Figure 4.2 Maternal mortality in Brazil, all states.
Source: IBGE

(*favelas*) located in the hills of the richest districts, provides another good illustration. As the study found: 'life expectancy at birth of men living in the richest parts of the city was 12.8 years longer than that of men living in deprived areas. For both men and women older than age 65 years, healthy life expectancy was more than twice as high in the richest sector as in the slum sector'.[14]

***

The picture that emerges from the past three decades under the constitutional right to health is one of significant average improvement but persistent inequalities. In the words of a recent comprehensive study of Brazil's so-called burden of disease published in the Lancet: 'although health outcomes in Brazil improved overall between 1990 and 2016, these improvements were not sufficient to eliminate health inequities'.[15] To use Célia Szwarcwald and her colleagues' apt phrase, there is an 'excess burden of poor health experienced by populations in the less developed regions'.[16] The same conclusions are reached in another recent comprehensive study:

> The decline of age-standardized mortality rates is not uniform and is less impressive in the Northeast and North states, in which there are more non-white inhabitants as well as more poor and vulnerable populations. Previous studies showed that the decline in age-adjusted mortality rates differs according to race, sex, and socioeconomic status with black individuals and lower income populations suffering the greatest impact.[17]

What needs to be done and how can the right to health help?

4.2 The Limits of the Right to Health

That health inequalities in Brazil continue to be too high three decades after the establishment of a right to health in the Constitution

[14] C. L. Szwarcwald et al., 'Health Inequalities in Rio de Janeiro, Brazil: Lower Healthy Life Expectancy in Socioeconomically Disadvantaged Areas', (2011) 101(3) *American Journal of Public Health*, 517–523.

[15] F. Marinho et al., 'Burden of Disease in Brazil, 1990–2016: A Systematic Subnational Analysis for the Global Burden of Disease Study 2016', (2018) 392(10143) *The Lancet*, 760–775.

[16] C. L. Szwarcwald et al., 'Inequalities in Healthy Life Expectancy by Brazilian Geographic Regions: Findings from the National Health Survey, 2013', (2016) 15 (1) *International Journal for Equity in Health*, at 141.

[17] E. B. França et al., 'Cause-Specific Mortality for 249 Causes in Brazil and States during 1990–2015: A Systematic Analysis for the Global Burden of Disease Study 2015', (2017) 15(1) *Population Health Metrics*, at 39. The same conclusion is reached in many other studies, e.g., 'the burden of disease is generally higher in the states of the north and northeast regions than in the south and southeast', Marinho et al., 'Burden of Disease in Brazil, 1990–2016'.

is therefore clear. But it is important to emphasise that the right to health alone, even if perfectly implemented, would still not be sufficient to address the problem. To overlook this is to ignore one of the crucial messages of the Sanitary Movement's campaign. As we saw in Chapter 2, the aim of the movement was not 'simply' to extend health actions and services to the whole population but also to expose and address the underlying *social determinants* that made people ill in the first place.

The provision of health actions and services, as important as it is, is only a part of any adequate and comprehensive strategy to improve population health. A country may have a magnificent network of hospitals, complete with the most updated equipment, the best health professionals one can train and the largest supply of state-of-the-art medicines one can imagine, and still the health of its population will not improve much if people lack access to clean water and basic sanitation, lack basic health knowledge and education, work in poor conditions and earn less than the minimum needed to eat, dress and be housed properly.

The importance of this point within the movement's overall project was such that its draft proposal for the Constitution broke down the right to health into several components, each representing a different social determinant of health, as can be seen in one of its submissions to the constituent assembly, *Emenda Popular* (Popular Amendment) no. 50. Its first article read as follows:

> Art. 1. Health is an inalienable right of the person, without any discrimination, guaranteed by the state to the whole population.
> Paragraph 1. The right to health entails the following fundamental rights:
> I – access to land and the means of production;
> II – dignified working conditions, basic sanitation, housing, food, education, transport and leisure;
> III – respect to the environment and control of environmental pollution;
> IV – development of domestic basic sanitation, including in substandard housing until urban reform eliminates them;
> V – information about health risks, including on individual and collective health conditions;
> VI – dignified, free and quality health actions and services, with the right to consent and refuse;
> VII – refusal to work in unhealthy, dangerous or risky environments, being forbidden any sanctions or payment cuts;
> VIII – free choice as to the size of ones off-spring.[18]

[18] Popular Amendment (*Emenda Popular*) no. 50, submitted by the Sanitary Movement and allied groups to the constituent assembly. As we saw in Chapter 2, Section 2.4, this proposed article did not make it into the final text. Several other proposals had social determinants in

Brazil's stratospheric historical levels of inequality not only influenced the strong focus of the movement on social determinants, it presented (and still does) important challenges to the achievement of its broader aims. The attainment of more radical and sustainable change within health policy is strongly dependent on social transformation in all social determinants, in particular, income distribution, which is extremely resistant to change.[19] There has been progress towards more health equality in all areas in the past three decades as we saw in Chapter 3. But without a more radical egalitarian transformation of Brazilian society, even a perfect public health system, that is, one that is adequately funded, efficiently managed and easily accessible to everyone will not suffice to address Brazil's health problems.[20]

4.3 Brazil's Socioeconomic Gulf

Brazil has consistently occupied a top position in the unflattering ranking of the most unequal countries in the world. Although the focus

their text, such as the one submitted by parliamentarian Carlos Sant'Anna to the 8th National Health Conference in 1986, the one from the Commission of Pro-Constituent Studies of the Municipal Chamber of São Paulo, also from 1986 and the one from the National Commission for the Sanitary Reform from 1987. For a useful compendium of all relevant proposals of texts for the Health chapter of the constitution, see E. Rodriguez Neto, *Saúde: Promessas e limites da constituição* (Rio de Janeiro: Fiocruz, 2003). Express recognition of the importance of social determinants was made in the ordinary law that regulated Art. 196 of the Constitution (Law 8.080/1990) Article 3. The levels of health express the social and economic organisation of the country, whose determinants and conditions are, among others, food, housing, basic sanitation, environment, work, income, education, physical activity, transportation, leisure and access to essential goods and services.

[19] As Szwarcwald and colleagues note: 'Health inequalities found nationwide may therefore be considered a product of the poor living conditions experienced by a considerable fraction of the Brazilian population.' Szwarcwald et al., 'Inequalities in Healthy Life Expectancy'.

[20] As some of the leading experts on social policies and the public health system in Brazil have noted, the Sanitary Movement has not succeeded in fully implementing its ambitious goals of radically transforming not only the health conditions of the population but society as a whole. J. S. Paim, *Reforma sanitária brasileira: Contribuição para a compreensão e crítica* (Salvador: Edufba; Rio de Janeiro: Editora Fiocruz. 2008). Sonia Fleury, for instance, argues that the reform did not manage to build the aspired 'new civilizatory standard', that is, one that would definitely consolidate the idea of health as a public good. S. Fleury, 'Revisitando a questão democrática na área da saúde: Quase trinta anos depois', (2009) 33 *Saúde em Debate*, 156–164; see also J. S. Paim, 'A Reforma Sanitária Brasileira e o Sistema Único de Saúde: Dialogando com hipóteses concorrentes', (2008) 18(4) *Physis Revista de Saúde Coletiva*, 625–644, at 633, explaining how the Sanitary Movement aimed at a comprehensive 'social reform', a reform of the 'way of life'.

of these rankings is income and wealth, it is well-known that inequality in this realm tends to correlate strongly with inequalities in health, education, housing conditions and food consumption, that is, all the important determinants of well-being.[21] Even if we take the (increasingly contested) reported reduction in inequality of the past two decades at face value, the fact is that Brazil has remained a very unequal country, with a Gini of 0.53 in the latest estimate available (2017) (see Figure 4.3).[22]

All countries that adopt a market-based economic system tend of course to experience economic inequality. Yet, how much inequality the market generates and how much of that inequality consolidates can vary significantly according to several contextual factors, among which state taxation and redistribution policies occupy a crucial place. To see this clearly, we can compare pre- and post-state intervention levels of inequality. Whereas OECD countries reduce market inequalities by an average of 16 per cent through taxation, and some reduce it even further,

[21] See D. Rasella et al., 'Impact of Income Inequality on Life Expectancy in a Highly Unequal Developing Country: The Case of Brazil', (2013) 67(8) *Journal of Epidemiol Community Health*, 661–666; M. B. Barros et al., 'Trends in Social and Demographic Inequalities in the Prevalence of Chronic Diseases in Brazil. PNAD: 2003–2008', (2011) 16(9) *Cien Saúde Colet.*, 3755–3768; D. Chor et al., 'Prevalence, Awareness, Treatment and Influence of Socioeconomic Variables on Control of High Blood Pressure: Results of the ELSA-Brasil Study', (2015) 10(6) *PLoS One*, available at: doi:10.1371/journal.pone.0127382. B. P. Nunes et al., 'Socioeconomic Inequalities in the Access to and Quality of Health Care Services', (2014) 48(6) *Rev Saúde Pública*, 968–976; I. O. Miquilin, 'Inequalities in Health Services Access and Use among Formal, Informal, and Unemployed Workers, Based on Data from the Brazilian National Household Sample Survey, 2008', (2013) 29(7) *Cad. Saúde Pública*, 1392–1406; M. C. Louvison et al., 'Inequalities in Access to Health Care Services and Utilization for the Elderly in São Paulo, Brazil', (2008) 42(4) *Rev Saúde Pública*, 733–740; R. A. Carvalho et al., 'Inequalities in Health: Living Conditions and Infant Mortality in Northeastern Brazil', (2015) 49(5) *Rev Saúde Pública*, available at: doi.org/10.1590/S0034-8910.2015049004794.

[22] The Gini coefficient is the standard measure of inequality representing the income distribution of the population within a given country. It takes the value of 0 when everybody has the same income and 1 when one person has all the income. More recent studies with more comprehensive and perhaps reliable data have put in question earlier reports that income inequality had decreased significantly in Brazil in the past decade. See M. Medeiros, P. H. G. F. Souza, F. A. Castro, 'A estabilidade da desigualdade de renda no Brasil, 2006 a 2012: Estimativa com dados do imposto de renda e pesquisas domiciliares', (2015) 20(4) *Ciênc. saúde coletiva*, available at: doi.org/10.1590/1413-81232015204.00362014.

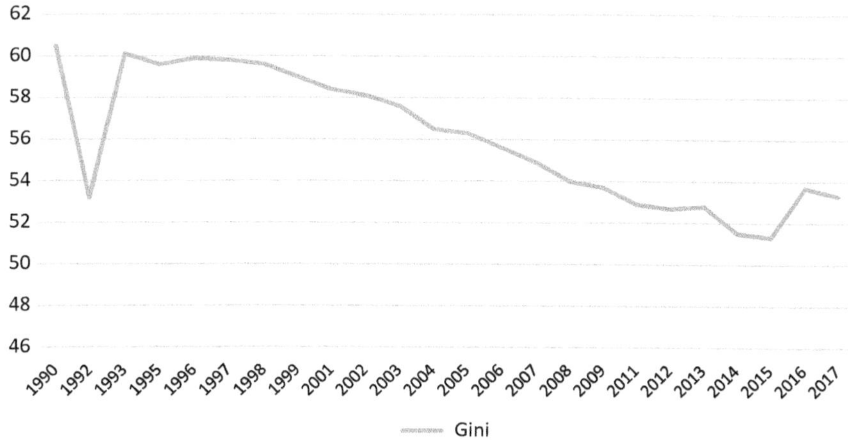

Figure 4.3 Inequality in Brazil.
Source: World Bank Poverty and Equity Database

above 20 per cent,[23] the Brazilian taxation system is thought to make inequalities even worse due to its low rates of taxation of income and wealth and strong focus on so-called indirect consumption taxes.[24] Brazil is the country where the top 10 per cent holds the largest share of total income when compared to other countries in the world (41.9 per cent) and where the ratio between the top and bottom quintiles is one of the highest, at 15.6 times (see Figure 4.4).[25] To put this into context, the

[23] The effects of income redistribution policies can be measured by comparing the Gini coefficient before and after taxes and transfers. Income inequalities are reduced through taxes and transfers in all OECD countries. In about a third of OECD economies, inequality is cut by more than 20 per cent through public transfers and tax systems. See OECD, Government at a Glance 2017 (Paris: OECD Publishing, 2017), available at: http://dx.doi.org/10.1787/gov_glance-2017-en, accessed 23 June 2019.

[24] See R. C. Fernandes et al., 'The Distributive Impact of Income Taxes in Brazil', Working paper number 171, International Policy Centre for Inclusive Growth (IPC-IG) (2018). Some studies estimate that those who earn up to two times the minimum wage pay indirect and direct taxes of 27 per cent, whereas those earning more than thirty times the minimum wage pay 18 per cent. See S. Dain, 'Os vários mundos do financiamento da Saúde no Brasil: Uma tentativa de integração' ('Healthcare Financing Options in Brazil: An Attempt at Integration'), (2007) 12 Suppl. *Ciência & Saúde Coletiva*, 1851–1864.

[25] The World Bank, income share held by highest 10 per cent https://data.worldbank.org/topic/poverty, accessed 23 June 2019. Such high levels of inequality make the rich in Brazil richer than the rich in some of the most developed countries, such as France. See J. Cunha, 'Renda média dos brasileiros ricos é maior que a dos franceses', *Folha de*

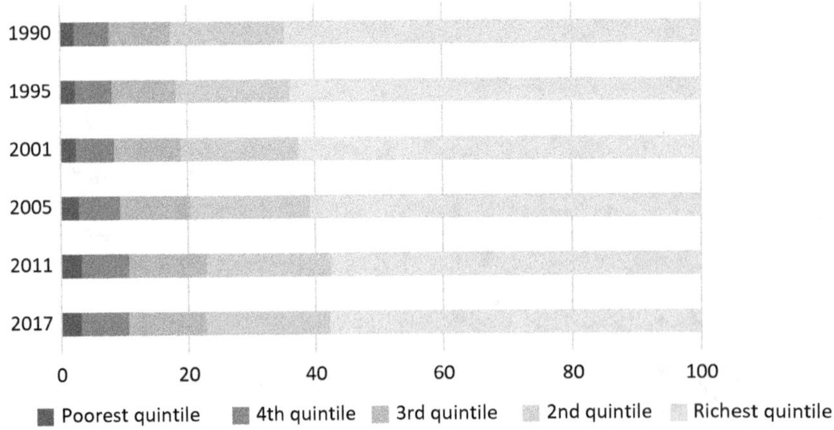

Figure 4.4 Distribution of income by quintile in Brazil.
Source: World Bank Poverty and Equity Database

United States, which is the most unequal among developed countries, has a top – bottom quintile ratio of 9.4. The United Kingdom, one of the most unequal European countries, has a top – bottom ratio of 5.4. As the Brazilian GDP per capita is almost three times lower than the United Kingdom and four times lower than the United States, these large inequalities result in even starker deprivation at the bottom quintile (see Figures 4.3 and 4.4).[26]

***

Such high levels of income and other socioeconomic inequalities in social determinants of health, such as education, nutrition, housing conditions, access to water and sanitation, are not solvable through health actions and services. Without deeper structural changes in the labour market, the education system, taxation and redistribution policies, the root causes of

S. Paulo (newspaper), 29 October 2017, www1.folha.uol.com.br/mercado/2017/10/1931198-renda-media-dos-brasileiros-ricos-e-maior-que-a-dos-franceses.shtml, accessed 21 June 2019.

[26] In 2017, Brazil's GDP per capita ppp was US$15,553, the UK's was US$44,920 and the US US$59,927, https://data.worldbank.org/indicator/NY.GDP.PCAP.PP.KD?locations=PY-BR-AR-UY-GB.

health inequalities will remain. The health system cannot provide the income required for individuals to eat, dress and be housed properly. The health system can try to educate people on basic hygiene measures but cannot provide them with the solid basic schooling that affects health so positively.[27]

Universal health actions and services can and do mitigate these inequalities to some extent, but are insufficient, in themselves, to eradicate them. As much as the health system is capable of achieving, only a more radical and structural attack on Brazil's deep and historical economic inequalities can deliver the egalitarian aims of the Constitution. It is important to be aware of these limitations of the right to health. The problem, which is clear in the phenomenon of judicialisation (see Part II), is that the health system is attributed a power that it does not have and then blamed for failing to achieve what it could not.

Having highlighted this important *external* limitation to the ability of the health system to improve health, we must now discuss another crucial but *internal* challenge also often overlooked or minimised in judicialisation debates: *limited resources*. All health systems have to grapple with the problem of limited resources. The Brazilian public health system has felt this challenge in a particularly stark manner due to chronic underfunding.

4.4 Chronic Underfunding

To achieve its necessarily limited yet still important potential to improve population health, a health system needs to be able to dispose of a minimum amount of resources. What that amount should be is of course a complex and contested matter. The title of a recent report of the WHO summarises this well: *Spending Targets for Health: No Magic Number*.[28] But Brazil's investment patterns on health are so low (whatever standard one uses) that it is hard not to conclude (i) that it could invest much

[27] As Szwarcwald notes: 'To mitigate the effects of social exclusion, the development of strategies at the regional level is essential not only to provide health care to all persons in need, but also to reduce risk exposures and to support prevention policies for adoption of healthy behaviors, prioritizing the disadvantaged population groups that will have the greater impact of interventions.' Szwarcwald et al., 'Inequalities in Healthy Life Expectancy', at 7.

[28] M. Jowett et al., *Spending Targets for Health: No Magic Number* (Geneva: WHO, 2016).

more given its economic capacity and (ii) that underinvestment is one of the main problems of the system.

Brazil's *total* health expenditure (i.e., the aggregate expenditure incurred by government and individuals privately) is not that low by international standards. According to the WHO Global Health Expenditure database, it is currently 11.77 per cent (2016), which is higher than the world average (10.021 per cent) and even higher than that of more developed countries such as the United Kingdom (9.762 per cent).[29] But total health expenditure is not a very good indicator of the actual beneficiaries of health expenditure nor of the priority that a given country gives to health. For that, of course, we need to know how these resources are distributed among the population. The first thing we need to do, thus, is disaggregate between public and private expenditure. Once we do that, it becomes immediately clear that Brazil is much more of an outlier than it appears at first.

As Figure 4.5 shows, health expenditure in Brazil is extremely imbalanced towards private expenditure by international standards. Only 33 per cent of total expenditure is public compared to between 74 per cent and 80 per cent in the other countries included in the graph.[30] A high proportion of private expenditure is not by necessity evidence of health inequality. Nothing prevents, in principle, a country to display a very high proportion of private expenditure in its total health expenditure, even 100 per cent, and still have a very equal distribution of that expenditure. In practice, however, given the tendency of private health markets to reinforce economic inequality and of state intervention to mitigate it, the higher the proportion of private health expenditure the more unequal health expenditure tends to be.[31] A fortiori, such

[29] WHO Global Health Expenditure database, Current health expenditure (% of GDP), https://data.worldbank.org/indicator/SH.XPD.CHEX.GD.ZS, accessed 23 June 2019.

[30] The challenge is to come out of what Sérgio Piola, a leading Brazilian expert in health financing, aptly calls a paradox: 'With this level of public spending Brazil is in a paradoxical situation: it is the only country with a public health care system that has a responsibility to care for all, but which spends more on private health care.' S. Piola et al., 'The Effects of Constitutional Amendment 29 on the Regional Allocation of Public Funds for the National Health Service in Brazil', (2016) 21(2) *Ciência & Saúde Coletiva*, 411–421, at 419.

[31] See A. S. Ke Xu et al., *Public Spending on Health: A Closer Look at Global Trends* (Geneva: WHO, 2018): 'public funding sources (taxes, typically) enable revenues to be pooled and spent more equitably and efficiently to meet health needs and reduce the reliance on out-of-pocket spending', at 7 and 'A health system that relies mainly on high levels of government funding, as well as a high share of public sources in overall health spending, generally provides better and more equitable access to services and better financial protection.', at 35. See also Jowett et al., *Spending Targets for Health*, at 34.

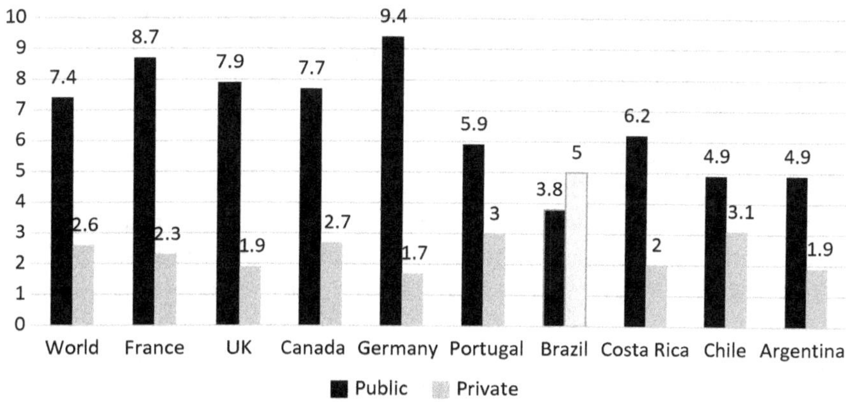

Figure 4.5 Public and private health expenditure as % of GDP.
Source: WHO Global Health Expenditure database[32]

inequalities will tend to be more pronounced the more economically unequal the country is, as the poor will have less to spend privately on health than the rich.

When we look into private health expenditure in Brazil in more detail, it becomes even clearer how unequal the system currently is. Given that a large proportion of private health expenditure is incurred by a relatively small fraction of the population (disproportionately those at the top quintile of income who use private health insurance), their per capita health expenditure is several times higher than that of those who rely almost exclusively on public expenditure, that is, on the actions and services of the public system. It is difficult to reach an exact number as there is some overlap between the beneficiaries of public and private expenditure, but it is possible to have a rough idea. According to the latest data released by the IBGE, Brazil as a whole spent R$546 billion (9.1 per cent of GDP) in 2015 on health. Of those, R$231 billion (3.9 per

[32] It is important to highlight that there are disputes over the exact figure of Brazil's total expenditure on health. According to the Brazilian Institute of Geography and Statistics (IBGE), Brazil's total expenditure in 2015 was 9.1 per cent of the GDP, that is, lower than the 11.46 per cent reported for that year by the WHO. The discrepancy is only in private expenditure and does not therefore affect my argument. I am grateful to Fabiola Sulpino Vieira for drawing my attention to this point. See IBGE, 'Conta-Satélite de Saúde Brasil: 2010–2015', available at: https://biblioteca.ibge.gov.br/visualizacao/livros/liv101437.pdf, accessed 31 May 2019.

cent of GDP) was public expenditure (i.e., by government) and R$315 billion (5.2 per cent of GDP) private (i.e., families and not for profit organisations). If we divide these amounts by the number of people in the population (204,470,000 in 2015), as the IBGE does, we reach the following expenditure per capita: R$1,538.79 – private; R$1,131.94 – public. This gives the false impression that private health expenditure per capita is 'only' 36 per cent higher than the public. The fact, however, is that whereas public expenditure is in principle for the benefit of the whole population, private expenditure is not. It goes only to those who actually incur it, that is, those who pay for the private health insurance plans, those who pay for the services of private doctors, those who buy medicines over the pharmacy's counter, etc.

To have a better idea of the discrepancy between public and private expenditure per capita we need to refine our calculation. The first step is to note that a big chunk of private expenditure goes to pay so-called health plans (*planos de saúde*), a form of pre-paid health insurance. In 2015, the total paid by holders of those private plans was R$143.3 billion, that is, 45 per cent of total private expenditure.[33] This expenditure benefited exclusively those who contracted those health plans – 71.5 million people in 2015 (34 per cent of the population).[34] The per capita expenditure for them was, thus, at least R$2,000 on average, that is, almost 90 per cent higher than public expenditure per capita. But it was certainly more. The IBGE figures also show that R$92.5 billion were spent with medicines ('out of pocket'). We know that everyone in Brazil, including those in the bottom decile of income, spends a lot on medicines as a proportion of their income, but as a proportion of total private expenditure, it is the richest who spend more.[35] All in all, thus, it is safe to assume that the large proportion of private health expenditure in Brazil as a percentage of GDP translates into even larger per capita

[33] ANS, Dados Gerais Beneficiários de planos privados de saúde, por cobertura assistencial (Brasil – 2009–2019), www.ans.gov.br/perfil-do-setor/dados-gerais, accessed 23 June 2019.

[34] The number is the sum of those who held a health plan (47,053,184) and those who held exclusively dental plans (24,479,494).

[35] T. Menezes et al., 'O gasto e a demanda das famílias em saúde: Uma análise a partir da POF de 2002–2003', in Silveira, F. G. et al., (eds.) *Gasto e consumo das famílias brasileiras contemporâneas* (Brasília: IPEA, 2006), 313–344. See also L. P. Garcia et al., 'Gastos com planos de saúde das famílias brasileiras: Estudo descritivo com dados das Pesquisas de Orçamentos Familiares 2002–2003 e 2008–2009', (2015) 20(1) *Ciênc Saúde Coletiva*, 1425–1434.

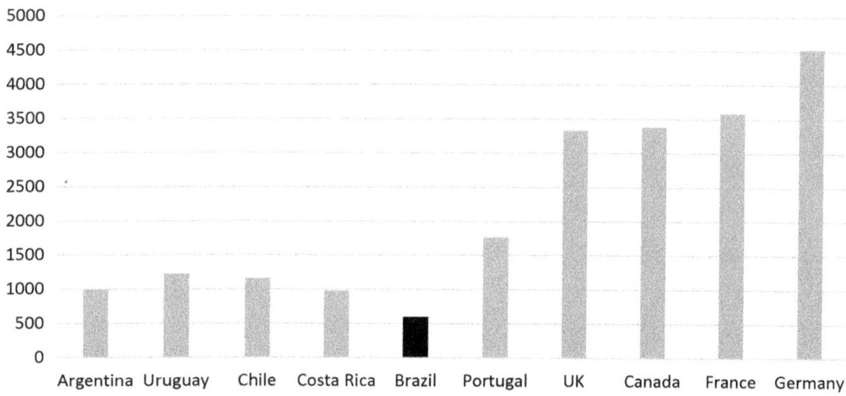

Figure 4.6 Health expenditure (public) per capita, in US$.
Source: WHO Global Health Observatory data repository

discrepancies between those who rely mostly on the public system and those who don't.[36]

It is not difficult to see how this scenario betrays the constitutional promise of an adequate, universal and egalitarian health system. The very low total (3.9 per cent of the GDP)[37] and per capita public expenditure (currently US$594.90) makes it virtually impossible to comply with the Constitution (see Figures 4.6 and 4.7). With this amount of resources, even if Brazil had the most efficient public health system of the world, it would still be impossible to offer the population the good quality and

[36] For a similar argument made as far back as 1986, see P. L. B. Silva, A. C. Medici, 'Considerações sobre o Gasto em Saúde no Brasil: Dilemas até o Final do Século', (1988) 1(4) *Cadernos de Saúde Pública*, 88–105, estimating that in 1986 total health expenditure in Brazil was US$10 billion (Cz$343.2 billion), or 3.9 per cent of GDP. Of those, 38 per cent were private, which leads the authors to a total per capita expenditure of Cz$2,469, divided into Cz$8,667per capita for the 15 million people then spending privately on health and Cz$1,719 for the population, at 95. The authors were dreaming, then, with a rise of total health expenditure to 6.5 per cent of GDP by the year 2000, of which about 4 per cent would be public. In 2000, Brazil's public expenditure on health was 2.89 per cent. It would reach almost 4 per cent only in 2009.

[37] The Pan-American Health Organization sets 6 per cent of GDP as a useful benchmark: 'increase efficiency and public financing of health, as appropriate, noting that in most cases, public expenditure of 6 per cent of GDP is a useful benchmark and that these resources should be allocated, as appropriate, on a priority basis to the primary level of care to expand the supply of quality services and quickly address unmet health needs'. See PAHO Proposed Resolution, 'Strategy for Universal Access to Health and Universal Health Coverage', 53rd Directing Council, 66th Session of the regional committee of WHO for the Americas, Washington, DC, 29 September–3 October 2014.

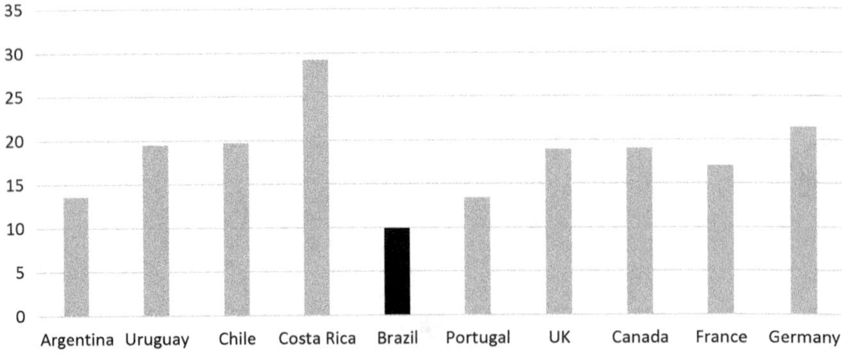

Figure 4.7 Health expenditure as % of general government expenditure.
Source: WHO Global Health Observatory data repository

comprehensive package of health actions and services promised by the idea of health as a human right. The existence of a private system alongside the public one, which spends a lot more and benefits between one quarter and one third of the population, makes a mockery of that idea. Leaving aside for the moment the debate about the actual differences in quality between the two systems, it is clear that the current situation is far from universalistic and egalitarian, as promised in the Constitution.[38] Public health expert Eugênio Vilaça Mendes puts it evocatively when he says that 'the dream of universalization is being transformed into the nightmare of segmentation'.[39]

To compound the problem, public health resources are not as equitably distributed across the country as they should be. To reduce the stark regional inequalities we saw earlier (which is something the Constitution actually pledges to do in Article 3),[40] there should be higher investment

[38] In this respect, Brazil's situation is not dissimilar to the situation of the world as a whole: Only 20 per cent of the world's population live in high income countries, and yet these countries account for close to 80 per cent of global health spending, Ke Xu et al., 'Public Spending on Health'.

[39] My translation from Portuguese: 'o sonho da universalização vem se transformando no pesadelo da segmentação'. E. V. Mendes, 'Vinte e cinco anos do Sistema Único de Saúde: Resultados Resultados e desafios', (2013) 27(78) *Estudos Avançados*, at 29. This is particularly problematic if we recall that the Brazilian state itself incentivises individuals to buy private health services through generous tax exemptions, see C. O. Ocké-Reis, F. N. Gama, *Radiografia do gasto tributário em saúde – 2003–2013* (Brasília: IPEA, 2016).

[40] 'Article 3. The fundamental objectives of the Federative Republic of Brazil are: I – to build a free, fair and supportive society; II – to ensure national development; III – to eradicate poverty and marginalization and *reduce social and regional inequalities*; IV – to promote

on health in the states where health conditions are worse, that is, those of the North and Northeast of the country (see Section 4.1). Yet the very opposite occurs. The average expenditure per capita in the Northeast is the lowest in Brazil (R$893.35), and some of the poorest states with the worse health indicators (see Figures 4.1 and 4.2) have the lowest expenditures: for example, Maranhão (R$750.45), Bahia (R$777.80), Alagoas (R$863.18). On the other hand, states of the South and Southeast, where health conditions are comparatively much better, have an average per capita expenditure of R$1,129.19 (Southeast) and R$1.159.05 (South), around 20 per cent higher than in the Northeast.[41]

***

There is simply too big a mismatch between the aims of the Constitution and the resources that are made available to the public health system. As an upper middle-income country, Brazil could invest much more in public health if the political will were there. To muster this political will is the greatest challenge for the consolidation of the important gains achieved so far (see Chapter 3) and for the further improvements still required.

4.5 The Battle for Resources

As we saw in Chapter 2, the Sanitary Movement and other supporters of the right to health knew only too well that, without legally guaranteed sources of funding, the dream of a genuinely universal and egalitarian public health system would not leave the paper of the Constitution. Accordingly, all their proposals for the Health chapter of the Constitution included specific provisions guaranteeing a minimum compulsory funding. With small variations, they all earmarked a significant proportion of total tax revenue (as much as 13 per cent) to be invested in health and set an ambitious goal of 10 per cent of Brazil's GDP as the aim to be achieved for an appropriately funded system.[42]

the well-being of all, without discrimination based on origin, race, sex, color, age and any other forms of discrimination' (my emphasis).

41 Conselho Federal de Medicina, 2018, available at: http://portal.cfm.org.br/index.php?option=com_content&view=article&id=27963:2018-11-12-18-36-26&catid=3, accessed 23 June 2019.

42 See, for all draft proposals, Rodriguez Neto, *Saúde*.

But that battle, as we also saw, was one of the few that supporters of the right to health lost in the constituent assembly, and the Health chapter ended up including only a generic clause stating that the system would be funded with 'resources from the Social Security budget, the Federal Union, states, municipalities, the Federal District and other sources'.[43] Another 'transitional provision' was added to the 'Transitional Chapter' at the end of the Constitution, establishing that 30 per cent of the Social Security budget would be invested in health in 1989 until the first budgetary law of the post-constitutional period was passed for 1990.[44] This transitional arrangement survived through the following five years, that is, until the Budgetary Laws of 1994, when then President Itamar Franco vetoed the provision, allegedly for 'national interest' reasons, reducing the federal resources of the Health budget for that year in about 50 per cent.[45]

An attempt to plug the hole was then spearheaded by then Health Minister Adib Jatene, a prominent heart surgeon. In great part due to his personal authority, prestige and connections, a temporary tax on financial transactions was created in 1996 (the CPMF – Contribuição Provisória sobre Movimentação Financeira), 80 per cent of whose revenue was earmarked to be invested in health.[46] The CPMF, as well as

43 According to some, the fiercest resistance against fixing minimum percentages of investment in health came from parliamentarians involved in the formulation of the Economic Chapter, led by José Serra, arguing that government revenue would become too inflexible. He would later become Minister of Health and suffer with underfunding. It is interesting to note that some states and municipalities went on to fix minimum rules of investments in their state constitutions and organic laws, which some thought was unconstitutional. See G. Carvalho, 'Financiamento da saúde pública no Brasil no pós-constitucional de 88', (2008) 2(1)*Tempus – Actas de Saúde Coletiva*, 39–51, at 43.

44 Art. 55 of the Ato das Disposições Constitucionais Transitórias (Transitional Constitutional Provisions), which reads: 'Article 55. Until the budget guidelines law is approved, at least thirty percent of the social security budget, excluding unemployment insurance, shall be allocated to the health sector.'

45 Carvalho, 'Financiamento da saúde pública', at 43. According to him, that veto resulted in a loss of 250 million US dollars monthly to the Health budget. Ibid., at 45.

46 The CPMF was created by Constitutional Amendment 12, of 15 August 1996, which inserted Art. 74 in the transitional provisions of the Constitution, allowing the Federal Union to create a provisional tax on financial transactions, for two years, at the maximum rate of 0.25 per cent, whose proceeds ought to be allocated 'in their entirety to the National Health Fund, to fund health actions and services'. The CPMF was regulated by Ordinary Law 9.311 of 24 October 1996, which was changed more than a dozen of times, including by three further constitutional amendments (21/1999, 37/2002 and 42/2003) until its extinction in 2007. Most typically, its proceeds were never allocated in their entirety to health, as from the very beginning 20 per cent were diverted through the

being a provisional measure (which would however last till 2007), was never seen as sufficient or adequate as a permanent solution for the funding of the health system.[47]

What campaigners kept seeking was the legally defined minimum of expenditure on health they were not able to guarantee during the constituent assembly of 1987–1988. With the newly elected Congress of 1999–2000, several proposals for constitutional amendment with different formulations were debated.[48] In the end, an agreement was reached and, twelve years after the enactment of the Constitution, health would finally secure constitutional rules for minimum investment through Constitutional Amendment 29 of 13 October 2000 (Amendment 29).[49] According to the new paragraphs included by Amendment 29 in Article 198 of the Constitution, the Federal Union has a duty to invest in public health actions and services every year, as a minimum, 'the amount invested in the previous year increased by the nominal variation of the

Fundo Social de Emergência (FSE), renamed (Desvinculação de Receitas da União – DRU in 2.000). These mechanisms allow the Federal Government to divert 20 per cent (30 per cent since 2016) of its earmarked tax revenues from health, education and social security to other areas, in particular to pay interests of the public debt. See Carvalho, 'Financiamento da saúde pública', at 44).

47 According to Carvalho, most of the money acquired via the new tax was taken away by the federal government, which led Adib Jatene to resign from his post as Health Minister in November 1996. Carvalho, 'Financiamento da saúde pública', at 44. See also interview of Adib Jatene with Josias de Sousa in 15 August 2007, https://blogs.ne10.uol.com.br/jamildo/2007/08/15/pai-da-cpmf-jatene-diz-que-lula-e-pt-eram-contra/, accessed 1 June 2019 where he states that his resignation was directly motivated by the reduction of resources for health and adds: 'it is said that the problem of public health is management. This is bullshit, the problem is lack of money'. According to him, if 30 per cent of the R$370 billion social security budget had been allocated to health in 2007, the health budget would have been R$111 billion and not R$46 billion as it was.

48 Constitutional Amendment Proposal (PEC) 169, from representatives Waldir Pires (PSDB/BA) and Eduardo Jorge (PT/SP), of 1993, set a minimum of 30 per cent of the revenue of Social Security contributions for health plus 10 per cent of other taxes revenue, as well as 10 per cent of the revenue of states and municipal taxes. Constitutional Amendment Proposal (PEC) 82, of 1995, from representative Carlos Mosconi (PSDB/MG), allocated to health all resources from contributions of employers to the Social Security system.

49 Ironically, in this period (1999–2000) the Ministry of Health was headed by José Serra, the constituent representative who opposed most fiercely the fixation of minimum revenues for health (see n. 43). It is also interesting to note that Amendment 29 was supposed to set temporary rules to be valid until 2004, when a infra-constitutional law should specify the criteria to calculate the minimum obligatory investment of each level of government. That law was approved only in 2012 (Complementary Law no. 141, of 13 January 2012).

GDP' (Art. 198, Paragraph 2, I).[50] States and municipalities are legally obliged to invest a minimum of 12 per cent and 15 per cent, respectively, of their total tax revenue.[51]

As we saw in Chapter 3, Amendment 29 was an important watershed in the financing of the Brazilian public health system. It consolidated public investment in health at a higher proportion of GDP (from 3 per cent to 3.9 per cent) and almost doubled the per capita public expenditure (from US$312 to US$594) from 2000 to 2015 (see Figures 3.9 and 3.10 in Chapter 3). It is still insufficient, as we saw in Section 4.4, but it is progress nonetheless.[52] Yet not even this limited progress is guaranteed, it never is.

Since 2016, Brazil has experienced economic crisis with fierce political disputes over the distribution of the pain. The result for health is expressed in the recent controversial Constitutional Amendment 95, of 2016, which froze public expenditure for twenty years.[53] According to the estimates of health economists Fabiola Vieira and Rodrigo Benevides, the freeze will result in a gradual decrease of the already low levels of the federal government's expenditure from 1.75 per cent of GDP to

[50] In the first year of operation, in 2000, the percentage fixed was 5 per cent, that is, a real boost as the GDP in 1999 grew by only 0.47 per cent.

[51] A transition period of five years was given to states and municipalities to reach those levels.

[52] Some are very critical about Amendment 29, seeing it as retrogression. See Carvalho, 'Financiamento da saúde pública', at 46. The burden on states and municipalities (12 and 15 per cent) is high, especially for municipalities, whereas the Federal Union, the richest entity in terms of tax revenues, was imposed no minimum in terms of revenues, ending up with what many see as a disproportionately low and decreasing burden. Whereas the Federal Union collects 60 per cent of the country's tax revenue, it is responsible only for 47 per cent of the health expenditure under the current arrangement. States are slightly overburdened, with 24 per cent of revenues and 26 per cent of expenditures, and municipalities are the most overburdened, with 16 per cent of revenues and 27 per cent of expenditures. This much lower contribution of the Federal Union to the health budget limits significantly the resources that could go to health. According to Soares and Santos, from 1994 to 2012 the participation of the Federal Union in the financing of the health system fell 38.4 per cent, whereas states increased their participation by 87.2 per cent and municipalities by 138.8 per cent. A. Soares, N. R. Santos, 'Financiamento do Sistema Único de Saúde nos governos FHC, Lula e Dilma', (2014) 38(100) *Saúde em Debate*, 18–25, at 22.

[53] Amendment 95 forbids any increase of so-called primary public expenditure above the inflation of the previous year until 2038, www.planalto.gov.br/ccivil_03/constituicao/Emendas/Emc/emc95.htm#art3. Amendment 95/2016 revoked another one, Amendment 86/2015, which had changed the way in which federal investment is calculated, www.planalto.gov.br/ccivil_03/constituicao/Emendas/Emc/emc86.htm#art1.

somewhere between 0.99 per cent and 1.45 per cent, depending on economic growth during the period. In absolute terms, the losses can add up to R$415 billion during the twenty years of the freeze.[54]

***

The protracted and perpetual battle over resources for the public health system recounted in this section is relevant for several different reasons. It confirms that the Constitution matters, otherwise political groups would not bother to fight so fiercely over changes to the constitutional text and their exact wording. As we saw, resources for health have changed, for better and worse (but overall for better) several times through constitutional amendments since 1988. It also shows that transformative campaigns are long-term processes, requiring sustained and continuous efforts to bear fruit. It took twelve years for supporters of the right to health to approve Amendment 29, which consolidated and increased resources for health, and another twelve for it to be duly regulated through Complementary Law 141, which further secured funds for health.

But as we saw in Section 4.4, the total public expenditure on health is still clearly insufficient to implement the right to health as promised in the Constitution. If we recall that the aim of the Sanitary Movement was for the state to gradually reach 10 per cent of GDP in public health expenditure, we can see that the current levels of funding are still far from that ideal, which is likely to be further delayed by the current scenario of austerity and the political leaning of the recently elected federal government.[55]

4.6 Conclusions: What Can the Right to Health Do?

This chapter has tried to put the achievements of thirty years of the right to health in Brazil into context. As we saw, despite the significant improvements in population health described in Chapter 3, the

[54] F. S. Vieira, R. P. S. Benevides, 'O Direito à Saúde no Brasil em Tempos de Crise Econômica, Ajuste Fiscal e Reforma Implícita do Estado', (2016) 10(3) *Revista de Estudos e Pesquisas sobre as Américas*, at 18.

[55] See 'Brazil Enters the Bolsonaro Zone', (editorial) (2019) 7(2) *The Lancet Global Health*, available at www.thelancet.com/journals/langlo/article/PIIS2214-109X(19)30002-6/fulltext, accessed 20 March 2019.

situation is still much worse than it could be given Brazil's economic possibilities as an upper middle-income country. The improved average health indicators mask persistent health inequalities across the main regions of the country, states, cities and even districts within cities. Part of the problem, as we saw, are resiliently high levels of inequality in so-called social determinants of health, that is, income, education, working and housing conditions, nutrition, etc. More radical improvements in population health can only be achieved as part of a systemic effort to address these broader inequalities. Those who fought to include the right to health in the Constitution knew that very well. The constitutional text partly reflected their vision, as Article 196 stresses the prominent role of social and economic policies as the main tools to implement the right to health.

Another part of the problem is the incapacity of the public health system to provide a genuinely universal and egalitarian package of health actions and services to the whole population. Problems of administrative efficiency abound, including corruption, but are dwarfed by more fundamental issues that have accompanied the public system since its inception: chronic underfunding and unequal distribution of resources. Both have been mitigated since the Constitution was adopted but remain high and represent an increasingly important challenge to further progress. Public expenditure on health in Brazil is still very low however you look at it. As a percentage of GDP (3.9 per cent), it is 35 per cent lower than the WHO recommends as a minimum benchmark (6 per cent) and less than half of what the countries that take health really seriously spend. It is lower than that of any of our Latin American neighbours of similar levels of economic development, not in itself a very high standard of comparison (see Figure 4.5). In per capita terms, Brazil's public expenditure on health is 7.6 times lower than Germany's, 5.6 times lower than the United Kingdom's and 3 times lower than Portugal's. These countries are of course richer than Brazil, but not to that magnitude. Germany's GDP per capita is 3 times the Brazilian, the United Kingdom's is 2.6 times and Portugal's 1.8. Costa Rica, a Latin American neighbour of similar GDP per capita, spends 64 per cent more on health than Brazil (see Figure 4.6).

To compound the problem, as we saw, public health resources are not as equitably distributed across the country as they should be, and the better off everywhere have all but deserted the public health system in favour of private health insurance plans, in no small part incentivised by generous tax exemptions that currently add up to approximately 30 per cent of the federal health budget.[56] In the aggregate, private expenditure in Brazil exceeds government expenditure by a large margin, but benefits only between one quarter and one third of the population.

Chapters 3 and 4 have tried to provide a reasonably comprehensive picture of the right to health in Brazil in the past three decades. The Constitution has worked, improving significantly the health of the population, in particular, the most disadvantaged. A lot more could be done given Brazil's economic capacity, but structural socioeconomic inequalities and political obstacles pose serious challenges. What else can be done through the right to health? One option is to continue the political fight. As the history of the constituent assembly, Amendment 29, Complementary Law 141 and so many other initiatives show, well-organised and sustained political campaigning can pay important dividends in the medium to longer term.[57]

Can the process be accelerated? One increasingly popular tool thought to be capable of contributing to that endeavour is litigation. As the Brazilian Supreme Federal Tribunal Justice Carmen Lucia has dramatically put it to justify the assertive stance of the Brazilian judiciary in health litigation: 'Pain does not wait'.[58] Part II of this book critically analyses the potential of health litigation to bring about social change through an in-depth discussion of the that phenomenon in Brazil.

[56] Ocké-Reis, Gama, *Radiografia do gasto tributário em saúde – 2003–2013.*

[57] The most recent campaign started in 2013 with the mobilisation of various sectors of society for the strengthening of the SUS (The 'Saúde+10' movement), resulting in a Popular Bill (Projeto de Lei de Iniciativa Popular, PLC no. 321/2013) being submitted to the National Congress with more than 2.2 million signatures to guarantee 10 per cent of federal revenues to be invested on health, see www.camara.leg.br/proposicoesWeb/fichadetramitacao?idProposicao=589775, accessed 23 June 2019.

[58] Statement made on 7 November 2018 when opening a course on health for judges organised by the National Council of Justice, available at: http://agenciabrasil.ebc.com.br/geral/noticia/2016-11/carmen-lucia-diz-que-sentencas-que-dao-acesso-remedios-sao-parte-da-democracia, accessed 26 July 2019.

PART II

The Judicialisation of the Right to Health

5

The Judicialisation of Health in Numbers

My aim in this chapter is chiefly descriptive and explanatory. What is the scale of the judicialisation of health in Brazil? How is it geographically distributed in such a large and diverse country? What kinds of health interventions are mostly claimed in the courts? Who are its main actors? How much does it cost the public coffers? I will try to build as comprehensive a picture as possible with the currently available data.

The task is not simple. Comprehensive and reliable data are limited, a problem for empirical studies in general made worse by the complex and fragmented organisation of the Brazilian public health and judicial systems. The constitutional duty to implement the right to health is held concurrently by the Federal Union, the 27 states[1] and the 5,570 municipalities currently in existence across the country.[2] Individuals are therefore able to bring claims against any of these three government entities (i.e., the municipality where they live, the state in which that municipality is located and the federal government) together or separately.[3]

[1] I am counting the Federal District – where the capital, Brasilia, is located – as a state, as its legal status is that of a state although, technically, it is a territory controlled by the federal government.

[2] The number of municipalities keeps increasing in Brazil with the creation of new ones, often for public finance reasons (municipalities can collect property taxes and receive funds from the central government). This joint responsibility to respect, protect and fulfil the right to health flows from the interpretation of the constitutional text and the Organic Law of Health (Law 8.080/1990), which makes no distinction related to the level of government, mentioning simply 'the state' as the duty holder and leaving the distribution of specific responsibilities for regulations and agreements among the entities under so-called Tripartite and Bipartite Commissions. As we shall see in Chapter 8, this can cause significant problems, in particular, for municipalities, as they are often condemned in health litigation to provide treatment and medicines whose agreed responsibility lies with the state or Federal Union and for which they have no allocated funds.

[3] Nothing in the law, as far as I know, prevents claimants from suing a different municipality or state from that in which they reside but I assume this is not a frequent phenomenon. Most claimants seem to sue the state or the municipality and less often the federal government. The choice between suing the state or the municipality is strategic and seems

A complete picture of the judicialisation of health in Brazil would require data on all the lawsuits filed across the country, from the Amazon region in the North to the southernmost state of Rio Grande do Sul in the border with Uruguay, against all municipalities, states and the Federal Union.

Perhaps unsurprisingly, no such comprehensive data is currently available. Yet increasingly, more studies have been and are being conducted at the federal level and in a few specific states and municipalities where litigation seems to be mostly concentrated as we will see; such studies are significantly enhancing our knowledge. Moreover, with the increasing development of new tools of information technology, more data is becoming accessible even from the remotest parts of the country, and an effort is under way by the National Council of Justice (Conselho Nacional de Justiça, or simply 'CNJ') to provide aggregate data from all courts of the country.[4]

I resort to this still incomplete and fragmented but increasingly richer data in my attempt to build a reasonably comprehensive picture of the judicialisation of health in Brazil.

5.1 Number of Cases

Until very recently, we had to rely on data erratically released by the government and on a few empirical studies carried out by academics to try to build a picture of health litigation in Brazil. In a study I carried out in 2009 and 2010 for a project coordinated by Alicia Yamin from Harvard and Siri Gloppen from Bergen ('the Harvard-Bergen study'),[5]

partly driven by the jurisprudence of the respective Court of Appeal, partly by the posture of the local executive in terms of compliance with judicial orders. see: M. Scheffer et al. (eds.), *O Remédio via Justiça: Um estudo sobre o acesso a novos medicamentos e exames em HIV/Aids no Brasil por meio de ações judiciais*, Série Legislação no. 3 (Brasília: Ministério da Saúde, 2005), at 118.

4 The National Council of Justice is an organ created by Constitutional Amendment No. 45, 2004 and installed on 14 June 2005, pursuant to Art. 103-B of the Constitution to control the administrative and financial activities of the judiciary as well as discipline its members. It is composed of fifteen members, including the president of the Supreme Federal Tribunal (STF), another eight judges from across the Justice system, two members of the Public Prosecutor's office (Ministério Público), two lawyers and two lay citizens.

5 The project resulted in several publications, including A. Yamin, S. Gloppen (eds.), *Litigating Health Rights: Can Courts Bring More Justice to Health?* (Cambridge, MA: Harvard University Press, 2011), in which I authored the chapter on Brazil, 'Health Inequalities, Rights and Courts: The Social Impact of the "Judicialization of Health" in Brazil'.

I used this strategy to estimate, conservatively, that approximately *40,000 cases a year* were reaching the courts in Brazil at the end of the 2000s claiming some health intervention from the state. The estimate was somewhat conservative because it was based on data on only 5 of the 27 states in Brazil, and litigation against municipalities was estimated through a survey responded to by 1,337 of them, that is, 24 per cent of the total. But it did include the states and municipalities then perceived as the 'leaders' of health litigation and also the official numbers of claims against the federal government.

Since 2004, to gauge the levels of what they call 'litigiousness' across the country, the CNJ has been publishing yearly reports called *Justiça em Números* (*Justice in Numbers*) including data on the number of new cases that arrive at the justice system every year.[6] In its first yearly reports, the data were not disaggregated in much detail. They included only the total number of cases in each state and their distribution among the broad spheres of the Brazilian judiciary (e.g., state, federal, labour courts, etc.).[7] It was therefore not possible to know the volume of right to health litigation from the CNJ database, nor of any other specific object of litigation for that matter. Since 2007, however, the CNJ has been trying to increase the level of disaggregation and specificity of its reports by *object* of lawsuits,[8]and since 2010, it has been making a conscious effort to improve the data on health litigation, having established the Fórum Nacional da Saúde (National Health Forum), whose remit is to help in the 'monitoring and solution of health claims'.[9]

[6] All reports are available for public consultation on their website, some with English summaries, available at www.cnj.jus.br/pesquisas-judiciarias/justicaemnumeros/2016-10-21-13-13-04/pj-justica-em-numeros.

[7] The aim of the reports was more to elicit an idea of the workload of courts and judges (so-called congestion rates) than to provide a profile of litigation.

[8] In 2006, the CNJ started an effort to standardise information on lawsuits through what they called 'basic tables of process classification' (*tabelas básicas de classificação processual*). See Resolution CNJ no. 12, of 14 February 2006. These tables were officially implemented a year later through Resolution CNJ no. 46, of 18 December 2007, under the name 'Tabelas Processuais Unificadas' (Unified Process Tables), available at www.cnj.jus.br/images/stories/docs_cnj/resolucao/rescnj_46.pdf, accessed 31 March 2019.

[9] My free translation from the Portuguese of Resolution CNJ no. 107 of 6 April 2010, www.cnj.jus.br/atos-normativos?documento=173, accessed 31 March 2019, which establishes as further aims of the National Health Forum 'carrying out studies and suggesting concrete measures towards improving procedures, reinforcing the effectiveness of litigation and preventing new conflicts'.

Although still incomplete and imperfect, the most recent reports provide us with a much better idea of right to health litigation across Brazil than was possible a decade ago when the Harvard-Bergen study was conducted.[10] According to data from the latest available CNJ report (*Justiça em Números 2019*), from 2014 to 2019 there were approximately 1.7 million new proceedings involving *health* in some way or another. Of those, the vast majority were claims against the state grounded on the right to health.[11] It is important to re-emphasise that these cases include only claims *against the state*, which is the focus of this book. There is also a significant number of cases addressed against private providers of health insurance or medical negligence cases, which may also invoke the right to health but are normally decided according to consumer protection legislation.[12] The majority of cases against the state involved claims for medicines and hospital treatment, which together added up to 1.3 million cases between 2014 and 2019 (about 76 per cent of the total of

[10] The reports rely on each of the twenty-seven state Courts of Appeal to input the information, some of whom (increasingly fewer though) do not comply, and also on categories that, as we will see below, may unfortunately cause some confusion, duplication and inaccuracies in the reports.

[11] It is important to note that, due to the manner in which the CNJ classifies health cases using potentially overlapping categories, in particular, 'hospital treatment *and/or* medication', there is the possibility that the same case could be reported twice, depending on how the Tribunal inputting the information interprets the categories 'hospital treatment and/or medication' and whether it follows or not the express request of the CNJ that cases involving medicines and hospital treatment are registered under both categories. A very conservative estimate would bring down the total number of cases to 702,739 between 2014 and 2019, that is, counting only medication cases, assuming that all hospital treatment cases, which are fewer in number, are also medication cases and have thus been counted twice in all states (an unlikely scenario). It also discards all cases classified in the category medicines and/or hospital treatment assuming they were all double counted (again, an unlikely scenario). The number given in the text (1.3 million cases) may be overestimated yet in my view not significantly. The state of Goiás' Court of Appeal, for instance, consistently reports *no* cases for either medicines or hospital treatment exclusively, which we know from local studies is not accurate, but reports a sizeable number of cases in the 'and/or' category (1,532 in 2017), indicating that they simply lump together all cases. On the other hand, some Tribunals clearly under-report litigation happening in their state. Take Ceará, for instance. We know from studies and news reports that it has experienced a significant increase in health litigation, with some reports indicating between 4,000 and 5,500 cases in 2015, 2016 and 2017. Yet, in the CNJ database, we see less than 1,000 cases in those years. See: https://diariodonordeste.verdesmares.com.br/editorias/metro/judicializacao-da-saude-cai-no-estado-e-gastos-sao-reduzidos-em-quase-50-1.1731371 and https://diariodonordeste.verdesmares.com.br/editorias/metro/judicializacao-se-torna-alternativa-para-carencia-de-atendimento-1.2029751, both accessed 19 March 2019.

[12] Some claim that such private health provider litigation is even larger than claims against the state, but I have found no comprehensive and reliable data on this.

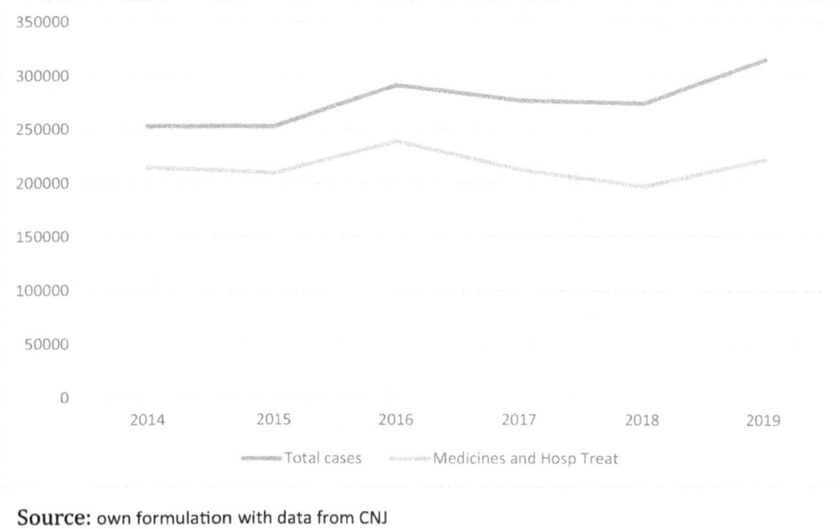

Figure 5.1 Volume of health litigation 2014 to 2019.
Source: Own elaboration with data from CNJ, Justiça em Números, 2019

claims reported by the CNJ.[13] Less frequent claims include those related to improvements in hospital facilities and other health units, mental health, organ and tissue donation and transplantation. (see Figure 5.1).

The number of lawsuits invoking the right to health is therefore reasonably high in absolute terms, but it should of course be borne in mind that Brazil is a very populous country, with 209 million inhabitants as of 2017 (I will return to this issue below).[14]

The data also confirms that right to health claims have grown significantly in the past two decades. Although such comprehensive data as the CNJ's has only recently become available, we know from other studies and reports that the current numbers are significantly higher than they were ten and twenty years ago. The estimate I made for the Harvard-

[13] See A. H. S. Lima Jr., C. J. Schulze, 'Os números do CNJ sobre a judicialização da saúde em 2018', Consultor Juridico, 10 November 2018, available at: www.conjur.com.br/2018-nov-10/opiniao-numeros-judicializacao-saude-2018, accessed 25 November 2018.

[14] By 'new cases', the CNJ database Justiça em Números means all cases registered in that year in all instances of the judiciary system, that is, the lower courts, state and federal tribunals and the highest courts. It is possible, though unlikely given the relative slowness of the judicial process, that the same case is registered more than once in any given year.

Bergen study almost a decade ago, even if somewhat conservative, put right to health litigation at about 40,000 cases a year, which would mean a growth of 500 per cent in the past decade or so. Even if I have underestimated the volume of litigation by half, the growth would still have been of 250 per cent in one decade.

This significant increase seems to have occurred at all government levels. Between 2003 and 2009, the Federal Union reported to have responded to 'only' 5,323 right to health lawsuits.[15] By 2012, a study showed that cases had risen to 13,051.[16] According to data from the CNJ 2018 report, there were almost 18,877 lawsuits in the federal courts in 2017 only related to medicines. If we add the other two categories (hospital treatment and/or medicines) we reach 26,572, indicating a growth of more than 400 per cent in the past two decades.[17]

The same significant growth can be observed at the state and municipal levels. In the Harvard-Bergen study, information collected from different sources revealed 1,144 cases in 2002 and 2,245 cases in 2006 in the state of Rio de Janeiro. The CNJ 2018 report estimates 7,319 new cases in 2017 in that state. In Rio Grande do Sul, there were 1,846 cases in 2002, 7,970 in 2007 and a staggering 34,921 in 2017. In Santa Catarina, there were a meagre 24 cases in 2002, 2,511 cases in 2007 and 11,140 in 2017. In the state of São Paulo, seemingly the champion of judicialisation in absolute numbers, there were 4,123 lawsuits in 2006 and a staggering 43,313 in 2017, a growth of more than 1,000 per cent in just over ten years.[18] It is unfortunately not possible to

15 O. L. M. Ferraz, 'Health Inequalities, Rights and Courts: The Social Impact of the "Judicialization of Health" in Brazil', in Yamin, A. and Gloppen, S. (eds.), *Litigating the Right to Health: Can Courts Bring More Justice to Health Systems?* (Cambridge, MA: Harvard University Press, 2011), 76–102.

16 Advocacia Geral da União, 'Intervenção Judicial na Saúde, Panorama no Âmbito da Justiça Federal e Apontamento na Seara das Justiças Estaduais', Consultoria Jurídica Ministério da Saúde, 2013, available at http://portalarquivos2.saude.gov.br/images/pdf/2014/maio/29/Panorama-da-judicializa—-o—2012—modificado-em-junho-de-2013.pdf, accessed 6 December 2018.

17 My own formulation using the data available from the CNJ website. https://paineis.cnj.jus.br/QvAJAXZfc/opendoc.htm?document=qvw_l%5Cpainelcnj.qvw&host=QVS%40neodimio03&anonymous=true, accessed 25 November 2018. It is important to emphasise again that these numbers are far from perfect and should therefore be taken with some caution. There is some indication that the numbers may at the same time be both under- and overestimated.

18 I arrived at those numbers by adding all the cases registered under medicine, hospital treatment and medicine and/or hospital treatment from the CNJ 2018 Justiça em Números database. In relative numbers, that is, adjusted for the size of the population,

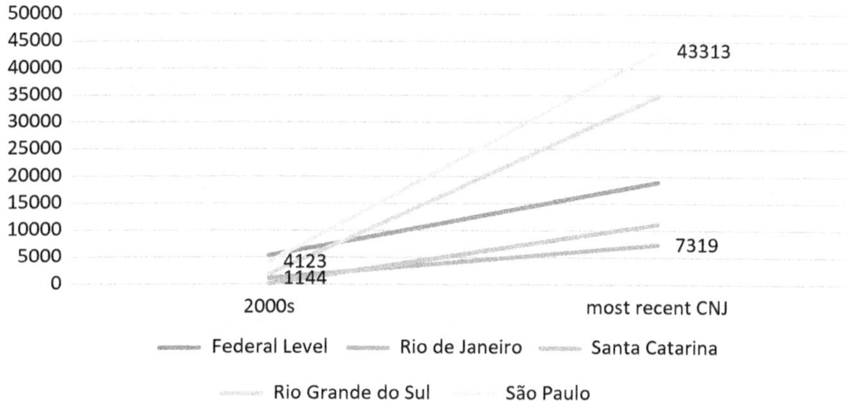

Figure 5.2 Growth in health litigation against the Federal Union and in selected states.
Source: Own formulation with data from various sources[19]

disaggregate the lawsuits against the municipalities within each state in order to have a more precise sense of the actual growth at the state level, but the total numbers are so much higher in 2017 compared to the early and even late 2000s that we can confidently conclude that there was a significant rise in litigation against all levels of government (see Figure 5.2).

As regards the municipal level, that is, lawsuits addressed exclusively against Brazil's 5,570 municipalities, it is expectedly much harder to get information. For the Harvard-Bergen study, an electronic survey was conducted with municipal secretariats of health between November 2009 and March 2010. We sent questionnaires to all 5,566 Brazilian municipalities then in existence asking whether the judicialisation of health was an important issue in that municipality and, if so, requesting

Rio Grande do Sul is the 'champion' of litigation given that its population, 11,329,605, is about four times smaller than that of São Paulo (45,538,936), https://g1.globo.com/economia/noticia/2018/08/29/brasil-tem-mais-de-208-milhoes-de-habitantes-segundo-o-ibge.ghtml.

[19] For the most recent data, see CNJ *Justiça em Números 2019*. For the earlier data see, Ferraz, 'Health Inequalities, Rights and Courts', and the sources cited therein. Note that early 2000s data included only lawsuits against the state, whereas most recent data include lawsuits against states and municipalities.

data on the volume and costs of health litigation.[20] Responses were received from 1,337 municipalities (24 per cent of the total). Of these, 34 per cent said that the judicialisation of health was growing and was an important issue; 23 per cent responded that it was growing but was not yet an important issue; and 43 per cent stated that they did not have that problem. Only 624 municipalities (11 per cent of the total) reported on the number of estimated lawsuits. The aggregate total for two and a half years was 43,061 (an average of 71.64 per respondent municipality), 12,766 in 2007, 15,735 in 2008 and 14,560 in the first six months of 2009.[21] A recent study of health litigation against municipalities reports a total of approximately 100,000 cases in 2015, that is, a growth of almost 800 per cent.[22]

***

The available data just presented, even if still incomplete and fragmented, are improving and allow us to reach increasingly more robust conclusions about the number of cases reaching the courts in Brazil invoking the right to health. From an almost insignificant level in the first ten years after the enactment of the 1988 Constitution, it started to gradually rise in the late 1990s and early 2000s and then accelerated significantly in the past 15 years, stabilising at an average of approximately between 117,000 (conservative estimate) and 215,000 cases a year in the past four years for which data is available (2014–2019). As we know from several studies that I will discuss further below, a very high percentage of these cases are successful, that is, judges accept the claim and order the state (the Federal

[20] I owe Daniel Wang, then my research assistant for the Harvard-Bergen project, for the excellent idea of the survey with municipal health secretariats. We both owe the CONASEMS – Conselho Nacional de Secretarias Municipais de Saúde (National Council of Municipal Health Secretariats) a huge debt for contributiong to the execution of the survey.

[21] Ferraz, 'Health Inequalities, Rights and Courts', at 84. Costs had also grown, according to the respondents, from R$47 million (US$24 million) in 2007 to R$73 million (US$37 million) in 2008 and had already reached R$57 million in the first six months of 2009. In addition, most of the claims were for medication, confirming the same trend found at the federal and state levels.

[22] For a more recent study of judicialisation against municipalities, see C. E. Albert, 'Análise: Sobre a Judicialização da Saúde nos Municípios', (2016) 101 *Revista Técnica CNM* 101, at 157 and 165, reporting approximately 100,000 lawsuits in municipalities across Brazil with a high concentration (36,766 lawsuits, 37 per cent) in twenty municipalities (ten from Sao Paulo, three from Minas Gerais, three from Rio Grande do Sul, two from Santa Catarina, one from Mato Grosso and one from Bahia), seventeen of them with high HDI (78 per cent claiming medicines; 10 per cent hospital treatment; 2 per cent ICU; and 10 per cent special treatment).

Union, the state or the municipality, often all of them together) to provide the claimant with the requested health intervention (medicine, hospital treatment, etc.). One important consequence of this significant growth in judicialisation is of course its costs to the state's coffers, that is, its budgetary impact. I will present and discuss the available data on this later in this chapter (see Section 5.5). Before that, however, I want to present a more granular picture of health litigation by looking behind these aggregate numbers to see *where* these cases are located within the vast territory of Brazil (Section 5.2), *what* is actually claimed in terms of health actions and services in those cases (Section 5.3) and *who* are the actual claimants behind these lawsuits (Section 5.4).

5.2 The Geographic Distribution of Health Litigation

In such a vast and diverse country, it would be extremely surprising if right to health litigation presented a similar, let alone identical pattern across the whole of Brazil. The available data confirm this intuition, revealing a lot of variation among different regions, states, municipalities and even districts within municipalities.

The first thing to note is that right to health litigation is very disproportionately concentrated in some places. This is a consistent finding of the studies that attempted to gauge the volume of litigation in Brazil as a whole and is confirmed by the more recent and comprehensive data of the CNJ. In the Harvard-Bergen study of almost a decade ago, for instance, I was given access by the Federal Ministry of Health to data on all 4,343 lawsuits responded to by the federal government between 2005 and 2009 claiming medicines, which represented then 80 per cent of all health-related suits.[23] Of all these lawsuits, a very high proportion (85 per cent) originated in the seven states of the South and Southeast, whose population represents 56.8 per cent of the country's total. The North and the Northeast together, with 36 per cent of the Brazilian population, accounted for only 7.5 per cent of all lawsuits. Recall that Brazil's 27 states are divided into five large regions (the South, the Southeast, the Centre-West, the North and the Northeast).[24]

[23] Of those, only 124 (less than 3 per cent) were collective ones. The vast majority of lawsuits (97 per cent) were individual ones in which the claimant was a single person demanding some medicine. Ferraz, 'Health Inequalities, Rights and Courts', at 87. See more on this in Section 5.4.

[24] Ibid., at 88.

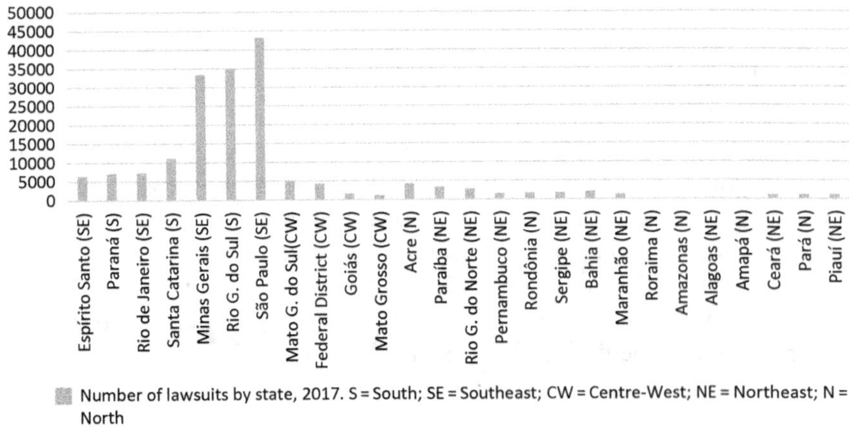

Figure 5.3 Number of lawsuits by state (absolute), 2017.
Source: Own formulation with data from CNJ 2018

To allow a more precise understanding of this significant concentration I built an indicator of *lawsuits per population*, which resulted in the following picture of the country. Brazil's average was then one health lawsuit for every 42,364 inhabitants. The North had the lowest ratio (1 per 406,203) – almost ten times lower than the country's average – whereas the South had a ratio of 1 per 11,902 – almost four times higher than the country's average. The Southeast had the second highest ratio, of 1/52,404 and the Centre-West (1/46,395) were just above the country's average, while the Northeast was over four times lower (1/177,704).[25]

The CNJ's more recent and more complete data confirm those early findings, revealing a very similar distribution of 'champions' and 'laggards'. When we disaggregate cases by state courts (which include lawsuits against the state and all its municipalities), the same pattern of high concentration of cases in the states of the South and Southeast and low concentration in the states of the North and Northeast emerges (see Figures 5.3 and 5.4).[26]

[25] Ibid., at 90.

[26] Note that in the Harvard-Bergen study, the litigation – population ratio was drawn exclusively from cases against the federal government. In the CNJ database, we have a more complete picture, including all cases, that is, also cases against states and municipalities. As the cases in the federal courts are not disaggregated by state, I had to leave them out of the table (they represent approximately 15 per cent of the total).

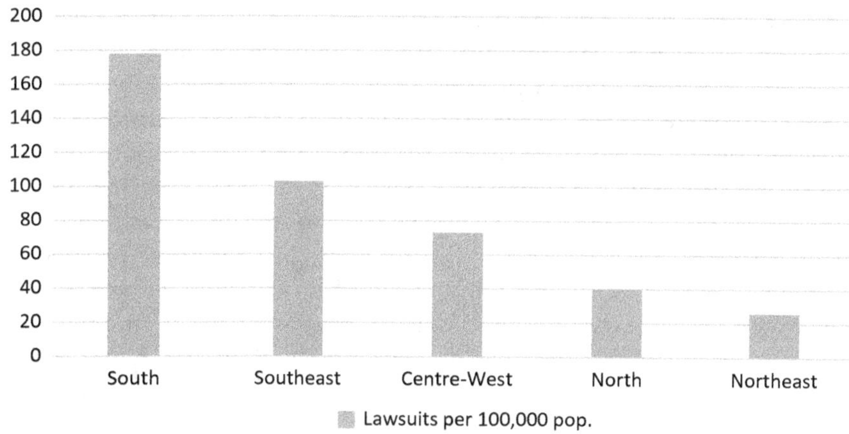

Figure 5.4 Lawsuits per 100,000 population by region.
Source: Own formulation with data from CNJ 2018

It seems clear, thus, that the so-called explosion of right to health litigation witnessed in the past couple of decades is not a phenomenon that affects the whole of Brazil with the same intensity. It has certainly grown almost everywhere, but it is significantly concentrated in a handful of states, mostly from the Southeast and South of Brazil, both in absolute numbers (Figure 5.3) and when adjusted for population size (Figure 5.4). If we add all the lawsuits of the South and Southeast states in 2017, we reach 143,570, that is, 81 per cent of all the lawsuits in the country, while the aggregate population of these states represents 56.4 per cent of the total population of Brazil. Conversely, at the other end of the spectrum, when we add all states of the North and Northeast, which together represent 36 per cent of the Brazilian population, we reach only 12.7 per cent of right to health litigation (22,544 cases). The Centre-West is the most balanced state with around 7 per cent of the population of the country and 7 per cent of litigation (11,856 cases).

Although it is currently impossible to disaggregate further the CNJ data into municipalities, we know that further concentration occurs at that level (and even in districts within municipalities), as some studies have shown.[27] I will discuss this in much more detail in Chapter 7

[27] In the survey with municipalities for the Harvard-Bergen study, as we saw earlier, 43 per cent of respondents said that judicialisation was not an issue. In a recent survey conducted by the National Council of Municipalities (CNM), 51 per cent responded in

(Section 7.2.1), but let me give a couple of examples here just to illustrate the point. The Health Department of the State of São Paulo, where the litigation rate is one of the highest in the country as we have just seen, has created an interesting index, the São Paulo index of judicialisation, which measures litigation by population across the seventeen health administrative regions in which the São Paulo state is divided. The variation is significant, from around 1,000 cases per 100,000 in some areas to as little as 12 in others (see Figure 5.5).[28] In the same state, thus, we have areas where litigation is more than ten times the Brazilian average and others where it is almost ten times less. In fact, some areas in the state of São Paulo have litigation rates that are lower even than the rates of the

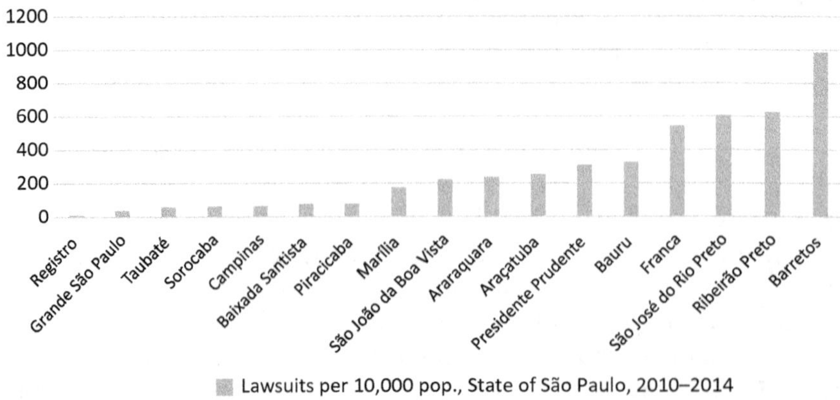

Figure 5.5 Lawsuits per 100,000 population, by region of the state of São Paulo.
Source: Own formulation with data from Chieffi, 2017[29]

the same way, confirming that health litigation is concentrated in some municipalities, see Albert, 'Análise'. The response rate was very high (4,168 municipalities) and confirmed that judicialisation is much lower in the North (40 per cent of respondents said there was health litigation in their municipality) and Northeast (35.7 per cent) compared to the South (52.8 per cent), Southeast (58.5 per cent) and Centre-West (58.2 per cent). Ibid., at 157.

[28] Secretaria de Estado da Saúde de São Paulo, 'Perfil das Ações Judiciais no Estado de São Paulo', PowerPoint presentation, September 2016, on file with author. See also A. L. Chieffi, 'Análise das demandas judiciais de medicamentos junto a Secretaria de Estado da Saúde de São Paulo à luz da política de assistência farmacêutica', PhD thesis, University of São Paulo (2017).

[29] Chieffi, 'Análise das demandas judiciais de medicamentos junto a Secretaria de Estado da Saúde de São Paulo à luz da política de assistência farmacêutica'.

Northeast region, the lowest in the country, as we have just seen (see Figure 5.4).

Even within single municipalities, significant variation was detected among districts. Chieffi and Barata, for instance, have looked at the addresses of litigants from 2,927 lawsuits that originated in the city of São Paulo in 2006 and clustered them into 6 different groups of districts, classified according to level of socioeconomic development. More than 50 per cent of the claims originated from two groups of districts whose population adds up to less than 25 per cent of the total, whereas 25 per cent of the claims originated from three groups of districts whose population adds up to almost half of the city's total population.[30] Fabiola Sulpino Vieira, in her pioneering study of São Paulo City in 2005, also found a concentration of litigation originating from central districts of the municipality and virtually no litigation in the more peripheric districts of the south and the east.[31]

We will see in Chapter 7 that such concentration is not peculiar to the state and municipality of São Paulo. It repeats in almost every state and municipality studied in more depth. It would be inaccurate, therefore, to describe health litigation as a national, or even a regionally widespread phenomenon. What we really see is a much more varied picture, with *pockets* of high-intensity litigation in some places, areas where litigation exists and has grown but not 'exploded' and yet other areas where it barely happens or does not occur at all.

What explains this significant geographical variation in health litigation in Brazil? I discuss this in more detail in Chapters 6–8, which are dedicated to the drivers and social impact of litigation. Before this, I must try to complete the picture so far presented with data on the *types of claims* that are most often taken to the courts (Section 5.3), on *the actors*

[30] A. L. Chieffi, R. Barata, 'Judicialização da política pública de assistência farmacêutica e eqüidade', (2009) 25(8) *Cadernos de Saúde Pública*, 1839–1849. F. F. C. Gomes et al., 'Access to Medium and High-Complexity Procedures in the Brazilian Unified National Health System: A matter of Judicialization', (2014) 30(1) *Cadernos de Saúde Pública*, 31–43.

[31] F. Vieira, P. Zucchi, 'Distorções causadas pelas ações judiciais à política de medicamentos no Brasil', (2007) 41(2) *Revista de Saúde Pública*, 214–222; see also D. W. L. Wang, O. L. M. Ferraz, 'Reaching Out to the Needy? Access to Justice and Public Attorneys' Role in Right to Health Litigation in the City of São Paulo', (2013) 10(18) *SUR International Journal on Human Rights*, 159–179; O. L. M. Ferraz, 'The Right to Health in the Courts of Brazil: Worsening Health Inequities?', (2009) 11 *Health and Human Rights*, 33–45; Ferraz, 'Health Inequalities, Rights and Courts'.

who make these claims (Section 5.4) and on the *costs* that they entail to the state's coffers (Section 5.5).

5.3 What Is Claimed in Courts?

We have already seen in Section 5.1 that a large portion of right to health litigation involves claims for medicines and hospital treatment, that is, curative health benefits (or secondary and tertiary healthcare). But we know little from that aggregated data about what exact types of medicines and treatments feature most often in the judicialisation of health in Brazil. In this section, I start to present a more detailed picture of the *objects* of litigation (further detail and analysis is provided in Chapter 8). As we shall see, there is also some geographical variation in *what* is litigated and also what we could call *temporal variation* in the kinds of claims that are made, that is, the health benefits that are most prevalent in health litigation change over time.

5.3.1 Medicines

One of the few constants across time and regions in health litigation in Brazil is the high prevalence of medicines as the most claimed benefit almost everywhere.[32] What varies somewhat are the exact drugs claimed across time and in different places, yet not that much, as we shall see in Chapter 8.

Recent and comprehensive CNJ data confirms this trend. In the aggregate, that is, adding all lawsuits against the Federal Union and the states, there were at least 420,000 claims exclusively for medicines and another 240,000 for medicines and/or hospital treatment out of the approximately 820,000 claims from 2014 to 2017. When we disaggregate the data by states, we can confirm that medicine claims are the clear leader in at least fourteen (out of twenty-six)[33] states and in *all* of those

[32] See D. Diniz et al., 'Consequências da judicialização das políticas de saúde: Custos de medicamentos para as mucopolissacaridoses', (2010) 28(3) *Cadernos de Saúde Pública*, 479–489, at 479; M. Ventura et al., 'Judicialização da saúde, acesso à justiça e à efetividade do direito à saúde', (2010) 20 *Physis*, 77–100; E. Andrade et al., 'A judicialização da saúde e a política nacional de assistência farmacêutica no Brasil: Gestão da clínica e medicalização da justiça', (2008) 18(4) *Revista Médica de Minas Gerais*, 46–50 and virtually all other studies cited in this book.

[33] The Court of Appeal of Tocantins has consistently failed to report to the CNJ, thus the total of twenty-six rather than twenty-seven states in the table.

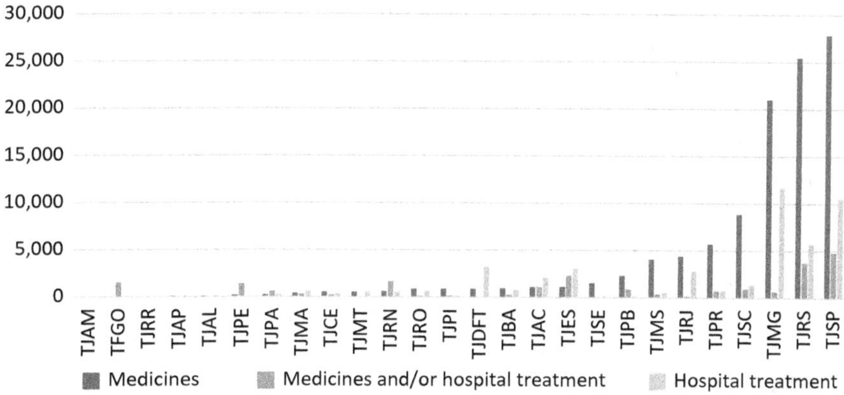

Figure 5.6 Number of claims in state courts in 2017 by three most prevalent types.
Source: Own formulation using data from CNJ, 2018

with the highest volume of litigation. If we also take into account the category of 'medicines and/or hospital treatment', twenty-one states would present a majority of cases involving a claim that may include medicines. In only four states (Espírito Santo, Amapá, Acre and the Federal District) reported claims for hospital treatment supersede the other two categories in terms of volume.[34] Figure 5.6 disaggregates claims by each of the three main categories reported by states to the National Council of Justice in 2018 (data from 2017).

But what kinds of medicines are being claimed? Here, unfortunately, we do not have a comprehensive picture of the whole country, as the CNJ database does not include that piece of information. We need to rely on other more detailed and inevitably less comprehensive studies, which almost never cover more than one single state or municipality nor more than a year. According to such studies, a great variety of medicines for all kinds of conditions have been claimed through litigation, yet some conditions and specific drugs stand out both in terms of number of cases and in terms of costs imposed on the state (more on this in Section 5.5).

[34] The high number of hospital treatment claims compared to medicines claims in the Federal District is somewhat surprising and would warrant further investigation. For a good study, see D. Diniz et al., 'A judicialização da saúde no Distrito Federal', (2014) 19(2) *Ciênc. saúde coletiva*, 591–598.

Among the most recurrent conditions in the past ten years are diabetes, hypertension, chronic obstructive pulmonary disease (COPD), chronic hepatitis C, cancer, rheumatoid arthritis and kidney disease. In terms of most frequently requested medicines, we find insulin glargine, for diabetes and adalimumab, etanercept and infliximab for rheumatoid arthritis.[35]

The most requested medicines vary somewhat among different states and municipalities. Diabetes drugs, for instance, in particular, analogue insulins, have made up approximately one-third of the tens of thousands of suits against the São Paulo state in the past few years.[36] In the southern state of Paraná, however, the most claimed drugs were oncological ones (23.4 per cent), followed by medicines for respiratory diseases (13.3 per cent) and immunosuppressant agents (for rheumatoid arthritis, 11.7 per cent).[37] In Minas Gerais, the most claimed drugs from 1999 to 2009 were for rheumatoid arthritis (38.4 per cent), followed by diabetes (24 per cent) and COPD (20.6 per cent).[38] In Rio Grande do Sul, a study found less concentration in any type of condition or medicine, but still a sizeable number of claims for the most frequent conditions cited above, in particular, COPD.[39]

Interestingly, anti-retroviral drugs for HIV-AIDS, which, from the mid-1990s to the early 2000s were perceived as the most claimed drugs in several states,[40] do not feature any longer in any study as among the

[35] According to a meta-analaysis of studies published between 2005 and 2013. See V. S. Gomes, T. A. Amador, 'Studies Published in Indexed Journals on Lawsuits for Medicines in Brazil: A Systematic Review', (2015) 31(3) *Cadernos de Saúde Pública*, 1–12, at 5.

[36] Chieffi, 'Análise das demandas judiciais de medicamentos junto a Secretaria de Estado da Saúde de São Paulo à luz da política de assistência farmacêutica'.

[37] J. G. Pereira, V. L. E. Pepe, 'Acesso a medicamentos por via judicial no Paraná: Aplicação de um modelo metodológico para análise e monitoramento das demandas judiciais', (2014) 15(2) *Revista de Direito Sanitário*, 31–45, at 39. Note that the study focuses only on 2009.

[38] In another study of that state, a similar pattern was found during 2005 and 2006: rheumatoid arthritis (23.1 per cent), followed by diabetes (6.5 per cent) and hypertension (5.5 per cent); see M. A. A. Machado et al., 'Judicialization of Access to Medicines in Minas Gerais State, Southeastern Brazil', (2011) 45(3) *Revista de Saúde Pública*, at 3.

[39] J. Biehl et al., 'The Judicialization of Health and the Quest for State Accountability: Evidence from 1,262 Lawsuits for Access to Medicines in Southern Brazil', (2016) 18(1) *Health and Human Rights*, 209–220.

[40] Scheffer et al. (eds.), *O Remédio via Justiça*. See also F. Leite, 'Justiça faz política de medicamentos em SP', *Folha de S. Paulo* (newspaper), 18 August 2002.

most prevalent, illustrating the point I made above about the changing profile of litigation across time.[41]

There seems to be, therefore, surprisingly small variation in the most prevalent types of medicines claimed in different states for such a large and diverse country. They are mostly medicines for a handful of chronic conditions. In Chapter 8, we shall try to understand why these few groups of medicines feature so often in health litigation.

5.3.2 *Hospital Treatment*

Given the significant prevalence of claims for medicines in the judicialisation of health in Brazil, most studies have understandably focused on them. This is somewhat unfortunate as it prevents us from building a more comprehensive picture of health litigation. As we saw above, though not as numerous as medicines claims, there is also a sizeable amount of cases claiming some kind of hospital treatment.

Interestingly, there is no close correlation between the number of claims for medicines and hospital treatment in different states. Although São Paulo and Rio Grande do Sul, the two leaders in claims for medicines, also report some of the largest amounts of claims for hospital services, putting them in second and third places with 10,582 and 5,718 claims respectively, it is the state of Minas Gerais that leads the table on hospital treatment claims, with 11,701 such claims (see Figure 5.6).[42]

The CNJ database also includes an interesting subcategory under hospital treatment that helps us to disaggregate the data, namely, that of litigation for places in Intensive Care Units (ICUs) in hospitals. Almost 20 per cent of the total within hospital treatment, that is, 10,319 cases, are of that sort. Minas Gerais appears again in the lead here, with 2,452 cases, but the rest of the table looks very different from that of medicines or even hospital treatment in general. When the focus

[41] Although it is often repeated that judicialisation of health in Brazil started in the mid-1990s with claims for HIV drugs and tests, the fact is that the first case to reach the Supreme Federal Tribunal was actually about a rare disease called Duchenne Muscular Dystrophy (DMD). It seems to have been in that case that the highest court in Brazil (The Supreme Federal Tribunal, or simply STF from its Portuguese name Supremo Tribunal Federal) changed its usual deferential approach and granted the medicines requested by the claimant for the first time, as I discuss in more detail in Chapter 6 (see Section 6.3.1).

[42] I re-emphasise the possibility that reporting issues may have distorted some of these numbers.

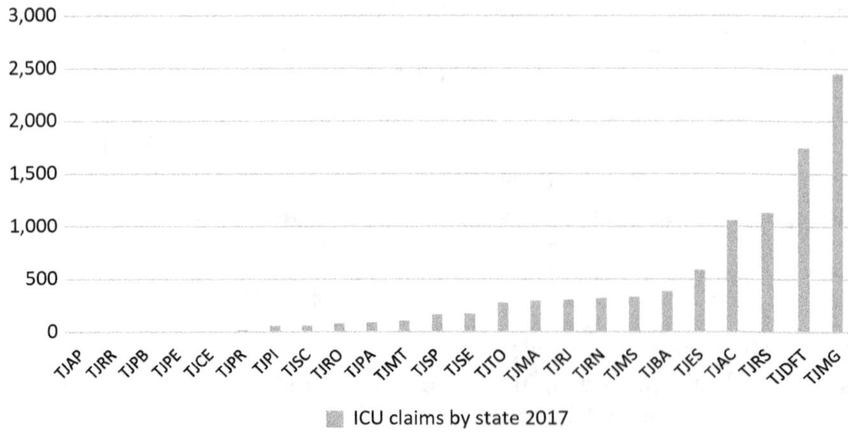

Figure 5.7 Intensive care unit claims by state, 2017.
Source: Own formulation using data from CNJ, 2018

is exclusively on ICUs, some states with an otherwise high volume of litigation do not appear to have a litigation problem in this specific area. São Paulo, for instance, which we saw is the 'champion' in medicine claims, with almost 30,000 cases in 2017 alone, reports only 166 cases of claims for a place in ICUs. Other states of the South and Southeast with a relative low prevalence of claims for ICUs are Santa Catarina (59), Paraná (14) and Rio de Janeiro (303). The Federal District (1,748) and Rio Grande do Sul (1,132) have a sizeable amount of cases. Some of the states in the North and Northeast regions, where medicines are not as high in the ranking of litigation, have a relatively high number of claims for ICUs, for example, Acre, with 1,059 claims, the fourth highest among all states, and Bahia (394), Rio Grande do Norte (319) and Maranhão (296) (see Figure 5.7).

As mentioned earlier, the strong focus on medicines left little space for studies focusing on hospital treatment, but a couple of rare ones from some of the states with the highest numbers of cases offer some interesting insights. In Minas Gerais, of 1,002 procedures claimed via courts from 1999 to 2009, the most frequent claims were for surgical procedures (37.2 per cent overall) of the circulatory system (11.2 per cent of the total), the eye (7 per cent), bones and muscular systems (6.3 per cent) and the digestive system (5.7 per cent). There was also a sizeable number of claims for diagnostic procedures (26.6 per cent) such as ultrasonography, endoscopy, interventionist radiology and MRI scan and for clinical consultations and treatment (16.8 per cent).[43] Another frequent claim was for a bed in an ICU (14.2 per cent), a common object of litigation in several states as Figure 5.7 shows.

Fewer, but interesting studies have focused on claims for a bed in an ICU. In the Federal District, the state that reported the second highest number of these claims in 2017, Gizele Mota analysed a sample of 440 lawsuits from 2012 to 2015.[44] Of these, the most prevalent request was for a place in a generic ICU (n=194, 43.99 per cent), followed by ICU with support for neurological trauma (n=88, 19.95 per cent) and ICU with dialysis assistance (n=71, 16.10 per cent). All requests were granted by the court. In Espírito Santo, another state with relatively high numbers of such claims, Stephanie Moulin and colleagues conducted an interesting analysis of all 26,489 requests for an ICU bed in 2014 and 2015, out of which 20,533 resulted in an effective admission of the patient. They then compared regular requests made by the doctors of the public system (20,075) with those ordered by courts via health litigation (458), finding a disproportionately high number of judicialised requests for beds in generic ICUs and neurosurgical ones.[45]

5.3.3 *Other Claims*

Of the 820,000 cases reported in the CNJ database involving the right to health from 2014 to 2017, the vast majority 799,463 (97 per cent) involved either medicines (420,930 – 52 per cent), hospital treatment (135,849 – 16.5 per cent) or both (242,684 – 29.5 per cent).[46] Much less frequent, yet not totally insignificant in absolute terms, were claims related to improvements in hospital facilities and other health units (13,125 – 1.6 per cent), mental health (6,739 – 0.8 per cent),[47]

[43] Gomes et al., 'Access to Medium and High-Complexity Procedures in the Brazilian Unified National Health System', at 31–43. The total number of lawsuits found by the authors in that period was 6,112, confirming that medicines are by far the most claimed benefit in Minas Gerais.

[44] G. P. Mota, 'Judicialização do acesso a leitos de UTI no Distrito Federal: Dimensões clínica, ética e legal', MPhil dissertation, University of Brasilia (2017). See also Diniz et al., 'A judicialização da saúde no Distrito Federal'.

[45] S. R. A. Moulin et al., 'Judicialização do Acesso à Internação em UTI no SUS: Análise Concreta de Pacientes do Estado do Espírito Santo', in Gebran Neto, J. P. (ed.), *Direito da Saúde em Perspectiva. Judicialização, Gestão e Acesso*, vol. 2 (Vitória: Editora Abrages, 2017), 73–90 (on file with the author).

[46] Lima Jr., Schulze, 'Os números do CNJ sobre a judicialização da saúde em 2018'.

[47] It is unclear if under mental health there might also be medicines and hospital treatment cases, or whether cases are related mostly to compulsory internment measures.

and organ and tissue donation and transplantation (1,255 – 0.15 per cent).

Conspicuously absent from almost all reports and studies about right to health litigation are claims related to primary care and public health issues such as basic sanitation and access to primary care programmes such as the Family Health strategy, which we saw in Chapters 3 and 4 are some of the most important policies for the most disadvantaged population but are still not universalised in Brazil.

I will discuss this imbalanced profile of health litigation in much further detail in the next chapters of this part of the book. In this descriptive chapter, I want to finish this section by briefly reporting the findings of a rare and interesting study focused on basic sanitation by Ana Paula Barcellos. She looked at all cases she could find between 2003 to 2013 and ended up with a total of 258 cases across the courts of Brazil involving basic sanitation: 47 per cent dealt with requests for sanitation services for communities (community cases), 7 per cent involved lack of sanitary infrastructure in public buildings (for instance, public hospitals and prisons), and 46 per cent were claims that could be described as environmental cases, mainly dealing with pollution of water from the discharge of untreated sewage.[48]

Cases were concentrated in 177 municipalities (i.e., 3.17 per cent of the municipalities of Brazil). As with health litigation in general, the rate of success was very high (76.6 per cent) but the rate of full implementation was very low (4 per cent).[49]

5.4 The Main Actors in Health Litigation

We have seen so far that the amount of right to health litigation in Brazil is reasonably large in terms of the absolute number of lawsuits – (approximately between 117,000 [conservative estimate] and 215,000 cases a year in the past six years for which data is available [2014–2019], see Section 5.1) – occurs more intensely in some regions of the country (the South and Southeast) and focuses on curative health interventions, mostly medicines and hospital treatment, with a higher prevalence of the former in most places. But who are the actors behind these hundreds of thousands of claims? This is a crucial piece of information in the puzzle, especially for

48 A. P. Barcellos, 'Sanitation Rights, Public Law Litigation, and Inequality: A Case Study from Brazil', (2014) 16(2) *Health and Human Rights*, 35–46.

49 Ibid., at 38.

the questions about the drivers and social impact of health litigation that we will address in the following chapters.

As a fundamental (and thus universal) right, the right to health is in principle claimable in courts by everyone in the country. Yet, in practice, one would expect only a small proportion of the population in any country to actually resort to the courts and claim rights, for several different reasons ranging from lack of necessity (the ideal scenario) to lack of opportunity (the regrettable scenario). We will discuss this latter issue in great length in Chapters 6 and 7, which focus on access to justice in Brazil and analyse the socioeconomic profile of the individuals who manage to reach the courts (and, by exclusion, those who don't). Here, my aim is to briefly describe in more general terms the different types of actors that may initiate health litigation.

We must distinguish, first, between individualised (or individual) and collective litigation. By individualised litigation, I mean claims brought to the judiciary by individuals or small groups of individuals on their own behalf, that is, for their own benefit. In this type of claim, the individual is (most of the time) represented by a lawyer, either a state-funded one (a public prosecutor or a public defender) or a private one retained directly by the claimant.[50] In what I call collective litigation,[51] a restricted number of institutional actors (e.g., a public prosecutor, a public defender, a political party, an NGO) can invoke the right to health on behalf of a larger group of people to claim a certain benefit (e.g., people suffering from a certain condition, people lacking basic sanitation) or in view of dealing with a problem in the public health system (e.g., the repair or improvement of the facilities of a hospital, a challenge to the funds allocated to and in the health budget). For those more familiar with Anglo-American legal systems, *class actions* are the closest, though not perfect equivalent here.[52]

[50] In the Brazilian system, unlike in other countries, such as Colombia, Costa Rica and India, a claimant must be represented in court by a lawyer with the exception of cases that fall below a certain threshold monetary value and are litigated in a small claim court. I discuss this in further detail in Chapter 6, showing that even in small claims courts litigants are almost always represented by a lawyer.

[51] I call collective litigation what others may prefer to call regulation or structural litigation as my aim is to emphasise the larger number of people these cases usually cover. For these other classifications, see V. Gauri, D. Brinks, 'The Law's Majestic Equality? The Distributive Impact of Litigating Social and Economic Rights', Policy Research Working Paper 5999 (2012), at 11; D. Landau, 'The Reality of Social Rights Enforcement' (2012) 53(1) *Harvard International Law Journal*, 189–247, passim.

[52] Note that public defenders and public prosecutors, whom I name together as state lawyers as they are both public servants funded by the state (see Chapter 6 for a detailed explanation), can initiate both collective and individual lawsuits.

Any of the types of claims described in Section 5.3 (medicines, hospital treatment, basic sanitation) can in principle be the subject of both kinds of litigation; for example, an individual can claim a health intervention for herself only, or the same health intervention can be claimed through a collective suit for the benefit of a group, sometimes a whole city, state or even the whole country.[53] Most litigation for medicines and hospital treatment, according to available data, features a single individual as the claimant-beneficiary. In the Harvard-Bergen study already mentioned above, for instance, I found that less than 3 per cent of lawsuits against the federal government were collective ones (and even those may have been 'false' collective ones, as state lawyers often use the collective form of action to represent a single individual).[54] Other studies have found a similar pattern in several states and municipalities.[55] The more comprehensive data of the CNJ report *Justice in Numbers* is unfortunately not fine-grained enough for us to know the precise proportion of individualised and collective health litigation across Brazil. But it seems plausible to extrapolate from the available studies that collective cases are likely a small minority.[56] I offer further explanation for this hypothesis in Chapter 6.

[53] In one of the leading collective cases on health, a political party from the opposition, the Brazilian Social Democratic Party – PSDB, challenged a decision of the then President Lula of the Workers' Party for alleged disrespect of the constitutional minimum investment on health by vetoing an article of the Budgetary Law of 2004. See Argüição de Descumprimento de Preceito Fundamental (ADPF) 45, Federal District, decided on 29 April 2004.

[54] It is well-known that the collective remedy of the Ação Civil Pública is often used by the Ministério Público to represent single claimants in right to health cases. Though precise data is not available, it is plausible to conclude that the proportion of genuine collective cases is even lower than that reported in studies.

[55] See, for instance, the study by Fernanda Terrazas, who found only 2 per cent of collective suits among all claims for hepatitis C medication in São Paulo from 1998 to 2005. F. V. Terrazas, 'O poder judiciário como voz institucional dos pobres: O caso das demandas judiciais por medicamentos', MPhil dissertation, University of São Paulo (2008). For other studies reaching the same finding, see F. Hoffmann, F. R. N. M. Bentes, 'Accountability for Social and Economic Rights in Brazil' in Gauri, V. and Brinks, D. M. (eds.), *Courting Social Justice: Judicial Enforcement of Social and Economic Rights in the Developing World* (New York: Cambridge University Press, 2008) 100–145; D. Sartoni Jr. et al., 'Judicialização do acesso ao tratamento de doenças genéticas raras: A doença de Fabry no Rio Grande do Sul', (2012) 17 *Ciências & Saúde Coletiva*, 2717–2728; O. H. Campos Neto et al., 'Médicos, advogados e indústria farmacêutica na judicialização da saúde em Minas Gerais', (2012) 46 *Revista de Saúde Pública*, 784–790; Conselho Nacional de Justiça, *Justiça Pesquisa: Judicialização da saúde no Brasil – dados e experiências* (Brasília: CNJ, 2015).

[56] In a very recent study of more than 300,000 decisions spread across 21 Tribunals it was found that, again, only around 3 per cent of them were collective suits. The percentage varied across states, with Mato Grosso, Pará and Rondônia having the highest

Why should we bother with this in the first place? The relevance of the individual-collective litigation distinction resides in the different potential social impact of each of these types. Collective suits are by definition more capable of directly affecting a larger number of people than individual ones. They are also (again in principle) more likely to generate equitable outcomes, as, when successful, they benefit everyone similarly situated and not just the individual litigant. So, if the right to health litigation ought to be a tool to fix problems in the system for everyone and not just the litigant, the argument goes, collective suits seem in principle more appropriate than individual ones, particularly so in legal systems where courts' decisions have effect only *inter partes* and not *erga omnes*, as is the case in Brazil with few exceptions and where poorer individuals face significant difficulties to access the courts, again, as is the case in Brazil (see Chapter 6).[57]

I will return to this discussion in greater detail later in the book (see, in particular, Chapters 6 and 7). Let me emphasise here a couple of important general points. Firstly, as I indicated earlier, these two advantages of collective suits over individual ones are only potential. Depending on *what* is litigated in a particular lawsuit, be it individual or collective, its social impact will vary. A collective suit whose object is regressive, for example, claiming something that is not a priority to the most disadvantaged and should not be provided in the public system will have greater regressive effects than individual ones. Secondly, depending on the effectiveness of enforcement and on so-called indirect effects of litigation, collective lawsuits may not produce larger effects than individual ones. As we saw in Section 5.3, only 4 per cent of basic sanitation claims, most of which were collective, were effectively implemented according to Barcellos' study.[58] Lastly, health collective suits in Brazil have a lower

percentages: 15.79 per cent, 25.66 per cent and 18.18 per cent, respectively, and some states having registered no collective suit whatsoever. Conselho Nacional de Justiça, *Judicialização da Saúde no Brazil. Perfil das Demandas, Causas e Porpostas de Solução*, (Brasília: CNJ, 2019), at 129–135.

57 For an excellent discussion of this issue in Brazil, see Terrazas, 'O poder Judiciário como voz institucional dos pobres: O caso das demandas judiciais de medicamentos', (2010) 253 *Revista de Direito Administrativo*, 79–115, at 111, arguing that: 'The individual implementation of this right [health] – which happens through the courts as claims are almost always individual – is a problem in itself, as it results in differentiated 'unjustified' treatment' (my translation from the original in Portuguese). For a detailed and insightful analysis of this issue in Colombia, including an interesting discussion of health litigation in Brazil, Landau, 'The Reality of Social Rights Enforcement'.

58 Barcellos, 'Sanitation Rights, Public Law Litigation, and Inequality'.

rate of success in court than individual ones. As Hoffmann and Bentes have aptly noted in their study:

> To be sure, one successful public class action may, because of its collective effect, count for many hundreds or thousands of individual actions on the same subject matter. Yet, as is also still evident from the quantitative study, the courts have applied two levels of scrutiny for either type of action. Whereas in individual (access to medicine and treatment) actions the mere showing of prima facie evidence of medical need is usually accepted as sufficient for a claim to stand, courts are very reticent to appear to directly influence executive policy administration by considering *erga omnes* claims.[59]

As a general conclusion, thus, we can say that the main actors of health litigation in Brazil are individuals, public defenders and public prosecutors and that individual litigation predominates in numbers, have higher rates of success in courts and are more effectively implemented than collective ones. The implications of this in terms of the drivers and social impact of litigation will be discussed in greater detail in the next chapters.

5.5 The Costs of Health Litigation

To complete the overview of health litigation in Brazil, I will turn now to the costs that it generates to the state's coffers. As with the number of cases (Section 5.1), it is not easy to get a full and accurate picture of the costs of judicialisation. Similar difficulties related to the vastness of the country and the fragmented nature of government (27 states, 5,570 municipalities) apply here. The following data should therefore be assessed with this caveat in mind.[60]

[59] Hoffmann, Bentes, 'Accountability for Economic and Social Rights in Brazil', at 141. I would not go as far as they do and say that, 'as a result, the litigation "success story" only applies to individual access to medicines and treatment'. The rate of success of collective suits, though lower than individual ones, is still quite high. The main obstacle in my view is difficulties of enforcement. See also Wang, Ferraz, 'Reaching Out to the Needy?', for success rates of collective suits in São Paulo; O. L. M. Ferraz, 'Right to Health Litigation in Brazil: Are Collective Suits Harder to Enforce?', in Langford, M. and Rodríguez-Garavito, C. (eds.), *Making It Stick: Social Rights Judgments and the Politics of Compliance* (Cambridge: Cambridge University Press, 2018).

[60] For the expenditure at the federal level, researchers have been able to gauge part of the costs with judicialisation through publicly accessible data from the Ministry of Health, in particular, the Department for Judicially Determined Purchases (Coordenação de Compras por Determinação Judicial, CDJU) and the National Fund

In the Harvard-Bergen study, I reported that judicialisation costs had risen from US$1.2 million in 2005 to US$26.5 million in 2009 at the federal level, whereas at the state level some larger states such as São Paulo were already spending significantly more (US$200 million in 2008). The total estimated costs of litigation across Brazil (i.e., including the federal, state and municipal levels) in 2009 were around R$2 billion (US$1.545 billion in 2009), approximately 0.4 per cent of the total health budget then and 4 per cent of the medicines budget.[61] We know from the numbers reported above that litigation rose even more intensely in the last few years, so we should expect its costs to have also risen accordingly. According to the latest widely publicised estimate by the Ministry of Health, the total cost of judicialisation across the whole country rose to R$7 billion by the end of 2016 (roughly US$3.5 billion), a 126 per cent rise since 2009.[62]

The most precise data available relates to the costs at the federal level. In 2017, a detailed sixty-five-page report published by the TCU – Tribunal de Constas da União (Federal Audit Tribunal) covering the period from 2008 to 2015 prompted by concerns with the growing financial impact of health litigation, estimated a rise of 1,300 per cent in the expenses of the federal government with medicines litigation in that period, from R$70 million to R$1 billion (US$58 million to US$538 million), an almost tenfold increase.[63] In a more comprehensive and

of Health (Fundo Nacional de Saúde, FNS), see http://portalms.saude.gov.br/institucional/o-ministerio, http://portalms.saude.gov.br/consultoria-juridica/biblioteca-eletronica, and www.conasems.org.br/wp-content/uploads/2019/03/Dilemas_do_Fenomeno_da_Judicializacao_da_Saude-1.pdf, accessed 1 April 2019. See also C. A. Xavier, 'Judicialização da Saúde: Perspectiva Crítica sobre os Gastos da União para o Cumprimento das Ordens Judiciais', in CONASS (eds.), *Coletânea Direito à Saúde Dilemas do Fenômeno da Judicialização da Saúde*, 1st ed. (Brasília: Conselho Nacional De Secretários De Saúde – CONASS, 2018).

61 Ferraz, 'Health Inequalities, Rights and Courts', at 82–83.

62 For the R$7 billion figure, see, among others: B. Pierro, 'Demandas Crescentes', (2017) 252(18) *Pesquisa Fapesp*, 18–25, at 20. For municipalities, the budgetary impact can be even higher. In Campinas (state of São Paulo) 86 lawsuits for medicines in 2009 consumed R$2,505,762, of a total budget of R$16,929,316, that is, 16 per cent. See Advocacia Geral da União (2013), 'Intervenção Judicial na Saúde, Panorama no Âmbito da Justiça Federal e Apontamento na Seara das Justiças Estaduais', at 50. For the exchange rates, see OECD (2019), Purchasing power parities (PPP) (indicator), doi: 10.1787/1290ee5a-en, accessed 5 June 2019.

63 Tribunal de Contas da União – TCU (Federal Union Audit Tribunal), Acórdão 1787, of 2017, TC 009.253/2015-2017, on file with author and also reported in several media outlets, https://noticias.uol.com.br/saude/ultimas-noticias/estado/2017/08/21/despesa-judicial-no-ministerio-da-saude-avanca-1300-em-7-anos.htm, accessed 26 November

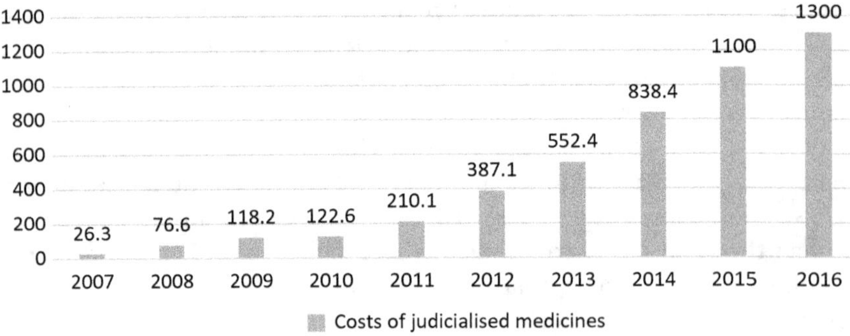

Figure 5.8 Costs of judicialised medicines, federal government, in R$ millions.
Source: Xavier, 2018

detailed recent study by Christabelle-Ann Xavier, a rise of almost 5,000 per cent is estimated in federal costs from R$26.3 million in 2007 to R$1.3 billion in 2016.[64]

Recall that these are only the costs at the federal level and are likely underestimated.[65] Note, too, that they represent only a part of the total costs, since the bulk of health litigation in Brazil takes place at the state level, and a sizeable proportion at the municipal level, as we saw in Section 5.1. There are unfortunately no comprehensive data on these levels, that is, including the whole country. Figure 5.9 puts together very limited and incomplete, yet still instructive, available data on selected states that I could find from several sources.[66]

2018 and www.cnj.jus.br/noticias/cnj/85911-tcu-e-estados-apontam-aumento-dos-gastos-com-a-judicializacao-da-saude. The aggregate costs of the last five years with available data added up to R$2.7 billion. Ibid.

64 Xavier, 'Judicialização da Saúde'.

65 They include only the costs incurred with the actual price of the medicines, excluding other expenses, such as administrative ones, of the process of purchase and delivery, often involving importation. See Xavier, 'Judicialização da Saúde', at 55. The TCU report adds to these expenses another R$605.4 million in 2014, 2015 and 2016 in air freight, cash deposits, direct payments and payments to private entities, see paragraphs 151–153. It is not clear, though, if there is some overlap between this and Xavier's data.

66 The TCU audit (see n. 63) reported on costs for three states: Sao Paulo, Santa Catarina and Minas Gerais (three of the champions of judicialisation as we saw in Section 4.1). Together, they spent R$1.5 billion in two years (2013 and 2014), paragraph 120.

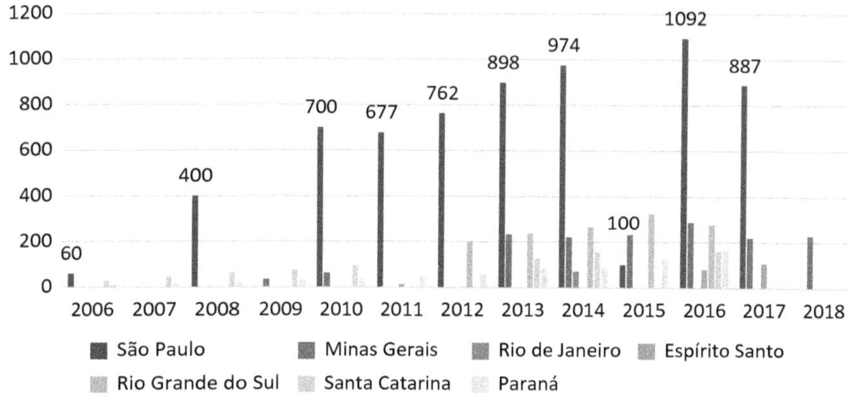

Figure 5.9 Costs of health litigation, selected states and selected years, in R$ millions.
Source: Own formulation with various sources[67]

The seven states depicted in Figure 5.9 are among the states with the highest numbers of health litigation (see Section 5.1), all located in the South and Southeast regions of the country. I could find no data for several states for several years. These costs are therefore clearly underestimated. They nonetheless add up to R$11 billion in the past thirteen years. (Note that I haven't updated this to account for Brazil's high inflation.) To put this into some context, it is estimated that a 'walk-in' health clinic (Unidade de Pronto Atendimento – UPA), which is the main primary care facility in the public health system, costs around R$21 million to serve 120,000 patients in one year. To take 2016, the year with most complete data, the costs of judicialisation in the seven states (approximately R$2.1 billion) plus the cost at the federal level (R$1.1 billion) would be sufficient to fund 152 walk- in health clinics, capable of serving 18.2 million patients.[68]

[67] For Rio Grande do Sul, see https://setorsaude.com.br/estudo-revela-situacao-da-judicializacao-da-saude-no-brasil/. For Minas Gerais, see www.saude.mg.gov.br/judicializacao. For Rio de Janeiro, see https://cnj.jusbrasil.com.br/noticias/248395937/rj-cria-estrutura-propria-para-atender-casos-de-saude-que-chegam-a-justica, all accessed 12 March 2019.

[68] W. Fernandes, 'RJ cria estrutura própria para atender casos de saúde que chegam à Justiça', CNJ, 26 October 2015, available at https://cnj.jusbrasil.com.br/noticias/248395937/rj-cria-estrutura-propria-para-atender-casos-de-saude-que-chegam-a-justica, accessed 12 March 2019.

Even from the limited available data, thus, it seems clear that the costs of judicialisation have increased significantly, which is expected given the equally significant rise in litigation described in Section 5.1.

To finish this section, I would like to highlight a couple of important points about the rising costs of health litigation. The first, and most obvious, is that it concentrates in the same states of the South and Southeast where the numbers of litigation are concentrated. I found no consistent official data to report on the costs of health litigation in the states of the North and Northeast, which is a sign in itself, but some scattered reports indicate that they are much lower than those I reported above for southern and southeastern states.[69]

Another important point to bear in mind is that the costs of litigation seem to be highly concentrated on a limited number of medicines, some of which had not been approved by the regulatory agents (The National Agency of Sanitary Vigilance – ANVISA) and most of which had not been incorporated in the public health system at the time of litigation (see Chapter 8 for an in-depth discussion of the importance of regulatory approval and incorporation). In studies of the most costly judicially granted drugs in cases against the federal government, for instance, it was found that in 2012, eighteen drugs and in 2016, ten drugs generated approximately 85 per cent of the total costs of judicialisation (see Figures 5.10 and 5.11).[70]

The final point to be highlighted is that the number of patients for whom this expenditure is incurred are very low. The costs of the 18 medicines resulted from judicial requests of 523 patients, a per capita cost of R$416,000 (around US$210,000 at the time). In a more recent study, in 2016, a similar pattern emerges. It was found that the ten most expensive medicines granted via litigation (many of which were also in the 2012 list above) consumed R$1.1 billion with 995 patients, that is, approximately

[69] In the northeastern state of Alagoas, for instance, I found a report stating that a sizeable R$8.8 million were spent on litigation in 2010. This is almost 80 times less than São Paulo, and a lot lower even in relative terms, as the population of Alagoas is only 13.2 times smaller than the population of São Paulo. In the northern state of Roraima, which is 90 times smaller than São Paulo in size, litigation costs were more than 700 times lower. See AGU – Advocacia Geral da União (2013), 'Intervenção Judicial na Saúde, Panorama no Âmbito da Justiça Federal e Apontamento na Seara das Justiças Estaduais' for data on litigation costs (on file with the author).

[70] For an excellent discussion of some of the judicialisation of some of these drugs, see Diniz et al., 'Consequências da judicialização das políticas de saúde'.

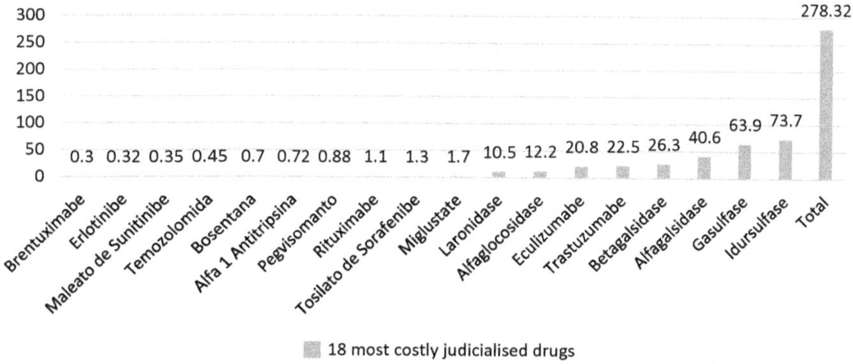

Figure 5.10 18 most costly judicialised drugs, cases against federal government, 2012, in R$ millions.
Source: AGU, 2013

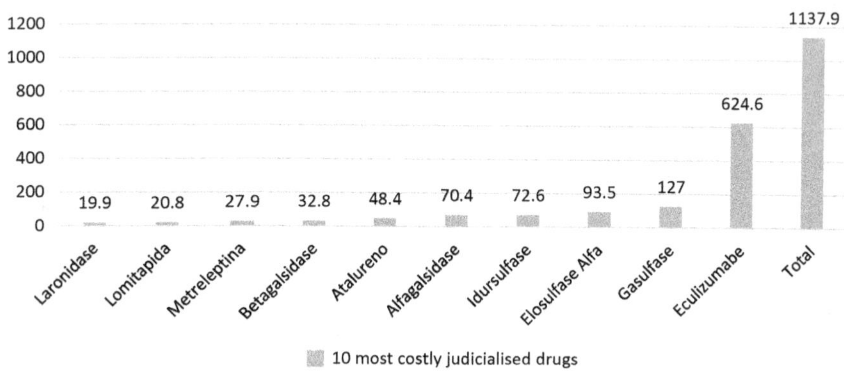

Figure 5.11 10 most costly judicialised drugs, cases against federal government, 2016, in R$ millions.
Source: Xavier, 2018

R$1.1 million in per capita terms (around US$300,000 at the time).[71] To put this in perspective, recall, from the discussion in Chapter 4, that the Brazilian public health system has very limited resources, having spent

[71] The exact amount was R$1,138,519,335. See Xavier, 'Judicialização da Saúde', at 56. For the historical exchange rates between the Brazilian Real, R$, and the US dollar, US$, I used www.x-rates.com/, accessed 1 April 2019.

R$1,255.73 per capita in 2012 and R$1,237.31 in 2016, that is, 331 and 889 times less per capita on average than the costs of these judicially granted medicines.[72]

The opportunity costs of such expenditure are therefore high, which has of course important implications for the issues of equity and social impact that will be discussed in great detail in the next chapters.

5.6 Conclusion

This opening descriptive chapter of Part II of the book attempted to provide as detailed and comprehensive a picture of the judicialisation of health in Brazil as is possible with the still limited and imperfect yet increasing available data on the subject. The most salient features that emerge from the data are these.

First, it seems difficult to deny that the phenomenon of health litigation has achieved significant proportions in Brazil, even if the terms 'explosion' and 'epidemic' seem a little overstated in light of the large population of the country and the existence of many other areas (e.g., labour issues, pensions, consumer protection) where litigation is even higher, and significantly so, than in health.

With an estimated number of between 702,739 (conservative estimate) and 1,293,625 new cases in the past four years of available data (2014 to 2019) and a total cost of around R$7 billion a year (approximately US$3.545 billion), around 3 per cent of the total aggregate health budget of the country (up from 0.4 per cent in 2009), the right to health litigation cannot be easily dismissed as a marginal issue. On the contrary, it has become a central preoccupation for the Ministry of Health and several state and municipal secretariats across the country, especially so given the harsher economic environment of the past few years, which compounds the historical funding challenges of the public system discussed at length in Chapter 4.

The available data also shows a prevalence of individual claims and a focus on curative medical treatment, in particular, medicines, followed by hospital treatment, as the most litigated interventions. Although comprehensive data is less readily available on what types of medicines and hospital treatments are claimed, some studies show a high concentration

[72] Data from the Brazilian Federal Council of Medicine (Conselho Federal de Medicina), available at https://portal.cfm.org.br/index.php?option=com_content&view=article&id=27961:2018-11-12-17-57-13&catid=3, accessed 1 April 2019.

of claims and costs on a limited number of drugs, an issue I explore in much further detail in Chapter 8.

We can also conclude with reasonable confidence from the available data that the judicialisation of health is not a homogeneous phenomenon, that is, one that evenly distributed across the country. It is rather disproportionately concentrated in states and municipalities of the South and the Southeast, which, together, account for approximately eight of every ten lawsuits in the country, well above their share of Brazil's total population (56.4 per cent). Conversely, all states of the North and Northeast, which together represent 36 per cent of the Brazilian population, accounted for less than 13 per cent of right to health litigation. Moreover, litigation concentrates further in some municipalities within states and even districts within municipalities, whereas large areas of the country experience little or no litigation at all, an issue explored in further detail in Chapter 7.

Rather than a widespread national manifestation that percolates through all corners of Brazil and involves all types of health interventions (including primary care and public health measures that affect most Brazilians), health litigation is more appropriately described as a niche phenomenon, to be found only in some pockets of the country and focused significantly on a limited range of curative health benefits.

Why does the judicialisation of health in Brazil have this profile? What is its social impact? The aim of the next chapters is to explore these questions and offer plausible hypotheses.

6

How the Haves Come Out Ahead in Health Litigation

> Justice in Brazil, in the sense of rights guarantees, exist only for the small minority of 'doutores' [the great and the good]. It is inaccessible to the multitude of believers and sorcerers [the poor], that is, the great majority of Brazilians. For them, there is the Criminal Code, not the Civil Code, just as to the 'doutores' there is only the Civil Code.[1]
>
> José Murilo de Carvalho

> Many discussions of the relationship between the Supreme Court and litigants assume that the resources necessary to support litigation are easily generated and that, as a result, litigants of all kinds have always stood ready to bring forward any kind of case that the Court might indicate a willingness to hear and decide. But that presumes a pluralism of litigating interests and an evenness of the litigation playing field that is wholly unjustified.[2]
>
> Charles R. Epp

Having presented as complete a picture of the judicialisation of health in Brazil as I could with the available data in Chapter 5, I now turn to the interpretation of that picture. Why has judicialisation grown so much in the past couple of decades? Why are the hundreds of thousands of cases now reaching the courts every year concentrated in the states of the South and Southeast, and mostly in some cities and districts? Who gains, and who loses, from the approximately R$7 billion (3 per cent of the total health budget) spent annually as a result of litigation? These are the main

[1] J. M. de Carvalho, *Cidadania no Brasil: O Longo Caminho*, 7th ed. (Rio de Janeiro: Civilização Brasileira, 2001). My translation from the original in Portuguese. The expression 'doutores', which means literally 'doctors', is used in Brazil liberally for anyone with relatively high socioeconomic status (the 'great and the good'), as a sign of distinction. By 'believers and sorcerers', Carvalho refers to the poor.

[2] C. R. Epp, *The Rights Revolution: Lawyers, Activists, and Supreme Courts in Comparative Perspective*, 1st ed. (Chicago: University of Chicago Press, 1998), at 3.

questions addressed in Chapters 6–8 in an attempt to shed some light on the drivers and social impact of health litigation in Brazil.

Many try to explain health litigation through what we could call a *rights revolution narrative.* According to that narrative, litigation is a *transformative tool* that benefits by and large the most disadvantaged and neglected by the Brazilian public health system. Its main driver is the state failure to comply with its constitutional duties towards those who most need it and its social impact is therefore extremely positive. It represents an important form of legal (constitutional) accountability and results in benefits to the most disadvantaged. Others see health litigation as mostly a disruptive and *iniquitous tool* used by economic elites that diverts precious scarce resources from the public health system, preventing the state from doing more for the poorest. Rather than progressive legal accountability, it is rights opportunism at its worst. (Let's call it the *elite capture narrative.*)[3]

Although the truth in Brazil is likely much closer to the latter narrative, it too oversimplifies the drivers and social impact of health litigation. Socioeconomic inequality, with its inevitable consequences on access to justice, does go a long way to explain why health litigation varies so much across Brazil, as should become clearer by the end of this and the next two chapters. But it is worth looking at the data more carefully for the following reasons.

There have been some important efforts in the past three decades to enhance access to justice for the poor in Brazil (to 'democratise' access to justice to use the evocative language of campaigners), which have

[3] For a summary of this polarised debate in Brazil, see O. L. M. Ferraz, 'Moving the Debate Forward in Right to Health Litigation', (2016) 18(2) *Health and Human Rights*, 265–268; J. Biehl, M. P. Socal, J. J. Amon, 'On the Heterogeneity and Politics of the Judicialization of Health in Brazil, (2016) 18(2) *Health and Human Rights*, 269–271. For a general discussion, see D. Brinks, V. Gauri, 'The Law's Majestic Equality? The Distributive Impact of Litigating Social and Economic Rights', Policy Research Working Paper 5999, Washington DC, World Bank (2012), at 4–5: 'From questioning the courts' capacity to accomplish anything at all (Rosenberg 1991), the literature is now returning to the Galanterian (1974) concern that somehow the haves must be coming out ahead in all this (Da Silva and Terrazas 2011; Ferraz 2011). Who is right? Are the juriskeptical academics right, that insofar as this activity is not irrelevant, it can only be harmful? Or are the constitution writers and activists right that courts and rights can be powerful tools for advancing the interests of the underprivileged? Are all these constitutions and legal actions, to the extent they are effective at all, covert vehicles for preserving privilege, or should we revise our understanding of the conventional wisdom?'.

widened somewhat the traditionally narrow doors of the judicial system.[4] Two initiatives in particular seem to merit deeper investigation and analysis in the context of health litigation in Brazil: (i) the enhancement of free legal services to the poor through the expansion and strengthening of the Public Defensory (Defensoria Pública) across the country and the widening of the remit of the Attorney General's Office (Ministério Público);[5] and (ii) the creation and expansion of the Special Courts (Juizados Especiais) system (a type of 'small claims' court), whose aim is to make access to justice simpler and cheaper.

As the picture that emerged in Chapter 5 indicates, these initiatives have clearly not been able to fuel a widespread and large-scale health rights revolution across Brazil. But it is worth investigating if they have nonetheless made some difference, that is, if they have helped at least some disadvantaged groups to reach the courts. The sizeable number of health claims filed by state lawyers, in particular public defenders in many states and the proportion of claims processed by the Special Courts seem to provide some indication that this may be occurring at least to some extent. (see Figure 6.1 and Figure 7.2 in Chapter 7).

This and the next chapters will probe this hypothesis. This chapter focuses on access to justice to gauge how much more accessible litigation has really become for the poor in Brazil in light of the developments just mentioned. Chapter 7 looks in greater detail at the socioeconomic profile of litigants and beneficiaries of litigation to test the hypothesis further.

6.1 The 'Opportunity Structure' for Health Litigation

To discuss how easy (or difficult) it is for the poor to access justice in Brazil, I will use the analytical framework developed by social and

[4] For two among many valuable civil society initiatives, see the organisations Terra de Direitos, https://terradedireitos.org.br/acoes/democratizacao-da-justica/4 and Instituto Pro Bono, https://probono.org.br, accessed 22 June 2019.

[5] After the 1988 Constitution, the functions of legal advice and representation of the Brazilian government were transferred from the Ministério Público to a newly created institution named Advocacia-Geral da União (Articles 131 and 132 of the Constitution). The Ministério Público remained with its primary function of prosecuting crime but also had additional competences consolidated by the new Constitution such as the protection of the environment, consumers, combat of corruption and general 'defense of the juridical order, the democratic regime and social and individual inalienable interests'. (Article 127 of the Constitution). I use the expression 'Attorney General's Office' throughout this book to refer to the Ministério Público as it is more familiar to those acquainted with the American and British legal systems, but the reader should be aware of this important difference.

political scientists often referred to as the 'opportunity structure for legal mobilisation' or simply the 'legal opportunity structure'. As noted by Lisa Vanhala, the idea is deployed differently by different scholars, but the following simple insight unites them: the decision to resort to litigation in order to pursue a certain claim is importantly determined by what we may call the degree of *openness* (*or receptiveness*) of that route in the particular context in question. The more open (or receptive) the litigation route is, the more likely it is that people will resort to litigation as a tool to further their interests.[6]

What makes the litigation avenue more or less open is a combination of factors that vary significantly from context to context. But some conditions seem to feature almost universally in reasonably developed legal systems where litigation is an option in the first place. These include *procedural rules* (e.g., rules of standing, of legal representation, of evidence); *prospects of success* (i.e., likelihood not only of winning in court but also, importantly, of actually managing to enforce the court order); and *access to the resources needed to litigate*, not only financial resources (e.g., funds to cover legal representation and other litigation expenses) but also intellectual and psychological ones (e.g., knowledge of one's rights and litigation options, familiarity and ease with the judicial world, etc.). All of these factors will exert some influence on the openness of the litigation route, that is, on the 'opportunity structure' of potential claimants. Or, to put it in more straightforward terms, on the ability and willingness of individuals to use litigation as a means to further their interests.

Another way of articulating the same idea is through the opposite angle of *closeness* rather than openness, that is, by focusing on the traditional *barriers* often lying on the path of litigation that potential litigants must be able and willing to overcome. One rather useful formulation along such lines has been developed by Siri Gloppen. As she aptly

[6] L. Vanhala, 'Legal Opportunity Structures and the Paradox of Legal Mobilization by the Environmental Movement in the UK', (2012) 46(3) *Law & Society Review*, 523–556, at 527. As Vanhala properly emphasises, the legal opportunity structure is not static but can be influenced by social movements. We also need to look beyond litigation and the legal opportunity structure to understand why litigation takes place or does not take place, as the case may be. A judicial system may well be very open but still not the ideal strategic option if other better avenues exist. Chapters 2 and 3 of this book discuss extensively the political avenues used by campaigners instead of, or as a complement to, litigation to advance the right to health.

notes, 'for social rights litigation to succeed, those whose social rights are violated must be able to articulate their concerns and effectively voice them in court as legal claims, or have someone else do so on their behalf'.[7] As she goes on to clarify:

> [Potential litigants'] opportunity situation is defined by the formal or 'systemic' and informal *barriers* to seeking justice or redress through the judicial system. Some of the barriers preventing people from assessing the justice system are *practical.* These include the costs of litigating, rules of standing, geographical distance, language barriers, and lack of information.
>
> Other barriers keeping people from pursuing a legal strategy are motivational and psychological. Fear and distrust of the courts is often widespread among poor and socially marginalized groups due to cultural and social distance.[8] (Italics in the original)

The 'legal opportunity structure' framework can help us in our endeavour to better understand the drivers of right to health litigation in Brazil. It departs from the plausible assumption, grounded on decades if not centuries of empirical observation, that litigation is hardly ever, in most societies, an easy route to take given the traditional barriers mentioned by Gloppen. It directs our focus to the factors that, in particular scenarios, help litigants to overcome these barriers.[9] What are the main barriers on the path of right to health litigation in Brazil? How have they been overcome by the hundreds of thousands of litigants that are now reaching the courts every year? Is it likely that among these hundreds of

[7] S. Gloppen, 'Courts and Social Transformation: An Analytical Framework', in Gargarella. R. et al. (eds.), *Courts and Social Transformation in New Democracies: An Institutional Voice for the Poor?*, 1st ed. (Oxford: Routledge, 2006), at 46.

[8] Gloppen, 'Courts and Social Transformation'. As she continues: 'For courts to play a transformative role, the claims of the poor and marginalized must be channelled into the legal system. A crucial parameter of the poor's ability to defend rights or seek redress through the legal system is their opportunity situation, which defines the poor as litigants in the legal process.'

[9] The interest in opportunity structures seems to have originally been sparked, or intensified, by the so-called rights-revolution in the United States. The challenge then was to try to explain how, in the 1950s, more and more African American individuals started to resort to courts to demand protection for their rights, in particular, the right to non-discrimination in education and transport (the famous desegregation cases). As is well-known, the right to non-discrimination had been part of the American constitution since the passage of the fourteenth amendment ('the equal protection of the laws') in 1868. Yet the explosion of litigation (or 'rights revolution') took place only in the middle of the next century, in the 1950s. See: Epp, *The Rights Revolution.*

thousands (still a small proportion of the Brazilian population) we can find representatives of the most disadvantaged?[10]

To help us to address these questions, I will discuss in turn each of the following three main aspects of the legal opportunity structure: *procedural rules* (Section 6.2), *prospects of success* (Section 6.3) and *access to resources* (Section 6.4).

6.2 Procedural Rules of Standing

In Chapter 5, I explained that right to health litigation can take two main forms in Brazil: *individualised* and *collective litigation.* I also mentioned that the vast majority of the hundreds of thousands of claims reaching the courts every year are individualised ones (see Chapter 5, Section 5.4). I will discuss the implications of this for the issue of social impact in Chapter 8. Here my aim is to explain the different procedural rules in terms of standing and legal representation that each of these types of claim must follow, as these are relevant aspects of the opportunity structure for litigation.

Anyone in Brazil is in principle apt, that is, has legal standing to start an individualised lawsuit in the lower courts to claim a health benefit against the state invoking the right to health. The only formal barriers, which are quite low, are that the claimant demonstrates compliance with the so-called action conditions (condições da ação), which in Brazilian civil procedural rules are two: 'legitimacy and necessity to act' (legitimidade e

[10] The literature on the obstacles faced by litigation strategies as an effective progressive tool is now large. To cite just one classic, see M. Galanter, 'Why the Haves Come Out Ahead? Speculations on the Limits of Legal Change', (1974) 9(1) *Law & Society Review*, Litigation and Dispute Processing: Part One, pp. 95–160. For a good summary see Brinks, Gauri, 'The Law's Majestic Equality?', at 3, recalling that: 'Since well before 1974, when Galanter wrote – Why the Haves Come out Ahead (Galanter 1974), it is probably fair to summarize the conventional wisdom as follows: economic, social, and procedural barriers prevent the great majority of poor people from making claims in courts (Cappelletti and Garth 1978–1979); accumulated experience gives the rich and the powerful advantages in the courtroom (Galanter 1974); patterns of judicial recruitment and retention, which reflect prevailing configurations of political power, significantly affect the attitudes and calculations of judges (Dahl 1957); and without the active support of elected officials, opponents can easily limit and undermine the implementation of pro-poor rulings (Rosenberg 1991).' For classic studies focused on access to justice in Brazil, see: M. T. A. Sadek, 'Controle Externo do Poder Judiciário', in Sadek, M. T. A. (ed.), *Reforma do Judiciário* (São Paulo: Fundação Konrad Adenauer, 2001); B. S. Santos, 'The Law of the Oppressed: The Construction and Reproduction of Legality in Pasargada', (1977) 12(1) *Law and Society Review*, 5–126.

interesse para agir) (Art. 17 of the Civil Procedural Code, CPC).[11] The legitimacy to act condition requires that the claimant, ordinarily, must invoke a benefit for herself, that is, on her own behalf and not on behalf of someone else, although there are exceptions to this rule that need not detain us here (see Art. 18 of the CPC). The interest to act condition requires that the claimant has an actual need to litigate, that is, that he cannot get what the law entitles him to without resource to the courts.

These are rather low procedural barriers for the potential health litigant to overcome. Anyone with a health need not fulfilled by the public health system easily qualifies.

A much higher barrier in terms of procedural rules is the requirement that no one can litigate without being represented by a lawyer, with the exception of claims filed at the 'Special Civil Courts' (Juizados Especiais Cíveis) (a type of 'small claims' court),[12] whose monetary value is below a certain threshold (twenty times the value of the minimum wage, or R$19,960 at the time of writing, approximately US$5,200 or £4,000). According to the data of the National Council of Justice (CNJ) about 38 per cent of right to health litigation takes place in these courts (see Figure 6.1), yet, as I will explain further below, it is likely that a sizeable proportion of those are nonetheless filed by lawyers and not the claimants themselves.

Although partly a formal, procedural barrier, the need to be represented by a lawyer is of course also a substantive one, as access to lawyers require significant financial and informational resources and represent, as a consequence, one of the most important barriers to litigation as we will see in more detail later (see Section 6.4).

[11] The full text of the Civil Procedural Code in Portuguese can be found at: www.planalto.gov.br/ccivil_03/_Ato2015-2018/2015/Lei/L13105.htm, accessed 22 June 2019.

[12] The first law to establish more accessible courts in Brazil did name them Small Claims Courts (Juizados de Pequenas Causas). See Law 7.244, approved in 1984 at the very end of the military regime. When the 1988 Constitution imposed the obligation on the Federal Union and all states to create such courts, it used the language of 'special courts' for the 'settlement, adjudication and enforcement of civil cases of lesser complexity and criminal offences of lesser harmful potential'. The constitutional mandate was to be implemented only seven years later through Law 9.099, of 26 September 1995. Later laws established special courts at the Federal level (Law no. 10.259, of 2001) and for administrative issues (Fazenda Pública, Law no. 12.153, of 2009). For a very good account of the constitutional debates and the first few years of the operation of the new system, see L. W. Vianna et al., *A judicialização da política e das relações sociais no Brasil* (Rio de Janeiro: Revan, 1999). See also L. W. Vianna et al., 'Dezessete anos de judicialização da política', (2007) 19(2) *Tempo Social, Revista de Sociologia da USP*, 39–85.The main criterion for admission of cases in the special civil courts is that the claim's value is less than forty times the minimum wage (sixty for the special federal courts).

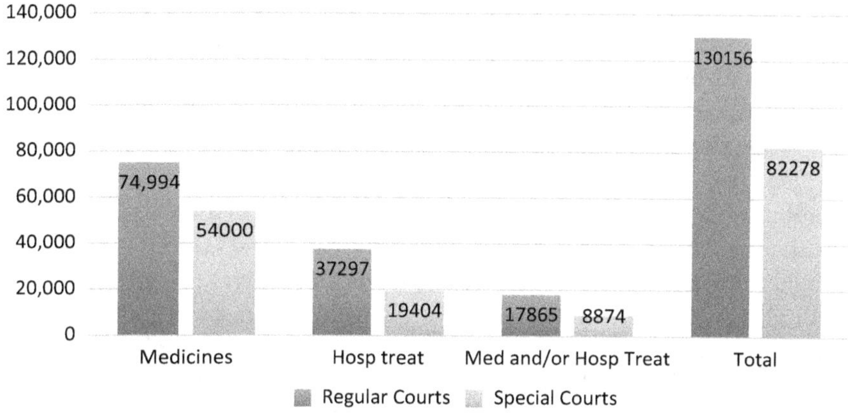

Figure 6.1 Proportion of claims in regular and special ('small claims') courts, 2017.
Source: Own formulation with data from CNJ, Justiça em Números, 2017

Collective suits, which I defined in Chapter 5 as suits whose beneficiaries are a larger group of individuals, potentially whole cities, states or even the whole country, must comply with much more restrictive rules of standing. The main type of collective suit available in right to health cases is the 'Public Civil Action' (Ação Civil Pública, or simply ACP), a type of class action[13] aimed at protecting collective interests.[14]

Only a limited number of institutional actors have standing to file an ACP: members of the Attorney General's Office (Ministério Público, or simply MP), of the Public Defensory (Defensoria Pública, or simply DP), the Union, states and municipalities, public entities such as universities (autarquias), state companies, foundations and civil society associations that comply with certain conditions. In practice, however, it is virtually only the MP and the DP that use ACPs in right to health cases.

13 Under my definition, general challenges to the constitutionality of legislation and policies would also qualify as collective suits and therefore also have very restrictive rules of standing.

14 Legislation on Ação Civil Pública (ACP) distinguishes between three types of interests: (i) collective interests; (ii) so-called homogeneous individual interests; and (iii) so-called diffuse interests (defined in legislation as interests that cannot be easily attributed to specific individuals or groups). For the legal sources of the ACP, see Art. 129, III, of the Constitution of 1988 and Law no. 7.347/85. Public prosecutors have been using ACPs, controversially, also to represent the interests of single patients, with the approval of the Supreme Federal Tribunal. See Notícias STF, 15 August 2018, 'STF afirma legitimidade do MP para postular fornecimento de medicamentos por meio de ação civil pública', www.stf.jus.br/portal/cms/verNoticiaDetalhe.asp?idConteudo=386926, accessed 23 June 2019.

As regards the potential barrier of procedural rules of standing, we must therefore distinguish between individualised and collective suits. The former has rather lower standing requirements, whereas the latter can only be filed by a very limited number of institutional actors and for the protection of certain types of so-called collective interests.

These rules of standing help to explain, in part, the relatively low number of collective suits involving health in Brazil (see Chapter 5). As we shall see in Section 6.4, the number of litigants and lawyers potentially available to initiate individual litigation is infinitely higher than those with standing to file collective suits. As collective suits are also usually harder to prepare in terms of time and research and are slightly less well received by judges and much harder to enforce, it is not surprising that their volume is relatively low. On the other hand, given that 'collective interests' are very loosely interpreted by courts, members of the DP and the MP have a significantly large scope of freedom to file collective suits and do so from time to time, especially the MP. It is fair to conclude, thus, that from the exclusive perspective of procedural rules of standing, neither collective nor individual suits face very significant barriers in Brazil.

6.3 Prospects of Success

Another important element in the opportunity structure for litigation is the likelihood of winning in court and of having that victory actually enforced. There is of course also the possibility of benefiting from litigation indirectly, and even when a case fails in court, for instance, when the state changes its policy to avoid the threat of further litigation or when litigation helps to put an issue in the political agenda (what some call 'winning by losing'). I return to the issue of indirect effects in Chapter 8.[15] But winning in court and having the court order effectively implemented is surely the best possible outcome for any litigant and one likely to incentivise other potential litigants to pursue claims (so long, of course, as the other elements of the opportunity structure are also in place).

The significant rise in numbers of health litigation experienced in Brazil in the past two decades seems to be partly driven by courts'

[15] See Vanhala, 'Legal Opportunity Structures', discussing this issue in the context of environmental litigation in the UK. I discuss the indirect effects of health litigation in Brazil in detail in Chapter 8, Section 8.6.

receptiveness to health claims and the state's relative capacity and willingness to comply with judicial orders (though the latter is more variable across the country).

As regards courts receptiveness to health claims, a clear correlation can be observed in the trajectory of growth of these claims in Brazil. Health litigation, unlike other areas, did not start to grow immediately after the adoption of the new Constitution in 1988, even though the right to health was there from the start (see Chapter 2). As we saw in Chapter 5, health litigation picked up much later, sometime around the mid-1990s and the early 2000s, and only accelerated to the higher levels we see today from the middle to the end of the 2000s.[16] It is around that time that we can also observe a drastic change in courts' receptiveness to right to health claims due to an important change in the courts' jurisprudence on the legal status of social and economic rights in general and the right to health in particular. From seeing these rights as constitutional directives to the legislature (so-called programmatic norms) not to be enforced by courts (with the exception of rather weak remedies such as the declaration of unconstitutionality by omission), the judiciary started to consider social rights as fully enforceable, just as more traditional civil and political rights had always been.[17]

This jurisprudential change is in my view extremely relevant not only as a driver of health litigation but also in the social impact that health litigation has had and continues to have (see Chapters 8 and 9). It seems useful, thus, to describe it in greater detail.

6.3.1 *From Programmatic Norms to Enforceable Rights*

In the first decade or so after the Constitution came into force, the articles of the Constitution that recognise the right to health and other

[16] Confirming that judicialisation grew faster towards the end of the 2000s, more than 80 per cent of the lawsuits in Gomes et al. sample occurred in the last three years of the period they research (2007–2009). Gomes et al., 'Access to Medium and High-Complexity Procedures in the Brazilian Unified National Health System: A Matter of Judicialization', (2014) 30(1) *Cadernos de Saúde Pública*, 31–43.

[17] There is no consistency though in the jurisprudence, with some social rights still largely regarded as non-justiciable by many judges, such as the rights to housing or to the minimum wage. See O. L. M. Ferraz, 'Between Activism and Deference: Social Rights Adjudication in the Brazilian Supreme Federal Tribunal', in Alviar Garcia, H., Klare, K. and Williams, L. A. (eds.), *Social and Economic Rights in Theory and Practice: Critical Inquiries* (London: Routlegde, 2015).

social rights have been widely interpreted by courts as so-called programmatic norms, that is, norms addressed to the legislator and thus not amenable to direct judicial enforcement, particularly not in individualised lawsuits.[18] The prevalence of this traditional and more deferential approach throughout the first decade of the new Constitution has likely disincentivised litigation as the chances of winning were rather small. The following summary (ementa) of a case decided in the late 1990s provides a good illustration:[19]

> Claimants with chronic kidney disease. Provision of medicine (CELLCEPT) by the state. The programmatic norms of the Federal Constitution *do not confer on the citizen an individual right* to demand from the state the provision of high-cost medicines, at the cost of other patients, who are equally needy. In its public health duty, the executive must attend to more pressing interests of the population.[20] (my emphasis)

Between the mid- and the late 1990s, however, this view began to change with more and more academics and judges arguing that social and economic rights, as *constitutional norms*, should be just as enforceable by courts as any other legal norm.[21] The first case in which the Supreme Federal Tribunal (Supremo Tribunal Federal, or simply STF), the highest court in the land, adopted the new approach seems to have been decided in 1997. Unlike it is widely believed, it did not involve HIV-AIDS but rather treatment for a rare and degenerative disease called Duchenne

[18] See J. A. da Silva, *Aplicabilidade das normas constitucionais* (São Paulo: Malheiros, 1999), at 83–84: The only judicial procedure available, yet rare and difficult to pursue, was the action of unconstitutionality for omission.

[19] See L. R. Barroso, 'Da falta de efetividade à judicialização excessiva: Direito à saúde, fornecimento gratuito de medicamentos e parâmetros para a atuação judicial', (2009) 60 (188) *Revista Jurisprudência Mineira*, 29–60. See also: Apelação Cível 27.522-5, São José dos Campos/SP, Nona Câmara de Direito Público do Tribunal de Justiça de São Paulo, Relator Yoshiaki Ichihara, 28 April 99, cited in M. Scheffer et al. (eds.), *O Remédio via Justiça: Um estudo sobre o acesso a novos medicamentos e exames em HIV/Aids no Brasil por meio de ações judiciais*, Série Legislação no. 3 (Brasília: Ministério da Saúde, 2005), at 107.

[20] TJRJ, December 1998, MS 220/98, Rel. Des Antonio Lindberg Montenegro, cited in Barroso, 'Da falta de efetividade à judicialização excessiva', at 44.

[21] This was not a phenomenon restricted to Brazil, of course. For a very similar development in Costa Rica, see: O. F. Norheim, B. M. Wilson, 'Health Rights Litigation and Access to Medicines: Priority Classification of Successful Cases from Costa Rica's Constitutional Chamber of the Supreme Court', (2014) 11(16) *Health and Human Rights*, 47–61. See, for the global trend, C. N. Tate, T. Vallinder,*The Global Expansion of Judicial Power* (New York: New York University Press, 1997).

syndrome.[22] The STF, or rather the justice who single-handedly decided that case, Justice Celso de Mello, accepted the claimant's argument that the right to health recognised in Article 196 of the 1988 Constitution entitled him to receive from the state, at no cost, the very expensive drug recently developed by a pharmaceutical company and not offered by the public health system. Justice Mello's reasoning in that case became what I call a *de facto* precedent,[23] cited hundreds if not thousands of times as the legal ground for later decisions across the country, in particular, the following passage of a later case, this time involving HIV-AIDS, where he largely repeats the 1997 decision:

> The right to health – as well as a fundamental right of all individuals – represents an inextricable constitutional consequence of the right to life . . .. *The interpretation of a programmatic norm cannot transform it into a toothless constitutional promise* . . .. Between protecting the inviolability of the right to life and to health, an inalienable fundamental right guaranteed by the Constitution itself (Art. 5 and Art. 196) or ensuring, against this fundamental prerogative, a financial and secondary interest of the state, I believe – once this dilemma is established – ethical and legal reasons impose on the judge one single and possible option: that which privileges unswerving respect for life and human health.[24] (my emphasis)

That position was soon adopted by most other Justices in the Supreme Federal Tribunal and across the country in other cases involving different health conditions, including but not exclusively HIV-AIDS cases.[25] The significant rise in right to health litigation observed from the early 2000s is likely, in my view, to have been strongly influenced by this change in the jurisprudence of the STF that cascaded down to almost the whole of the judiciary. It was not just that judges became more willing to entertain individual claims based on the constitutional right to health. They started

[22] See PET 1.246-SC (1997).

[23] I say 'de facto' precedent as the Brazilian system, belonging to the so-called civil law family, does not recognise precedents apart from exceptional cases.

[24] RE 271.286 AgR-RS (2000), involving HIV-AIDS, citing several other cases of the STF where the same view was expressed, e.g., AG 232.469-RS Marco Aurelio AG 236.644-RS Mauricio Correa; AG 238.328-RS Marco Aurelio, AG 273.042-RS Marco Aurelio; ARE 730.741/SP. My translation from the Portuguese. Full text, in Portuguese, available at the STF website: www.stf.jus.br/portal/processo/verProcessoPeca.asp?id=133345682&tipoApp=.pdf, accessed 23 August 2107.

[25] See D. R. Coutinho, A. M. Vojvodic (eds.), *Jurisprudência Constitucional: Como decide o STF?* (São Paulo: Malheiros, 2009), V. A. da Silva, F. V. Terrazas, 'Claiming the Right to Health in Brazilian Courts: The Exclusion of the Already Excluded', (2011) 36(4) *Law & Social Inquiry*, 825–853.

to decide in favour of the claimant in a very large proportion of those claims. This was due to the extremely expansive interpretation of that right adopted, as the passage quoted shows. I call it the 'right to everything' interpretation, as it prevents the state from raising any justification, not even resource scarcity, to refuse the provision to individuals of whatever health benefits they claim to need. The only condition imposed on litigants is that they produce a prescription from a medical doctor attesting their need. The following passage of a case decided by the second highest court in Brazil, the Superior Tribunal of Justice (Superior Tribunal de Justiça, or simply STJ), also often cited in lower courts, illustrates the point:

> The medical prescription, signed either by a private physician or by a public doctor, is sufficient to prove the necessity of the medicine. To accept the argument of the state, which intends to challenge the medical prescription, would be to *unduly interfere* in the realm of the physician responsible for the treatment of the patient. Only when there is an evident error in the medical report-prescription, that is, when the prescription is absurd, it is inappropriate to the administrator, as well as to the Judiciary, to question whether this or that medication would be the most appropriate.[26] (my emphasis)

Under this 'right to everything' interpretation of the right to health (see also Chapter 8, section 8.2.1), the success rate in health litigation is unsurprisingly high, many studies reporting success rates of 100 per cent and none reporting success rates lower than 80 per cent.[27]

I must now briefly discuss the other important aspect of what I call prospects of success that does not always receive the deserved attention in the literature: the capacity and willingness of the state to comply with the decisions emanating from the courts.

[26] My translation from the Portuguese. See Decision of STJ Justice Mauro Campbell Marques, Agravo de Instrumento no. 1.114.613/MG, 8 May 2009. See also Voto no. 05215 Reexame Necessário no. 1002469-71.2.018.8.26.0066 by Court of Appeal Judge Carlos Fakiani Macatti, citing it with approval and reemphasising: 'As it is known, a medical doctor's prescription, from the private or public system, is sufficient as evidence that the treatment in question is needed. Neither the public administration nor the judiciary can challenge this, as they would be interfering unduly in the medical arena.' (see Appeal No. 1.114.613/MG, 8 June 2005).

[27] For a comprehensive meta-review of judicialisation studies citing nine studies showing success rates above 90 per cent across Brazil, including four citing 100 per cent, see: I. Torres, 'Judicialização do acesso a medicamentos no Brasil: Uma revisão sistemática', MPhil dissertation, Universidade Federal da Bahia, Instituto de Saúde Coletiva (2013), at 52.

6.3.2 Compliance

If judicial orders are not implemented by the state – as it seems to happen not infrequently in several countries, for reasons that range from outright defiance to genuine difficulties related to resource limitations and other practical issues – judicial receptiveness alone will not be sufficient to motivate and sustain litigation.[28] It would disincentivise potential litigants to invest their hopes and resources in litigation if it was clear that compliance with court orders would not be forthcoming, or would be erratic, too time and resource consuming, etc.

Not many studies try or manage to collect reliable and comprehensive information on this important aspect. It is much easier, of course, to collect information on the outcome of litigation (i.e., the final decision) than on whether the decision has been complied with.[29] It is nonetheless plausible to assume that implementation of the hundreds of thousands of successful right to health cases across Brazil is neither perfect nor uniform across states. There is anedoctal evidence that many successful claimants face difficulties to actually receive the health benefits granted by courts. In an interview I conducted in the state of Bahia with a claimant who was also an activist in the field of rare diseases, I was told that the medicinal product she was granted for her son's rare condition was often significantly delayed or delivered in smaller amounts than was necessary for his treatment.[30] When I interviewed those responsible for complying with the court order in the state health department, they mentioned recurrent difficulties with suppliers and limitation of funds as the most common causes for the delays, especially when the health benefit granted by the courts was not available in Brazil and had to be imported, which was the case in the claim in question.[31]

[28] Compliance is also relevant, of course, for the issue of impact discussed in Chapter 8.

[29] Epp, *The Rights Revolution*, at 7 lists 'implementation' as the third of the three main components of the rights revolution process, alongside judicial attention to the new rights and judicial support for the new rights. But his impressive book discusses this component in much less detail than the other two, likely because, as he properly notes, 'implementation of judicial decisions is a complex and multifaceted matter', ibid., at 7–8.

[30] Interview with Ms Lindamar M. Lima, 17 November 2014. That led a group of patients suffering from the same condition and also benefited by court orders to create a network to share the product when necessary. Ibid.

[31] Interview with officials at the Health Secretariat of the State of Bahia, 18 November 2014. See also F. Hoffmann, F. Bentes, 'Accountability for Economic and Social Rights in Brazil', in Gauri, V. and Brinks, D. (eds.) *Courting Social Justice: Judicial Enforcement of Social and Economic Rights in the Developing World* (New York: Cambridge University

The problem seems to be even worse when complex collective suits are at stake. In a study I conducted on a large class action filed by the MP on behalf of all autistic children of the state of São Paulo, implementation of the successful decision, issued more than thirteen years ago, is still ridden with problems.[32] Many of the children with autism nominally benefited by the decision still don't receive the special education, health and assistance from the state that they were granted by the courts. Some go back to the courts, individually, through a private lawyer or a public defender, turning, in effect, a collective suit into an individual one, while many simply continue to wait for state compliance or have lost any hope of ever benefiting from the judicial order.[33]

We also know, for instance, that some better resourced states, such as São Paulo, have created a whole department only to deal with judicialisation and thus manage, by and large, to comply with the tens of thousands of court orders, whereas other less well-resourced, such as Bahia, face difficulties even to maintain an accurate record of the orders issued by courts against it.[34] These differences in compliance rates are likely to have some impact on the volume of litigation and may help to explain, to

Press, 2008), 100–145, at 133. They report a similar pattern: 'in some states such as Rio de Janeiro (but much less so in Rio Grande do Sul), there is a considerable compliance problem'. As they go on to explain, 'the usual pattern is not that the public pharmacy in question will deny outright the provision of the medicine, but that it will either promise delivery in the future or dispense the medicine but later discontinue dispensation; in both cases, logistical difficulties will be cited. As a result, many indigent plaintiffs become persuaded that even enforcement action through the Defensoria Pública is not going to make any difference'.

32 See O. L. M. Ferraz, 'Right to Health Litigation in Brazil: Are Collective Suits Harder to Enforce?', in Langford, M. and Rodríguez-Garavito, C. (eds.), *Making It Stick: Compliance with Social Rights Judgments in Comparative Perspective* (Cambridge: Cambridge University Press, 2018). See also, Sobre as mudanças na execução da ação civil pública de autismo, 20 January 2017, https://aliberdadeehazul.com/2017/01/20/sobre-as-mudancas-na-execucao-da-acao-civil-publica-de-autismo/, accessed 11 December 2018.

33 See also A. P. Barcellos, 'Sanitation Rights, Public Law Litigation, and Inequality: A Case Study from Brazil', (2014) 16(2) *Health and Human Rights*, 35–46, showing that collective suits involving basic sanitation have a very low implementation rate (4 per cent).

34 I visited both state health departments on separate occasions for separate research projects and was given extensive access to officials and documents. Whereas the state of São Paulo currently has thirty-five employees dealing only with the administration of lawsuits and has created a dedicated Pharmacy to dispense judicially ordered drugs ('The Judiciary Pharmacy'), the health department in Bahia, despite the goodwill and effort of the employees who received me, wasn't even able to provide me with an accurate and comprehensive record of the claims in existence against it. See also B. Pierro, 'Demandas Crescentes', (2017) 252(18) *Pesquisa Fapesp*, 18–25.

some extent at least, why São Paulo and other better resourced states of the South and Southeast have not only much higher numbers of lawsuits against them but also report very high costs incurred to comply with judicial orders (see Chapter 5, Section 5.5).

In conclusion, my view is that effective implementation is an important complementary component of judicial receptiveness in the opportunity structure for health litigation. When potential claimants know that the chances not only of winning in court but also of effectively benefiting from the court order are high, as they seem to be in some states of Brazil, such as São Paulo and Rio Grande do Sul, litigation is likely to rise. When the prospects of actually benefiting from court orders are much lower, as seems to be the case in other less well-resourced states, such as Bahia, a further disincentive to litigation seems to arise.

***

The relatively low procedural barriers and the jurisprudential change of the mid-1990s, in which courts abandoned a more deferential view of social rights as programmatic norms and adopted a very expansive and assertive interpretation of the right to health, seem to constitute important components of the legal opportunity structure in Brazil and important aspects of the explanation of the rise in health litigation witnessed in the past two decades. But it cannot alone explain that rise. As political scientist Charles Epp aptly notes, although it is true that 'litigants pursue rights claims if judges indicate a friendliness toward those claims . . . cases do not arrive in supreme courts as if by magic'.[35] As he appropriately adds:

> The process of legal mobilization – the process by which individuals make claims about their legal rights and pursue lawsuits to defend or develop those rights – is not in any simple way a direct response to opportunities provided by constitutional promises or judicial decisions . . .. Legal mobilization also depends on resources, and resources for rights litigation depend on a support structure of rights-advocacy lawyers, rights-advocacy organizations and sources of financing.[36]

The remainder of this chapter focuses on this further crucial (perhaps the most crucial) aspect of the opportunity structure for legal mobilisation.

[35] Epp, *The Rights Revolution*, at 18.
[36] Ibid.

6.4 Resources for Legal Mobilisation

Permissive procedural rules of standing, a highly receptive judiciary and a reasonably compliant state are certainly helpful yet not sufficient to generate health litigation. In the absence of what Charles Epp calls 'resources for legal mobilization' no litigation will materialise for the simple reason that litigants will not be able to reach the courts in the first place. This provides us with a strong clue to explain the picture that emerged in Chapter 5 of health litigation in Brazil. Since the two other components of the opportunity structure just discussed – favourable procedural rules and high prospects of success – obtain more or less equally everywhere in Brazil, differences in *resources* emerges as the most likely explanation for the significant variation in the volume of health litigation experienced across the country.[37]

Going to court to claim rights is not as trivial a matter as it is sometimes portrayed to be in debates on the judicialisation of health. For a large part of the population in Brazil, litigation is something that doesn't ever come to mind as a realistic option. Even among those who may consider litigation as a potential tool, it is mostly as something exceptional, a last resort and one often to be discarded rather than actually used.[38]

Such attitudes are not really surprising once one reflects a moment on what is usually required in terms of *knowledge*, *time*, *energy* and *money* (I will refer to all these collectively as *resources* here) to pursue a claim in court.[39] I suppose this is true of most countries, but it is certainly the case in Brazil. To even consider litigation as an option, one needs to have command of a reasonably comprehensive basket of resources that is not easily assembled even by middle class citizens, let alone by the less

[37] Another potential explanation would be of course disparities in the quality of the public health system in different regions, but this hypothesis can be easily dismissed as health litigation currently concentrates in comparatively better, not worse, served areas of the country. See Chapters 4 and 5.

[38] Studies of judicial review elsewhere have found similar scenarios, in particular, where potential beneficiaries are vulnerable groups, such as the homeless and the mentally incapacitated. See the studies by Loveland and Halliday cited by J. King, *Judging Social Rights*, 1st ed. (Cambridge: Cambridge University Press, 2012), at 71.

[39] As a lawyer myself who spent several years representing clients in the courts of São Paulo, I quickly learned that, for them, none of the thrill I felt when facing the opposing legal counsels and arguing their case before the judge was very exciting, if at all. All they seemed interested in was to conclude the case as quickly and as cheaply as possible, often through settlements.

advantaged. As Charles Epp has aptly noted in the context of the United States, perhaps the most litigious society of all, 'not every issue is now, or has been in the past, the subject of extensive litigation in lower courts, due in part to limitations in the availability of resources for legal mobilisation'.[40]

These resources, it is worth emphasising, are not simply money, but also time, energy, knowledge and even confidence, as not everyone is psychologically prepared to face the arcane and often hostile environment of the judicial system. In short, litigation is almost always a very limited, costly and unattractive option, for anyone, but especially for the poor, as they tend to possess none or little of all these resources.

Awareness of this traditional problem led to initiatives aimed at enhancing access to justice in Brazil, many of which are included in the Constitution of 1988, such as the expansion of the small claims system, the so-called Special Courts (Juizados Especiais) for civil and criminal issues (Art. 98, I), the expansion of the remit of the Attorney General's Office (Arts. 127 and 129) and the recognition of the Public Defensory as an essential organ of the justice system (Art. 134) to provide legal representation for those unable to afford the notoriously high costs of litigation.

These important initiatives, however, have not yet been able to significantly address the resource barriers faced by a large part of the population, as the data on some of the key resources for legal mobilisation discussed in the following subsections demonstrate.

6.4.1 *Knowledge ('Rights Awareness')*

It seems evident that without knowledge about legal rights and how they work (I will refer to it simply as *rights awareness* or *rights consciousness* here) a person will likely not litigate. As political scientist Siri Gloppen concisely puts it, litigation 'requires, firstly, that potential litigants should be aware of their rights, the right-violation and the possibility for redress through the courts'. Yet, as she goes on to note, 'often, those whose social rights are most severely violated lack this knowledge'.[41] Lack of or insufficient rights awareness is one of the main resource barriers to legal mobilisation. Once one is aware of one's rights and the possibility to litigate one can at least try to overcome the other obstacles. One can try

[40] Epp, *The Rights Revolution*, at 3.
[41] Gloppen, 'Courts and Social Transformation', at 46.

to find the time and the energy, muster the courage, save the financial resources to go to court. Without awareness, one is virtually paralysed, incapacitated to take any action.

It is likely that the growth in right to health litigation experienced in Brazil in the last two decades is at least partly due to a rise in rights consciousness among the population. As we have seen in Chapter 2 and have emphasised earlier in this chapter, an important part of the post-military Constitution's project (the evocatively dubbed, even if somewhat overcast, 'Citizen Constitution'), was precisely to foster more rights awareness among the population, that is, to foster citizenship. After thirty years of the enactment of the Constitution it seems plausible to assume (though difficult to measure) that increasingly more people have become familiar with the rights that the Constitution recognises. More reports and discussion in the news have taken place, more government programmes referring to these rights have been implemented, more political campaigns promising to fulfil these rights have occurred, etc. The rise in right to health litigation is likely to be at least in part a positive reflection, thus, of an enhanced rights culture encouraged by the 1988 Constitution.

But it would be highly implausible to argue that this enhanced rights culture has widely spread across the whole population. It most likely fails to reach large sections, especially those least educated, who tend of course to be also those with lower income and worse health conditions.

A brief overview of Brazil's situation in terms of educational level and educational inequalities helps us to see the magnitude of the challenge. Despite some improvements in the past couple of decades, the general level of education of the Brazilian population is still rather low. The mean schooling years of those above 25 years of age is still as low as 7.8, with 40 per cent having no secondary education whatsoever and only 26.3 per cent having completed secondary education.[42] The illiteracy rate is higher than it could be for Brazil's level of economic development, at 8.3 per cent of the population. To put this into context, Figure 6.2 compares Brazil with three other Latin American neighbours and one more developed country, the United Kingdom.

[42] See United Nations Development Programme, Human Development Reports, http://hdr.undp.org/en/indicators/103006 and http://hdr.undp.org/en/indicators/23806, both accessed 12 December 2018. See also data from the Brazilian Institute of Geography and Statistics – IBGE at: http://hdr.undp.org/en/indicators/69706, accessed 20 July 2020. The average number of years of schooling that a child of school entrance age can expect to receive if prevailing patterns of age-specific enrolment rates persist throughout the child's life is also still low (15.4).

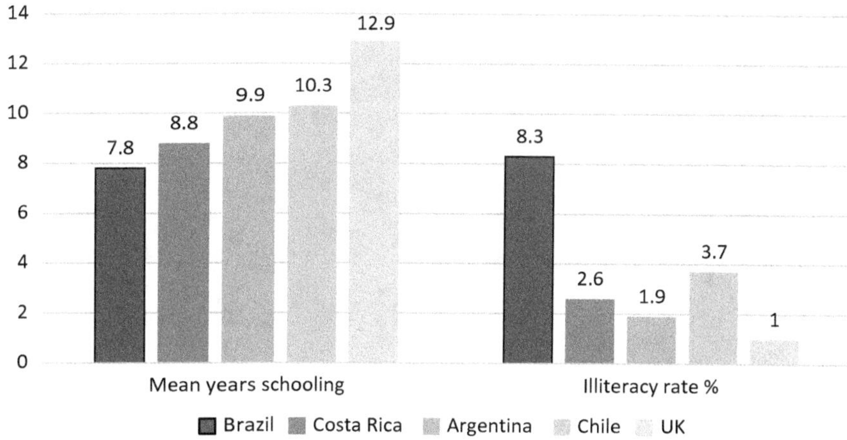

Figure 6.2 Selected educational indicators.
Source: UNDP, Human Development Reports, http://hdr.undp.org/en

These are, of course, quantitative measures of access that say little about the quality of education in Brazil. When more qualitative indicators are taken into account, the picture worsens considerably. In the Programme for International Student Assessment – PISA, which tests the skills and knowledge of fifteen-year-old students in mathematics, reading and science, Brazil has fared consistently poorly (see Figure 6.3). When literacy is assessed through more detailed functionality tests, the picture also deteriorates significantly, with another 22 per cent of the population achieving only the so-called rudimentary level, which is slightly above complete illiteracy. Thirty per cent of the Brazilian population is therefore 'functionally illiterate', that is, either incapable of reading (8 per cent) or of understanding texts of more than a very rudimentary and literal nature, such as calendars, simple tables and posters. Those who achieve the top level ('proficient'), that is, who are capable of reading more complex texts, understanding the context and expressing an opinion about the style of the author are a very small minority of 12 per cent. The bulk of the population falls in the second and third brackets ('intermediate', 25 per cent) and ('elementary', 34 per cent).[43]

[43] INAF – Indicador de Analfabetismo Funcional, BRASIL 2018 Resultados preliminares, at 8. Available at: http://acaoeducativa.org.br/wp-content/uploads/2018/08/Inaf2018_Relat%C3%B3rio-Resultados-Preliminares_v08Ago2018.pdf, accessed 23 June 2019. For a

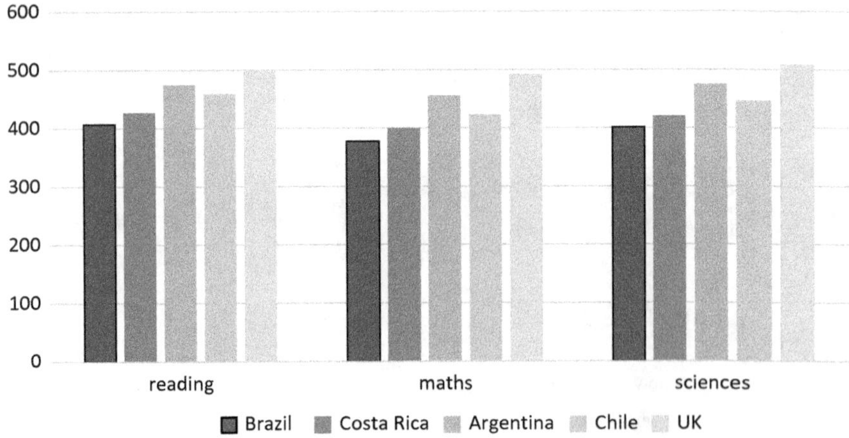

Figure 6.3 PISA 2015 results.
Source: UNDP, Human Development Reports, http://hdr.undp.org/en

It would be surprising if such low general levels of educational achievement and high levels of educational inequality did not translate into low and unequal rights awareness in Brazil. As political scientist Maria Tereza Sadek, one of Brazil's leading experts on access to justice, aptly noted after reviewing earlier but not very dissimilar data on Brazil's education profile: 'even acknowledging that the current socioeconomic situation is better than in the past, this is not a favourable state of affairs for the real expansion of rights and the ability to invoke them when violated'.[44]

good summary in English, see 'Brazil's Failed Educational System Creates Illiterate Students', The Brazilian Report, 27 October 2017, available at https://brazilian.report/society/2017/10/27/brazil-educational-system-illiteracy-stats/, accessed 2 April 2019.

[44] M. T. A. Sadek, 'Acesso à Justiça: Um Direito e seus Obstáculos', (2014) 101 *Revista USP*, 55–66, at 59. My translation from the original in Portuguese. She discusses the slightly worse but not dissimilar data of the Census of 2010 (9.6 per cent illiteracy) and further interesting disaggregated data showing the significant regional inequalities that persist in Brazil, which I have emphasised several times in this book, in particular, in Chapter 4. In 2010, 53.3 per cent of illiterates were from the Northeast. In Brazil as a whole, illiteracy was much higher in rural areas (23.2 per cent) than in urban ones (7.3 per cent). She also stresses Brazil's poor performance in PISA in 2013, achieving the thirty-eighth position out of forty-four countries in the ability of students to solve problems of logic and reasoning.

Some interesting specific surveys conducted in the past few decades support this hypothesis, showing a general lack of rights awareness in the Brazilian population and an unsurprising social gradient in this field. The findings of the innovative survey *Índice de Confiança na Justiça* (Index of Trust in the Justice System, or simply FGV-ICJ) carried out by the Law School of the Fundação Getúlio Vargas in São Paulo are particularly interesting for our purposes. They asked respondents in 2014 to name any of the rights recognised in Brazilian law. Sixty-one per cent of respondents could not name a single one. Of the 39 per cent who could, civil liberties were by far the most mentioned (46 per cent). The right to health was mentioned by 20 per cent of those 39 per cent, that is, by just above 8 per cent of the sample (exactly the same rate as the right to education).[45]

The FGV-ICJ survey also revealed significant inequalities in rights awareness among different socioeconomic groups. Unsurprisingly, knowledge about rights was positively correlated with income and schooling, ranging significantly from a rather low level of knowledge among the poorest (23 per cent) and least educated (27 per cent) to reasonably high levels of knowledge among the richest (70 per cent) and most educated (75 per cent) (see Figure 6.4).

Other more generic surveys seem to confirm the finding that most of the Brazilian population does not have a deep knowledge of their legal rights. In 2010, the Núcleo de Estudos da Violência da USP (Centre for the Study of Violence of the University of São Paulo, NEV-USP) asked a sample of more than 4,000 interviewees in 11 capitals across Brazil several questions about human rights, violence and the criminal law system. The most specific question about human rights was whether respondents had heard of the existence of the Universal Declaration of Human Rights.[46] Fifty-five per cent of respondents had never heard of it.

[45] See F. L. Oliveira, L. G. Cunha, 'Medindo o acesso à Justiça Cível no Brasil', (2016) 22(2) *Opinião Pública*, 318–349, at 342. The FGV-ICJ corroborates an earlier survey by the Centro de Pesquisa e Documentação de História Contemporânea do Brasil (Brazilian Centre for Research and Documentation of Contemporary History, CPDOC) of the late 1990s carried out in Rio de Janeiro, asking people to enumerate three of the most important rights of Brazilian citizens: 56.7 per cent of respondents could not name any. As cited by Oliveira, Cunha, 'Medindo o acesso à Justiça Cível no Brasil', at 343.

[46] See N. Cardia, R. Cinoto et al., *Pesquisa nacional, por amostragem domiciliar, sobre atitudes, normas culturais e valores em relação à violação de direitos humanos e violência: Um estudo em 11 capitais de estado* (São Paulo: Núcleo de Estudos da Violência da Universidade de São Paulo, 2012), at 361. The full report is available at: www.nevusp.org/downloads/down264.pdf, accessed 5 April 2019.

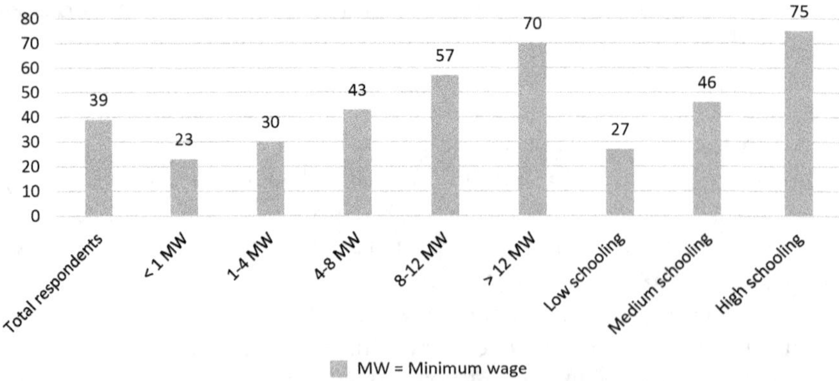

Figure 6.4 Percentage of respondents who could name one right recognised in Brazilian law, by income and schooling levels.
Source: Own formulation with data from FGV-Índice de Confiança na Justiça

These rather low rates of knowledge about rights instruments such as international declarations and constitutions (which are probably overestimated as most of these surveys are carried out through landline phone calls in capitals where the population tends to have higher levels of education), are likely to translate into even lower genuine rights awareness.[47] It is one thing to know that a constitution or laws that recognise certain rights exist, another to know which rights are in fact recognised and yet another, and much more complex, to know what exactly one can do with this information. For rights awareness to trans-

[47] In the NEV-USP survey, a high percentage of the sample (42 per cent) contained interviewees who had completed the secondary level of education, a much higher level than in the general population (26.3 per cent in 2017). See: https://agenciadenoticias.ibge.gov.br/agencia-sala-de-imprensa/2013-agencia-de-noticias/releases/18992-pnad-continua-2016-51-da-populacao-com-25-anos-ou-mais-do-brasil-possuiam-apenas-o-ensino-fundamental-completo, accessed 5 May 2019. Most of these surveys are conducted through landline phone calls, which many poorer Brazilians don't have access to. The total aggregate in the country, as of January 2019, was 53.8 per cent, varying significantly, as everything does in Brazil, across regions. In the poorest North and Northeast regions, the density of access is 6.82 and 8.02 lines per 100 inhabitants, in the richest South and Southeast regions, it is 23.59 and 28.43 respectively. See Dados, Agência Nacional de Telecomunicações – ANATEL, available at: www.anatel.gov.br/dados/destaque-1/331-telefonia-fixa-acessos-janeiro-2017, accessed 5 April 2019.

late into ability and willingness to litigate, this latter, deeper knowledge seems necessary.[48]

We need to look now at another important resource for legal mobilisation that is an essential complement to (and may perhaps also mitigate somewhat the lack of) rights awareness, namely, access to legal advice and representation. A person's initial awareness that she has certain legally recognised rights will only be fully converted into actual motivation and ability to resort to litigation if she is also able to carry out a relatively complex assessment of whether her right has been violated and whether the route of litigation is a promising one. Such assessment demands some degree of expert knowledge. Moreover, should this hurdle be overcome, most right to health claims will also require the intervention of lawyers to file and follow the lawsuit in court on behalf of the claimant (i.e., legal representation). Section 6.4.2 turns to this important aspect of the opportunity structure of legal mobilisation.

6.4.2 *Access to Legal Advice, Representation and Courts*

Any citizen considering right to health litigation in Brazil (or any type of litigation for that matter) will likely need to consult a lawyer first and, if decided to go ahead, will probably be represented by one in court as well. As we saw in Section 6.2, legal representation is a requirement in Brazil for any claim not filed in one of the Special Courts ('small claims') in operation across the country *and* whose monetary value exceeds twenty times the minimum wage (about US$5,200 or £4,000 at the time of writing). In 2017, as we saw, around 38 per cent of all right to health claims were processed in those courts (see Figure 6.1). We can be certain, thus, that 62 per cent of the claims in 2017 (around 130,000) did have a lawyer behind them, but we cannot be sure that the other 38 per cent did not. On the contrary, it is rather likely that even in the Special Courts most claimants are still represented by lawyers. This is due, in part, to the fact that health litigation, in particular, access to medicines litigation, can

[48] An interesting yet also limited poll carried out in 2016 to mark twenty-five years of the Consumer Protection Code found a higher level of awareness of consumer rights among the interviewed but a low propensity to complain even among those who claimed to know their rights. See: IDEC (Instituto Brasileiro de Defesa do Consumidor), 'Brasileiros conhecem seus direitos de consumidor, mas não reclamam de forma efetiva, mostra pesquisa', IDEC, 15 March 2016, available at: www.idec.org.br/em-acao/em-foco/brasileiros-conhecem-cdc-e-seus-direitos-de-consumidor-mas-no-reclamam-de-forma-efetiva-mostra-pesquisa, accessed 5 April 2019.

easily supersede the twenty-times minimum wages threshold.[49] As studies have shown, a significant number of claimants arrived at these courts already represented by a lawyer, as many as 78.42 per cent in Rio de Janeiro, and many Special Courts have the practice of recommending that those who arrive without a lawyer should seek the services of the Public Defensory.[50]

I will discuss in greater detail below how Special Courts are unfortunately still far from fulfilling their aim of addressing the significant restrictions to access to justice in Brazil (the 'democratisation of justice' to use the evocative terminology of those who admirably fought for their creation and still fight for their expansion and improvement). My point here is simply to highlight that access to legal advice and representation is still (and will likely remain) an essential resource for potential right to health litigants even in the 38 per cent of cases that are processed in Special Courts. If we want to gauge how significant a barrier access to legal resources are within the larger opportunity structure for litigation, we need to understand the barriers of access to legal representation in much more detail.

Different Types of Legal Representation

There are three different types of lawyers who can advise and represent claimants in right to health lawsuits in the Brazilian system. There are *independent*, or 'private lawyers' (*advogados particulares*) as they are called in Brazil, who work either individually or as part of private law firms and normally charge fees for their services and there are *state lawyers*, that is, public servants paid by the state.[51] State lawyers are

[49] Given that the monetary ceiling to litigate in Special Courts (forty times the minimum wage in *state* Special Courts and sixty times in *federal* ones) is much higher than the ceiling to be able to litigate without a lawyer, many cases in Special Courts will also require legal representation. Moreover, the Brazilian Superior Tribunal of Justice has decided that a judge can issue a condemnation above those limits in Special Courts, and even companies can litigate there. Some argue that the high thresholds in Special Courts have a deleterious effect on access to justice, as they have become as clogged as regular courts. See A. Goldemberg, 'Juizado Especial Cível: Reflexos do elevado limite do valor da causa', Ambra, 9 May 2012, available at: https://blog.ambracollege.com/juizado-especial-civel-reflexos-do-elevado-limite-do-valor-da-causa/, accessed 22 June 2019.

[50] See IPEA, *Diagnóstico sobre os Juizados Especiais Cíveis* (Brasília: IPEA, 2013), mentioning also access problems such as geographical locations that are difficult to reach and a lack of infrastructure to attend the population. The study looked at Special Courts in the states of Amapá, Ceará and Rio de Janeiro.

[51] There is an increasing trend for private lawyers, especially in large firms, to also litigate pro bono. Studies about the magnitude of such work do not exist as far as I am aware, but I assume it does not represent a significant proportion of a lawyer's time. Until very recently, the National Bar Council (OAB) prohibited pro bono litigation. Those closely

further subdivided into two types: *public defenders* (*defensores públicos*, who are members of the Public Defensory – Defensoria Pública, or simply DP) and *public prosecutors* (*promotores* and *procuradores públicos*, members of the Ministério Público, Attorney General's Office, or simply MP). Public defenders' constitutional remit is to provide legal services and representation in court in any type of case for the so-called needy (*necessitados*), defined by law as those unable to afford the costs of litigation.[52] As we shall see below, how 'need' in this technical sense ought to be assessed and determined is a matter of dispute. Public prosecutors, as well as their traditional role of prosecuting crimes, are also tasked since the 1988 Constitution with the somewhat vague missions of 'protection of the legal order', 'protection of the democratic regime' and 'protection of individual and social inalienable interests' as well as protection of several vulnerable groups (children and adolescents, the elderly, the disabled, workers, indigenous people, consumers) and the environment.[53] One can easily imagine the large scope for interpretational disputes that such broadly defined functions give rise to, but public prosecutors have developed and consolidated a vast array of specialist areas of intervention over the last three decades, one of which

involved with the campaign to establish pro bono advocacy in Brazil share my assumption that it is not yet very developed in Brazil. (Interview with Oscar Vilhena Vieira, London, 9 May 2019).

52 Article 134 of the 1988 Constitution: 'Art. 134. The Public Defender's Office is a permanent institution, essential to the jurisdictional function of the State, entrusted with, fundamentally, legal guidance, the promotion of human rights and the defence, judicial and extrajudicial, of individual and collective rights, comprehensively and for free, to those in need, as an expression and instrument of the democratic regime, in the form of clause LXXIV of art. 5 of this Federal Constitution.' Clause LXXIV of the Constitution reads as follows: 'LXXIV. The State will provide full and free legal assistance to those who prove insufficiency of resources.' My own translation.

53 Article 127 of the 1988 Constitution: 'Article 127. The Attorney General's Office is a permanent institution, essential to the jurisdictional function of the State, which is responsible for defending the legal order, the democratic regime and the inalienable social and individual interests.' Unlike in some countries, public prosecutors are not only entrusted with criminal cases but have a whole set of other attributions, such as the protection of the environment, children, the elderly, the disabled, the consumer and of so-called collective and diffuse interests, which includes public health. There is some dispute about whether public prosecutors should also initiate individual litigation or should only focus on collective suits. The fact is that many do represent single individuals in health litigation, as studies show. See, as an example, O. H. Campos Neto et al., 'Doctors, Lawyers and Pharmaceutical Industry on Health Lawsuits in Minas Gerais', (2012) 46 *Revista de Saúde Pública*, 784–790, showing public prosecutors in many cases requesting certain drugs for individuals (Tiotropium bromide, Clopidogrel, Losartan).

is the protection of both society and individuals in public health issues. Unlike public defenders, whose main role is to represent claimants in court at their request, public prosecutors have greater autonomy in defining their own portfolio of cases as they act on their own behalf, that is, without the need of a mandate by any claimant. In other words, their standing is institutional.

If we want to gauge how easy or difficult it is for claims based on the right to health to reach the courts, we need to investigate in some detail these three main conduits of litigation: private lawyers, public defenders and public prosecutors. How accessible are these legal professionals in Brazil? How proactive and well-resourced are public defenders and public prosecutors in the field of health? Here lies a very important key to the understanding of the drivers and social impact of health litigation in Brazil.

Availability of Legal Advice and Representation

An important initial piece of information is the actual numbers of legal professionals actively working in each of the three different categories in relation to the size of the population, that is, in per capita terms. The more professionals per capita the greater the likelihood, in principle (*ceteris paribus*), that they will be available to take right to health claims to the courts. As we shall see, private lawyers are by far the largest group among the three types of lawyers under consideration here, followed very distantly by public prosecutors. In third place, we find public defenders, the youngest of the three institutions and the latest to be properly recognised and organised as an essential part of the justice system.

Private Lawyers Brazil is a veritable haven of private lawyers. According to some studies, it is the third country in the world in absolute numbers of these professionals (behind only India and the United States) and the first in per capita terms (see Figure 6.5).[54] It has breached the one

[54] See R. Duran, 'Lawyers and Law Schools in Brazil', *The Brazil Business*, 13 February 2014, https://thebrazilbusiness.com/article/lawyers-and-law-schools-in-brazil. See also FGV Exame da Ordem em Números for interesting data on the socioeconomic profile of those seeking to be admitted to the Bar, available at: www.conjur.com.br/2015-mai-29/pesquisa-fgv-mostra-perfil-candidatos-exame-ordem. It is also interesting to note that Brazil is perhaps one of the few countries to celebrate every year the Day of the Lawyer, on 11 August, the date when the first two Faculties of Law were established in Brazil back in 1827, one in São Paulo and another in Recife, for more information, see: www.scielo.br/scielo.php?pid=S0104-87752017000200419&script=sci_abstract&tlng=pt, all above accessed 22 June 2019.

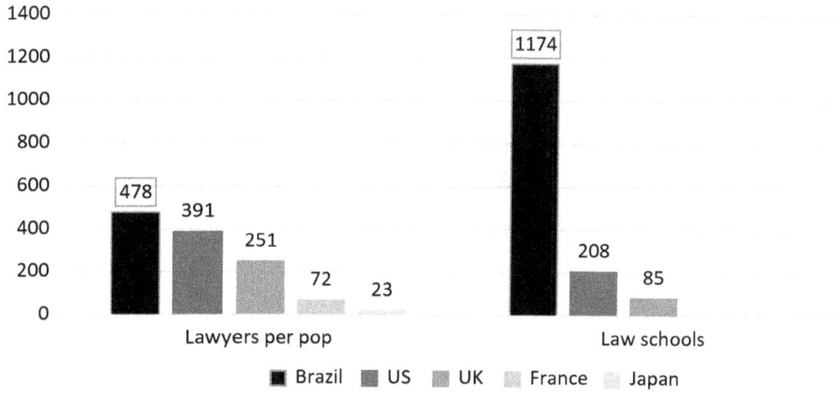

Figure 6.5 Number of lawyers per 100,000 inhabitants and absolute number of law schools.

Source: Own formulation with data from the Brazilian Bar Association, 2018, Nexo Jornal, 2017 and Harvard 2010[55]

million barrier in 2016, which, in per capita terms, means one lawyer for every 209 inhabitants, or 478 per 100,000 inhabitants, to use a more common measure.[56] For comparison, in the United States, renowned for being a very litigious society, the ratio is 391 per 100,000; in the United Kingdom, it is 251 per 100,000. Brazil is apparently also the country with the largest number of law schools in the world, a staggering 1,174 (208 in the United States for a population 30 per cent larger than the Brazilian; 85 in the United Kingdom for a population between three and four times smaller).[57]

We should of course not jump to the conclusion that private lawyers are therefore easily accessible in Brazil to represent potential claimants in right to health litigation. Availability and accessibility are not the same thing. These aggregate numbers tell us little about their distribution

[55] OAB, Cadastro Nacional de Advogados, available at: www.oab.org.br, accessed 22 June 2019; also see: J. M. Ramseyer, E. B. Rasmusen, 'Comparative Litigation Rates', Discussion Paper No. 681/11, John M. Olin Center for Law, Economics, and Business, Harvard Law School (2010), at 5.

[56] The most updated data shows already 1,131,769 lawyers registered in Brazil, available at: www.oab.org.br/institucionalconselhofederal/quadroadvogados, accessed 4 April 2019.

[57] B. Lupion, 'Por que o Brasil tem tantos advogados', *Nexo Jornal*, 2 November 2017, available at: www.nexojornal.com.br/expresso/2017/01/02/Por-que-o-Brasil-tem-tantos-advogados, accessed 1 December 2018.

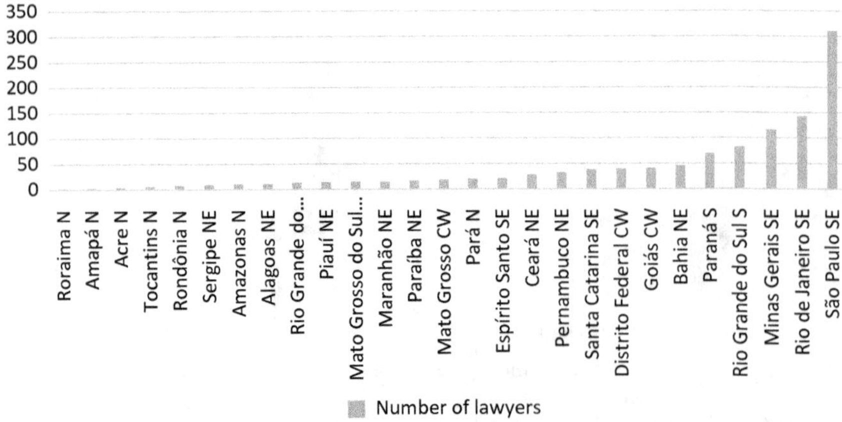

Figure 6.6 Number of lawyers in Brazil by state, in thousands, 2019.
Source: OAB, 2019

across the country and their costs, two important indicators of accessibility.[58] When we disaggregate the data by state, we find a concentration of private lawyers in the Southeastern states of São Paulo (310,851 lawyers), Rio de Janeiro (142,675), Minas Gerais (116,338) and the Southern states of Rio Grande do Sul (82,803), Paraná (69.259) and Santa Catarina (38.174), yet not as pronounced as we found with health litigation volume (see Chapter 5, Section 5.1). These seven states host together 760,000 lawyers (67 per cent of the total) and have an aggregate population of 56 per cent.[59] Moreover, as the total numbers are so high, there are plenty of lawyers elsewhere in the country as well, including in the less developed states of the North and Northeast, such as Bahia (45,413), Pernambuco (32,612), Ceará (28,818), Pará (19,506) and Amazonas (10,663). The least developed region of the Northeast counts 185,238 lawyers, that is, 326 per 100,000 inhabitants, similar to the ratio in the United Kingdom as we saw above.

It seems plausible to conclude, thus, that lack of private lawyers is not, per se, an important barrier to right to health litigation in Brazil, not even

[58] Not all of them, moreover, actually practice, though data on this is hard to collect. The numbers reported by the Bar Association are of those regularly registered and therefore apt to practice.

[59] Official data from the Brazilian Bar Association, available at: www.oab.org.br/institucionalconselhofederal/quadroadvogados, accessed 4 April 2019.

in the less developed states of the North and the Northeast. What may and does prevent large sections of the population from accessing private lawyers is their high average fees vis-à-vis the average income of the population, as we shall see in Section 6.4.3. The accessibility of state lawyers' services become even more relevant to the opportunity structure of legal mobilisation in such a scenario.

State Lawyers Public defenders and public prosecutors are much less abundant than private lawyers in Brazil. Let us start with public defenders, who, according to available studies, are behind a relatively high proportion of health claims in some states across the country (see Figure 7.2 in Chapter 7) and whose remit, as we saw, is to represent those who are 'needy', that is, unable to afford the costs of litigation.

It falls to each state, and to the Federal Union, to organise its own Public Defensory and define the parameters of neediness through a threshold that sets the so-called presumption of economic necessity. In most states across the country, it is fixed at three times the official monthly minimum wage, currently just below R$3,000 (roughly US$800 or £600 at the time of writing).[60] As we shall see in greater detail below, this is a relatively high threshold when compared to more traditional thresholds of socioeconomic deprivation or even the average monthly income of the Brazilian population (R$1,373 in 2018). To highlight this point, I will refer to 'legal need', 'legal neediness' and the 'legally needy' when talking about the population that qualifies for the services of the Public Defensory.[61]

[60] See for the shift of parameters of neediness in the Public Defender's Office, G. F. Oliveira, 'A alteração dos parâmetros objetivos de hipossuficiência das pessoas naturais no âmbito da DPU, Blog Ebeji', https://blog.ebeji.com.br/a-alteracao-dos-parametros-objetivos-de-hipossuficiencia-das-pessoas-naturais-no-ambito-da-dpu/. See for the Rio de Janeiro Public Defender's Office, www.defensoria.rj.def.br/legislacao/detalhes/5485-DELIBERACAO-CS-DPGE-N%C2%BA-124-DE-20-DE-DEZEMBRO-DE-2017. See also Constitutional Amendment 80, 4 June 2014: www.planalto.gov.br/ccivil_03/constituicao/Emendas/Emc/emc80.htm#art1. At the Federal level, the threshold is currently R$2,000 (equivalent to approximately US$530 or £400 a month) for the income of the 'núcleo familiar'. See 'Resolução nº 134, de 07 de dezembro de 2016', available at: www.lex.com.br/legis_27403541_RESOLUCAO_N_133_DE_7_DE_DEZEMBRO_DE_2016.aspx and www.dpu.def.br/conselho-superior/resolucoes/37083-resolucao-n-134-de-07-de-dezembro-de-2016-fixa-o-valor-de-presuncao-de-necessidade-economica-para-fim-de-assistencia-juridica-integral-e-gratuita, all accessed 22 June 2019.

[61] Note that in the legislation of some states, the Public Defensory's remit is also described as to provide assistant to vulnerable populations, including children, the elderly, people with disabilities and women victims of domestic violence. It is not clear if

When looking at the per capita availability of public defenders, it is therefore necessary to focus on this restricted group of the population (the 'legally needy') and not the whole of the population. According to the Public Defensory, the minimum ideal number of public defenders to serve the legally needy population would be 1 defender for every 10,000 people, that is, 10 per 100,000 to use the metrics already employed above for private lawyers (recall that the ratio of private lawyers is 478 per 100,000 people, see Figure 6.6).

According to the most recent available data, there was a deficit of around 10,000 public defenders in Brazil at the end of 2017, almost twice the actual number currently active (around 5,800).[62] There is a severe shortage, thus, of public defenders in Brazil. And this seems to be a conservative estimate, in my view, for reasons that will become clearer when we look at the income profile of the Brazilian population later on (see Section 6.4.3).

The geographical distribution of public defenders (and of their deficit), is uneven across Brazil. The latest comprehensive study to map the deficit across all regions and states of the country was conducted by Instituto de Pesquisa Econômica Aplicada (the Institute of Applied Economic Research – IPEA) in 2013. It found a shortage of 10,791 public defenders across Brazil (see Figure 6.8). Seventy-two per cent of the 2,680 'comarcas' (administrative regions where at least one court is headquartered, or simply 'judicial district') had no public defender at all. The number of people potentially affected is huge: 17 million people in the Northeast, 2.7 million in the North, 5.1 million in the Centre-West, 13.9 million in the South and 13.8 million in the Southeast (see Figure 6.9). We are talking,

the income thresholds apply to these groups as well or not. See, as an example, the remit of DP in the state of Rio de Janeiro: www.defensoria.rj.def.br/legislacao/detalhes/5485-DELIBERACAO-CS-DPGE-N%C2%BA-124-DE-20-DE-DEZEMBRO-DE-2017, accessed 22 June 2019.

62 Although it is true that every year more posts are opened for public defenders across Brazil, the situation reported here is unlikely to have changed significantly in the past five years since the IPEA study. For more recent but much less comprehensive accounts of the persistent challenges of the DP to attend the population, see J. Piva, 'Quando a Justiça não alcança: Faltam quase 10 mil defensores públicos no Brasil', Lupa, 19 April 2017, reporting that the deficit remains near 10,000 and telling the poignant difficulties of Edineia, a 27-year-old, trying to use the services of the DP in the state of Goiás on behalf of her imprisoned brother and the story of Eudália's right to health litigation saga. Available at: http://piaui.folha.uol.com.br/lupa/2017/04/19/falta-defensoria-publica-brasil/, accessed 4 April 2019.

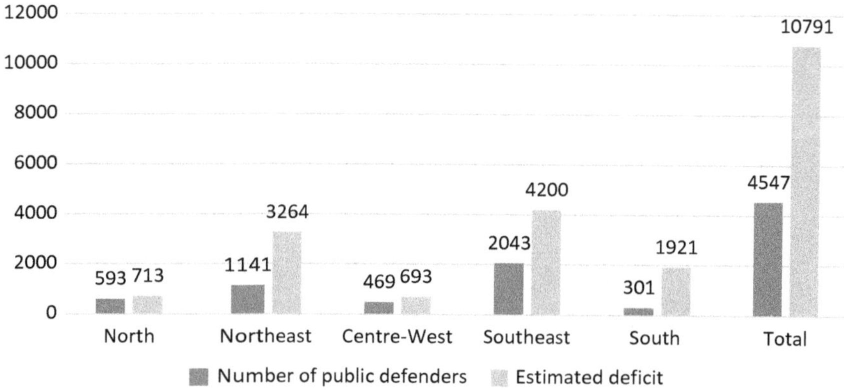

Figure 6.7 Number and estimated deficit of state public defenders by region and total.
Source: Own formulation with data from IPEA, 2013

thus, of almost *53 million* people who in 2013 resided in a place where no public defender was available within the corresponding judicial district. This is more than one quarter of the Brazilian population and 37 per cent of the 142.3 million people who qualified then for the services of the Public Defensory, that is, those earning less than three times the minimum wage. It is important to note that a judicial district can encompass several municipalities and cover a large territorial area, which creates a significant barrier to access to these services, as anyone intent on visiting a public defender will need to travel, often long distances, to do so (which assumes of course that they know the service is available in the first place ['rights awareness'], not to be taken for granted as discussed earlier in Section 6.4.1).

This large number of people with no or very restricted access to public defenders is in reality underestimated. To reach the 53 million figure, I counted only judicial districts with no *fixed* Public Defensory, excluding a large number of regions where public defenders come only from time to time (so-called *itinerant services*) and those where one single public defender covers more than one region. If we add the population who live in such regions to the total (roughly 6 million), we reach 59 million people with no or very limited access to the Public Defensory.[63]

[63] I have only discussed here public defenders of states, as the vast majority of right to health litigation promoted by the Public Defensory is represented by them. For a complete analysis, one would need to add also the Federal Public Defensory, yet the outcome would not change significantly given its much smaller size and similar problems of deficit. There

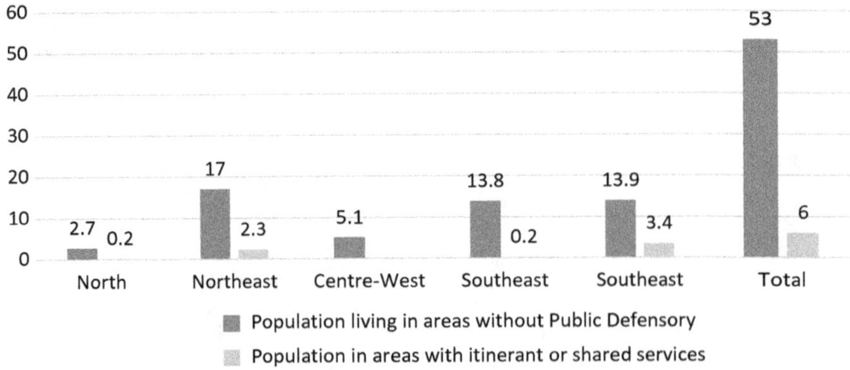

Figure 6.8 Population living in judicial districts without public defensory, in millions.
Source: Own formulation with data from IPEA, 2013[64]

The picture is not dissimilar as regards public prosecutors, the other kind of state lawyer in principle available to represent poorer claimants in right to health litigation. There were 12,193 such public prosecutors active in Brazil in 2017, a rate of 6.84 per 100,000 inhabitants, with significant regional variation in their geographical distribution, ranging from 4.17 in the northeastern state of Bahia to 11.65 in the northern state of Amapá.[65] Figures 6.9 and 6.10 display data on absolute and per capita numbers for the whole country.

Unfortunately, no comprehensive study of the deficit of public prosecutors by region is available as far as I could establish. From the data just cited and some further data easily accessible on the internet, however, it is possible to deduce that the shortage of public prosecutors, though

are currently 627 federal public defenders in Brazil, that is, about 10 per cent of the number of state public defenders. The deficit of federal public defenders is estimated at 70 per cent, a little higher than that of state public defenders. See: www.dpu.def.br/noticias-defensoria-publica-da-uniao/29526-numero-de-defensores-federais-cresce-mas-deficit-da-dpu-ainda-e-de-72, accessed 5 April 2019.

64 *Mapa da Defensoria Pública no Brasil*, (Brasília: IPEA, 2013), available at: www.ipea.gov.br/sites/en-GB/mapadefensoria/deficitdedefensores, accessed 4 April 2019.

65 *Ministério Público, Um Retrato*, Volume 7, dados 2017, Ano 2018 (Brasília: Conselho Nacional do Ministério Público, 2018), at 31, available at: www.cnmp.mp.br/portal/images/Anu%C3%A1rio_um_retrato_2017_internet.pdf, accessed 4 April 2019. I have excluded from the total 772 public prosecutors that deal exclusively with labour issues and 79 that deal exclusively with military issues.

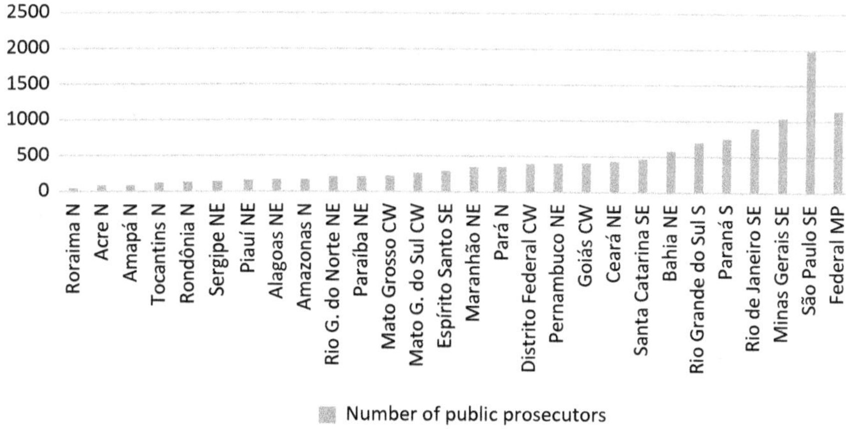

Figure 6.9 Number of public prosecutors total = 12,193.
Source: Own formulation with data from CNMP, 2018[66]

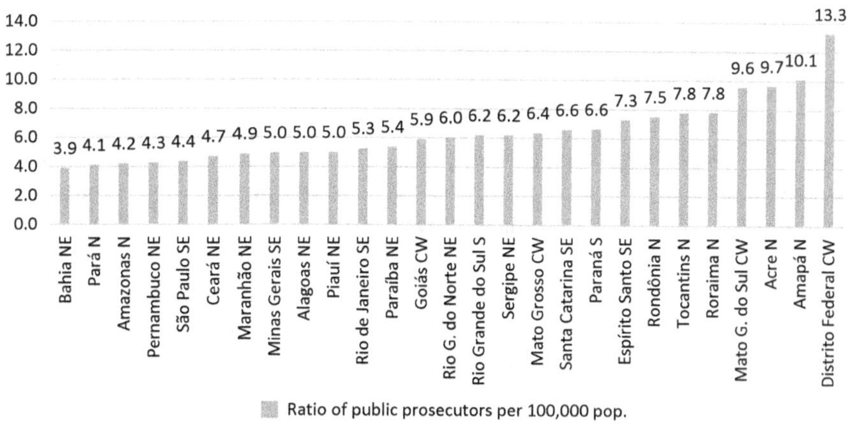

Figure 6.10 Ratio of public prosecutors per 100,000 pop.
Source: Own formulation with data from CNMP, 2018 and IBGE, 2019[67]

66 *Ministério Público, Um Retrato.*

67 The ratios per 100,000 in my chart are lower than those found in *Ministério Público, Um Retrato*, at 34–35, as I used updated IBGE data on the Brazilian population whereas the report used data from 2010, when the Brazilian population was roughly 10 per cent lower than in 2018.

smaller, is still significant and affects particularly badly some of the least developed states of the North and the Northeast. The shortage is particularly acute, for instance, in the northeastern states of Bahia, Ceará, Pernambuco, Alagoas and Piauí and the northern states of Amazonas, all of which have ratios of 5 prosecutors per 100,000 inhabitants or below. To compound the problem, the ratios vary significantly within states, being very low in some of the most deprived areas. Take the state of Amazonas as an example. According to the Conselho Nacional do Ministério Público (National Council of the Attorney General's Office – CNMP) report of 2018, there were 171 public prosecutors in total in Amazonas. A brief look at their webpage shows that at least 102 (60 per cent) are located in the capital, Manaus, whereas the other 61 judicial districts of that huge state share the remainder 40 per cent or so. In Santo Antônio do Içá, one of the most deprived areas, with a Human Development Index of 0.409 (very low), there is only one public prosecutor for the circa 41,560 inhabitants, or 2.4 per 100,000 inhabitants.

***

The picture of the raw availability of legal representation that emerges in this section does not in itself provide sufficient information for us to reach any definite conclusions about what ultimately interests us, that is, how *accessible* the three existing types of legal representation are in Brazil. It does however help us to add an important piece to the puzzle. Given that most potential right to health claims will require legal advice and legal representation to materialise into a concrete lawsuit, availability of legal services is an important indicator of prima facie accessibility. In places where more legal services are available, they will also tend to be more accessible.

As we saw, private lawyers are infinitely more abundant in Brazil than public defenders and public prosecutors. On average there are 478 private lawyers per 100,000 population and only 3.4 public defenders and 5.3 public prosecutors. Table 6.1 provides the data for all states in the country. The discrepancy (probably underestimated) is colossal and likely to affect accessibility to legal services across the country, especially limiting access to public defenders and prosecutors who are not only very low in numbers but also sparsely distributed across the country.[68]

[68] To calculate the ratio of public defenders, I used only the subgroup in the population that can use their services, that is, those earning less than three times the minimum wage, whereas for private lawyers and public prosecutors I used the whole population. If we calculate the ratio of private lawyers using only the subgroup whose income is, say, in the

I will go back to this issue later at the conclusion. Before that, we need to further refine the picture so far provided by looking at two other factors that may affect people's opportunity structure for legal mobilisation: the geographical distribution of courts (in particular, small claims courts, that is 'Special Courts') and the financial capacity of potential litigants to afford not only lawyers' fees but the other inevitable costs involved in initiating and sustaining litigation.

Geographical Distribution of Courts

The preceding sections have shown how private lawyers, public defenders and public prosecutors (i.e., the professionals that can provide legal advice and representation in right to health litigation) are very unevenly distributed across Brazil. It has also become clear how the latter two, on which most of the population depends, are much scarcer than the former, whose services can be afforded only by a minority, as we shall see in Section 6.4.3. We must now complete the picture with an analysis of the availability of courts (i.e., judges) across the country, as this is obviously also relevant for access to justice.

To assess the availability of judges, we need to look into the same two main factors already discussed in relation to lawyers: (i) their geographical distribution across the country and (ii) their numbers in relation to the population they serve. There may be plenty of judges in a country. If most are sitting in a building in the capital hundreds of miles away from where a large proportion of the population lives, their accessibility will be significantly limited.[69] Conversely, the distribution of judges across a country may be very good yet their numbers so low in relation to the population they should serve that their availability and accessibility will be rather restricted. Availability and accessibility of judges (or any resource for that matter) requires both sufficient numbers, physical reach[70] and, most importantly, resources, in particular, financial resources, the topic of Section 6.4.3.

so-called class A of income (see Figure 6.13), the 12.8 million people (6.19 per cent of the population) earning above R$3,566, the average ratio would go up to a staggering 8,841 private lawyers per 100,000 inhabitants in Brazil.

69 Recall that I distinguish availability from accessibility as the latter involves many other additional factors such as money, time, etc., discussed under Resources below (see Section 6.4.3).

70 Physical reach may of course diminish in importance with information technology. Yet, I believe it is plausible to assume it will remain a relevant factor for some time yet, especially in unequal countries where large sections of the population don't have access to

As the data reveal, the availability of judges is better than the availability of public defenders and public prosecutors, but not that much, and still way below the availability of lawyers. Brazil's judicial system, as we saw earlier, is organised around so-called comarcas (I call them simply 'judicial districts' here). These are geographical areas encompassing one or more (often several) municipalities, in which at least one judge is located.[71] A judicial district may have a single judge or several, depending on its territorial size and population, and these can be located all in the same municipality or even in the same building, or in several municipalities within the judicial districts. Each of these buildings, called 'fóruns', can hold, again, one or more judges, depending on factors such as territorial size and population density. To illustrate, the city of São Paulo, the largest in population in Brazil (12.1 million), is a judicial district (comarca) with several judicial units, including ten just in the centre and another twelve regional units spread across the city.[72] Some of them, such as the largest for civil and family law issues, Fórum João Mendes Jr, houses hundreds of judges.[73] At the other end of the spectrum, there are thousands of small places across the country with only a few judges, some with only one. I will call each of these buildings (fóruns) a 'judicial unit' (unidades judiciárias), following the classification of official statistics.

Let us start, then, by looking at the population density of judicial units and judges across Brazil. The report of the Conselho Nacional de Justiça (National Council of Justice – CNJ) *Justiça em Números* (*Justice in*

that technology. According to the most recent available data, more than 25 per cent of households in Brazil had no access to the internet. Most people have access through mobile phones though, as only 43.4 per cent of households have microcomputers and 13.7 per cent tablets. See IBGE, Estatísticas Sociais, 'PNAD Contínua TIC 2017: Internet chega a três em cada quatro domicílios do país', IBGE, 20 December 2018, available at: https://agenciadenoticias.ibge.gov.br/agencia-sala-de-imprensa/2013-agencia-de-noticias/releases/23445-pnad-continua-tic-2017-internet-chega-a-tres-em-cada-quatro-domicilios-do-pais, accessed 8 May 2019.

71 The actual number of 'comarcas' is not clear. Some refer to 2,682. L. Aquino, 'O Território como Referência para (Re)pensar o Judiciário: O caso da Justiça da Infância e da Juventude', in IPEA (eds.), *Boletim de Análise Potítico-Institucional* (Brasília: IPEA, 2012), at 61, available at: http://repositorio.ipea.gov.br/bitstream/11058/6756/2/BAPI_n02_p61-67_NP_Territorio_Diest_2012-ago.pdf, accessed 5 April 2019.

72 Information from Instituto Brasileiro de Geografia e Estatística, available at: https://cidades.ibge.gov.br/brasil/sp/sao-paulo/panorama, accessed 8 May 2019.

73 See the list at Fóruns Centrais e Regionais, Tribunal de Justiça do Estado de São Paulo, available at: www.tjsp.jus.br/Download/PrimeiraInstancia/FolhetosInformativos/Capital/FolhetoForunsCentraiseRegionais.pdf, accessed 8 May 2019.

Numbers) provides a good initial picture.[74] According to the latest report, there were 15,398 first instance judicial units in Brazil at the end of 2017. Of those, 10,035 (65.2 per cent) were state ones; 2,771 (18 per cent) were electoral ones, 1,572 (10.2 per cent) were labour courts and 988 (6.4 per cent) were federal ones. The remaining 0.2 per cent, or 32 units, were military courts. For our purposes, we should focus only on state and federal judicial units (i.e., discard electoral and labour units as they cannot process right to health cases). We must also exclude courts that deal exclusively with criminal prosecutions (1,348) and penal execution (113), reaching a final number of 11,023 judicial units (10,035 state and 988 federal) across the country in principle apt to process right to health litigation and 12,417 state judges and 1,939 federal ones, a total of 14,356. As a first inference from the data, we can note that there is approximately 1 judicial unit for every 19,000 inhabitants or, to keep using the indicator employed above for lawyers, there are 5.3 judicial units per 100,000 inhabitants on average in Brazil. Of this total number of units, 1,606 are Special Courts ('small claims'), that is, 14.5 per cent of the total. In per capita terms, there is one Special Court for every 130,000 inhabitants, or 0.8 per 100,000.

If we take the number of judges instead of judicial units, these ratios go up a little, as there is on average 1.3 judges for each judicial unit in Brazil. There are therefore 6.9 judges per 100,000 inhabitants in the country as a whole. If we focus only on Special Courts, there are 5,577 judges (4,474 state and 1,103 federal), that is, 1 per 37,384 inhabitants, or 2.7 per 100,000 inhabitants.

But these aggregate numbers, low by international comparisons, do not tell us enough.[75] As with lawyers, the geographical distribution of judicial units is far from balanced across Brazil (see Figure 6.11). The states of the South and Southeast are the leaders in absolute

[74] There is no clear definition of 'judicial unit' in the report, but one can assume from several passages that it refers to each separate facility where one can find a first instance judge. Of the state and federal units, the ones that deal with right to health litigation, 1,391 are state small claims courts and 215 federal small claims courts ('Juizados Especiais'). See: Conselho Nacional de Justiça, *Justiça em Números 2018* (Brasília: CNJ, 2018), at 31.

[75] See Ramseyer, Rasmusen, 'Comparative Litigation Rates', at 17, reporting the number in the United States to be 10.81, but 2.83 in Japan and 2.22 in England and Wales. According to other sources, Germany's rate is around 25, Costa Rica, 26, Chile, 10.4 and Argentina, 4.9. See https://en.actualitix.com/country/wld/professional-judges.php, accessed 22 June 2019.

number of judicial units, which is expected as they are also amongst the most populous. When adjusted by population size, we find much less discrepancy among the big regions than we did with health litigation. There are 5,213 judicial units in the South and the Southeast (51.9 per cent of the total); 3,751 in the North and the Northeast (37.3 per cent) and 1,071 in the Centre-West (10.7 per cent).[76] A higher discrepancy appears, though, when we disaggregate the data by state and municipality. The states with the lowest number of judicial units per population are the northern ones of Amazonas and Pará and the southeastern one of Rio de Janeiro. The states with the lowest number of judges per population are Alagoas (NE), Pará (N) and Bahia (NE). At the other end of the ranking we see Mato Grosso (CW), Roraima (N) and Espírito Santo (SE) as those with the highest number of judicial units per population and Distrito Federal (CW), Rondônia (N) and Amapá (N) as leaders in the number of judges by population. Table 6.1 shows data for all states.

This indicator is rather useful to give us an initial idea of the density of the judicial system across Brazil, but it is still a little crude for our purposes of assessing the availability of judges to the population. We can already see that even in the comparatively better states, the density of judicial units and, most importantly, judges, is not very high, though slightly higher in some states than the ratio of public defenders and public prosecutors (see, for comparison, Table 6.1).[77]

To achieve a sharper picture of availability and accessibility we need to try to disaggregate the data further. As Brazil is such a vast country (8.5 million square km), each of its states, including the smallest, Piauí, with 22,000 square km, is larger than many whole countries around the world.[78] Some of its largest states are colossal, such as Amazonas (1.5

[76] Recall, from Chapter 5, that the distribution of the population among these regions is 57 per cent SE and S, 36 per cent NE and N, and 7 per cent CW.

[77] One of the main limitations for the expansion of the Brazilian judicial system is its very high costs, driven mainly by the very high salaries of judges, public prosecutors and public defenders, higher than in richer countries than Brazil, such as France, Germany and Sweden. For illustration, whereas the Brazilian judicial system consumes 1.30 per cent of the GDP with what we saw are very limited services, Germany consumes 0.32 per cent, the United Kingdom, 0.14 per cent, Chile, 0.22 per cent and Argentina 0.13 per cent. See the superb discussion of this issue by Luciana Zaffalon, L. Z. L. Cardoso, *A Política da Justiça: Blindar as Elites, Criminalizar os Pobres* (São Paulo: Hucitec, 2018), at 240ff.

[78] To illustrate with examples from Europe, Piauí is much larger than Malta, Luxembourg and Cyprus, a bit larger than Slovenia (circa 20,000 sq km) and only 25 per cent smaller than Belgium (circa 30,000 sq km).

Table 6.1 *Ratio of public defenders, public prosecutors and private lawyers per 100,000 inhabitants*

	Public defenders	Public prosecutors	Private lawyers	Judges	Population
Brazil	3.4	5.3	481.8	8.2	**208,494,900**
Acre (N)	8.4	9.7	389.9	4.5	869,265
Alagoas (NE)	3.0	5.0	340.8	9.4	3,322,820
Amapá (N)	18.8	10.1	369.0	5.1	829,494
Amazonas (N)	1.7	4.2	261.3	3.9	4,080,611
Bahia (NE)	1.9	3.9	306.6	4.9	14,812,617
Ceará (NE)	3.7	4.7	317.5	13.1	9,075,649
Distrito Federal (CW)	11.7	13.3	1328.7	8.6	2,974,703
Espírito Santo (SE)	5.4	7.3	526.0	6.1	3,972,388
Goiás (CW)	1.3	5.9	582.5	4.7	6,921,161
Maranhão (NE)	2.0	4.9	214.6	8.4	7,035,055
Mato Grosso (CW)	6.0	6.4	540.3	7.8	3,441,998
Mato Grosso do Sul (CW)	8.1	9.6	528.5	4.9	2,748,023
Minas Gerais (SE)	3.9	5.0	552.9	4.0	21,040,662
Pará (N)	4.5	4.1	229.1	6.9	8,513,497
Paraíba (NE)	8.9	5.4	412.2	7.9	3,996,496
Paraná (S)	1.0	6.6	610.3	5.7	11,348,937
Pernambuco (NE)	1.9	4.3	343.4	5.5	9,496,294
Piauí (NE)	3.1	5.0	413.5	5.3	3,264,531
Rio de Janeiro (SE)	6.3	5.3	831.4	7.1	17,159,960
Rio Grande do Norte (NE)	1.6	6.0	364.8	7.2	3,479,010
Rio Grande do Sul (S)	3.8	6.2	730.9	10.0	11,329,605
Rondônia (N)	3.1	7.5	437.0	9.2	1,757,589
Roraima (N)	11.7	7.8	341.9	7.0	576,568
Santa Catarina (SE)	2.2	6.6	539.5	5.8	7,075,494
São Paulo (SE)	1.9	4.4	682.6	6.7	45,538,936

Table 6.1 (*cont.*)

	Public defenders	Public prosecutors	Private lawyers	Judges	Population
Sergipe (NE)	4.4	6.2	408.9	8.3	2,278,308
Tocantins (N)	9.0	7.8	405.7	8.2	1,555,229

Source: Own formulation with data from IPEA, 2013, CNMP, 2018, OAB, 2019, CNJ, *Justice in Numbers*, 2018[79]

million sq km), Pará (1.2 million), Minas Gerais (586,000) and Bahia (564,000) to cite just the four largest. To effectively gauge the availability and accessibility of judges for the population in each of these states, we need to know much more about where judicial units and judges are located.[80] From the map produced by the CNJ (Figure 6.11) we have a good visual perspective and can see that judicial units concentrate significantly on the coast, leaving vast areas of the hinterland uncovered. This is again expected, as the Brazilian population has historically concentrated on the coast.[81] But the concentration is clearly disproportionate, as we shall see further below.

79 As four states did not have a Public Defensory at the time of IPEA's comprehensive study in 2013, namely, Alagoas, Goiás, Paraná and Santa Catarina, I used the numbers provided by the Ministry of Justice in its *IV Diagnóstico da Defensoria Pública no Brasil* (Brasília: Ministério da Justiça, 2015). As the numbers for public defenders were collected in 2013 (twenty-three states) and 2015 (the four mentioned states), it is possible that the table underestimates the current ratio, as we know the numbers went up in some states. I decided to use these numbers because they are the most comprehensive and official and also because they probably underestimate only slightly the ratios. The population used by IPEA in its study was 190,755,799, whereas in 2018, it was already 208,494,900, a 9.3 per cent increase. The slightly higher number of private lawyers per 100,000 inhabitants reported in this table in comparison to Figure 6.5 is due to the use of a more updated primary source here.

80 Whether to establish judicial districts or units in distant and lowly populated areas is a debatable question that involves a trade-off between more access to courts and resources (similar issues arise of course with any public service, such as health, education, etc.). See: G1 Ceará, 'Poder Judiciário aprova o fechamento de 34 comarcas no Ceará', Globo, 3 July 2017, available at: https://g1.globo.com/ceara/noticia/poder-judiciario-aprova-o-fechamento-de-34-comarcas-no-ceara.ghtml, for the type of debate entailed when judicial districts are closed, accessed 23 June 2019.

81 The construction of Brasília and the move of the capital there from Rio de Janeiro was of course in part an effort to populate the hinterland. For the persistent concentration of the population on the coast, see: *Mapa de Densidade Demográfica de 2010* (Rio de Janeiro: Instituto Brasileiro de Geografia e Estatística, 2010).

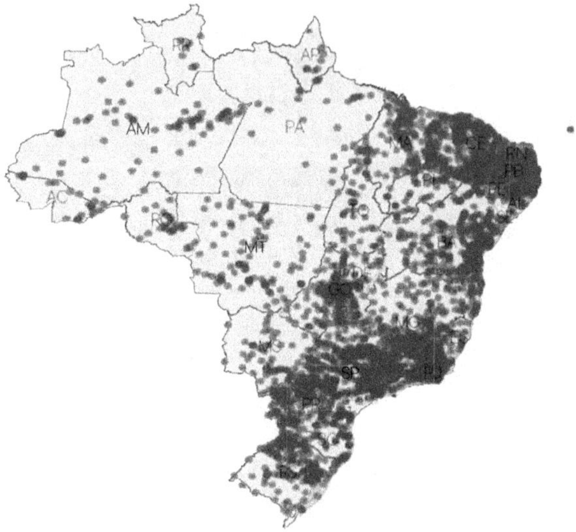

Figure 6.11 Distribution of judicial units across the Brazilian territory.
Source: CNJ, 2018, p. 24

Another important piece of information would be the concentration of judicial units and judges in the capitals and other municipalities of each state.[82] The CNJ report unfortunately does not provide the exact number of judges by municipality as we have for public defenders. It is plausible to assume, however, that some municipalities, in particular, the twenty-seven capitals, do overconcentrate judicial units and judges. The CNJ report provides the number of municipalities within each state where judicial units are headquartered. They add up to 2,697 according to the latest data, covering therefore just about 48.4 per cent of Brazilian municipalities.[83] It is possible to conclude, thus, that the population living in half of the municipalities in Brazil either need to travel to go to a court or need to wait for the so-called itinerant courts to visit their municipality, which is not a regular occurrence and often not an

[82] The most recent census established that 24 per cent of Brazilians live in the capitals. See D. Silveira, 'Brasil tem mais de 208,5 milhões de habitantes, segundo o IBGE, G1', 29 August 2018, available at: https://g1.globo.com/economia/noticia/2018/08/29/brasil-tem-mais-de-208-milhoes-de-habitantes-segundo-o-ibge.ghtml, accessed 22 June 2019.

[83] New judicial districts are created and closed from time to time. As you will recall from the IPEA study on public defenders cited above, there were 2,682 judicial districts in Brazil in 2013. IPEA, *Mapa da Defensoria Pública no Brasil.*

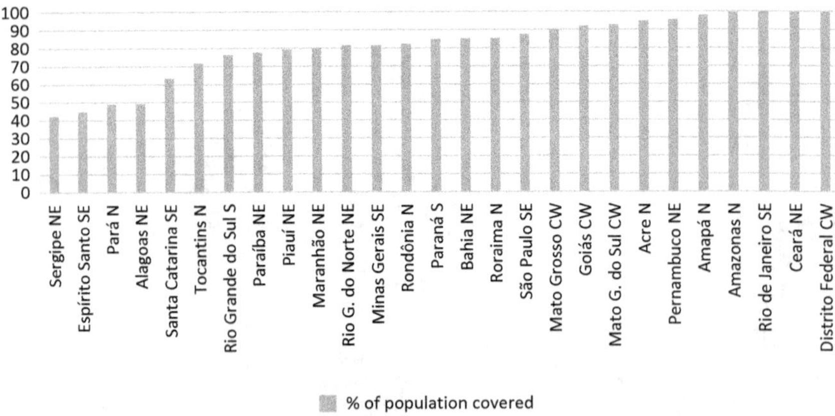

Figure 6.12 Percentage of population living in municipalities where a judicial unit is headquartered, by state.
Source: CNJ, *Justice in Numbers*, 2018

occurrence at all.[84] In terms of how many people are in that unfavourable situation, it varies from state to state, from as many as 57.8 per cent of the population in Sergipe (NE), to as little as 0.3 per cent in Ceará (NE). Figure 6.12 shows the percentage in all 27 states.

One should be cautious not to conclude, too hastily, that the percentages in Figure 6.12 translate perfectly into levels of access to courts. Although having to travel across municipalities is in itself a barrier, the magnitude of such a barrier will differ of course according to other factors, such as the actual distance of their residence to the nearest court and the availability and costs of transport, which can vary a lot in Brazil given the large differences in the territorial area and transport infrastructure among states. In a comparatively smaller (in territorial terms), densely populated and more developed state like São Paulo, where municipalities have an average size of 384 sq km and an average density

84 The establishment of so-called Itinerant Justice was mandated by Constitutional Amendment 45, of 2004, which enacted the 'Judiciary's Reform' (and regulated by Law 12.726, of 2012, which changed Art. 95 of Law 9.099, of 1995) but which has so far been very inconsistently implemented. For empirical studies, see: *Democratização do acesso à Justiça e efetivação de direitos: A Justiça Itinerante no Brasil* (Brasília: Instituto de Pesquisa Econômica Aplicada, 2015); IPEA, L. S. Ferraz, 'Challenges and Limitations for Legal Empirical Research in Brazil: Exploring a Study on Itinerant Justice', (2017) 4(1) *Revista de Estudos Empíricos em Direito*, 37–56.

of 166.2 inhabitants per sq km, and where roads and the public transport system are reasonably well-developed, someone living in one of the 326 municipalities without a judicial unit will have comparatively lesser difficulties to reach a court than someone living in one of the larger states, such as Amazonas, where the average size of municipalities is 25,000 sq km (65 times larger than in São Paulo) and the population density is 2.23 inhabitants per sq km (75 times lower than São Paulo) and where the transport system is much less well-developed and some places are only accessible by boat or airplane.

What is also important, thus, and perhaps more so than the actual number of judicial units in a given state, is their geographical location, that is, their distance from the residence of the inhabitants (i.e., potential claimants). Even in densely populated states and cities where judicial units exist in reasonable numbers, their geographical location is likely to restrict access for large segments of the population given large distances, well-known limitations of the public transport system and incapacity of many to afford the time and costs of the required travel (see Section 6.4.3).[85]

***

The data on the availability and geographical distribution of judicial units and legal services (i.e., private lawyers, public defenders and public prosecutors) presented in this section add further important pieces to the overall picture of the opportunity structure for legal mobilisation in Brazil. The availability of these resources, as we saw, is significantly limited in general, as the numbers of public defenders, public prosecutors and, to a lesser extent, judges and judicial units is low in general and significantly so (often non-existent) in some areas of the country. The exception to this rule is private lawyers, the only resource that is available in relative abundance, as Brazil has the highest per capita ratio in the world (see Figure 6.5).

These significant limitations are compounded by a lack of rights awareness, as we saw in Section 6.4.1, and, as we shall see in Section 6.4.3, by lack of sufficient financial resources to initiate and sustain litigation by a large proportion of the Brazilian population.

[85] See IPEA, *Diagnóstico sobre os Juizados Especiais Cíveis*, emphasising the problems of geographical location.

6.4.3 Financial Resources

One may be deeply knowledgeable about one's rights, live right next door to a lawyer and a court and yet be incapable to resort to litigation as a tool to make claims against the state. The most likely reason for that is lack of the financial resources required to initiate and sustain litigation. Such resources are far from trivial, even for those who can in principle resort to the limited numbers of state funded lawyers available in the country.

Financial resources to initiate and sustain litigation include not only the direct costs of litigation (e.g., legal counsel's fees, court's fees, photocopy and other administrative expenses, etc.) but also what we may call indirect costs. These include time off work (to attend meetings with legal counsel, court hearings, preparation of documents to be used in court) and the costs of transportation, accommodation and subsistence expenses (which vary according to the distance of legal services and courts to the potential litigant's residence). I am not able to offer any precise figure of the costs that initiating and sustaining litigation entails – often through several years and instances of the Brazilian judiciary system. This will vary significantly anyway according to particular circumstances of the claimant, such as the distance of her place of residence from available legal services, the rate of legal counsel in the region, availability of state legal services, etc.. This final section will nonetheless provide further substantiation to a point I made at the beginning of the chapter, that is, that litigation is almost always a very limited, costly and unattractive option, for anyone, but especially for the poor.[86]

Let me start by providing an overview of the general level of income of the Brazilian population and the level of economic inequality among groups. As I have already emphasised in Chapter 4, Brazil is not a poor country.[87] Brazil is in fact what the World Bank classifies as a middle

[86] It is perhaps not surprising, thus, that a very limited number of actors feature in a large proportion of lawsuits in Brazil as plaintiffs (so-called repeat litigants). The finance system (i.e., banks) and the public administration at all levels (municipalities, states and the Federal Union) initiated 34.4 per cent of all lawsuits in state courts in Brazil in 2011. See: M. T. A. Sadek (ed.), *Acesso à Justiça no Brasil: Índice de Fragilidade dos Municípios* (2012), available at: www.cidadessustentaveis.org.br/arquivos/acessoajusticanobrasil.pdf, accessed 22 June 2019.

[87] See Chapter 4 for a more detailed discussion of Brazil's levels of poverty and inequality and its impact on health. For a very good summary of the data, see: IBGE, 'Síntese de Indicadores Sociais: Indicadores apontam aumento da pobreza entre 2016 e 2017', IBGE, 5 December 2018, available at: https://agenciadenoticias.ibge.gov.br/agencia-sala-de-

upper income country.[88] Yet, due to high levels of inequality, it still has a lot of poor people for its level of economic development. As we saw in Chapter 4, in 2017, almost 55 million people (26.5 per cent of the population) was below the national poverty line, of whom 15.2 million (7.4 per cent of the population) were under the lowest 'one dollar a day' threshold of extreme poverty of the World Bank.[89]

According to the latest official data from the Brazilian Institute of Geography and Statistics (IBGE), the average monthly income per capita in Brazil was R$1,373 (roughly US$350 or £270), varying significantly across the country from a very low R$605 (US$155 or £120) in the northeastern state of Maranhão to R$2,460 (US$635 or £490) in the Federal District (Centre-West).[90] These averages conceal further important variations between those at the top and those at the bottom in each state. To illustrate, let us use a standard measure of inequality, the income of the top 10 per cent and the bottom 40 per cent ratio.[91]

imprensa/2013-agencia-de-noticias/releases/23298-sintese-de-indicadores-sociais-indicadores-apontam-aumento-da-pobreza-entre-2016-e-2017, accessed 22 June 2019.

88 Upper middle-income economies are those with a GNI per capita between US$3,896 and US$12,055, Brazil's was US$8,600 in 2017, down from US$12,730 in 2013, see: https://data.worldbank.org/country/brazil for Brazil's data, and https://datahelpdesk.worldbank.org/knowledgebase/articles/906519-world-bank-country-and-lending-groups for the criteria of classification of countries. Both accessed 4 April 2019.

89 The national poverty line is calculated at US$5.50 dollars a day, adding up to R$406 a month in 2017. See: 'No Brasil,15,2 milhões vivem abaixo da linha da pobreza', IBGE, G1, 5 December 2018 https://g1.globo.com/jornal-nacional/noticia/2018/12/05/no-brasil-152-milhoes-vivem-abaixo-da-linha-da-extrema-pobreza-diz-ibge.ghtml, accessed 23 June 2019. The extreme poverty threshold is equivalent to R$140. To qualify for the Bolsa Família, the Brazilian conditional cash transfer programme, a person must prove to have income below R$85, or below R$170 if the family has children below the age of seventeen. See: Ministériodo Desenvolvimento Social, http://mds.gov.br/area-de-imprensa/noticias/2017/setembro/bolsa-familia-saiba-quais-sao-as-regras-para-participar-do-programa, accessed 10 May 2019.

90 The monthly median income per capita is equivalent to US$4,200 a year and US$11.50 a day (Brazil's average). In Maranhão, the poorest state, the median is US$1,860 a year and US$5.09 a day.

91 The so-called Palma ratio, defined as the ratio of the richest 10 per cent of the population's share of gross national income divided by the poorest 40 per cent's share, based on the work of Chilean economist Gabriel Palma. See J. G. Palma, 'Homogeneous Middles vs. Heterogeneous Tails, and the End of the 'Inverted-U': The Share of the Rich Is What It's All About', Cambridge Working Papers in Economics (CWPE) 1111 (2011), available at: www.repository.cam.ac.uk/bitstream/handle/1810/241870/cwpe1111.pdf;jsessionid=AC5FCB0249571F5EEEB23261583E6F8E?sequence=1. See also: A. Cobham, A. Sumner, 'Putting the Gini Back in the Bottle? "The Palma" As a Policy-Relevant Measure of Inequality', King's International Development Institute, King's College London (2013), available at: https://web.archive.org/web/20130423083249/https://www.kcl

Taking Brazil as a whole, we see that the average income of the bottom 40 per cent is R$376 (US$97 and £75) whereas those at the top 10 per cent average R$6,629 (US$1,716 or £1318), that is, 17.6 times higher.[92] For comparison, in the United Kingdom, which is one of the more unequal countries in Western Europe, the median income of the top 10 per cent is about four times the income of the bottom 40 per cent. The variation in income across the country is even larger. In the poorest state of Maranhão, the bottom 40 per cent average income is a meagre R$167 (US$43 and £33, or US$1.40 a day) whereas the top 10 per cent in the richest 'state' of Brasília (the Federal District), the average is R$13,905 (US$3,600 or £2,762, or US$118.30 a day), that is, 83.2 times more.

To have a better idea of the whole distribution of income in the country, we can make use of the concept of 'income classes' (or income groups) often used in the literature.[93] This approach divides the population into five socioeconomic classes (A to E), showing how many people or families fall into each of them. According to a recent study, the Brazilian population has 12.8 million people in the top income class A, 63.9 million in class B, 82.8 million in class C, 28.3 million in class D and 19.1 million in class E (see Figure 6.13).[94]

These data seem sufficient to demonstrate that economic incapacity is another, and perhaps the most important, barrier to litigation for a very large proportion of the Brazilian population. If we recall that the current minimum wage, which is deemed by many to be insufficient to cover even basic necessities, is currently R$998, we see that the vast majority of Brazilians (130.2 million, i.e. 62 per cent of the population) earn bellow

.ac.uk/aboutkings/worldwide/initiatives/global/intdev/people/Sumner/Cobham-Sumner-15March2013.pdf, both accessed 4 April 2019.

92 A Palma ratio of 3.5 in aggregate terms. According to IBGE, the top 10 per cent amassed 43.3 per cent of the total R$263.1 billion of the country's income in 2017. M. Benedicto, M. Marli, 'PNAD Contínua: 10% da população concentram quase metade da renda do país', IBGE, 11 April 2018, see: https://agenciadenoticias.ibge.gov.br/agencia-noticias/2012-agencia-de-noticias/noticias/20844-10-da-populacao-concentram-quase-metade-da-renda-do-pais, accessed 22 June 2019. See world ranking produced by the World Bank: http://hdr.undp.org/en/composite/IHDI, accessed 22 June 2019.

93 See, for instance, Fundação Getúlio Vargas, Centro de Políticas Sociais, available at: https://cps.fgv.br/qual-faixa-de-renda-familiar-das-classes, accessed 22 June 2019.

94 B. Villas Boas, 'Estudos apontam que até 900 mil pessoas deixaram classes A e B', *Valor Econômico*, 10 May 2018, available at: www.valor.com.br/brasil/5515501/estudos-apontam-que-ate-900-mil-pessoas-deixaram-classes-e-b, accessed 4 April 2019. Different studies use slightly different thresholds.

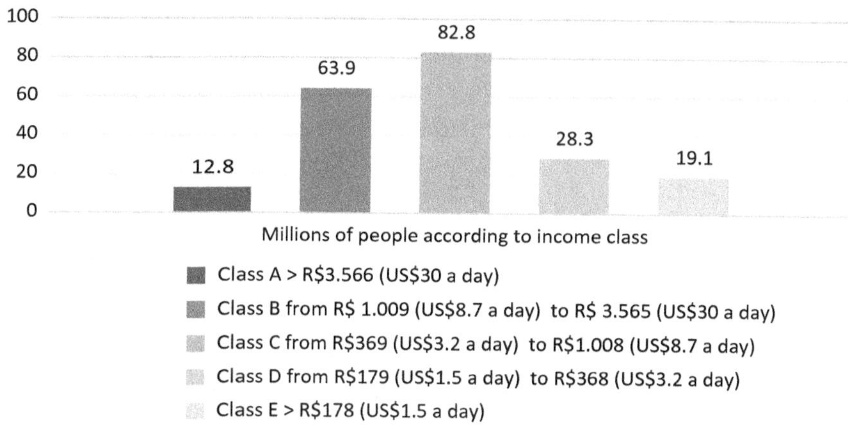

Figure 6.13 Distribution of Brazilian population by income 'classes'.
Source: Valor Econômico, 2018[95]

that threshold (i.e., all those in classes C, D and E).[96] Even the 63.9 million people belonging to class B, another 30 per cent of the population, earn just over 3.5 times the minimum wage (recall that the threshold to qualify for the free legal services of the Public Defensory is 3 times the minimum wage). There are approximately 190 million people in Brazil (over 90 per cent of the population), thus, who are deemed by law to be 'needy', that is, not to be sufficiently affluent to pay for private legal services without jeopardising their ability to afford basic necessities.

One may want to question if the threshold of the Public Defensory is not perhaps too high, especially in a country where, as we have seen, the vast majority does not earn even half that threshold and the availability of public defenders is so low (see Section 6.4.2). The problem is that any lower threshold would deprive millions of people from access to legal

[95] Ibid.

[96] Since 1994, the DIEESE – Departamento Intersindical de Estatística e Estudos Socioeconômicos (Trade Unions Department for Statistics and Socioeconomic Studies), a research body funded by trade unions, calculates what in their view would be the appropriate amount of the minimum wage in Brazil to cover basic necessities as determined by the Brazilian constitution. The value varies across the country, but it is more than three times higher than the official minimum wage. In São Paulo, the most expensive city, it should be R$3,928.73 according to the DIEESE, that is, 3.93 times higher than it is. See J. P. Caleiro, 'Salário mínimo "necessário" é quase quatro vezes maior do que o nominal', *Exame*, 10 February 2019.

services, as even those who earn at or above the DP's threshold would find it hard to afford the costs of private legal advice and representation, though they are comparatively rich by Brazilian standards.[97] An interesting recent study provides a good sense of the affordability of private legal services in Brazil. It compares the average income of the population in each state with the minimum hourly legal fees recommended by the corresponding state's Bar Association.[98] The fees varied widely, as predictable, yet not according to the expected criterion of affluence of the general population of the corresponding state. The highest fee was in the northeastern state of Piauí, one of the poorest of Brazil, at R$1,200/hour (US$311 or £240). This *hourly* rate is 20 per cent above the current *monthly* minimum wage in Brazil (R$998), almost 40 per cent above the average *monthly* income in Piauí (R$817) and almost 600 per cent above the average income of the bottom 40 per cent (R$209) in that state.[99] To afford a single hour of legal advice at the minimum price recommended by the local Bar, an individual earning the average income in Piauí would need to spend what he or she takes 1.4 months to earn.

Even if we discard Piauí as an aberration and take other states with more reasonable recommended minimum hourly fees and higher average income, we still find a generalised picture of very low accessibility to private legal services across the country. Table 6.2 shows what percentage of individuals *monthly* income the recommended *hourly* legal fees represents by different income groups in every state in Brazil. There are, as expected, significant variations, but even if we take only the 'most affordable', we can see that private legal services are not within the reach of the vast majority of the population.

Take one of the richest states in Brazil as an example, the southeastern state of São Paulo. One hour of legal advice at the local bar recommended rate would consume 15 per cent of the monthly income of the average 'paulista',[100] 52 per cent for someone at the bottom 40 per cent and

97 See, for example, Defensoria Pública da União, 'Perfil dos assistidos é tema de pesquisa realizada em Minas Gerais', https://dpu.def.br/noticias-minas-gerais/19977-perfil-dos-assistidos-e-tema-de-pesquisa-realizada-em-minas-gerais, accessed 22 June 2019.

98 K. Coura, S. Spagnuolo, 'Honorários: DF tem a tabela mais barata, PI, a mais cara', *Jota*, 7 April 2017, available at: www.jota.info/advocacia/honorarios-df-tem-a-tabela-mais-barata-pi-a-mais-cara-07042017, accessed 4 April 2019.

99 Brazil, Instituto Brasileiro de Geografia e Estatística – IBGE, Cidades e Estados, available at: www.ibge.gov.br/cidades-e-estados/ce.html, accessed 22 June 2019.

100 People who were born or who live in São Paulo.

Table 6.2 *Affordability of private legal services*

Recommended hourly *rate of private lawyers' fees as a percentage of average monthly income of population, by different income groups in all states of Brazil*

Brazilian states	Legal fees hourly rate recommended by local bar association in R$	Average monthly income by income groups in R$ and *hourly* legal fees as % of *monthly* income									
		Whole population		Bottom 20%		Bottom 40%		Top 20%		Top 10%	
Brazil	383	1,373	**28%**	203	**188%**	376	**102%**	4 491	**9%**	6 629	**6%**
Acre	140	909	15%	94	149%	200	70%	2 987	5%	4 422	3%
Alagoas	440	714	62%	104	423%	210	209%	2 356	19%	3 522	12%
Amapá	300	857	35%	136	221%	235	128%	3 621	8%	5 282	6%
Amazonas	350	791	44%	107	326%	214	164%	4 038	9%	6 446	5%
Bahia	240	841	29%	98	245%	212	113%	3 540	7%	5 601	4%
Ceará	350	855	41%	118	296%	230	152%	2 941	12%	4 435	8%
Distrito Federal	570	2460	23%	350	163%	583	98%	9 928	6%	13 905	4%
Espírito Santo	150	1295	12%	227	66%	397	38%	3 925	4%	5 666	3%
Goiás	280	1323	21%	283	99%	456	61%	4 098	7%	5 972	5%
Maranhão	300	605	50%	76	396%	167	179%	1 986	15%	2 890	10%
M. Grosso	420	1386	30%	301	140%	481	87%	3 759	11%	5 301	8%
M.G. do Sul	395	1439	27%	293	135%	480	82%	3 938	10%	5 456	7%
Minas Gerais	300	1322	23%	248	121%	424	71%	4 091	7%	5 969	5%
Pará	525	863	61%	123	428%	225	233%	2 498	21%	3 681	14%

Table 6.2 (*cont.*)

Brazilian states	Legal fees hourly rate recommended by local bar association in R$	Average monthly income by income groups in R$ and *hourly* legal fees as % of *monthly* income									
		Whole population		Bottom 20%		Bottom 40%		Top 20%		Top 10%	
Paraíba	280	898	31%	146	192%	261	107%	3 318	8%	5 031	6%
Paraná	300	1607	19%	333	90%	542	55%	4 640	6%	6 677	4%
Pernambuco	282	871	32%	126	224%	248	114%	2 995	9%	4 522	6%
Piauí	1200	817	147%	101	1187%	209	574%	2 531	47%	3 606	33%
Rio de Janeiro	980	1689	58%	290	337%	483	203%	4 975	20%	7 176	14%
Rio Grande N	440	956	46%	132	334%	255	172%	2 913	15%	4 199	10%
Rio Grande S	230	1705	13%	361	64%	599	38%	5 140	4%	7 335	**3%**
Rondônia	300	1113	27%	222	135%	368	81%	2 707	11%	3 724	8%
Roraima	620	1204	51%	163	380%	291	213%	3 574	17%	5 177	12%
Santa Catarina	350	1660	21%	462	76%	695	50%	4 421	8%	5 998	6%
São Paulo	290	1898	**15%**	331	**88%**	553	**52%**	5 831	5%	8 577	3%
Sergipe	150	906	17%	108	138%	230	65%	2 863	5%	4 185	4%
Tocantins	150	1045	14%	193	78%	323	46%	3 013	5%	4 386	3%

Source: Own formulation with data from Jota, 2017 and IBGE[a]

[a] See: www.ibge.gov.br/cidades-e-estados.html and www.ibge.gov.br/estatisticas-novoportal/sociais/populacao/9221-sintese-de-indicadores-sociais.html?=&t=resultados, accessed 22 June 2019.

88 per cent for someone at the bottom 20 per cent. If we take the Brazilian average, we would see these ratios go up to 188 per cent (bottom 20 per cent), 102 per cent (bottom 40 per cent) and 28 per cent (average income). Even those at the top 20 per cent and the top 10 per cent of income would not find it easy to afford private legal services. For the top 20 per cent, the weight of an hour with a private lawyer would vary from 4 per cent of the top 20 per cent monthly income in the 'most affordable' states (Espírito Santo and Rio Grande do Sul) to 21 per cent in Pará (leaving out Piauí as a potential aberration, 47 per cent). For the top 10 per cent, it varies from 3 per cent in Espírito Santo, Rio Grande do Sul, Acre, São Paulo and Tocantins, to 14 per cent in Rio de Janeiro and Pará (again, leaving Piauí out – 33 per cent). If we recall that we are talking about percentages of people's *monthly* income to afford a *single hour* of legal advice and that health litigation is a long process likely to consume tens of hours of a lawyers' time, it seems plausible to conclude that not even the top 10 per cent in Brazil are in a comfortable position to afford private legal advice and representation in court (recall that lawyers' fees are only a part of the costs of litigation).[101]

***

When one compares private legal services' costs with the income profile of the Brazilian population, it becomes clear that, for most people in Brazil, private lawyers' fees are simply unaffordable, let alone the total costs of litigation, which include court fees, transportation and also indirect costs such as time off-work to prepare for litigation, attend meetings with lawyers, court hearings, etc.[102] As a consequence, for most

[101] It is true that these are only recommendations which may or may not be followed by private lawyers. How strictly they are followed is impossible to know. But the data provide a reasonably good sense of the (lack of) affordability of private lawyers services in Brazil vis a vis the income of the population.

[102] It is not surprising that opinion surveys consistently find a large proportion of respondents, always above 80 per cent, stating that the costs to access the courts are either 'high' or 'very high', see: Fundação Getúlio Vargas, *Índice de Confiança na Justiça – ICJ* (São Paulo: Fundação Getúlio Vargas, 2017). All reports are available at: https://direitosp.fgv.br/publicacoes/icj-brasil, accessed 22 June 2019. In the latest report, of 2017, 81 per cent of respondents mentioned that justice is too expensive. Ibid., at 17. The index is based on interviews with 1,650 people distributed across 7 states representing around 40 per cent of the total population (83,918,659). Ibid., at 26.

potential litigants in Brazil, access to state funded lawyers, that is, public defenders and prosecutors is crucial to make litigation a realistic option.

Yet, as we saw earlier, state lawyers are not available in sufficient numbers to attend the large demand for their services, far from it (see Section 6.4.2 and Figures 6.7, 6.8, 6.9 and 6.10). Moreover, the small number available are outside of the reach of a large section of the population, often the poorest (72 per cent of judicial districts had no public defender as of 2013, affecting 53 million people according to my conservative estimate, see Figure 6.8). And even in places where public defenders and prosecutors are comparatively more available, actual access to their services remain challenging for large segments of the population. High lawyers' fees are only one of the barriers that prevent individuals from litigating.[103] Other factors, such as the possibility to take time off work or other activities such as childcare or care for an elderly, the distance from one's residence to the state lawyer's office, rights awareness, etc. all influence accessibility to litigation.[104]

The overall picture that emerges on *resources*, the final and important component of the opportunity structure for legal mobilisation, is thus not very auspicious. The financial resources controlled by a vast majority of the Brazilian population are clearly insufficient for litigation to constitute a realistic option, including for many of those who are in principle able to reach the limited services of public defenders and public prosecutors. As we saw, 130.2 million Brazilians (62 per cent of the population) earn less than the minimum wage. Even if state lawyers were waiting for them in abundance and at close reach of their homes (not the case by a long shot

[103] See Oliveira and Cunha, 'Medindo o Acesso à Justiça Cível no Brasil', stating that the majority of people do not resort to lawyers and courts to solve legal problems, irrespective of income level, citing C. R. Albiston, R. L. Sandefur, 'Expanding the Empirical Study of Access to Justice', (2013) 101 *Wisconsin Law Review*, 101–120.

[104] A quick browse through some of the websites of the DP and MP to check their opening times gives a good illustration of further access limitations. Some DPs are not even open to the public every day of the week, others have very limited opening hours. Some schedule interviews with public defenders only once a week. For a random example, see the Public Defensory of Jaraguá do Sul, Santa Catarina, which is open for meetings with the public only on Tuesdays and Thursdays from 1:30 PM to 4:00 PM, available at: www.defensoria.sc.gov.br/index.php/atendimento#nucleo-de-jaragua-do-sul, accessed 5 April 2019. In Pará, where a large number of municipalities do not have public defenders as seen above, the opening times in the capital, Belém are from Monday to Friday, 8:00 AM until 2:00 PM according to their website, available at: www2.defensoria.pa.def.br/portal/, accessed 22 June 2019.

as we saw), it would be rather unlikely that most would be able to afford all other indirect costs of litigation highlighted above (in particular, time off work).

6.5 Conclusion

This chapter has begun to assess the drivers and social impact of the judicialisation of health in Brazil. What drives the hundreds of thousands of cases that reach Brazilian courts every year? What impact do they have on the health of the population and on the public health system?

I was sceptical, from the outset, of the very popular, yet in my view implausible, hypothesis that litigation is a reaction of the most vulnerable and neglected to force the public health system to guarantee their constitutional right to health (which I call the 'rights revolution narrative'). If that were the case, we should witness a flood of litigation in the poorer regions of the country, that is, the states, municipalities and districts with the worse health indicators and more precarious health services (discussed at length in Chapter 4). I also doubted the opposite hypothesis that it is *only* the economic elite in Brazil who can reach the courts. Again, if that were the case, we should not see a reasonably sizeable proportion of health litigation involving public defenders and, to a lesser extent, public prosecutors, in many states (see Figure 7.2 in Chapter 7).[105]

[105] Moreover, as we saw in Chapter 5, health litigation against private healthcare providers and insurers in Brazil, whose services anyone from the economic elites certainly uses, is even higher than litigation against the state, indicating that those at the very top of economic income probably sue private providers much more often than they sue the state. As we saw in Chapter 4, the public health system is used mostly by the 75 per cent poorest in the population (the richest 25 per cent tend to have private health insurance). This does not mean that users of private health insurance never sue the state at all. Studies show that they actually do at high rates (see Chapter 7). For some medicines and procedures, it is easier to convince the judge that the state ought to provide them given the expansive ('right to everything') interpretation explained in Section 6.3.1. Though judges also tend to interpret contracts in favour of the consumer, it may be less risky for a claimant to sue the state when the health benefit sought is clearly excluded from the coverage according to the contract with the private provider. According to the FGV-ICJ opinion survey, when it comes to seeking a solution via courts, a very large proportion of those reporting problems with the public health system say that they do *not* use litigation (63 per cent), whereas of those reporting problems with their private health insurance, a significant proportion (70 per cent) say that they *do*. As reported by Oliveira and Cunha, 'Medindo o acesso à Justiça Cível no Brasil', at 341.

The challenge for those interested in a more accurate and nuanced picture of the drivers and social impact of litigation is to understand who exactly, then, are behind these hundreds of thousands of claims that concentrate in some pockets of the country. The extended empirically supported analysis of this chapter has hopefully helped us to advance towards a more plausible explanation. The following chapters will complete the picture.

That the haves come out ahead in the health litigation race in Brazil seems difficult to deny.[106] Given the copious availability of private lawyers (478 per 100,000 inhabitants) and the significantly limited availability of public defenders and public prosecutors (3.4 and 5.3 per 100,000 respectively) we must conclude that health litigation is within much closer reach of those capable of hiring a private lawyer, a very small minority (below 10 per cent of the population as I argued). The other 90 per cent of the population who must rely exclusively on the limited services of state lawyers, sparsely distributed across the country, face significantly higher barriers to litigate. To compound the problem of access to legal representation, the number of courts and judges is not only limited but also unevenly distributed across the country. Large sections of the population of almost every state reside in municipalities that have no court (and therefore no judge), no public defender or no public prosecutor, and many of them have none of these at the same time.

Perhaps the most significant limitation for those unable to hire the services of private lawyers is the so-called deficit of public defenders across Brazil. According to moderate estimates, there should be at least 10 public defenders per 100,000 inhabitants. The average across Brazil is 3.4; in several states it is barely above 1. According to the latest comprehensive study available, 53 million Brazilians lived in judicial districts without a single public defender as of 2013, and we know the situation, though better, has not improved significantly.

Further limitations in the opportunity structure for legal mobilisation are still considerable for a large proportion of the Brazilian population, in particular, rights awareness and financial resources to cover the other indirect costs of litigation (e.g., time off from work, travel expenses, etc.).

[106] The phrase is borrowed from the well-known article by Marc Galanter, which makes similar arguments about the advantages of the 'haves' in using litigation. See: Galanter, 'Why the "Haves" Come Out Ahead'.

The levels of poverty and inequality in Brazil are still so high that large sections of the population are automatically disenfranchised from litigation as a realistic option. As we saw, 30 per cent of the population is 'functionally illiterate' and another 34 per cent achieves only the grade 'elementary' in functional literacy tests (see Section 6.4.1). As regards income, 130 million (62 per cent of the population) earn less than the minimum wage, 55 million people (26.5 per cent) are below the national poverty line and 15.2 million (7.4 per cent) are extremely poor according to the lowest threshold of the World Bank (the meagre 'one dollar a day' threshold).[107] Unsurprisingly, in my view, a recent study of the UN Development Programme and the University of Brasilia, the *Access to Justice Atlas*, found a strong correlation between the Index of Human Development and access to justice across states in Brazil.[108]

My conclusion, thus, is that health litigation in Brazil is driven mostly by two different groups, both minorities of a sort. In the large proportion of cases represented by private lawyers, the litigant behind the case is most likely within the top 10 per cent of the income distribution in each state (see Table 6.2). In the sizeable (yet in most states smaller) proportion of cases represented by public defenders and public prosecutors and the fewer represented by university legal clinics, the litigant or beneficiary (in collective cases), it is harder to make a precise estimate of their socioeconomic profile but still possible to make reasonably accurate

[107] See UN Brazil, 'PNUD: Diferenças regionais no acesso à justiça chegam a 1000% no Brasil' ('UNDP: Regional Differences in Access to Justice Reach 1000% in Brazil'), published on 28 May 2015, available at: https://nacoesunidas.org/pnud-diferencas-regionais-no-acesso-a-justica-chegam-a-1000-no-brasil/, accessed 10 May 2019.

[108] See Ministério de Justiça, Governo do Brasil, *Atlas de Acesso à Justiça: Indicadores Nacionais de Acesso à Justiça* (Brasília: Ministério da Justiça, 2013), at 29. It is important to emphasise that my analysis focuses on the particular conditions of Brazil. Although they seem to recur elsewhere, this is a contextual issue and thus can vary from place to place. For a superb discussion of the United Kingdom, see the seminal book by King, *Judging Social Rights*, at 80, where he cites studies that found no disadvantage for the poor in resorting to courts: in particular, H. Genn, S. Beinart, *Paths to Justice: What People Do and Think about Going to Law* (Oxford: Hart Publishing, 1999); H. M. Kritzer, 'To Lawyer or Not to Lawyer: Is That the Question?', (2008) 5(4) *Journal of Empirical Legal Studies*, 875–906, claiming even that 'the poor in Britain are actually more likely to consult a lawyer in a grievance against the government than are the wealthy or middle classes'. But he admits that this is 'dependent to some extent on legal aid provision, which fluctuates within and between countries' and that this is likely going to worsen given legal aid cuts at the time the book was going to press (ibid).

predictions. Given the significant limitation of these state-funded legal services and the further cultural and financial barriers discussed in this chapter, it is plausible to assume that also in this second group (which is much larger in population terms – about 90 per cent – but smaller in terms of claims) there will be a strong social gradient, that is, the haves within this group will likely also come ahead.

This hypothesis is supported by the findings of several empirical studies and surveys, some of which will be discussed in more detail in Chapter 7. In the PNAD – Pesquisa Nacional por Amostra de Domicílios of 2009 (The National Household Sample Survey), the largest official household survey conducted periodically by the federal government across the whole country, it was found that of those who report having sought a solution to their 'serious problems' via ordinary courts in the past five years, the average income was relatively high, that is, R$1,454 (3.12 times the minimum wage then and approximately 60 per cent higher than the average income in the country, then at R$893.48). Even for those seeking a solution in the Special Courts, the average income was quite high (R$1,416), corroborating the findings of other studies that Special Courts have not managed to expand significantly access to justice to the poor in Brazil. The same was true for their levels of education, which was between 0.88 and 1.3 years higher than the country's average. Conversely, those reporting *not* to have sought a solution through the courts had much lower income and education levels, close to or below the country's average. Interestingly, those seeking help from family, friends or the church had the lowest levels of income and education.[109]

When asked why they did not seek a solution for their serious problems in the judiciary, a social gradient emerges again. The average income of those who answer that they did not know they even could ('rights awareness') was the lowest (R$762, i.e., 15 per cent below the country's average then). Those reporting that 'it would cost too much' or 'it is too far' from their residences had the second and third lowest average incomes of the sample (R$787 and R$885 respectively).[110] A very similar pattern was found with educational levels.[111]

[109] See: Conselho Nacional de Justiça, *Panorama do Acesso à Justiça no Brasil* (Brasilia: Conselho Nacional de Justiça, 2011), at 13–16. For an interesting discussion, see also: Oliveira and Cunha, 'Medindo o acesso à Justiça Cível no Brasil', at 328.

[110] Conselho Nacional de Justiça, *Panorama do Acesso à Justiça no Brasil*, at 31.

[111] Ibid., at 33.

According to the innovative ICJ (Index of Trust in Justice) opinion survey coordinated by political scientist Luciana Gross Cunha of Fundação Getúlio Vargas in São Paulo, when it comes to seeking a solution via courts, a very large proportion of those reporting problems with the public health system say that they do *not* use litigation (63 per cent), whereas, of those reporting problems with their private health insurance, a significant proportion (70 per cent) say that they *do*.[112] To quote political scientist Maria Tereza Sadek, one of Brazil's leading experts on access to justice: 'the entrance door attracts a type of litigant and discourages – or closes to – the great mass of individuals who are incapable of using litigation to make their rights effective, producing a paradox: too many claims, and too little claims'.[113]

A final piece of data seems to corroborate the narrative just presented. Though seemingly very high in absolute numbers, health litigation in Brazil is still only a fraction of total litigation in the country (around 0.7 per cent) and, in terms of the percentage of the population that reaches the court, about 0.1 per cent.[114]

Health litigation in Brazil is, thus, neither a rights revolution nor an exclusive tool of the richest. Rather, it is an instrument that is available to small groups of individuals who have a favourable opportunity structure for legal mobilisation, that is, those who can muster the demanding set of resources needed to reach the courts: rights awareness, access to legal services, psychological preparedness, time and money. Although things have certainly improved in the past three decades with the expansion of the Public Defensory, the Attorney General's Office and the Special Courts, it seems clear that the haves still come out way ahead in this race and that the have-nots struggle to reach the finishing line. To paraphrase the historian José Murilo de

112 As reported by Oliveira and Cunha, 'Medindo o acesso à Justiça Cível no Brasil, at 341.

113 Sadek, 'Acesso à Justiça', at 60, arguing that: 'From this picture [of litigation across Brazil] results a grave imbalance, characterised by a distinction between, on one side, those who litigate too much – i.e. those who know their rights and how to claim them – and, on the other side, those who don't even know their rights and who don't claim them. Reaching the courts in Brazil contributes, therefore – as contradictorily as it may seem – to exacerbate the socioeconomic distances, acting as yet another element among the triggers of a situation qualified as cumulative inequalities.' My translation from the original in Portuguese.

114 My own calculations using the approximate number of new cases in 2017 according to the least conservative estimate (200,000), see Section 5.1 in Chapter 5.

Carvalho cited at the beginning of the chapter, the path to the democratisation of justice, like any other progressive goal of the Brazilian Constitution, is a long one.[115]

[115] Carvalho, *Cidadania no Brasil*. As he explains in another of his books: 'The equality of all before the law, established in Article 5 of the current Constitution, is bullshit' ("balela"). Citizenship, in practice, is determined by the police. In the short ten-minute conversation with a law enforcement official, with someone who should implement the constitutional provisions, we find that he distinguishes on his own behalf three classes of citizens, namely: the doctor, the believer, and the sorcerer ("macumbeiro"). The doctor is the citizen of first class, holder of the constitutional rights, deserving of the respect and deference of the agents of the law. The believer comes second: he may have some rights violated, but he still deserves some respect. Finally, the "macumbeiro": has no rights, nor can be considered a citizen. In the real life of that locality, what really counts is the constitution of Animal Farm, the famous literary creation of George Orwell. As everyone knows, after the constitutional reform of Animal Farm implemented by pigs, the constitution of that seemingly imaginary country has been reduced to an article: "All animals are equal, but some animals are more equal than others."' J. M. de Carvalho, *Pontos e bordados: Escritos de história e política* (Belo Horizonte: Editora da UFMG, 2005), at 276.

7

Islands of Rights Revolutions?

> José Bonifácio affirmed in a letter sent to the constituent assembly of 1823 that slavery was a cancer that eroded our civic life and prevented the construction of the nation. Inequality today is our slavery, the new cancer that prevents the construction of a democratic society.[1]
>
> José Murilo de Carvalho

In Chapter 6, I discussed the broader picture of access to Justice in Brazil using the analytical framework of the 'opportunity structure for legal mobilisation' developed in the political sciences' literature. I argued that, despite some advances in the past thirty years, the opportunity structure of most Brazilians (in particular, the poorest), has not improved sufficiently to make their traditionally hard path to the courts much easier. Although procedural barriers such as rules of standing are rather low in Brazil, and the prospects of success in court are very high, crucial resources needed for legal mobilisation are still rather scarce across the population, in particular, financial resources, rights awareness and access to legal services and courts. As regards the latter, improvements did take place through the expansion of the free legal services of state attorneys (the Public Defensory and the Attorney General's Office) and the extension of the Special Courts ('small claims' courts), which are cheaper and less formal. The scale and depth of such changes, however, was well below what would be necessary to produce significant transformation in access to justice, especially as the vast majority of the population have very limited income and education, two other crucial components of the

[1] J. M. de Carvalho, *Cidadania no Brasil: O Longo Caminho*, 7th ed. (Rio de Janeiro: Civilização Brasileira, 2001). My translation from the original in Portuguese: 'José Bonifácio afirmou em representação enviada à Assembléia Constituinte de 1823, que a escravidão era um câncer que corroía nossa vida cívica e impedia a construção da nação. A desigualdade é a escravidão de hoje, o novo câncer que impede a constituição de uma sociedade democrática.'

opportunity structure for legal mobilisation (see Sections 6.2 and 6.3, Chapter 6).

Chapter 6 offered a plausible hypothesis, thus, for why health litigation has so far concentrated in a few pockets of the country and has occurred in disproportionately higher intensity in the comparatively richer states of Brazil, in particular, in the South and Southeast, than in the poorer ones, being notably low in some of the states of the poorest regions of the North and Northeast. The opportunity structure for legal mobilisation is weaker in poorer areas. We can unfortunately discard, thus, the optimistic view that health litigation is (or can be in the foreseeable future) a transformative tool at the disposal of the most disadvantaged and neglected by the Brazilian public health system (the 'rights revolution narrative'). The most disadvantaged and historically most neglected in the country, those who live in its least developed states, are not reaching the courts in any significant numbers, if they are reaching them at all.

Is it possible that health litigation is within reach of the most disadvantaged *at least* in the states and cities where it happens so intensely? Could it be the case that the opportunity structure for legal mobilisation of the poor has achieved a minimum critical mass to propel them to the courts at least in those places where pockets of litigation are found? If this is indeed happening, we would have at least some 'islands' of rights revolutions to be encouraged about. Perhaps, with time and further improvements in the opportunity structure of the poor, the islands would enlarge, link together and become one day a genuine rights revolution of continental proportions across Brazil.

The data presented and analysed in the previous two chapters give us plenty of reasons to be sceptical of this possibility. High concentration of health litigation in states with higher levels of socioeconomic development (Chapter 5) plus severe limitations of access to justice (Chapter 6) strongly indicate that *the haves are coming out ahead*. But we must probe this hypothesis further for two reasons. Firstly, because the rights revolution narrative is very popular. It is fiercely believed by many judges and endorsed by activists and even some academics who have conducted empirical research on health litigation.[2] We must therefore give it the

[2] For the view of judges and prosecutors endorsing the rights revolution narrative, see L. Buíssa, L. Bevilacqua, F. H. B. B. Moreira, 'Impactos Orçamentários da Judicialização das Políticas Públicas de Saúde', in CONASS (eds.), *Dilemas do Fenômeno da Judicialização da Saúde* (Brasília: CONASS, 2018), 26–51. For a recent academic study that has endorsed the rights revolution narrative and claimed that those studies that say

benefit of the doubt. Secondly, because looking more closely at the beneficiaries of health litigation where it occurs with higher intensity will give us a better understanding of the phenomenon, its drivers and social impact.

This chapter will therefore look closer at the socioeconomic profile of beneficiaries of health litigation than we have done so far. Who are the actual people behind the hundreds of thousands of cases reaching the courts every year? Where do they fit in the highly stratified socioeconomic profile of Brazilian society? What is their level of education, how much income do they possess? Who represents them in court? Are those represented by state attorneys really the most disadvantaged or also a privileged minority in the Brazilian context?

Addressing these questions will help us to sharpen further our picture of the drivers and, in particular, of the beneficiaries of health litigation.

7.1 Who Benefits from Health Litigation?

A comprehensive and accurate picture of the beneficiaries of health litigation is not simple to produce. It would require detailed information not only on the characteristics of claimants of individualised lawsuits but also on the beneficiaries of collective lawsuits. Moreover, it would also require information on the actual implementation of judicial orders, as we cannot simply assume that court orders are effectively implemented.[3] Last but not least, we would also need information on the potential broader effects of judicial orders, such as policy changes induced by

otherwise are stating 'myths', see J. Biehl et al., 'The Judicialization of Health and the Quest for State Accountability: Evidence from 1,262 Lawsuits for Access to Medicines in Southern Brazil', (2016) 18(1) *Health and Human Rights*, 209–220.

[3] As Hoffmann and Bentes note: 'Even in successful individual access to medicines and health actions, the number of claimants who actually obtain the granted remedy for the required period is lower than the winning case count implies. In some of the sampled states, like Rio de Janeiro, there is a considerable compliance problem, and enforcement action tends to depend on the personal initiative either of the individual claimant or a particular defensor publico who is then transformed into a compliance agent. And even enforcement action does not always lead to the remedy actually being provided. In this sense, the de facto hurdles for obtaining medication or treatment through the courts are relatively high and require a considerable investment of time and money, even for nominally indigent claimants.' F. Hoffmann, F. R. N. M. Bentes, 'Accountability for Social and Economic Rights in Brazil', in Gauri, V. and Brinks, D. M. (eds.), *Courting Social Justice: Judicial Enforcement of Social and Economic Rights in the Developing World* (New York: Cambridge University Press, 2008) 100–145, at 141.

litigation (so-called indirect effects, discussed further in Chapter 8). This Herculean information-gathering task has not been attempted and perhaps never will. We need to content ourselves, therefore, with a much less comprehensive picture, built with data available from more limited yet often very insightful studies.

These studies allow us to sharpen further the picture emerging from Chapters 5 and 6. We know already that health litigation concentrates disproportionately in the most developed states of the South and the Southeast regions and on curative treatment, mostly medicines and hospital care (Chapter 5). We also know that resources for litigation and, as a consequence, access to justice, are very unevenly distributed and virtually lacking for large segments of the Brazilian population (Chapter 6). We were able to arrive at these conclusions through macro-data available from nationwide databases. Studies focused on smaller units, such as single states and municipalities, can complement nicely that macro-data and give us important insights into the details of health litigation.

There is a growing number of studies on health litigation in Brazil in the states and municipalities where it occurs with greater intensity. Most try to shed some light on the question that interests us here (i.e., on which socioeconomic groups actually benefit most from such litigation) using interesting and innovative methods. As it is difficult to access data on the actual income and education of litigants, studies have employed a number of interesting proxy indicators in their effort to gauge the profile of the beneficiaries of health litigation. These include the place of residence of litigants, the type of legal representation (private or state lawyers) and the type of health services (private or public) they use. I discuss each of these in turn, presenting findings from different studies and explaining their strengths and weaknesses. After that, I present and analyse a couple of rare studies that managed to collect some data on the actual income and education of litigants.

7.2 Place of Residence

Brazil's high levels of inequality and the socioeconomic stratification of its territory (see Chapter 4 for a more detailed discussion) facilitates the use of place of residence as a reliable proxy for income and other socioeconomic indicators such as health and education. In such a context of inequality and stratification, it is possible to predict with a high level of certainty the socioeconomic profile of a person by her address.

We have seen already in Chapter 5 that most individual litigants and beneficiaries of collective suits live in certain more developed states of the country. To have a better idea of their socioeconomic profile, we also need to know at least their municipality and, ideally, the district within their municipality where they live. In principle, though unlikely, most litigants could be people living in the poorest municipalities within more developed states and in the poorest districts within municipalities.

Let us organise our inquiry, then, moving from the broader to the narrower geographical units, that is, starting with studies that disaggregate health litigation by municipalities within states and then districts within municipalities.

7.2.1 Intra-State Distribution of Health Litigation

The same socioeconomic indicator we have used at the national level, the UN Human Development Index (HDI) can be used to assess the intra-state distribution of health litigation, as, helpfully, it is available for each of the 5,570 municipalities currently in existence across Brazil.[4] To recall, the HDI aggregates indicators on health, education and income into a summary measure that goes from 0 (worst possible case) to 1 (best possible case). Municipalities are currently divided into five different groups according to the level of their HDI: very high (from 0.8 to 1), high (from 0.7 to 0.799), medium (from 0.6 to 0.6999), low (from 0.5 to 0.5999) and very low (below 0.4999). In the latest report available for the whole of Brazil, of 2010, the average state HDI varied from 0.631 in Alagoas, the lowest in Brazil, to 0.824 in the Federal District (Brasília), the highest. These averages, as already noted, hide significant discrepancies. When disaggregated by municipality, the lowest HDI in Brazil is Melgaço, in the state of Pará (North), at 0.418 and the highest is in São Caetano do Sul, in the state of São Paulo (Southeast), at 0.862. When we disaggregate further by smaller units within municipalities, some districts within municipalities in all states reach HDI levels higher than 0.965. Within Brazil, thus, there are places whose HDI are higher than Norway's, the country with the highest average in the world (0.953 in 2018) and places with a HDI lower than Sierra Leone (0.438 in 2018), the country with the sixth lowest HDI in the world.

[4] The data has been published by PNUD since 1991 and can be easily accessed here: www.br.undp.org/content/brazil/pt/home/idh0/rankings/idhm-municipios-2010.html, accessed 21 June 2019.

Where data on health litigation in a certain state is disaggregated by municipality, we can therefore compare it with the corresponding HDI to gauge if any correlation emerges. As we shall see, it does. Just as with regions and states (see Map 1.1 in Chapter 1), municipalities with a higher HDI tend to have higher health litigation per capita.

In the southern state of Santa Catarina, for instance, Boing et al. found, in a sample of almost 2,600 cases filed between 2000 and 2006 that 'the municipalities with better socio-economic indicators presented a larger number of lawsuits per inhabitant'.[5] A similar pattern can be observed in the same state in a study conducted by Ronsein with a random sample of 716 medicines requests from 2005 to 2008. Although she herself does not make this point in her study, we can identify a significant concentration of lawsuits in municipalities with high HDI in her sample, such as the capital, Florianópolis, whose HDI is the highest in that state (0.847) out of the 293 existing municipalities of Santa Catarina. Many other municipalities cited in her study as concentrating high number of cases have high HDI, such as Joinville (0.809/4th highest HDI in the state), São José (0.809/4th), Tubarão (0.796/12th), Itajaí (0.795/14th), Braço do Norte (0.778/35th) and Criciúma (0.788/20th). As Santa Catarina is one of the most developed states in Brazil, there is no municipality with a low HDI in that state, only medium and high. It is telling, though, that no municipality among the sixty with a medium HDI feature in Rosein's sample, that is, no health litigation seems to take place in those municipalities.[6]

In the southern state of Paraná, a study by Pereira and Pepe of 649 lawsuits claiming medicines in 2009 found that such lawsuits occurred only in 74 (52.1 per cent) of the 142 judicial-administrative areas in which the state is subdivided ('comarcas') and were heavily concentrated in a few of those, namely, the capital Curitiba (20.5 per cent), Londrina (16.3 per cent), Metropolitan Region of Curitiba (8.9 per

[5] A. C. Boing et al., 'The Judicialization of Access to Medicines in Santa Catarina State: A Challenge for the Management of the Health System', (2013) 14(1) *Revista de Direito Sanitário*, 82–97.

[6] J. G. Ronsein, 'Análise do perfil das solicitações de medicamentos por demanda judicial no Estado de Santa Catarina no período de 2005 a 2008', MPhil dissertation, Universidade Federal de Santa Catarina (2010). The lowest HDIs in municipalities with high litigation were Içara (0.741/125th) and Morro da Fumaça (0.738/132nd), see www.atlasbrasil.org.br/2013/pt/ranking, accessed 18 March 2019.

cent), Cascavel (6.2 per cent) and Maringá (6.2 per cent).[7] Although they too do not make that correlation in their article, these are among the most developed in the state of Paraná (all among the top 6 HDIs out of the 399 municipalities of that state, with HDIs between 0.778 and 0.823).[8]

Gomes et al. found a similar picture in the state of Minas Gerais (Southeast).[9] From a universe of more than 6,000 cases registered at the State Secretariat of Health from 1999 to 2009, they focused exclusively on those claiming medical procedures rather than medicines, reaching a universe of 783 cases. In line with other studies, they found that cases concentrate in a small number of municipalities (14 per cent, 122 out of the 853 municipalities of Minas Gerais) and the ones cited as concentrating the highest proportion of cases are ones with high HDI, such as Belo Horizonte, the capital and with the second highest HDI in Minas Gerais (0.810) and almost 1 in every 4 cases (22.3 per cent) followed by Divinópolis (19.8 per cent), the 21st highest HDI in Minas Gerais (0.764), out of 853 municipalities.

An earlier study of the state of Rio de Janeiro (Southeast), from 2005, found a very high concentration of cases in the capital (70 per cent), which has the second highest HDI of the 92 municipalities of that state (0.799).[10] If we add cases from municipalities surrounding the capital, so-called Grande Rio, we reach more than 90 per cent of claims originating from 10 municipalities. Among these, most have high HDI: Niterói (1st / 0.837), Nilópolis (9th), São Gonçalo (14th), Mesquita (16th), São João de Meriti (34th), Nova Iguaçu (43rd) and Duque de Caxias (49th). Only two stand out as having lower, yet still medium, HDI: Belford Roxo (70th/ 0.684) and Queimados (73rd/0.680).[11]

[7] J. G. Pereira, V. L. E. Pepe, 'Acesso a medicamentos por via judicial no Paraná: Aplicação de um modelo metodológico para análise e monitoramento das demandas judiciais', (2014) 15(2) *Revista de Direito Sanitário*, 31–45.

[8] See also the more recent study of Nisihara et al., in 2017, finding that 65 per cent of the lawsuits filed against the Federal Union in the state of Paraná were from litigants resident in the capital, Curitiba. R. M Nisihara et al., 'Demanda judicial de medicamentos na Justiça Federal do Estado do Paraná', (2017) 15(1) *Einstein*, 85–91, at 87. See also: www.ipardes.gov.br/index.php?pg_conteudo=1&sistemas=1&cod_sistema=5&grupo_indic=2, accessed 6 March 2018.

[9] F. F. C. Gomes et al., 'Access to Medium and High-Complexity Procedures in the Brazilian Unified National Health System: A Matter of Judicialization', (2014) 30(1) *Cadernos de Saúde Pública*, 31–43.

[10] A. M. Messeder, C. G. S. Osorio-de-Castro, V. L. Luiza, 'Mandados judiciais como ferramenta para garantia do acesso a medicamentos no setor público: A experiência do Estado do Rio de Janeiro', (2005) 21(2) *Cadernos de Saúde Pública*, 525–534, at 527.

[11] Ibid.

In the state of São Paulo (Southeast), where data is perhaps the most comprehensive and detailed of all due to a long-standing effort of the state Health Department to understand and manage health litigation, there is also great variation among regions and municipalities. As the data is divided into its seventeen Regional Health Departments (DRS), which amalgamate municipalities of different levels of HDI, it is not possible to know exactly if a lawsuit comes from one of the better off or comparatively worse off municipalities within each DRS.[12] It is conspicuous, though, that a high volume of litigation occurs in DRSs that include some of the cities with the highest HDIs of the state of São Paulo, such as Presidente Prudente, Ribeirão Preto, Bauru, São José do Rio Preto, Barretos and Franca. Conversely, in the DRS headquartered in the municipality with the lowest HDI (Registro), litigation is also the lowest. (see Figure 5.5 in Chapter 5).[13]

These data on five of the seven states of the South and Southeast, which, as we saw, concentrate most health litigation in Brazil (81 per cent of the total, see Section 5.2 in Chapter 5), indicates that health litigation is not only concentrated in states with comparatively higher levels of socioeconomic development but also, within these states, in *municipalities* with comparatively higher levels of socioeconomic development.[14]

[12] Secretaria de Estado da Saúde, 2012, www.saude.sp.gov.br/ses/institucional/departamentos-regionais-de-saude/regionais-de-saude, accessed 17 March 2019

[13] In an recent survey carried out by the National Confederation of Municipalities, it was found that, among the twenty municipalities reporting the largest volume of litigation involving medicines, ten (50 per cent) were from the state of São Paulo, three (15 per cent) from Rio Grande do Sul, three (15 per cent) from Minas Gerais, two (10 per cent) from Santa Catarina, one (5 per cent) from Bahia and one from Mato Grosso (5 per cent), available at: www.cnm.org.br/cms/biblioteca_antiga/An%C3%A1lise%20sobre%20a%20Judicializa%C3%A7%C3%A3o%20da%20Sa%C3%BAde%20nos%20Munic%C3%ADpios.pdf, accessed 17 March 2019.

[14] The only detailed study of Rio Grande do Sul (RS) has unfortunately not presented sufficiently enough disaggregated data on volume of litigation by municipality. See Biehl et al., 'The Judicialization of Health and the Quest for State Accountability'. The binary classification they use, the capital (6 per cent) versus 'inland' ('interior') municipalities (94 per cent) is unfortunately not very useful to gauge the socioeconomic profile of litigants, as RS is the Brazilian state with the largest number of inland municipalities with an HDI in the 'high' and 'very high' brackets. No less than 310 municipalities out of the 496 in that state have an HDI above 0.7. The distance between Porto Alegre, the capital, whose HDI is 'very high', at 0.805 and the municipality with the 100th highest HDI, Osório (0.751) is barely 0.05. Moreover, in RS only 1 out of the 496 municipalities, Dom Feliciano, scores below 0.6, and only just slightly (0.587). There are 181 municipalities in that state that have an HDI in the 'medium' category, which goes from 0.6 to 0.7. So, without knowing exactly where the 94 per cent of the lawsuits in the inland municipalities

There are understandably fewer studies of states of the Northeast given the low concentration of health litigation there, yet in the most detailed one I could find, the same pattern repeats itself. In the state of Ceará, a study by Pessoa of 841 administrative and judicial medicine claims against that state found that 84 per cent of claimants resided in Fortaleza, the capital city and also the one with the highest HDI in Ceará (0.754). Another 4 per cent of claims originated in Maracanaú, the 6th in the HDI ranking (0.686) and another 4 per cent in Caucáia, the 8th (0.682).[15] Ceará has 184 municipalities, almost 50 of them with low HDI, some of them rather low, such as Salitre, the lowest, at 0.540, and no health litigation to its name. In a more recent study of the same state, Nunes and colleagues found a very similar picture with 750 (77.7 per cent) out of 965 of litigants residing in Fortaleza, 17 in Maracanaú (1.7 per cent), 13 in Caucáia (1.3 per cent) and no other municipality reaching 1 per cent of litigation.[16]

***

of RS come from, it is not possible to gauge how concentrated they are in the most developed ones, as we have done for the other states. Another study of one specific region of RS, with a high concentration of municipalities with comparatively low HDI for that state's standards, indicates that litigation in RS does not diverge from the pattern I identified in other states. It looked at all 400 medicines lawsuits against 25 municipalities of one of RS's health administrative regions in the northwest (12ª Coordenadoria Regional de Saúde), many of them in the bottom fifth of RS's HDI ranking, only 4 in the top 100, and the highest one, Santo Ângelo, ranking 29. If we recall that RS is one of the states with the highest volume of litigation, 400 cases is very low. See A. R. H. Silva, E. D. Corte, 'Judicialização na Assistência Farmacêutica do Sistema Único de Saúde', (2011) 8(27) *Ciência em Movimento*, 19–25. Another study of a single municipality of the same region (the northwest) with comparatively higher HDI, Santa Rosa, ranking 31st in the state, found 451 patients receiving drugs through the courts in 2013, that is, 51 more than the whole of that region in Silva and Corte's study. In terms of population, whereas 12ª Coordenadoria Regional de Saúde had 289,728 inhabitants in the 2010 census, Santa Rosa had 68,587, that is, about one quarter. See also the study by Anjos (2009), analysing 42 claims of the drug alfa interferon for Hepatites C in Porto Alegre and finding 40 claimants (95.2 per cent) belonging to socioeconomic class B (upper-middle) or C (middle) and two (4.8 per cent) belonging to class A (upper). No claimant belonged to classes D or E. See R. S. Anjos, 'Judicialização e eqüidade no tratamento da hepatite C: Estudo de caso sobre o tratamento com interferona alfa em um serviço de referência do SUS em Porto Alegre, RS', MPhil dissertation, Universidade Federal do Rio Grande do Sul (2009).

15 N. T. Pessoa, 'Perfil das solicitações administrativas e judiciais de medicamentos impetradas contra a secretaria de saúde do estado do Ceará', MPhil dissertation, Universidade Federal do Ceará (2007), at 87.

16 C. F. O. Nunes, A. N. Ramos Júnior, 'Judicialização do direito à saúde na região Nordeste, Brasil: Dimensões e desafios', (2016) 24(2) *Cadernos de Saúde Coletiva*, 192–199, at 195.

The data just presented are of course neither comprehensive enough nor sufficient to enable peremptory conclusions about the actual direct beneficiaries (let alone indirect ones) of health litigation. Yet they seem to weaken further the plausibility of the rights revolution narrative, showing that also in the high-intensity litigation states of the South and Southeast, and one of the Northeast, a large proportion of lawsuits concentrate in the most developed municipalities and is practically non-existent in those with the lowest levels of socioeconomic development.

If a rights revolution were actually occurring at least in these states, we would expect to see a significant number of cases in the least developed municipalities of these states and not such high concentration in the most developed ones. If we put together the macro-data presented in Chapter 5, the significant and persistent barriers to access to justice discussed in Chapter 6 and the more detailed data presented in this section it is difficult to be optimistic about even 'islands' of rights revolutions occurring across Brazil.

But let us probe the hypothesis further. If not 'islands', can we find at least 'islets' of rights revolutions somewhere? Perhaps at least in some of the municipalities where the services of public defenders are relatively more abundant the most disadvantaged are claiming health benefits in courts? Given that the HDI is an average and Brazilian municipalities are notoriously unequal, it would be possible in principle, though again unlikely, that the poor are behind some health litigation cases.[17]

To illustrate with an example we have used in Chapter 4, imagine two persons living in the two neighbouring districts in the city of Rio de Janeiro, Leblon and Rocinha, parts of which are only a few hundred meters apart. Rocinha, as we saw, is one of the largest shanty-towns of Brazil, with high levels of deprivation, whereas Leblon is one of Brazil's richest districts with some of the highest levels of well-being. Its HDI, at 0.944, is of Scandinavian levels. The average life expectancy gap between the two is more than twelve years. Given that residents of either district are in principle able to seek the services of lawyers to file a health claim in the courts of Rio de Janeiro, we cannot conclude with one hundred per

[17] For the actual data, see http://tabnet.datasus.gov.br/cgi/ibge/censo/cnv/ginibr.def, accessed 8 March 2019. Very few municipalities had a Gini lower than 0.4 in the latest measurement. Most had a Gini above 0.5 and many a Gini of 0.6, especially the large cities where a great part of litigation takes place: Rio de Janeiro (0.6391), São Paulo (0.6453), Belo Horizonte (0.6106), Florianópolis (0.5474), Porto Alegre (0.6144).

cent certainty, despite all the mounting evidence of Chapters 5, 6 and this section, that Rocinha dwellers are not flooding the courts with their urgent and copious health claims. The same could in principle be true of all the other municipalities analysed above, that is, it could perhaps be the poorest residents of these places that are reaching the courts in larger numbers, as the rights revolution narrative suggests.

Such microdata on the distribution of health litigation within municipalities is much less available but it exists. Let us see what it shows.

7.2.2 Intra-Municipal Distribution of Health Litigation

The pioneering study to investigate health litigation within municipalities seems to have been that of Vieira and Zucchi in São Paulo in 2005. They analysed the addresses reported by litigants in the universe of all 177 lawsuits filed against the municipality during that year claiming medicines.[18] Given that São Paulo, like many other places in Brazil as explained above, is a highly stratified city, it is possible to predict the socioeconomic profile of an individual from her district of residence with a large level of certainty. They found a strong positive correlation between high number of lawsuits and high level of socioeconomic development of the district where the claimants resided.[19] The map depicted in Figure 7.1, reproduced from the original article, provides a good graphic impression of their findings. They plot each lawsuit (the black dots) onto the map of the city divided by districts, on the exact address of the litigant. These districts are amalgamated into three different groups according to indicators of socioeconomic inclusion and exclusion. Most (63 per cent) of the litigants resided in districts of either low (white coloured) or medium (light grey) levels of exclusion. The rest (37 per cent) lived in districts of high level of socioeconomic exclusion (dark grey).

But 37 per cent, one may argue, is not a negligible proportion. Although not that impressive in absolute terms (around 60 litigants) given the small size of the sample (170), it certainly provides some prima

[18] In the first lines of any lawsuit, one can find the full name and qualification of the plaintiff, including her address and often also profession, marital status and identify card number.

[19] F. Vieira, P. Zucchi, 'Distorções causadas pelas ações judiciais à política de medicamentos no Brasil', (2007) 41(2) *Revista de Saúde Pública*, 214–222; V. L. E. Pepe et al., 'Characterization of Lawsuits for the Supply of "Essential" Medicines in the State of Rio de Janeiro, Brazil', (2010) 26(3) *Cadernos de Saúde Pública*, 461–71.

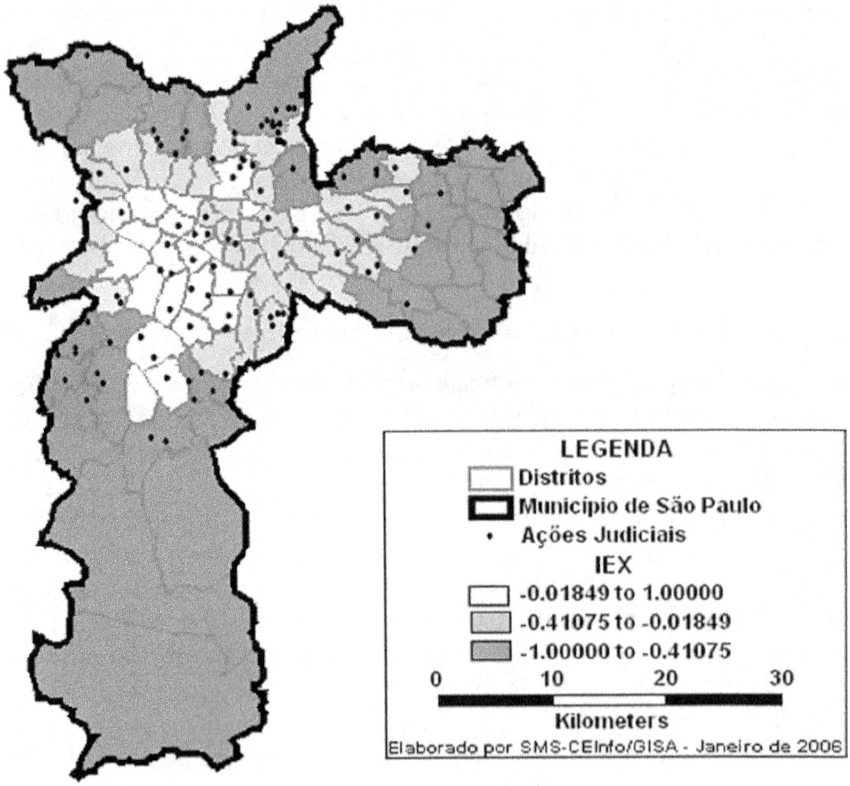

Figure 7.1 Distribution of health lawsuits across districts in the municipality of São Paulo, 2005.
Source: Vieira and Zucchi, 2007

facie evidence that litigation can also benefit the comparatively more disadvantaged in a rich city like São Paulo. If we look carefully at the distribution of lawsuits in the relatively more deprived ('high exclusion') districts, however, we notice an interesting fact. There is a significant concentration in some districts that are closer to central and less deprived ones (medium and high) and no lawsuit at all in the most distant districts of the south and the east of the city.

What could explain this disparity? One plausible explanation, in my view, is that the opportunity structure for legal mobilisation of these different groups varies significantly. The tripartite classification used by Vieira and Zucchi is perhaps not fine-grained enough to capture significant differences in education (rights awareness), income and access to legal services among these districts. When we use the HDI of each district, we see that no litigation occurred in the lowest ten districts in the city apart from a single case in Jardim Angela.[20] These are also the districts that are farthest from legal services and judicial units (an important barrier discussed in detail in Chapter 6).[21] Conversely, if we take two of the 'high exclusion districts' with the largest number of claims, Tremembé and Cangaíba, we see that they are not just closer to the centre, but also have much higher HDI than the average, at 0.826 and 0.825 respectively, which, in human development terms, are considered 'very high'.

Chieffi and Barata's study of São Paulo one year later (2006) and with a larger universe of lawsuits (2,604),[22] found a strong correlation again between higher levels of socioeconomic development and a higher volume of lawsuits: using a similar but more fine-grained index of socioeconomic development that divides the city into six areas rather than three, they found that 74 per cent of the lawsuits came from the three most developed areas of the city (more than 50 per cent from the two highest, with a further concentration in the second most developed area – 35 per cent).[23]

Menicucci and Machado carried out a study of a sample of 369 cases out of a total of 2,396 recorded between the years of 1995 and 2009 in the files of the municipality of Belo Horizonte, in the state of Minas Gerais.[24] To gauge the socioeconomic profile of litigants, they used the Health

[20] São Rafael, Cidade Tiradentes, Vila Curuçá, Itaim Paulista, Grajaú, Jardim Helena, Iguatemi, Jardim Ângela, Lajeado, Parelheiros and Marsilac are the ten districts with lowest HDIs in São Paulo, all geographically situated in the far South and far East.

[21] Someone from Marsilac, the southernmost district of São Paulo, would take 3 hours and 10 minutes and spend R$7.65 to get to the Public Defensory offices in the centre of Sao Paulo (Av. Liberdade, 32, São Paulo – SP, 01502-000, Brazil) according to google maps. That trip would involve walking, two buses, one train (CPTM) and the underground to cover about 50 km.

[22] Although their universe was lawsuits against the *state* of São Paulo, not the municipality as Vieira and Zucchi, their analysis of the socioeconomic profile of litigants also focused on those living in the municipality of São Paulo, exactly like Vieira and Zucchi. A. L. Chieffi, R. Barata, 'Judicialização da política pública de assistência farmacêutica e eqüidade', (2009) 25(8) *Cadernos de Saúde Pública*, 1839–1849. It is relevant to recall that Brazil is administratively divided into the Federal Union (which covers the whole of Brazil), 27 states and more than 5,570 municipalities. São Paulo is the largest municipality in the country, with a population of 11,253,503 (IBGE, Census 2010).

[23] Ibid.

[24] T. M. G. Menicucci, J. A. Machado, 'Judicialization of Health Policy in the Definition of Access to Public Goods: Individual Rights versus Collective Rights', (2011) 5 *Brazilian Political Science Review*, 33–68.

Vulnerability Index (Índice de Vulnerabilidade à Saúde), which the municipality employs to identify priority areas of intervention.[25] In their sample, 19.2 per cent (n=48) of litigants resided in areas of high or very high risk, whereas 42.4 per cent (n=106) resided in areas of medium risk and 38.4 per cent (n=96) in areas of low risk. The distribution of the population among these areas follows a reverse pattern (34 per cent of the population in Belo Horizonte lived in areas of high and very high risk, 38 per cent in areas of medium risk and 28 per cent in low risk at the time of their study), indicating, again, a positive correlation between socioeconomic status and ability and willingness to litigate.[26]

A similar pattern was found by Provin, who studied 1,378 lawsuits demanding different drugs from January 2003 to December 2007 in the city of Goiânia, in the state of Goiás (in the Centre-West region of Brazil). She divided the city into four socioeconomic regions according to the average estimated income of the head of the household. The bottom region in terms of income (from 0 to 3 minimum wages, 'mw') generated only 89 (7.1 per cent) lawsuits of the total 1,249. The remaining 93 per cent were distributed in the following manner: 417 (33.3 per cent) in region 2 (from 3 to 6 mw); 407 (32.5 per cent) in region 3 (6 to 9 mw) and 336 (26.9 per cent) in region 4 (9 mw and above).[27]

***

Studies that looked at the distribution of health litigation within municipalities are few and far between, but they all seem to go in the same direction of the conclusions of Chapters 5 and 6: ability and willingness to litigate is positively correlated with the socioeconomic profile of the litigant. Health litigation is consistently more common in districts with high levels of socioeconomic development in all cities studied (i.e., São Paulo, Belo Horizonte and Goiânia). Although a smaller proportion of claims do originate in less developed districts, these are never the least developed, are often closer to legal services and have a high HDI by

[25] As they explain: 'This index is a combination of different variables in an indicator that seeks to summarize relevant information which reflect intra-urban inequalities, pointing out priority areas for intervention and resource allocation and favouring the proposition of inter-sectoral actions (PBH 2005, 48).' Ibid., at 66.

[26] Ibid.

[27] M. P. Provin, S. N. Leite, R. G. Amaral, 'Social Inequalities in Lawsuits for Drugs', (2013) 43(3) *Brazilian Journal of Pharmaceutical Sciences*, 465–474.

Brazilian standards and even, in some cases, by international standards, as we saw in São Paulo.

7.3 Actual Income

As good as place of residence is as a proxy indicator of the socioeconomic profile of litigants, the best possible indicator would of course be the actual income and educational level of claimants. This is, unfortunately, not very easy to obtain,[28] but a few studies have tried and provide us with some further interesting insights. One such study was carried out by Fernanda Terrazas and Virgílio Afonso da Silva in the city of São Paulo.[29] Their strategy was to interview litigants and ask them directly to provide information on education, income and other details related to their lawsuit. It proved partially successful due to an interesting, if somewhat bizarre, development spurred by the high levels of litigation in São Paulo: to cope with the voluminous health litigation and the risks of falling into contempt of court, the State Secretariat for Health decided to create a separate special pharmacy, the 'Lawsuit Pharmacy' (Farmácia de Ação Judicial – FAJ), where beneficiaries of judicial decisions could collect their medicines, avoiding thus the need to queue in the ordinary public pharmacies across the city. That allowed the authors to find, in one place, all the individuals they wanted to interview, which would otherwise have proven very difficult if not impossible. Taking good advantage of this unusual opportunity, the authors applied a questionnaire that elicited a wide range of interesting information that goes well beyond the socio-economic profile of the litigants.[30] I will come back to some of that

[28] A good example is Pessoa's study of judicialisation in Ceará, (2007), which tried to find data on the income of litigants in the files of lawsuits but could not find any data in 93.7 per cent (n=788) of them. Pessoa, 'Perfil das solicitações administrativas e judiciais de medicamentos impetradas contra a secretaria de saúde do estado do Ceará'; see also Ronsein, 'Análise do perfil das solicitações de medicamentos por demanda judicial no Estado de Santa Catarina no período de 2005 a 2008', finding some information on litigants' income in only 28.2 per cent of her sample (n=201) and D. Diniz, T. R. C. Machado, J. Penalva 'A judicialização da saúde no Distrito Federal', (2014) 19(2) *Ciênc. Saúde Coletiva*, 591–598, finding data on litigants' income in 7 per cent of their sample (n=27/385)

[29] V. A Silva, F. V. Terrazas, 'Claiming the Right to Health in Brazilian Courts: The Exclusion of the Already Excluded', (2011) 36(4) *Law & Social Inquiry*, 825–853.

[30] The questions in the survey forms were related to (1) the age and gender of the beneficiary, (2) medicine requested, (3) where the medical prescription was issued, (4) the source of information through which the person interviewed had learned of the possibility of filing a lawsuit requesting medicine, (5) who filed the lawsuit, (6) the

broader data later, but here the focus will be on socioeconomic profile, in particular, income and education.

Of the 3,652 individuals who attended the Lawsuits Pharmacy from 27 March to 26 April 2007, the authors interviewed 160 (a sample of 4.38 per cent). In terms of education, they found that 30.63 per cent of interviewees had a university degree, 5.63 per cent of whom had post-graduate studies. Another 36.25 per cent had completed high school and a further 14.37 per cent had completed middle education. At the very bottom of their sample in terms of education, they found that 18.75 per cent had completed elementary schooling. No one seems to have reported not to have completed at least elementary schooling.

As regards income, the percentage of interviewees reporting income above the highest threshold used by the authors, that is 5 times the minimum wage (mw), was 11.88 per cent, with 10.63 per cent reporting income between 3 and 5 mw. At the lower levels of income, 21.88 per cent of their sample reported income between 1.5 and 3 mw, 13.75 per cent between 1 and 1.5 mw, 13.12 per cent between 0.5 and 1 mw and 14.37 per cent below 0.5 mw; 13.75 per cent of the interviewees did not respond. Table 7.1 puts all these findings together for ease of reference.

How should we interpret Silva and Terrazas' findings? Does it not indicate that, at least in the city of São Paulo, some poor people are able to reach the courts? How many? It depends of course on how one defines the poor and also on how much one can rely on self-reported income. Let us first take the self-reported income in their sample at face value and compare their findings with the distribution of income that prevailed in the city of São Paulo according to the UN Development Programme (UNDP) data of 2010 (the closest in time I could find to their study). According to the UNDP, 4.27 per cent of the population in São Paulo was poor in 2010 (those on a monthly household income per capita of R$140 or less). Silva and Terrazas' first threshold of 0.5 mw or less is unfortunately too high to allow for comparison (in 2010, it amounted to R$255). If we take the bottom 20 per cent of income in São Paulo in 2010 we have a better, yet still not ideal, match. Their income was on average R$204.10, that is, 25 per cent lower than that of Silva and Terrazas' first threshold. We can see already, though, that the bottom quintile is underrepresented in their sample, as 14.63 per cent in their sample reported income of less

frequency with which the beneficiary uses public hospitals, (7) her occupation, (8) household income (per capita), (9) her educational level, (10) information about housing and neighbourhood. Ibid.

Table 7.1 *Silva and Terrazas' findings on the income and educational profile of litigants*

Household income per capita in minimum wages	%	N	Educational level	%	N
Less than 0.5	14.37	23	–	–	–
From 0.5 to 1	13.12	21	Completed elementary schooling	18.75	30
From 1 to 1.5	13.75	22	Completed middle-education	14.37	23
From 1.5 to 3	21.88	35	Completed high school	36.25	58
From 3 to 5	10.63	17	University degree	30.63	40
More than 5	11.88	19	Post-graduate degree	5.63	9
No response	13.75	23	–	–	–
Total		160			160

Source: Silva and Terrazas, 2011

than 0.5 mw (R$255) whereas the bottom 20 per cent of the population earned on average R$204.10. The further we go up the income quintiles the more skewed towards the better off the sample seems. The average income of those at the fourth quintile of income, for instance, was only R$1,189.16 in 2010, whereas in their sample 22.51 per cent reported income equal or higher than R$1,530 and another 21.88 per cent between R$765 and R$1.530.[31] So, even if the income data in their sample did not suffer from the well-known problem of under-reporting,[32] we would still

[31] See Atlas of Human Development in Brazil, United Nations Development Programme – UNDP Institute of Applied Economic Research – IPEA João Pinheiro Foundation – FJP, www.atlasbrasil.org.br/2013/en/perfil_m/sao-paulo_sp, accessed 22 April 2019.

[32] M. E. Short et al., 'How Accurate Are Self-Reports? Analysis of Self-Reported Health Care Utilization and Absence When Compared with Administrative Data', (2009) 51(7) *Journal of Occupational and Environmental Medicine*, 786–796. It is not surprising, thus, that 13.75 per cent of those interviewed in Silva and Terrazas' sample did not respond (the only question out of the ten in the questionnaire that was not responded by all interviewees). Of those who responded, it is likely that many under-reported their income due to the problems cited above, as the expert literature consistently finds about income

find an important social gradient in health litigation in the city of São Paulo and not a great number of very poor people reaching the courts.

That Silva and Terrazas' sample did suffer from under-reporting of income is acknowledged by the authors themselves and is confirmed by the data on education, which shows a significantly higher level in the sample compared not only to the general population of Brazil but also in comparison to the population in São Paulo, one of the most developed cities of the country. To cite just one telling example, whereas less than 13.4 per cent of the population of São Paulo had university degrees at the time of the study, 36.26 per cent of the litigants did, 6 per cent of whom reported having postgraduate degrees.

It seems, thus, that the only available study with actual direct data on the socioeconomic profile of litigants within cities travels in the same direction we have been observing so far: the haves come out ahead in health litigation.

7.4 Other Proxy Indicators: Legal Representation and Health Services

Given the difficulties of accessing data on the personal economic and educational characteristics of litigants (not ordinarily available in the lawsuit files) and its low reliability due to under-reporting, researchers have made use of other proxy indicators in their attempt to assess the socioeconomic profile of litigants. As we shall see, none of these proxy indicators are as reliable as place of residence or educational attainment yet, as long as we are very clear about these limitations, they can help to shed some further light on our analysis.

7.4.1 Legal Representation

As discussed at length in Chapter 6, access to justice in Brazil is importantly determined by the potential litigant's access to the legal services of a

surveys and as Silva and Terrazas themselves state. As they note: 'Our perception during the survey was that the income values were underestimated, especially in the higher income range.' One hypothesis they mention to explain such perception is that litigants may be concerned not to undermine the legitimacy of their judicial claims, which are often justified by reported incapacity to afford the health benefits claimed. See also: J. C. Moore et al., 'Income Measure Error in Surveys: A Review', (2000) 16(4) *Journal of Official Statistics*, 331–361; L. H. Moyer et al., 'How Do People Answer Income Questions?', US Census Bureau (1997), at 355–356.

lawyer, which can be a private or a state one (i.e., a public defender or a public prosecutor). We saw how private lawyers are at the same time the most available but the least accessible in Brazil, an apparent paradox that is easily deciphered, once again, by the colossal levels of socioeconomic inequality in the country. The vast majority of the Brazilian population, and particularly the most disadvantaged, are simply not able to afford the services of a private lawyer. Most Brazilians are thus almost entirely dependent on the services of state lawyers in order to reach the courts.[33] This circumstance makes representation by a private lawyer a good proxy indicator of a litigant's high socioeconomic profile, as, at best, only 10 per cent of the Brazilian population is able to afford their services (see Section 6.4.3 in Chapter 6). Representation by a state lawyer, however, is not a reliable proxy indicator of low socioeconomic status, as we also saw in Chapter 6 and will become clearer soon.

As we saw in Chapter 6, in most studies that have collected data on this, the percentage of claims represented by private lawyers is very high, sometimes above 70 per cent and very often above 50 per cent (see Figure 7.2).

But these studies also show a sizeable number of claims represented by state lawyers, especially the studies of the states of Rio Grande do Sul and Rio de Janeiro. The detailed analysis carried out in Chapter 6 should help us to avoid unwarranted conclusions based on these findings alone, as some studies inadvertently make. As should be clear by now, the fact that the legal remit of state lawyers, in particular, public defenders, is to represent the 'needy', does not mean that any case represented by a state lawyer has a poor person as a litigant. The concept of 'neediness', as we saw, is a legal one that means simply incapacity to afford the costs of litigation. As this is very generously interpreted by courts and the Public Defensory, it ends up encompassing, in principle, about 90 per cent of the Brazilian population, if not more (see Chapter 6).

The threshold of three times the minimum wage officially adopted (but often disregarded) in most states is significantly higher than the medium income in the Brazilian population and, a fortiori, of those that can be regarded as poor by any definition. Take the somewhat

33 I say *almost* entirely rather than simply entirely to allow for the possibility that some in the group of the most disadvantaged have access to private lawyers through *pro bono* advocacy, or that some make use of the possibility of litigating without legal representation in the Special Courts. I find both cases unlikely to represent a significant proportion of litigation by the most disadvantaged as discussed in more detail in Chapter 6.

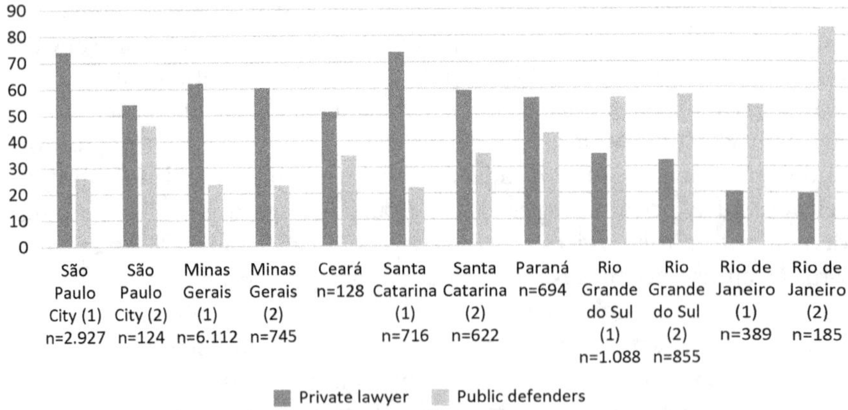

Figure 7.2 Percentage of lawsuits by legal representation (private lawyers and public defenders).
Source: Own formulation with data from several studies[34]

conservative definition of the most disadvantaged as those at the bottom 40 per cent of income. In Brazil as a whole, their average income is a meagre R$376 according to the latest data, that is, almost 8 times lower than the 3 times the minimum wage threshold. Even in the states of

[34] Chieffi, Barata, 'Judicialização da política pública de assistência farmacêutica e eqüidade'; Vieira, Zucchi, 'Distorções causadas pelas ações judiciais à política de medicamentos no Brasil'; O. H. Campos Neto et al., 'Médicos, advogados e indústria farmacêutica na judicialização da saúde em Minas Gerais', (2012) 46 *Revista de Saúde Pública*, 784–790; M. A. A. Machado et al., 'Judicialization of Access to Medicines in Minas Gerais State, Southeastern Brazil', (2011) 45(3) *Revista de Saúde Pública*, 590–598; Pessoa, 'Perfil das solicitações administrativas e judiciais de medicamentos impetradas contra a secretaria de saúde do estado do Ceará'; Ronsein, 'Análise do perfil das solicitações de medicamentos por demanda judicial no Estado de Santa Catarina no período de 2005 a 2008'; J. R. Pereira et al., 'Análise das demandas judiciais para o fornecimento de medicamentos pela Secretaria de Estado da Saúde de Santa Catarina nos anos de 2003 e 2004', (2010) 15 (Suppl. 3) *Ciência & Saúde Coletiva*, 3551–3560; Pereira, Pepe, 'Acesso a medicamentos por via judicial no Paraná'; J. Biehl et al., 'Between the Court and the Clinic: Lawsuits for Medicines and the Right to Health in Brazil', (2012) 14(1) *Health and Human Rights*, 36–52; Biehl et al., 'The Judicialization of Health and the Quest for State Accountability'; Messeder et al., 'Mandados judiciais como ferramenta para garantia do acesso a medicamentos no setor público'; Pepe et al., 'Characterization of Lawsuits for the Supply of "Essential" Medicines in the State of Rio de Janeiro, Brazil'. Note that the data for public defenders in the studies of São Paulo refers to prosecutors, as the DP was only created in 2006. The data does not add up to 100 per cent as I excluded lawsuits filed by the MP, legal clinics and cases where studies could not find the information for every lawsuit. As one can gauge from the chart, these are a minority of cases.

Brazil where the income of the bottom 40 per cent is highest, such as in Santa Catarina (R$695), Rio Grande do Sul (R$599) and São Paulo (R$553) it is still between 4 and 5.5 times lower than 3 times the minimum wage. Even if we take the medium income in Brazil, at R$1,511, we still have an amount twice as low as the 'legal neediness' threshold.[35]

I am not making any judgement here of the appropriateness of the current thresholds employed by the Public Defensory to determine 'legal neediness'.[36] It is perhaps arguable that the Public Defensory is correct in adopting a generous interpretation of 'neediness' given the inaccessibility of private lawyers to most of the population (see the discussion in Chapter 6). My point is simply that it is not appropriate to use representation by a public defender as automatic evidence of low socioeconomic status, as some studies do.[37] Given the explanations above and the

[35] It should also be noted that the Public Defensory's threshold is often not followed in right to health cases, especially those claiming drugs that are costly, when public defenders tend to relax the admissibility criteria due to medicines' high costs.

[36] There is an ongoing and heated discussion on the topic. The Federal Defensory has recently revised down its threshold from three minimum wages to approximately two (R$2,000) in order, according to their statement, to prioritise its finite resources targeting more vulnerable groups, available at: www.conjur.com.br/2017-mai-03/defensoria-publica-altera-valor-define-criterio-hipossuficiencia and http://pesquisa.in.gov.br/imprensa/jsp/visualiza/index.jsp?jornal=1&pagina=122&data=02/05/2017, both accessed 9 March 2019. There is also a bill in Parliament supported by the Ordem dos Advogados of São Paulo to impose a lower threshold valid for the whole of the country in order to, again according to their statement, prioritise the genuinely needy: 'Needy are those enrolled in the social programs of the federal government. This will end the situation of subjectivity of the Defensoria, of choosing who it serves, so that it serves those who in fact do not have resources to pay a lawyer', said the president of the section, Marcos da Costa. See 'Critério para definição de "necessitado" varia nas Defensorias Públicas', Migalhas, 26 January 2016, available at: www.migalhas.com.br/Quentes/17,MI232998,91041-Criterio+para+definicao+de+necessitado+varia+nas+Defensorias+Publicas, accessed 9 March 2019.

[37] For an example of such misuse, see Biehl et al., 'Between the Court and the Clinic'. In their study of Rio Grande do Sul, the authors have relied almost exclusively on type of legal representation and access to legal aid, which are perhaps the least reliable indicators available of the socioeconomic profile of the litigant. The indicator related to occupation used by the authors offers little help, as the five categories chosen are not fine-grained enough (professional, manual, retired, unemployed and student). If one adds the retired (32 per cent) who can be in any socioeconomic bracket to the 26.9 per cent of the sample where no information is available, one has 58.9 per cent of the sample where it is not possible to draw any conclusion whatsoever about socioeconomic status. Manual or service sector workers (14.5 per cent) could, again, fit into several different income brackets, although they tend to have lower salaries than professionals (4.7 per cent). Even the unemployed (21 per cent) are not in themselves a very good indicator without further data about their actual predicament in terms of income. Students fall into the

significant barriers faced by the poorest to access the services of state lawyers that we discussed in Chapter 6, we ought to be very cautious before drawing any conclusions about the socioeconomic profile of litigants from data on representation by state lawyers alone.[38]

As the analysis in Chapter 6 and the studies cited above show, the high percentages of claims originating in more developed municipalities and districts provide a good indication that public defenders and public prosecutors are not capable to reach the neediest in any large numbers. The only study I am aware of to have investigated this in more detail, carried out by Wang and Ferraz in the city of São Paulo, reached similar conclusions.[39] It looked at a sample of 340 health cases from 2006, the year when the Public Defender's Office went into operation in São Paulo, until February 2009 and 32 class actions (Ações Civis Públicas) filed by the Grupo de Ação Especial à Saúde Pública (Group for Special Action in Public Health – GAESP) of the Attorney General's Office (Ministério Público), from 1999, the year GAESP was created, until February 2009. The idea was to assess to what extent these state lawyers, whose remit is partly to represent the poor, actually did so, which tests the reliability of state legal representation as a proxy indicator for low socioeconomic profile.

Given the difficulties to access reliable data on the socioeconomic profile of litigants already discussed above, the study used three different indicators: self-reported income, human development and health need. The latter two were implied by the address of the litigant (i.e., a place of residence proxy indicator as discussed earlier, see Section 7.1). The findings can be summarised in the following manner: in terms of self-declared income, the Public Defensory (no data was available for the Attorney General's Office) seemed to represent mostly individuals who

same problem, but their participation in the sample is so negligible that one can safely disregard them (0.9 per cent). See also Diniz, Machado, Penalva, 'A judicialização da saúde no Distrito Federal', at 593, for an overreliance on legal representation by state lawyers as an inidicator of socioeconomic profile of claimants: 'There is no evidence that judicialization is a movement of elites. Virtually all cases (95%) were conducted by public defenders, which presupposes a lack of resources.' My translation from Portuguese.

[38] The same is true, if not more so, for the other kind of state lawyer: public prosecutors. As they have no threshold to follow and file lawsuits in their own name, as explained in Chapter 5, they are quite free to decide what cases they are going to take to court.

[39] D. W. L. Wang, O. L. M. Ferraz, 'Reaching Out to the Needy? Access to Justice and Public Attorneys' Role in Right to Health Litigation in the City of São Paulo', (2013) 10(18) *SUR International Journal on Human Rights*, 159–179.

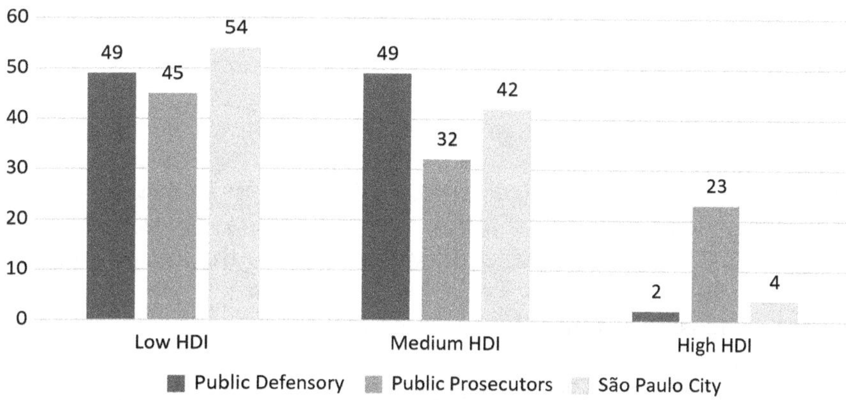

Figure 7.3 Distribution of lawsuits by HDI of litigants' district compared to the population.
Source: Wang and Ferraz, 2013.

should be regarded as either poor or extremely poor (varying from 80 per cent to 88 per cent depending on the year) according to a poverty definition widely used at the time in the city of São Paulo.[40] When HDI or HNI (Health Needs Index) were used, however, the picture changed. As regards the Public Defensory, 49 per cent of individuals came from districts with low human development and 42 per cent came from districts with high health needs. That is, most litigants resided in districts that had either medium or high human development (51 per cent) and either low or medium health needs (58 per cent), despite the income they reported in the documents. As regards the cases represented by GAESP, the study also found that litigation concentrated in districts with low and medium health needs, with only 27 per cent of lawsuits filed in districts with high health needs, but a sizeable, though not disproportionate, number of lawsuits in districts with low human development (45 per cent).

[40] The poverty and extreme poverty threshold we used in that paper was developed by Rocha (2009) for the urban area of the city of São Paulo. She defines the extreme poverty threshold as the amount of money needed by a person to purchase a minimum quantity of food. The poverty threshold is in turn calculated as the amount of money a person needs to fulfill her basic needs, such as food, transport, leisure, health, education and hygiene. S. Rocha, 'Pobreza e indigência', Instituto de Estudos do Trabalho e Sociedade (IETS) (2009).

It seems clear, thus, that representation by state lawyers is not a very good proxy indicator of low socioeconomic profile.

7.4.2 *Legal Aid ('Justiça Gratuita')*

Another proxy indicator often used in judicialisation studies is whether the litigant is granted the so-called Justiça Gratuita ('Free Justice', or 'legal aid'). This is a form of legal aid that exempts the litigant from all court fees and other expenses normally involved in litigation, including expert witnesses' fees and the legal costs of the other party in case of failure. Many studies, too hastily again as we shall see, interpret a high proportion of litigants benefiting from Justiça Gratuita as an indicator that they come from a lower socioeconomic group.

That seems at first plausible if one simply reads the legal provisions of Federal Law 1.060, which established the Justiça Gratuita, as far back as 1950, in their literal and most natural sense.[41] As Article 1 of that law establishes: 'State and federal public powers ... will grant judiciary assistance to the needy according to the provisions of this law.' Article 2 defines further what the term 'needy' (*necessitados*) should mean:

> Art. 2. Nationals and foreigners residing in the country will qualify for the benefits of this Law when they need to resort to Criminal, Civil, Military or Labour Justice.
>
> Sole Paragraph. By needy, for legal purposes, it is meant all of those *whose economic situation prevents them from paying the costs of the judicial process and lawyers' fees without jeopardising their own or their family livelihood.*[42] (my emphasis)

Exactly as we saw in Chapter 6, Section 6.4.2, when discussing the remit of public defenders, the legal definition of neediness is rather flexible, being related to the ability of the claimant to pay costs and lawyers' fees

[41] Federal Law 1.060, of 1950, has been recently partly revoked and amended by the new Civil Procedural Code (Federal Law no. 13.105/2015). As most litigation studies have been carried out while Law 1.060 was still fully in force and as the amendments have not been significant, I will focus the discussion in the text on that law and not the amended provisions.

[42] My translation from Portuguese. This article has now been revoked and replaced by Art. 98 of the New Civil Procedure Code, which reads: 'The natural person or legal entity, Brazilian or foreign, with insufficient resources to pay the costs, the process expenses and the lawyer's fees have the right to free justice, according to the law.' It is arguable that it will now become even easier to access Justiça Gratuita, as it expressly includes companies now.

and not to an objective threshold of income or any other criteria of socioeconomic deprivation. This has led courts across the country to interpret 'legal neediness' (or 'legal indigence' as some call it) in significantly varying terms, some more generous than others, but none in a manner that would make it a good indicator of socioeconomic disadvantage.[43]

Many judges across the country do not require any evidence to grant Justiça Gratuita beyond a simple self-declaration of the litigant that he or she qualifies according to the definition of the law. The law itself expressly requires only this self-declaration as evidence of neediness, applying a legal presumption of veracity to it,[44] and instructing the judge to grant Justiça Gratuita 'promptly' (no longer than 72 hours from the request), unless there are well-grounded reasons to reject it and dispensing the judge from offering any justification when conceding the benefit.[45] Under such liberal rules, it is a well-known fact that Justiça Gratuita is hardly ever rejected in Brazilian courts.

Few courts have set an objective income ceiling to grant Justiça Gratuita, but those that have, set it at relatively high levels. One of the chambers of the Court of Appeal of Rio Grande do Sul, for instance, has

[43] The original idea of Justiça Gratuita was to offer comprehensive legal assistance to the 'needy' in the form much later adopted through the institution of the Public Defender's Office. Most states never implemented it fully, though, and it remained a mere exemption of costs till the recent expansion of the Public Defender's Office explained in Chapter 6.

[44] The history of this provision, amended three times, is rather interesting, as the concession of legal aid was progressively made easier. The original provision in Law 1.060, of 1950, required from the litigant a declaration of his or her income and family expenses. 'Article 4. The party, who wishes to enjoy the benefits of legal aid, shall request the competent judge to grant them, mentioning, in the petition, the income or salary he perceives and his own expenses and those of the family.' In 1986, this was amended to allow the judge to grant the benefits of Justiça Gratuita through a 'simple affirmation' by the litigant that he or she qualified as needy according to the law's definition. 'Article 4. The party shall enjoy the benefits of legal aid by simply stating in the initial petition that it is not in a position to pay the costs of the proceedings and the lawyer's fees, without prejudice to himself or his family'(Law no. 7.510, of 1986). In the New Civil Procedural Code (Law no. 13.105, of 2015), the simple statement was kept, but the sanction previously imposed on false declarations (ten times the judicial costs, Art. 4, Paragraph 1) was eliminated. ('§3. The statement of insufficiency made exclusively by the natural person is presumed to be true.') It also made clear that even those represented by private lawyers can be granted the benefit. ('§ 4. Assistance of the applicant by a private lawyer does not prevent the granting of legal aid.').

[45] 'Art. 5. The judge, if he does not have reasonable grounds to reject the request, must decide it promptly, motivating or not the approval within the period of seventy-two hours.'

imposed a threshold of five times the minimum wage (approximately R$5,000), hardly a low one given the medium income of that state, as we saw (the bottom 40 per cent there have a medium income of R$599, i.e., about 60 per cent of the minimum wage). In Porto Alegre, the capital of Rio Grande do Sul, judges have come up with an even higher threshold, of ten times the minimum wage. When we note that the bottom 40 per cent in Porto Alegre have a medium income of approximately 80 per cent of the minimum wage (R$790) and the top 10 per cent have an medium income of about 13.7 times the minimum wage (R$13,771) we can see clearly that the concept of 'legal neediness' is very far from the socio-economic sense of disadvantage, even if we use the conservative definition of disadvantage as the bottom 40 per cent of income.[46]

But these thresholds are, as noted, exceptions. Most judges do not place any upper limit on the litigant's income to grant Justica Gratuita. This rather liberal and generous definition of legal neediness explains why even those resourceful enough to retain private lawyers are able to, and often do, litigate under the benefits of Justiça Gratuita, making it an even weaker indicator of socioeconomic disadvantage than representation by a state lawyer.[47] The most telling case was perhaps that of a Court of Appeals judge who requested Justiça Gratuita and was granted it (judges are the best paid public servants in Brazil, occupying the top 1 per cent of the income pyramid).[48]

7.4.3 Health Services Habitually Used by the Litigant

Another proxy that studies have employed in the endeavour to gauge litigants' socioeconomic profile is the kind of health services they

46 Statements of the Civil Coordination of Judges of Porto Alegre – RS. Statement (Enunciado) no. 2: 'The benefit of legal aid can be granted, without further investigation, to those who have a monthly income of up to ten (10) minimum wages' (approved at the meeting of 23 May 2002).

47 A good illustration can be seen in the study of Biehl et al., 'Judicialization of Heath and the Quest for State Accountability', in Rio Grande do Sul. Although 66.8 per cent in their sample were represented by state lawyers (public defender, 57.4 per cent, federal legal counsel, 7 per cent and university clinics, 2.4 per cent), 91 per cent of the lawsuits had requested Justiça Gratuita. A significant proportion of those represented by private lawyers (32.2 per cent in their sample) must therefore have requested Justiça Gratuita, likely successfully. Ibid., at 212.

48 M. Muniz, 'Desembargador pede Justiça gratuita e dois ministros do STJ votam a favor', JOTA, 10 May 2018, available at: www.jota.info/justica/desembargador-pede-justica-gratuita-ministros-votam-favor-10052018, accessed 20 March 2019.

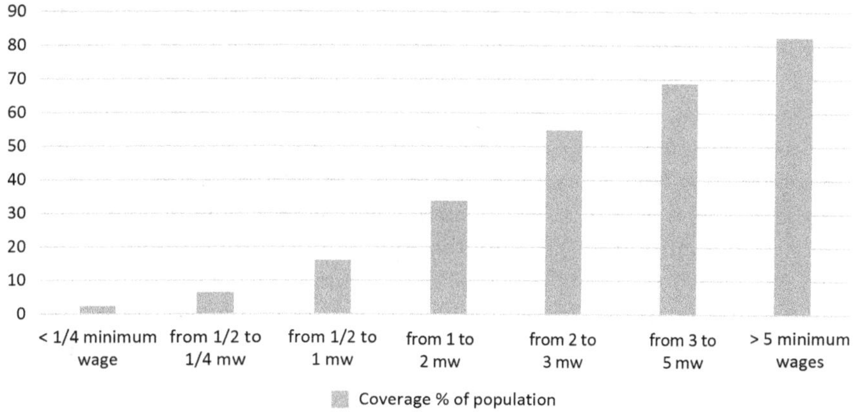

Figure 7.4 Percentage of population covered by private health insurance.
Source: IBGE, 2010

habitually use. Again, due to the high levels of inequality in Brazil, health services, just as legal services, are significantly segregated by financial capacity, as we saw in Chapter 4. Of those with income of less than one-quarter of the minimum wage, only 2.3 per cent have private health insurance, whereas 82.5 per cent of those with income above five times the minimum wage do (see Figure 7.4).[49] We can assume with some degree of confidence, thus, that beneficiaries of private health insurance tend to be much better off than those who rely exclusively on services provided by the public health system.

However, as Figure 7.4 shows, even those in the lowest income groups are covered by private insurance, though at a very low proportion and often with much lower coverage than those at the top. There are several potential explanations for this. One, already mentioned, is the under-reporting of income and wealth in surveys. Another is the fact that the private insurance market offers several tiers of contracts, with some at very low prices (and coverage, of course) to entice low income clients. Yet another is that companies, especially larger ones, tend to offer private health insurance coverage as part of their package to all employees, including those earning low wages. But this need not detain us much here. We just need to be aware that, compared to access to private legal

[49] IBGE, *Um panorama da saúde no Brasil: Acesso e utilização dos serviços, condições de saúde e fatores de risco e proteção à saúde, 2008* (Rio de Janeiro: IBGE, 2010).

services, access to private health services is slightly less strong as an indicator of high socioeconomic profile, yet still a strong one.

Access to the services of the public health system, on the other hand, are again not as good an indicator of disadvantage. As with state legal services, but much more intensely, many in the higher echelons of income can and do access public health services in Brazil. For one thing, here there is no legal restriction such as being 'needy' or having income below a certain threshold. On the contrary, as the health system is universal according to the 1988 Constitution, anyone is entitled, by law, to access it. It is of course less likely that someone with high income (say from the top quintile) who is a beneficiary of private health insurance with extensive coverage will habitually prefer to use the public system. It is not unlikely at all, though, that he or she may use it from time to time, in particular, for some services. Good examples are parents who may use the public system to vaccinate their children at no cost rather than pay for it privately (as private health insurance plans normally don't cover vaccines). Another good example is someone who lives near one of the better state general or specialist hospitals, often linked to good public universities, who may prefer to use them rather than the ones offered by his or her private insurance. The practice is so widespread that the government tries to recover from private insurance companies millions every year spent with beneficiaries of those companies who use the public system.[50] Finally, there is also the possibility of

[50] Data from the National Survey (PNAD) shows that 7.1 per cent of users of health services of the public system have private health insurance and that for some services even more do: e.g., chemotherapy, radiotherapy, blood therapy or haemodialysis (11.6 per cent), vaccination, injections and plasters (11 per cent). See I. S. Santos et al., 'Mix público-privado no sistema de saúde brasileiro: Realidade e futuro do SUS', in *A Saúde no Brasil em 2030 – prospecção estratégica do sistema de saúde brasileiro: Estrutura do financiamento e do gasto setorial* (Rio de Janeiro: Fiocruz/IPEA/Ministério da Saúde/Secretaria de Assuntos Estratégicos da Presidência da República, 2013), vol. 4, 73–131, at 114. This possibility is actually legally recognised in the law that regulates private health insurance (Law 9.656/1998) and was challenged by the companies in the Supreme Court under the argument that it went against the principle of universality of the constitution. See also: Messeder et al., 'Mandados judiciais como ferramenta para garantia do acesso a medicamentos no setor público', at 530, explaining another factor that makes university hospitals a driver of litigation: 'These hospitals are units that customarily evaluate new technologies; becoming, as such, units that prescribe innovative medicines and treatments. When university hospitals prescribe drugs that are not yet standardized by the rest of the system they generate a permanent unmet demand. This situation predisposes the use of court orders as a resource for access. This finding is in agreement with observations made by other authors.' See also, on this point, V. L. Luiza, 'Acesso a medicamentos

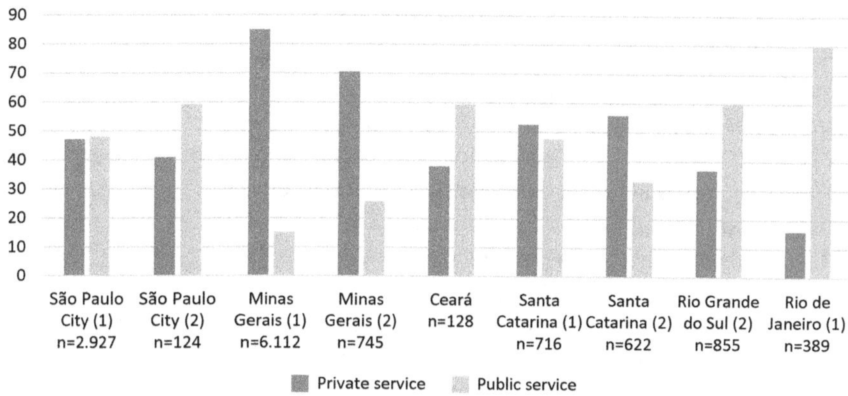

Figure 7.5 Percentage of lawsuits by health service that issued prescription used in litigation.
Source: Own formulation with data from several studies[51]

'validation' of private prescriptions by public services, that is, of claimants attending a public service for the exclusive purpose of getting a prescription to use in litigation.[52]

We need to be again careful, thus, when interpreting the data of Figure 7.5, not to automatically interpret that someone reporting to use the public system, or presenting a medical prescription from a doctor from a public hospital, is therefore a disadvantaged litigant. Silva and

essenciais no Estado do Rio de Janeiro', PhD thesis, Escola Nacional de Saúde Pública (2003).

[51] Chieffi, Barata, 'Judicialização da política pública de assistência farmacêutica e eqüidade'; Vieira, Zucchi, 'Distorções causadas pelas ações judiciais à política de medicamentos no Brasil'; Neto et al., 'Médicos, advogados e indústria farmacêutica na judicialização da saúde em Minas Gerais'; Machado et al., 'Judicialization of Access to Medicines in Minas Gerais State, Southeastern Brazil'; Pessoa, 'Perfil das solicitações administrativas e judiciais de medicamentos impetradas contra a secretaria de saúde do estado do Ceará'; Ronsein, 'Análise do perfil das solicitações de medicamentos por demanda judicial no Estado de Santa Catarina no período de 2005 a 2008'; Pereira et al., 'Análise das demandas judiciais para o fornecimento de medicamentos pela Secretaria de Estado da Saúde de Santa Catarina nos anos de 2003 e 2004'; Biehl et al., 'Between the Court and the Clinic'; Messeder et al., 'Mandados judiciais como ferramenta para garantia do acesso a medicamentos no setor público'. The data does not add up to 100 per cent, as I excluded from the chart cases in which the information was not available.

[52] Diniz, Machado, Penalva, 'A judicialização da saúde no Distrito Federal', at 594.

Terrazas' study is very illustrative of this point. To cover the possibility just explained, they decided to ask claimants in their sample not simply whether their medical prescription was issued by a doctor from a private or a public hospital (as studies normally do) but also what type of public hospital the claimant used, which they separated into 'ordinary' and 'reference' hospitals. What they called 'reference public hospitals' were those considered 'centres of excellence' within the public service, most of which, as mentioned, are linked to universities. Their findings show a high prevalence of private hospital prescriptions (60.63 per cent), but also a sizeable proportion originating from public hospitals (almost 40 per cent of their sample). When they disaggregate by type of public hospital, however, we see that two-thirds of those came from 'reference' hospitals and only one third from 'ordinary' ones.[53]

7.5 Conclusions

The high concentration of health litigation in the most developed states of Brazil (Chapter 5) and the significant barriers faced by most Brazilians to access justice (Chapter 6) seemed to confirm the well-established hypothesis that the haves tend to come out ahead in litigation. Given the strength of the contrary view in health litigation in Brazil, that is, that it represents a transformative tool that benefits by and large the most disadvantaged and neglected by the Brazilian public health system (the 'rights revolution' narrative), it was important to probe that hypothesis further. This chapter did so, looking closer at the socioeconomic profile of litigants to see if, at least in some of the pockets where health litigation happens so intensely in Brazil, it was perhaps reaching the most disadvantaged, or at least some of them.

The upshot of the inquiry is not very promising. All studies that tried to determine the socioeconomic profile of litigants through interviews or

[53] Not many studies disaggregate the data in this manner, but those that do also find a sizeable proportion of university hospitals among public hospitals used by claimants, e.g., Messeder et al., 'Mandados judiciais como ferramenta para garantia do acesso a medicamentos no setor público', finding 36.8 per cent in Rio de Janeiro, and Biehl et al., 'Between the Court and the Clinic', finding 14.7 per cent in Rio Grande do Sul. It is somewhat unfortunate that Silva and Terrazas' questionnaire did not include a direct question on whether the litigant had private health insurance or not. We would then be able to gauge how many of those with a public hospital prescription for the purposes of litigation were nonetheless covered by private health insurance.

using proxy indicators such as place of residence, type of legal representation (private or state lawyers) and type of health service habitually used (public or private) failed to detect, even on optimistic interpretations of the data, a high prevalence of poor litigants, whatever definition of poverty one uses, even if the relatively conservative definition of those at the bottom 40 per cent of income is employed.

According to the available data, a large proportion of litigants come from a relatively low number of municipalities and, within municipalities, a relatively low number of districts. These municipalities and districts tend to have the highest levels of socioeconomic development (as measured by HDI) of their already comparatively more developed regions, and therefore much higher than the average of Brazil as a whole. Within this already small universe, more appropriately described as a 'bubble', or a 'pocket' of health litigation, a large proportion of claimants are represented by private lawyers, use private health services and have high educational level by Brazilian standards. These are, as we saw, very strong indicators of high socioeconomic status in Brazil.

The data also show a sizeable proportion of cases represented by state lawyers where prescriptions backing the claim originate in the public health system. Yet these are much weaker indicators of low socioeconomic status, as explained in detail in this chapter. When all available data are put together and appropriately interpreted, it becomes clear that most of these litigants are still way better off than the average Brazilian, let alone the poorest.

The data presented and discussed in these three first chapters of Part II seem to weaken considerably, thus, the rights revolution narrative as a plausible account of the drivers of health litigation in Brazil. What we see so far, rather than transformative health litigation by large numbers of the poor, are a few pockets of claims driven by those who can either afford a private lawyer or access the limited services of a state one. Both groups are better off minorities in the Brazilian context – to different degrees of course, but still so.

In the final chapter of Part II (Chapter 8), the analysis of health litigation in Brazil will be completed by discussing in greater detail the *objects* of litigation, that is, the health interventions that feature most often in judicial claims. The focus will move, thus, from *who* litigates to *what* is litigated. This is crucial for a comprehensive understanding of the phenomenon for two main reasons. It will help us to grasp better both the drivers of health litigation (what motivates individuals to go to court) and its social impact (who benefits from litigation). As we shall see, depending on the kinds of health interventions that are most commonly litigated and how they are (or are not) incorporated into the public system, the social impact of litigation may vary considerably. It may even, as some claim, counter somewhat the regressive picture so far emerging through what is often called its *indirect* or *symbolic* effects.

8

Unequal Justice

What Is Litigated, Why, and Who Really Benefits?

The budget of the Brazilian health system is limited. When a judicial order forces the state to provide extremely expensive technologies, these resources will come out of other programmes and policies. More cost-effective and scientifically proven technologies may be unavailable for a great number of patients so that a small group of patients receive technologies of doubtful efficacy and effectiveness. This is the debate: whether the individual or the collective interest will prevail.[1]

José Gomes Temporão, public health expert and former Secretary of State for Health (2007–2011)

I do not ignore his responsibility. I am not Secretary of State for Health. I am a judge, I have the Constitution, which says that the right to health is guaranteed. I learn that Medicine can offer an alternative for this person to live with dignity. Let's be honest, the pain doesn't wait! I deal with the human, not with the coffer![2]

Justice Carmen Lucia, former President of the Supreme Federal Tribunal (2016–2018)

In this final chapter of Part II, my aim is to complete the analysis of the drivers and social impact of health litigation in Brazil carried out in Chapters 6 and 7. What makes people litigate and who really benefits from it? Is it mostly the poor, that is, those whose health is worse and who still lack access to important basic health actions and services, or is it

[1] Interview on 3 October 2016, Fundação Oswaldo Cruz, Agência Fiocruz de Notícias, 'Saúde Amanhã: Ex-ministro da Saúde, José Temporão fala sobre a Saúde na Justiça', https://agencia.fiocruz.br/saude-amanha-ex-ministro-da-saude-jose-temporao-fala-sobre-saude-na-justica, accessed 24 June 2019.

[2] Statement made on 7 November 2018 when opening a course on health for judges organised by the National Council of Justice, http://agenciabrasil.ebc.com.br/geral/noticia/2016-11/carmen-lucia-diz-que-sentencas-que-dao-acesso-remedios-sao-parte-da-democracia, accessed 26 July 2019.

by and large the better-off, the haves whose health conditions are already much better than the average?

I have argued so far that the truth seems closer to the latter hypothesis. I reached that conclusion by looking at the geographical distribution of health litigation across Brazil and at the available data on the socioeconomic profile of litigants. The data, neither perfect nor profuse, is nonetheless increasingly more comprehensive and points strongly towards a significant underrepresentation in health litigation of large sections of the Brazilian population, in particular, the most disadvantaged. As we saw in Chapters 5 and 7, health litigation occurs much more frequently in states, municipalities (and even districts according to some studies) with the highest indicators of socioeconomic development whereas it is low, or non-existent, in the rest of the country. Data on the socioeconomic profile of litigants (place of residence, levels of education and even self-reported income), although not easy to collect and therefore not very profuse, reinforce nonetheless that picture wherever it is available (see Chapter 7). When we add to the picture the significant limitations faced by a vast majority of Brazilians to access the justice system, caused by low levels of education, scarce possession of financial resources and difficulties to access legal representation, the hypothesis that health litigation benefits mostly the poor (the 'rights revolution narrative') becomes increasingly more implausible (see Chapter 6).

In this final chapter of Part II, the aim is to complete the analysis by discussing in greater detail a final important aspect of the question that we have only touched in passing till now: the *objects* of litigation, that is, the health interventions that feature most often in judicial claims. Our focus moves, thus, from *who* litigates to *what* is litigated. This is crucial for a comprehensive understanding of the phenomenon for two main reasons. First, it can help us to grasp better the drivers of health litigation, that is, *why* people litigate; what motivates individuals to go to court. Second, it allows us to arrive at a more robust and nuanced conclusion about the social impact of health litigation than we have so far. This is because, depending on the kinds of health interventions that are litigated and how they are (or are not) incorporated into the public system, the social impact of litigation may vary considerably. If, for instance, the health intervention claimed through litigation is one that could significantly benefit millions of deprived individuals and, due to individualised litigation promoted by some, become effectively incorporated in the system, its so-called *indirect* effects will be large and very positive. The haves may come out ahead in litigation, but everyone, including the poor, end up benefiting. A kind of 'judicial trickle-down' takes place. At the other end of the spectrum, if the health intervention litigated is one that only one or a few individuals can benefit from and never gets incorporated in the system because they are for instance extremely cost-ineffective, then the indirect effects of litigation are clearly negative. All it does is divert resources from the system to those able to litigate; a kind of 'judicial trickle-up'.[3]

8.1 Social Impact: A Framework

What is the social impact of health litigation? Is it positive, neutral, negative? This is of course a complex question whose answer depends on criteria on how to evaluate and measure social impact. There is not much agreement on this difficult issue, which may explain, to a great extent, why the literature on the judicialisation of health rarely ventures into this minefield. Without some agreement on this, however, it is simply impossible to make any assessment of the social impact of health litigation. In this and the next sections I will suggest an analytical framework to help us evaluate and measure the social impact of health litigation, which I hope may contribute to the advancement of the debate.

The central general question we are trying to answer seems to me the following: does litigation improve compliance by the state with its constitutional duty to guarantee the right to health? If it does, the social impact of litigation is positive. If it doesn't, it is neutral. In the worst possible scenario, litigation makes things worse; that is, its social impact is negative.

Though we speak rhetorically of health litigation's social impact as if it were one single homogenous phenomenon, it is clearly not. The overall social impact of health litigation is a composite of the different impacts that different types of litigation produce. If we find that a significantly large proportion of health litigation is of a similar type that produces a similar social impact then we can perhaps conclude that its overall impact is positive, neutral or negative. The prior step, however, is to identify all different types of litigation and assess their separate impact. This is what I aim to do here.

[3] As we shall see further in this chapter, these are only the two opposite ends of the spectrum. In between, there are at least two other possible scenarios.

To organise the inquiry and enable a reasonably nuanced analysis, I suggest that we look separately at the following two main aspects of the general question stated earlier. The first is whether litigation focuses on health interventions that the state should provide in light of its constitutional duty to guarantee the right to health (i). The second is whether judicially ordered interventions become effectively available to everyone (ii).

In the best possible scenario, litigation focuses on objects that should be provided by the public health system but aren't *and* induces effective policy changes that end up making these health interventions available to everyone. If we find that a significant proportion of health litigation in a certain country is of that kind, the conclusion is that its overall social impact is very positive. Litigation, in such a scenario, works at the same time as an important instrument of state accountability and progressive social change, extending to everyone in the population the benefits of the right to health.

At the opposite end of the spectrum (the worst possible scenario), health litigation focuses on objects that should not be provided by the public health system *and* do *not* benefit anyone except, perhaps, successful individual litigants themselves. Litigation here is neither an instrument of state accountability nor of progressive social change, quite the opposite. It forces the state to spend precious limited resources on health interventions that ought *not* to be part of the public system and benefits, at best, only those able to reach the courts (a small minority in Brazil, as we saw in Chapter 6).

Between these two extremes, we can think of at least two further intermediate scenarios that combine positive and negative answers to the two main questions of state accountability and social change. In the second-best possible scenario, litigation focuses mostly on objects that should be provided by the public health system *but* does *not* induce broad policy changes, benefiting only the litigants that manage to reach the courts. Although not very transformative, health litigation in this scenario is at least a legitimate tool of legal accountability to combat state failure. In the third-best (or second-worst possible scenario), litigation focuses on objects that should *not* be provided by the public health system *but does* induce effective policy changes that end up making these health interventions available to everyone in the population. Here, judicialisation is not a tool of legal accountability to combat state failure but at least affects everyone in the population equally. Not necessarily a great consolation depending on the opportunity costs involved, which can be very high.

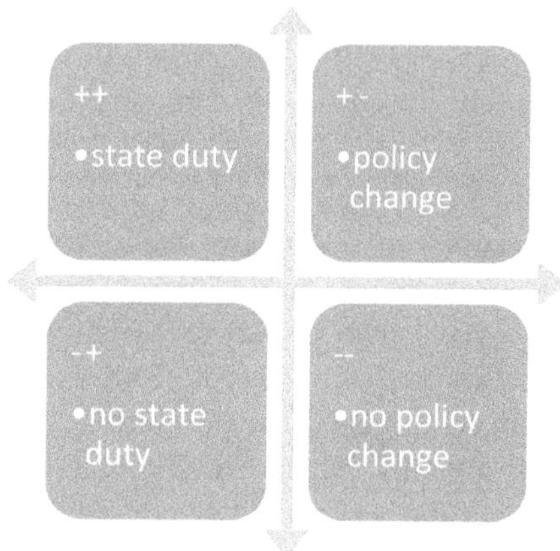

Figure 8.1 Four scenarios of social impact

We could of course imagine more scenarios and add much more detail to each of these scenarios to make our evaluation of social impact more fine-grained. We could, for instance, classify health interventions granted via litigation according to priority-setting criteria, as some interesting studies have started to do with promising results (see Section 8.5). But, for now, this more generic framework will suffice to allow us to proceed.

The next important step in our inquiry is to specify criteria to determine the crucial question of what the state should provide in the public health system in light of its duty to guarantee the right to health.

8.2 The Duty of the State

Although the question of what the public health system should provide to all citizens is crucial to a good analysis of the drivers, social impact and the very legitimacy of health litigation, it does not feature very often – nor in much depth when it does – in debates on the judicialisation of health in Brazil and elsewhere. The general assumption among supporters of health litigation in Brazil – especially among judges and activists, but also some academics – seems to be that whenever someone goes to court to claim the right to health, the state has obviously failed in its duty to guarantee the right to health. The following passage of a decision by the Brazilian Supreme Court repeatedly cited with approval by lower courts summarises this position:

> [The constitutional order legitimises] the Judiciary to act in those hypotheses in which the government, abnormally, *fails to respect the constitutional commandment*, frustrating, arbitrarily, the socio-juridical effectiveness, be it for intolerable omission, be it for any other unacceptable modality of governmental deviant behaviour.[4] (my emphasis)

In less convoluted terms,[5] Justice Celso Mello (the rapporteur of the decision) is saying that courts, when deciding against the state in health litigation, are simply forcing it to respect its constitutional duty. Nothing wrong with that idea *in itself*, of course. This is precisely what legal accountability is supposed to do. The problem is that Brazilian courts rarely specify what it actually means for the state to fail in its constitutional duties, that is, what precisely the constitutional right to health imposes on the state in terms of provision of health benefits to the population. The state is condemned, most of the time, on vague accusations of 'intolerable omission', 'unacceptable deviant behaviour', etc.[6]

This is hardly an appropriate exercise of the important judicial function to hold government accountable to its constitutional duties. In Part III, I discuss this in further detail and put forward what in my view courts can and ought to do to exercise that role appropriately (see Chapter 9).

[4] Supreme Federal Tribunal, RE 271.286 (2000), Ministro Celso de Mello.

[5] In my view, the unnecessarily convoluted language normally used by Brazilian judges represents an important psychological barrier to access to justice alongside the many others discussed in great length in Chapter 6. This is of course not a peculiarity of the Brazilian legal system. See S. Scheingold, *The Politics of Rights: Lawyers, Public Policy and Political Change* (New Haven: Yale University Press, 1974).

[6] Studies that analyse the reasoning of decisions in health litigation all find a similar pattern of lack of mention, let alone analysis of health policies, see D. C. L. Borges, M. A. D. Ugá, 'Conflicts and Impasses in the Judicialization of the Supply of Medicines: Circuit Court Rulings on Claims Brought against the State of Rio de Janeiro, Brazil, in 2005', (2010) 26 (1) *Cadernos de Saúde Pública*, 59–69, at 62: 'What is striking is that decisions do not mention criteria for medicines' selection, nor official programmes and lists, even though a large part of claims relate to medicines not included in these lists.' See, for confirmation of this point, the recent report of the Conselho Nacional de Justiça, of 2019, which scoured the text of 164,587 court of appeal decisions across the country in health litigation cases searching for any mention of the terms CONITEC (the organ that assesses and advises on technology incorporation), RENAME, REMUME and RENASES (government lists of actions, services and medicines) and also the general term 'protocols' (as in clinical protocols, see appendix). The results are very low, ranging from 0 per cent in some regions to 8.54 per cent in the highest, confirming that most judges either do not have much knowledge about incorporation, lists and how they work and/or do not think they are relevant in the adjudication of right to health cases. Conselho Nacional de Justiça, *Judicialização da Saúde no Brasil: Perfil das Demandas, Causas e Propostas de Solução* (São Paulo: Instituto de Ensino e Pesquisa – Insper, 2019), at 65–67.

My aim here is to tackle the more general question of what states are under a duty to provide to citizens in order to guarantee the constitutional right to health, which is crucial to complete our analysis of the drivers and social impact of health litigation.

8.2.1 A 'Right to Everything'?

Both the assumption that health litigation automatically involves state failure and the omission to define what state failure actually means seem to be influenced by a particular expansive interpretation of the right to health that is rather pervasive, certainly in Brazil, but also in other countries, in particular, in Latin America.[7] According to that interpretation, the right to health imposes a duty on the state to provide to individuals *any* health benefit they claim to need, so long as it is backed by medical opinion. Here is an example of this interpretation from a recent case decided in the second highest court in Brazil, the Superior Tribunal of Justice (STJ):

> As it is known, a medical doctor's prescription, from the private or public system, is sufficient as evidence that the treatment in question is needed. *Neither the public administration nor the judiciary can challenge this*, as they would be interfering unduly in the medical arena.[8] (my emphasis)

When the right to health is interpreted in this manner, it is not surprising that health litigation is seen by default as a response to state failure. If the

[7] See O. F. Norheim, B. M. Wilson, 'Health Rights Litigation and Access to Medicines: Priority Classification of Successful Cases from Costa Rica's Constitutional Chamber of the Supreme Court', (2014) 11(16) *Health and Human Rights*, 47–61. See also O. L. M. Ferraz, 'Health in the Courts of Latin America', (2018) 20(1) *Health and Human Rights*, 67–77.

[8] My translation from the Portuguese. Agravo de Instrumento no. 1.114.613/MG (decided on 8 May 2009), Min. Mauro Campbell Marques. ('Como se sabe, a prescrição feita por médico particular ou do serviço público se presta a comprovar a necessidade do tratamento em questão, não cabendo à Administração Pública, nem ao Poder Judiciário, discuti-la, uma vez que estaria adentrando no campo médico.') See also Voto no. 05215 Reexame Necessário no. 1002469-71.2.018.8.26.0066 Impetrante: Maria Rodrigues de Oliveira (Justiça Gratuita) Impetrado: Secretário Municipal de Sáude de Barretos 2ª Vara Cível da Comarca de Barretos Magistrado: Dr. Carlos Fakiani Macatti, citing precedent from the STJ: 'The medical prescription, signed either by a private doctor or by a public doctor, is sufficient to prove the necessity of the medicine. To accept the understanding of the state, which intends to discuss the prescription, would be to enter the realm of the doctor responsible for the treatment of the patient. Unless there is an obvious error in the medical report/prescription, that is, when the prescription is teratological, it is not appropriate for the administrator, nor for the Judiciary, to question whether this or that drug would be the most appropriate.'

public administration has to provide to every individual anything that his or her doctor believes to be medically beneficial, the role of the state becomes one of a mere supplier of health goods, a sort of a giant pharmacy.[9] Lack of supply, whatever its reason, is automatically seen as state failure. I call this the 'right to everything' conception of the right to health (see Chapter 6, section 6.3.1).[10]

This is not an appropriate way to interpret the right to health and the corresponding duties of the state. There are several good reasons for a health system – in particular, but not exclusively, a public one – not to provide everything that a person and her doctor demand as a health need. The most conspicuous is the fact that health resources are finite and claims on those resources always exceed them, often by a large margin. Another is that medical interventions can often be ineffective or unsafe, requiring therefore strict regulation by health authorities in terms of if and how they should be incorporated in the health system. A further related reason (more common than one may expect) is that doctors often issue inadequate prescriptions, for a set of reasons ranging from lack of knowledge to undue economic influence.[11]

9 See the excellent discussion of the difference between health needs and health demands in K. Syrett, *Law, Legitimacy and the Rationing of Health Care* (New York: Cambridge University Press, 2007).

10 See also O. L. M. Ferraz, 'What Course without Evils?: Rare Diseases, Children's Right to Health and the Sustainable Development Goals', in Fenton-Glynn, C. (ed.), *Children's Rights and Sustainable Development: Interpreting the UNCRC for Future Generations* (Cambridge: Cambridge University Press, 2019), 78–113; O. L. M. Ferraz, 'Two Conceptions of Social and Economic Rights: Basic Needs versus Equality', in Campbell, T. and Bourne, K. (eds.), *Political and Legal Approaches to Human Rights* (Oxford: Routledge, 2017). For studies showing that the only evidence required in most successful cases is a medical prescription, see: V. L. E. Pepe et al., 'Characterization of Lawsuits for the Supply of "Essential" Medicines in the State of Rio de Janeiro, Brazil', (2010) 26(3) *Cadernos de Saúde Publica*, 461–471, at 469; L. C. Romero, *Judicialização das políticas de assistência farmacêutica: O caso do Distrito Federal* (Brasília: Consultoria Legislativa do Senado Federal, 2008), at 41; F. Vieira, P. Zucchi, 'Distorções causadas pelas ações judiciais à política de medicamentos no Brasil', (2007) 41(2) *Revista de Saúde Pública*, 214–222; S. B. Marques, S. G. Dallari, 'Safeguarding of the Social Right to Pharmaceutical Assistance in the State of São Paulo', (2007) 41 *Revista de Saúde Pública*, 101–107; J. M. B. Sant'ana, 'Essencialidade e assistência farmacêutica: Um estudo exploratório das demandas judiciais individuais para acesso a medicamentos no Estado do Rio de Janeiro', MPhil dissertation, Escola Nacional de Saúde Pública, Fundação Oswaldo Cruz (2009).

11 As Pepe et al. aptly observe: 'It is worth remembering that several factors can negatively influence the quality of medical prescription and, therefore, inadequate prescriptions are not uncommon. Drug advertising, for example, has a strong influence on the prescribing pattern of physicians in the absence of effective tools to control the veracity of information.' Pepe et al., 'Characterization of Lawsuits for the Supply of "Essential" Medicines

Any health system, thus, justifiably excludes several health interventions from the package made available to the public for different valid reasons. Some health interventions will be left out because, after going through the regulatory process of approval, they are found not to be effective in dealing with the relevant health issue. Others will be rejected because they prove to be unsafe. Some will be both ineffective and unsafe. Others will be effective and safe, but only for particular groups in the population or for particular health conditions or when used in particular ways. Regulatory authorities will normally issue official instructions so that these interventions can be effectively and safely used in the system (so-called clinical protocols or clinical guidelines). Last but not least, some health interventions might be both effective and safe yet prove to be too expensive in light of its expected benefits and the limited resources available in any health system ('cost-ineffective' in technical parlance). The 'right to everything' conception overlooks all these possible valid justifications for the state not to provide a litigant with the medical intervention she or he demands through litigation, even when backed by a doctor's prescription.

8.2.2 A Right to Equitable Access to Safe, Effective and Affordable Interventions

As the public health system should not and cannot provide everything to everyone, the right to health is best seen as a right to equitable access to a package of safe and effective interventions that the state can afford to provide within its available resources. The challenge is to determine what should be provided and how this should be decided? These are not easy tasks. As regards effectiveness and safety, the regulatory agencies of the state need to review a myriad of studies, often incomplete and inconclusive, to decide, under conflicting pressures from private companies, patient associations, politicians and the public in general, whether a health intervention should be approved or not. As regards the limited availability of resources, the difficulties are perhaps even more daunting. Whether a health intervention will eventually be provided or not in the

in the State of Rio de Janeiro, Brazil', at 468. See also: G. H. Brundtland, 'Global Partnerships for Health', (1999) 13 *WHO Drug Information*, 61–64; M. J. D. Fagundes et al., 'Análise bioética da propaganda e publicidade de medicamentos', (2007) 12 *Revista Ciência & Saúde Coletiva*, 221–229.

public system depends on a web of complex and heavily contested political and technical interconnected decisions in the legislature and at different levels of government on how to allocate the limited health budget among infinite competing claims. (The Appendix to this chapter explains how each of these two complex processes of regulatory approval and incorporation take place in Brazil for those interested in their intricate details.)

How can we determine if the political and technical decisions taken by state authorities in these intractable areas are correct? This is, ultimately, the question that needs to be answered in order to establish if the state has complied or not with its duty to guarantee the right to health, which, in turn, is crucial for the assessment of the social impact of litigation. I carry out a fuller discussion of this difficult issue and a more detailed defence of my views in Chapter 9 when I analyse the appropriate role of courts in the adjudication of the right to health. Here I will only present a summary version of my arguments and conclusions in order to proceed in the analysis of the social impact of health litigation.

My view is that the concept of the right to health, as abstractly formulated in the Brazilian Constitution and international treaties ratified by Brazil, rarely provides clear guidance for the definition of the exact substantive content of the corresponding duties of the state. The constitution does not (and could not) specify in any detail what package of health interventions the state is under a constitutional duty to provide to all its citizens, as this involves answering, on a continuing basis across time, all those intractable political and technical questions just mentioned on how to set and spend the limited available resources of the health budget.[12]

Once this simple fact is acknowledged, it becomes clear that the government and the legislature should enjoy a great deal of freedom to arrive at appropriate substantive answers to these complex questions. That does not mean, I hasten to add, discretion to choose any answer whatsoever, or no answer at all. The right to health may not entail precise substantive answers but it does impose several important constraints on the political powers, including strict duties of diligence, rationality,

[12] As I explain in Chapter 9, this is not a problem with the way in which the right to health has been formulated in the Brazilian Constitution and international treaties that recognise that right, but rather in the nature of what I call distributive rights, that is, rights that depend on limited resources, which are virtually all rights. See also J. Tobin, *The Right to Health in International Law* (New York: Oxford University Press, 2012).

transparency, participation, non-discrimination and good faith in the discharge of their constitutional responsibility of advancing the health of the population as well as they can within available resources.

These are not trivial duties, as I discuss in greater length in Chapter 9 and unlike some supporters of social rights believe.[13] As I also discuss in that chapter, the concept of a 'minimum core' of the right to health can provide some substantive content to these more procedural duties, though it should not necessarily be defined by courts and imposed on the state through health litigation.

8.3 Government's Lists and Health Litigation

The elaboration and publication of so-called formularies (or simply 'lists') is arguably one of the most appropriate ways for states to discharge their constitutional duty to guarantee the right to health. They can constitute, in principle, a diligent, transparent, rational, participatory, non-discriminatory and good-faith process through which the package of health interventions to be provided to the population within the limited health budget is determined. Through this process, government health authorities, with the input of its health experts and, more and more often in several countries, including Brazil, members of civil society such as health professionals, academics, patients' representatives, deliberate about the introduction, utilisation or withdrawal of health interventions in the health system in light of the available evidence on effectiveness, safety and costs of interventions (see the Appendix for a detailed description of the process in Brazil). Once the lists are finalised and published, they serve as a transparent announcement to the public of the decisions made in the determination of the benefits available to everyone in the health system.[14]

The process of priority setting and formulation of lists is of course imperfect, as any institutional mechanism is, and can often fail in all

[13] See, for instance, D. Bilchitz, *Poverty and Fundamental Rights: The Justification and Enforcement of Socio-Economic Rights* (Oxford: Oxford University Press, 2007).

[14] They can also serve as an important instrument of equitable and effective management of any system, aiding the important collaboration between clinicians and managers, improving quality and reducing variations in clinical care, supporting the supply arrangements of medicines across a local health economy, supporting financial management and expenditure on medicines across health communities, encouraging prescribers to follow good practice, etc. See National Institute for Health and Care Excellence – NICE, 'Developing and Updating Local Formularies', 14 March 2014, available at www.nice.org.uk/guidance/mpg1, accessed 22 July 2020.

the important aspects mentioned (diligence, transparency, non-discrimination, etc.). But, in reasonably well-functioning democracies, inclusion and exclusion from a government's list should nonetheless constitute an important point of departure for any serious analysis of whether a certain health intervention ought to be provided by the state or not. It can offer, thus, a crucial piece of information for the assessment of the drivers and social impact of health litigation. A lawsuit demanding an 'on-list' health benefit provides prima facie evidence of state failure. By contrast, if the litigated intervention is 'off-list', the prima facie evidence is that the state should not provide it, that is, it has not failed in its constitutional duty.

I will explain in more detail in Section 8.4 why, unlike part of the literature, I am emphasising the prima facie, that is, non-absolute character of the on-list/off-list distinction as evidence of state failure. But let us have a glimpse, first, of what studies have found on this topic. Figure 8.2 shows the percentage of off-list medicines (most studies focus on medicines) claimed successfully through health litigation in several states of Brazil.

We should of course interpret these studies with some caution. They vary significantly in their sample sizes, methodologies, time span, etc. We also see significant variation in the findings of studies of the same place, that is, São Paulo (between 38 per cent and 77.4 per cent), Rio Grande do Sul (44 per cent and 63 per cent) and Rio de Janeiro (48 per cent and 66 per cent). But there is one convergence among all studies that is rather noteworthy. All of them find a sizeable volume of *off-list* medicines claimed through health litigation across several states: never below 38 per cent, above 50 per cent in all but three studies and often above 60 and 70 per cent of the medicines litigated.[15] There is extensive prima facie evidence, thus, for us to discard state failure as an obvious main

[15] The data collected by these studies completely contradict the following statement repeated by Justice Gilmar Mendes in several of his decisions after the 2009 Public Hearing on the judicialidation of health: 'In the majority of cases, judicial intervention does not occur on the face of an absolute omission of public policies aimed at protecting health, but rather in view of determining compliance with already established policies.' My translation from the original in Portuguese, 'Na maioria dos casos, a intervenção judicial não ocorre em razão de uma omissão absoluta em matéria de políticas públicas voltadas à proteção do direito à saúde, mas tendo em vista uma necessária determinação judicial para o cumprimento de políticas já estabelecidas.' See: Supremo Tribunal Federal, STF, SS 4045, rel. Min. Gilmar Mendes, decided on 7 April 2010. Dje-066 published on 14 April 2010.

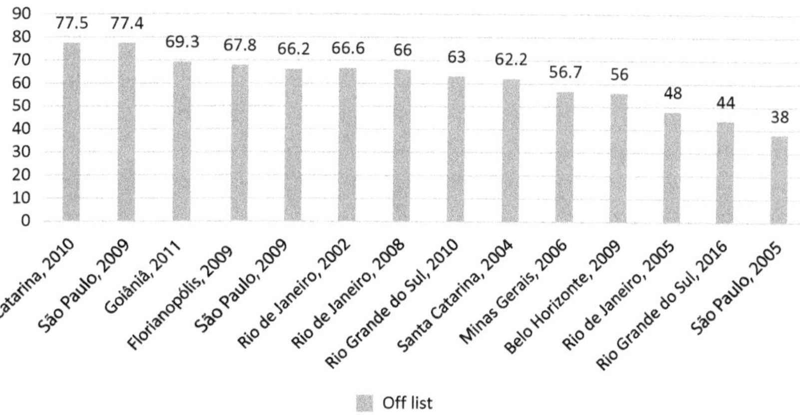

Figure 8.2 Percentage of off-list medicines claimed, different states and municipalities.
Sources: Own formulation with data from various studies[16]

driver of health litigation in Brazil, unless we adopt the implausible view that the federal Ministry of Health and the Health Departments of all these states are utterly incompetent and corrupt in the formulation of their pharmaceutical assistance policies.

16 A. L. Chieffi, R. Barata, 'Judicialização da política pública de assistência farmacêutica e eqüidade', (2009) 25(8) *Cadernos de Saúde Pública*, 1839–1849; Vieira, Zucchi, 'Distorções causadas pelas ações judiciais à política de medicamentos no Brasil'; O. H. Campos Neto et al., 'Médicos, advogados e indústria farmacêutica na judicialização da saúde em Minas Gerais', (2012) 46 Revista de Saúde Pública, 784–790; M. A. A. Machado et al., 'Judicialization of Access to Medicines in Minas Gerais State, Southeastern Brazil', (2011) 45(3) *Revista de Saúde Pública*, 590–598; N. T. Pessoa, 'Perfil das solicitações administrativas e judiciais de medicamentos impetradas contra a secretaria de saúde do estado do Ceará', MPhil dissertation, Universidade Federal do Ceará (2007); J. G. Ronsein, 'Análise do perfil das solicitações de medicamentos por demanda judicial no Estado de Santa Catarina no período de 2005 a 2008', MPhil dissertation, Universidade Federal de Santa Catarina (2010); J. R. Pereira et al., 'Análise das demandas judiciais para o fornecimento de medicamentos pela Secretaria de Estado da Saúde de Santa Catarina nos anos de 2003 e 2004', (2010) 15(Suppl. 3) *Ciência & Saúde Coletiva*, 3551–3560; J. G. Pereira, V. L. E. Pepe, 'Acesso a medicamentos por via judicial no Paraná: Aplicação de um modelo metodológico para análise e monitoramento das demandas judiciais', (2014) 15(2) *Revista de Direito Sanitário*, 31–45; J. Biehl et al., 'Between the Court and the Clinic: Lawsuits for Medicines and the Right to Health in Brazil', (2012) 14(1) *Health and Human Rights*, 36–52; J. Biehl et al., 'The Judicialization of Health and the Quest for State Accountability: Evidence from 1,262 Lawsuits for Access to Medicines in Southern Brazil', (2016) 18(1) *Health and Human Rights*, 209–220; A. M. Messeder et al., 'Mandados judiciais como ferramenta para garantia do acesso a medicamentos no setor público: A experiência do Estado do Rio de Janeiro', (2005) 21(2) *Cadernos de Saúde Pública*, 525–534; Pepe et al., 'Characterization of Lawsuits for the Supply of "Essential" Medicines in the State of Rio de Janeiro, Brazil'.

On the other hand, the volume of *on-list* medicines that are litigated is by no means negligible, being never below 20 per cent, and reaching more than 60 per cent in a couple of studies.[17] There is also prima facie evidence, thus, that at least part of health litigation in Brazil may be motivated by state failure.

But to reach a more robust and definite conclusion, we need to test these signals more deeply. We need to be particularly cautious not to use the on-list/off-list distinction too hastily as often seen in the literature. The distinction is useful, I emphasise, as initial, prima facie evidence, but it is too crude to capture the complexity not only of health policy but also of how the judicial system works, which in turn affects the motivations of those who litigate, that is, the drivers of litigation. On one hand, there are several plausible situations in which on-list medicines (or other on-list interventions) may feature in litigation without any failure of the state. On the other hand, there are also situations in which off-list medicines (or other off-list interventions) ought to be in the government lists but are not due to state failure. We need a much more fine-grained classification, thus, to capture all these potential situations.

In Section 8.4, I describe *eleven* different possible situations in health litigation, many of which contradict the on-list/off-list criterion.

8.4 Eleven Types of Health Litigation[18]

The first two situations, which I call types 1 and 6 for reasons that will become clear at the end, are the more straightforward cases, that is, those

[17] Although these percentages are lower when a different, and in my view more appropriate, measurement is used. See Figure 8.3 and Sections 8.5 and 8.6.

[18] I discussed some of these possibilities in a less systematic manner in O. L. M. Ferraz, 'Brazil: Health Inequalities, Rights and Courts', in Yamin, A. and Gloppen S. (eds.), *Litigating Health Rights: Can Courts Bring More Justice to Health?* (Cambridge, MA: Harvard University Press, 2011), at 95–96. Other contributors to the literature on health litigation, in particular, those more familiar with the public health system, have also presented more nuanced classifications of claims. See, for interesting analyses: E. I. Macedo et al., 'A Technical Analysis of Medicines Request-Related Decision-Making in Brazilian Courts', (2011) 45(4) *Revista de Saúde Pública*, 706–713; T. A. Figueiredo, 'Análise dos medicamentos fornecidos por mandado judicial na Comarca do Rio de Janeiro: A aplicação de evidências científicas no processo de tomada de decisão', MPhil dissertation, Escola Nacional de Saúde Pública (2010); T. A. Figueiredo et al., 'Evidence-Based Process for Decision-Making in the Analysis of Legal Demands for Medicines in Brazil', (2013) 29(1) *Cadernos de Saúde Pública*, 159–166.

in which the on-list/off-list classification matches perfectly the state failure/no state failure distinction.

> Type 1 (clear state failure). A claimant requests an *on-list* intervention in the exact specification of the corresponding clinical protocol for her condition after being denied it through the ordinary administrative procedures for no justified reason.
>
> Type 6 (clear no state failure). A claimant requests an *off-list* intervention that has been duly assessed and rejected by the health authorities (i.e., failed the incorporation process) for unquestionably justified reasons such as lack of safety and ineffectiveness.

There is both some evidence and strong indication that many of the claims pursued through health litigation in Brazil fall into one of these two clear-cut types. Type 1 cases are mostly caused by well-known problems of shortage of medicines, equipment and facilities in the public health system. Type 6 cases have several potential drivers, ranging from marketing strategies of pharmaceutical companies to patients hopes that a new medicine or technique may cure their condition.[19] Recent examples of such litigation include thousands of cases successfully claiming the infamous 'cancer pill' (based on the substance Phosphoethanolamine), which promised a cure for cancer, and several other cases requesting an eye surgery procedure performed in Cuba, which judges ordered the state to pay, including travel and accommodation costs, despite its rejection as unsafe by the Brazilian Federal Counsel of Ophthalmologists. In an infamous passage of a decision granting that procedure, Justice Luiz Fux of the SFT declared 'the right to have hope' as the grounds for his ruling. [20]

[19] See Macedo et al., 'A Technical Analysis of Medicines Request-Related Decision Making in Brazilian Courts', at 6. See also Figueiredo, 'Análise dos medicamentos fornecidos por mandado judicial na Comarca do Rio de Janeiro', at 103–104.

[20] For the 'cancer pill', see D. W. L. Wang, O. L. M. Ferraz, 'Fosfoetanolamina – A Proteção Judicial à Medicina sem Base em Evidência: Como os juízes devem proteger o direito à saúde?', Jota, 8 November 2015, available at: www.jota.info/paywall?redirect_to=//www.jota.info/opiniao-e-analise/artigos/a-protecao-judicial-a-medicina-sem-base-em-evidencia-08112015. For the case of eye surgeries in Cuba, in which Justice Luiz Fux infamously declared 'the right to have hope', see Recurso Extraordinário 368.564 (Rapporteur Min. Menezes Direito, decided on 13 April 2011). For earlier cases, see Messeder et al., 'Mandados judiciais como ferramenta para garantia do acesso a medicamentos no setor público', at 528, reporting that the medicine Gangliosídeo, banned from the market by ANVISA, was regularly granted by courts. Several other cases are reported in the media from time to time of judicial decisions granting experimental treatment abroad to claimants.

If all cases in health litigation were types 1 or 6, the on-list/off-list criterion would be perfectly reliable to distinguish between cases in terms of drivers and social impact and the findings reported in Figure 8.2 would represent a perfect summary of health litigation in Brazil. But the reality of health litigation is not that simple. There are at least *nine* other types of health litigation where the on-list/off-list distinction proves much less helpful, requiring further information to allow an appropriate evaluation of the causes and legitimacy of litigation.

Let us start with situations in which the public health system may reject the provision of *on-list* medicines for various potentially legitimate reasons related to the nature and design of health interventions and policies.

> Type 2a. A claimant being treated in a private hospital requests an on-list medicine that is available only for those treated in officially approved institutions.
>
> Type 2b. A claimant requests an on-list medicine yet in a different formulation or from a different make from the ones offered in the public system.
>
> Type 2c. A claimant requests an on-list medicine yet for a different use than that for which it is approved (so-called off-label use).

In all of these three types of health litigation, it would be wrong to automatically deduce that state failure is the driver of litigation simply because the medicine requested is on-list. The actual immediate driver of litigation is rather the desire of the litigant to be provided with a medicine from a different make, in a different formulation, for a different purpose or in a different setting than that established in the government's policies. Whether these demands are still legitimate and ought to be granted by the judiciary is a different discussion.[21] I will argue in Section 8.5 and in Chapter 9 that they are in principle not, in particular, in the case of type 2a. Here I simply note that the on-list status of the medicine says very little about whether it should be provided or not (i.e., whether there has been state failure), unlike in Type 1 cases described above. Type 2a, 2b and 2c cases are thus better classified as *off-list* cases, since they are not actually part of the package of interventions that the state has committed to provide to all citizens. To use a medical metaphor,

[21] These immediate drivers can have different determinants ranging from marketing strategies of pharmaceutical companies to genuine better suitability of the requested medicine to the patient's individual needs.

they are a sort of 'false positives', that is, cases that appear at first to fit the category of on-list interventions but are actually better described as off-list.

Examples of litigation of that sort abound. The provision of cancer drugs in the public system, for instance, is part of the National Policy for the Prevention and Control of Cancer and subject to the protocols and rules established by the Ministry of Health.[22] One of these rules establishes that cancer drugs can only be dispensed to patients being treated in officially approved hospitals.[23] As several studies have shown, many judicial claims for cancer medicines are filed by patients being treated in private hospitals (Type 2a cases).[24] A good example of Type 2b cases (on-list medicines requested in different formulations or makes) is the 'Aspirin case' (acetylsalicylic acid). It was initially somewhat of a puzzle why such a simple and cheap on-list medicine would feature so often in litigation. If supply problems were the actual driver, then the public health system would be in real dire straits. A more detailed study in the state of São Paulo in 2014 partially solved the puzzle. It showed that 1,725 lawsuits requested 22 different brand names or formulations of aspirin from the ones offered in the public system lists, many of them of particularly well-branded makes.[25] Examples of Type 2c cases were also found in several studies. Macedo et al., for instance, found several drugs 'requested for the treatment of medical conditions that were not supported by clinical protocols' in their meticulous analysis of eighty-one judicial claims filed in the state of São Paulo between 2005 and 2009.[26]

[22] Established in Portaria 874, of 16 May 2013, available at: http://pesquisa.in.gov.br/imprensa/jsp/visualiza/index.jsp?jornal=1&pagina=129&data=17/05/2013. The policy is of course not perfect. For an official report of some of its perceived problems see: www.cgu.gov.br/noticias/2018/06/cgu-avalia-politica-nacional-de-prevencao-e-combate-ao-cancer-no-sus, accessed 23 June 2019.

[23] The so-called Unacons or Cacons (Unidade de Assistência de Alta Complexidade em Oncologia [Unacon] and Centro de Assistência de Alta Complexidade em Oncologia [Cacon]), see also Portaria 140/2014.

[24] See Vieira, Zucchi, 'Distorções causadas pelas ações judiciais à política de medicamentos no Brasil'; Chieffi, Barata, 'Judicialização da política pública de assistência farmacêutica e eqüidade'; V. A. da Silva, F. V. Terrazas, 'Claiming the Right to Health in Brazilian Courts: The Exclusion of the Already Excluded', (2011) 36(4) *Law & Social Inquiry*, 825–853.

[25] See Secretariat of Health of the State of São Paulo, 'Judicialização em Saúde no Estado de São Paulo', presentation of 14 May 2015 (on file with author). Another potential explanation for such claims is that they fall on Type 3a cases explained below.

[26] See Macedo et al., 'A Technical Analysis of Medicines Request-Related Decision Making in Brazilian Courts', at 5. In three cases, they could not even find evidence of benefit to

Messeder et al. reached a similar conclusion, stating that 'the surge in litigation for certain medicines cannot be explained by the increase in the prevalence of that pathological condition but rather, at least in part, by the inobservance by doctors of clinical protocols'.[27] Again, whether these claims are legitimate and ought to be granted or not can be debated. What seems clearly inappropriate in my view is to classify such cases as what I call Type 1 cases, that is, on-list cases where state failure is the clear driver of litigation.

In the next two types of on-list cases, the claimant may be motivated to litigate for strategic reasons, in particular, because the judicial route entails some comparative advantage vis-à-vis the administrative route.

> Type 3a. A claimant's primary request is an off-list intervention but he/she includes, in the same claim, on-list medicines that the therapeutic programme also requires.
>
> Type 3b. A claimant requests an on-list intervention judicially as a faster way of obtaining it, that is, as a form of 'queue-jumping'.[28]

the patient to justify the use of the drugs, arguing convincingly that: 'According to the precepts of rational pharmaceutical use, the dismissal of such appeals would be more beneficial for the patients than granting them access to the requested medications.' See also M. G. M. Ferreira, 'Perfil das demandas judiciais para acesso a Medicamentos no Município de Itaperuna: Uma contribuição sobre novas perspectivas de acesso racional e igualitário', MPhil dissertation, Universidade Estácio de Sá (2007); see also R. Mapelli, *Judicialização da Saúde – Regime Jurídico do SUS e Intervenção na Administração Pública* (São Paulo: Atheneu, 2017).

27 See Messeder et al., 'Mandados judiciais como ferramenta para garantia do acesso a medicamentos no setor público', at 533. See also V. S. Gomes, T. A. Amador, 'Studies Published in Indexed Journals on Lawsuits for Medicines in Brazil: A Systematic Review', (2015) 31(3) *Caderno de Saúde Pública*, 1–12, at 10: 'The presence of such medicines [in litigation] can be justified since their supply is tied to the Clinical Protocols and Therapeutic Guidelines, and many patients may be using them for off-label treatment.' See C. S. Paula, 'Uso Off Label de Medicamentos: Análise das Demandas Judiciais no CEMEPAR e Conduta dos Farmacêuticos no Paraná', MPhil dissertation, Universidade Federal do Paraná (2010), reporting that 'out of 138 pharmacists surveyed, 76.81% said that received a prescription drug prescribed for an indication of use different from that stated in the package insert, 82.61%, related to dose or frequency of use and 63.77% for the patient in age other than those recommended in literature', (page number not available). A very recent example with a large cost to the public system is the request of Miglustate, approved for Gaucher disease, to be used for Niemann-Pick Type C, rejected for lack of evidence of efficacy by CONITEC in May 2019, see: http://conitec.gov.br/images/Consultas/Relatorios/2019/Relatiro_Miglustate_Niemann_Pick_CP_25_2019.pdf, accessed 27 May 2019.

28 Borges, Ugá, 'Conflicts and Impasses in the Judicialization of the Supply of Medicines'.

These two further situations show, again, that the presence of on-list medicines or other on-list interventions in litigation may have less to do with state failure to provide a particular intervention than with other drivers, in these cases litigants' strategies in the navigation of the legal and health systems. There is strong indication of Type 3a claims in the findings of many studies, as the majority of claims involve the request of more than one medicine (often several in the same claim)[29] and a large proportion of those include both on-list and off-list medicines.[30] When this happens, though it is impossible to determine for sure what made the claimant include on-list medicines in the judicial request, it is plausible to assume that in many cases the primary request is the off-list intervention. A good illustration is provided by Chieffi and Barata in their detailed study of health litigation in the state of São Paulo in a large sample of more than 3,000 lawsuits. As they report, many of those litigating for off-list medicines included on-list ones in their requests. As a common example, they cite off-list diabetes drugs (analogue insulins), which were often requested alongside several on-list medicines such as regular insulin, aspirin, atorvastatin or simvastatin in the same lawsuit 'despite the fact that these latter are accessible through the regular distribution of medications' in the public system.[31]

One way of testing the potential prevalence of Type 3a cases within a sample is to look not only at the proportion of off-list medicines out of the total of medicines litigated but also at the total of lawsuits in which at least one off-list medicine is requested as the proportion of the total sample. Unfortunately, not many studies have followed this reasonably easy to implement strategy. The few that have done so, however, provide us with interesting insights. I found three, all of them finding a significant difference between the two measures (see Figure 8.3).

As we can observe, the proportion varies significantly depending on what measure is used, being always higher when the measure is the proportion of lawsuits including at least one off-list medicine. Even in Rio Grande do Sul, it jumps from 44 per cent to 59 per cent. If a

[29] Macedo et al. found requests of as many as seven medicines in the same lawsuit in their study. See Macedo et al., 'A Technical Analysis of Medicines Request-Related Decision Making in Brazilian Courts'.

[30] See Chieffi, Barata, 'Judicialização da política pública de assistência farmacêutica e eqüidade'; Biehl et al., 'The Judicialization of Health and the Quest for State Accountability', among many studies with similar findings.

[31] Chieffi, Barata, 'Judicialização da política pública de assistência farmacêutica e eqüidade', at 1845–1846.

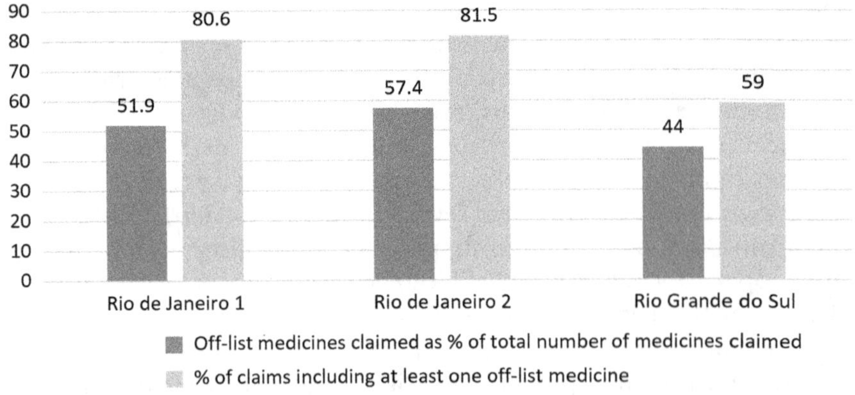

Figure 8.3 Two different measurements of off-list medicines claimed in health litigation.
Source: Own formulation with data from several studies[32]

significant proportion of these lawsuits are Type 3a cases according to the description above, it would seem that not even the few studies that found a majority of on-list medicines being claimed are really outliers.

The most common examples of Type 3b claims are requests for hospital beds, in particular, in intensive care units and surgical procedures such as organ transplantation. These are part of the package of interventions offered in the public system but are never sufficient to attend the existing demand, creating the traditional problem of long waiting lists. Some patients who are capable to resort to litigation (a minority as we saw in Chapters 6 and 7) end up taking their claims to the courts, most often successfully.[33]

***

[32] For Rio de Janeiro 1: Pepe et al., 'Characterization of Lawsuits for the Supply of "Essential" Medicines in the State of Rio de Janeiro, Brazil'. For Rio de Janeiro 2, see Sant'ana, 'Essencialidade e assistência farmacêutica'. For Rio Grande do Sul, see Biehl et al., 'The Judicialization of Health and the Quest for State Accountability'.

[33] See S. R. A. Moulin et al., 'Judicialização do Acesso à Internação em UTI no SUS: Análise Concreta de Pacientes do Estado do Espírito Santo', in Gebran Neto, J. P., Avanza, C. S. and Schulman, G. (eds.), *Direito da Saúde em Perspectiva: Judicialização, Gestão e Acesso*, vol. 2 (Vitória: Editora Abrages, 2017), 73–90; D. Diniz et al., 'A judicialização da saúde no Distrito Federal, Brasil', (2014) 19(2) *Ciênc. saúde coletiva*, 591–598. See also F. F. C. Gomes et al., 'Access to Medium and High-Complexity Procedures in the Brazilian Unified National Health System: A Matter of Judicialization', (2014) 30(1) *Cadernos de Saúde Pública*, 31–43, at 39.

Let me emphasise, once again, that I am not expressing a judgement here on the legitimacy of those claims described under Types 2 and 3 above. The point is simply to highlight that featuring on-list interventions among the requests is not, by itself, a very strong indicator that a judicial claim is driven by state failure. One should therefore avoid using the binary on-list/off-list classification as definitive evidence without first discussing and testing the several potential alternative drivers described above.[34] As we have seen, studies indicate that these alternative drivers are far from marginal and could represent a significant portion of litigation. I will go back to this important issue in Section 8.5.

Before that, we must turn now to cases featuring off-list requests that cannot be promptly dismissed as illegitimate, unlike the Type 6 cases explained above. Just as it would be hasty to infer state failure from all or most litigation involving *on-list* interventions, it would be equally unwarranted to conclude that litigation involving *off-list* interventions is automatically unjustified. The process of defining government's lists, like any institutional mechanism, is imperfect. There may well be many cases, thus, of litigation for off-list interventions that ought to be on-list but aren't due to some failure of the state. To use the medical metaphor again, these would be 'false negatives', that is, cases that appear at first to be unjustified but, on further investigation, may not be.

The trouble is to identify such cases, as it involves answering those intractable questions of what the health system ought to provide within its limited available resources that we saw have no clear-cut answers (see Section 8.2.2). Given the complexity of the task and the fierce disagreement it inevitably generates, my view is that a strong presumption of adequacy should be placed on the political and technical choices made at the legislative and administrative spheres of the state. In other words, if a health intervention is not on the government's list, the presumption

[34] For studies that seem to overlook this important caveat and adopt the on-list/off-list distinction in a definitive manner, see Biehl et al., 'The Judicialization of Health and the Quest for State Accountability', at 214: 'Our study found that the majority of patients requested low-cost drugs that were part of governmental drug formularies and that should have been publicly available.' Borges, Ugá, 'Conflicts and Impasses in the Judicialization of the Supply of Medicines', at 66: 'One observes omission from the Executive Branch – and the respective health agencies at each level of government responsible for the dispensation of medicines – since no less than 52 per cent of the drugs claimed in the lawsuits refer to products included in the pharmaceutical regulation [lists] of SUS.' My translation from the original in Portuguese.

ought to be that the state is not under a duty to provide it to the population.[35] Such presumption, though not absolute, should be rebutted only exceptionally, that is, when it is beyond doubt that a health intervention fulfils the appropriate criteria for incorporation but is nonetheless absent from government's lists. Type 4 cases describe this situation.

> Type 4. A claimant requests an off-list intervention that is safe and highly cost-effective according to the scientific consensus yet excluded from the government's list for no justified reason.

A good example of a case that in my view falls under Type 4 is the widely known South African case *Treatment Action Campaign* (or simply TAC), involving treatment for HIV-AIDS. If my reading of that case is correct, safe and highly cost-effective ART treatment against mother-to-child transmission of HIV was off-list in South Africa partly due to an unreasonable reluctance of the South African Health authorities to accept the consensual scientific evidence that it worked. As a result, hundreds of thousands of children were condemned to be infected by HIV during

[35] There has been a recognition of this point by some judges in the past few years, yet they seem often to be purely rhetorical. In a case decided at the STF in 2010 (STA 175), Justice Gilmar Mendes, then president of the court, stated that 'Compelling the public system to finance any and all existing health actions and services would create serious damage to the administrative order and would lead to the collapse of the SUS [public system], harming further the care of the portion of the population most in need. Therefore, we can conclude that, in general, the treatment provided by the SUS should be privileged instead of a different option chosen by the patient . . ..' The problem lies in the qualification of the general rule by the following condition that complements the passage quoted: 'whenever the ineffectiveness or the impropriety of the existing health policy is not proven'. The condition opens the possibility for the absolutist interpretation of the right to health to return through the back door (i.e., for the general rule to be practically swallowed by the exception). All it takes is for judges to interpret 'inefficiency' or 'impropriety' of the existing public policy as a mere synonym of non-incorporation by the public system of treatments and medicines available in the market that may somehow benefit the claimant according to the opinion of her or his doctor. This was precisely what happened in the case, as Mendes ended up granting the unincorporated drug Miglustat to the claimant on the basis of the 'exception' to the general rule (the drug has been recently rejected by the Brazilian incorporation agency, Conitec, for lack of evidence of efficacy). The decision of the general repercussion (repercussão geral) case RE 566.471 go in the same direction, as does the recent decision of the Superior Tribunal of Justice in the repetitive appeal [*recurso repetitivo*] case Recurso Especial no. 1.657.156 – RJ (2017/0025629-7). See my article, O. L. M. Ferraz, 'Para equacionar a judicialização da saúde no Brasil', (2019) 15(3) *Revista Direito GV*, dx.doi.org/10.1590/2317-6172201934.

birth.[36] It seems clear to me, thus, that the treatment should be on-list, that is, part of the package the South African state should provide to all citizens and that litigation in that case was driven by obvious state failure. It is a different, more complex question whether – and what kind of remedy – courts should issue against the state in such cases (a topic I discuss in Chapter 9).[37]

But these are extreme and gladly not very frequent cases in my view.[38] The following, much more common two situations are significantly more difficult to assess.

> Type 5a. A claimant requests an off-list intervention that is safe and effective according to the regulatory authorities yet has a therapeutic alternative that is less safe and/or less effective, yet more cost-effective.

The case of the new drugs for hepatitis C seems a good illustration of Type 5a claims. Although these new drugs were judged to be clinically safe and effective by regulatory authorities, their costs were so high that making them available for everyone, even in comparatively well-resourced systems such as the British NHS would be impossible to afford.[39] It is not at all clear, here, differently from Type 4 cases, whether such interventions should be off-list or on-list and also whether, being on-list, there should be some sort of limitation on who can have access to them (i.e., rationing).[40]

[36] See, for a good discussion of that case and comparison with cases in Brazil, Costa Rica and Colombia, O. F. Norheim, S. Gloppen, 'Litigating for Medicines: How Can We Assess Impact on Health Outcomes?', in Yamin, A. E. and Gloppen, S. (eds.), *Litigating Health Rights: Can Courts Bring More Justice to Health*? (Cambridge, MA: Harvard University Press, 2011).

[37] As I argue in Chapter 9, it is not obvious whether and how courts should intervene even in clear-cut state failure cases as they may cause more problems than they solve.

[38] In Brazil, Macedo et al., 'A Technical Analysis of Medicines Request-Related Decision Making in Brazilian Courts', at 6, describe a situation that may perhaps be classified as a Type 4 case: 'The lists of medications covered by SUS are limited to the first line of care and typically do not include alternative options for cases in which there are contraindications for the prescribed pharmaceuticals, such as cases of drug interactions in elderly patients taking multiple medications. This type of demand can be significantly reduced through improved training in pharmaceutical care services, enabling them to assess the individual needs of each patient, and by providing formal mechanisms in health management for accommodating claims based on the rational use of medications not covered by the SUS.'

[39] V. Charlton et al., 'Cost Effective but Unaffordable: An Emerging Challenge for Health Systems', (2017) 356 *BMJ*, 1402.

[40] Ibid.

Type 5b. A claimant requests an off-list intervention that is safe and effective according to the regulatory authorities, yet is extremely expensive and has *no* cheaper therapeutic alternative.

The best illustration of Type 5b cases are perhaps the so-called orphan drugs, that is, medicines developed to treat rare diseases whose price, due to the small number of patients suffering from the related condition, end up being extremely high in per capita terms and thus automatically fail cost-benefit assessments made by health authorities. This is in my view perhaps the hardest case of all. Though I sympathise strongly with claimants in that situation and tend to believe that the state should provide orphan interventions for the most serious conditions, I can also see how, from the perspective of the health system, it can be extremely challenging.[41] There is also an interesting debate on what duties, if any, the pharmaceutical companies have in facilitating access to the medicines they develop, in particular, to those patients who participate in their clinical trials.[42]

A final type of case, which is actually a variation of Type 5b but in my view not challenging at all, is Type 5c. The only, yet crucial difference is that in the latter there is a safe and more cost-effective therapeutic alternative in the public system.

Type 5c. A claimant requests an off-list intervention that is safe and effective according to the regulatory authorities yet is extremely expensive and *has* a safe and more cost-effective therapeutic alternative.

It seems difficult to see any valid reason to impose a duty on the state to provide the health interventions requested in claims of this type. They can therefore be added to Type 6 claims as ones in which there is clearly no state failure at the root of litigation. In both types, the state actually provides safe and effective options in the public system yet patients and doctors try to impose via litigation (and most often succeed as we will see

[41] See Ferraz, 'What Course without Evils'. For an account of litigation involving the rare Fabry disease and the participation of the pharmaceutical industry in such litigation, see: D. Sartoni Junior et al., 'Judicialização do acesso ao tratamento de doenças genéticas raras: A doença de Fabry no Rio Grande do Sul', (2012) 17 *Ciências & Saúde Coletiva*, 2717–2728. See also: D. Diniz et al., 'Consequências da judicialização das políticas de saúde: Custos de medicamentos para as mucopolissacaridoses', (2012) 28(3) *Cadernos de Saúde Pública*, 479–489.

[42] D. W. L. Wang, O. L. M. Ferraz, 'Pharmaceutical Companies vs. the State: Who Is Responsible for Post-Trial Provision of Drugs in Brazil?', (2012) 40(2) *The Journal of Law, Medicine & Ethics*, 188–196.

below) their own different preferences, at a very high opportunity cost to the public system.

***

It is possible that more types of health litigation can be identified beyond the eleven I have described above.[43] But these eleven types seem sufficient to cover most of the situations currently prevalent in Brazil (and likely elsewhere), allowing us a much more nuanced assessment of the drivers and social impact of health litigation than the binary on-list/off-list classification does. To sum up, there are cases in which the presence of a litigated intervention in a government's list does not automatically imply state failure ('false-positives' – Types 2a, b and c and 3a, b and c) and also cases in which the omission of an intervention from the government's list does not necessarily imply the contrary, that is, that the state has not failed ('false-negatives' – Type 4). Types 5a and b are more debatable. Types 1, 5c and 6 seem to be the only ones that correspond perfectly with the on-list (state failure)/off-list (no state failure) distinction. Table 8.1 summarises the discussion of this section.

If the analysis developed in this section is sound, using the on-list/off-list distinction in this more nuanced manner should help us to better assess the drivers and social impact of health litigation, including its *indirect effects*. It does not provide anything approaching a definitive answer to the intricate questions involved in this daunting task, of course not. For a truly comprehensive, accurate and definitive assessment we would need to look at each lawsuit, classify it according to each of the eleven types above, resolve all the 'not clear' types of cases (i.e., Types 2a, 2b, 2c, 3a, 3b, 5a and 5b) and then see if and how they became accessible in the public system (crucial, as we saw, to assess social impact). We would only then reach a reasonably nuanced classification of all cases into the four scenarios described at the beginning of this chapter (Section 8.1).

The information needed to carry out this Herculean exercise is unfortunately not available. But the analytical framework developed in this and

[43] Mapelli, for instance, mentions litigation driven by a lack of knowledge by patients and doctors of the administrative divisions of competence in the Brazilian state, leading many to claim against the state interventions whose administrative responsibility is of the municipality and vice-versa, *Judicialização da Saúde*, at 131.

Table 8.1 *A typology of health litigation claims*

Type	Description	State failure?
On-list cases		
Type 1	A claimant requests an on-list intervention in the exact specification of the corresponding clinical protocol for her condition after being denied it through the ordinary administrative procedures for no justified reason.	Clearly yes
Type 2a	A claimant being treated in a private hospital requests an on-list medicine that is available only for those treated in officially approved institutions.	Not clear/ likely not
Type 2b	A claimant requests an on-list medicine yet in a different formulation or from a different make from the ones offered in the public system.	Not clear
Type 2c	A claimant requests an on-list medicine yet for a different use than that for which it is approved (so-called off-label use).	Not clear
Type 3a	A claimant's primary request is an off-list intervention but he/she includes, in the same claim, on-list medicines that the therapeutic programme also requires.	Not clear/ likely not
Type 3b	A claimant requests an on-list intervention judicially as a faster way of obtaining it, that is, as a form of 'queue-jumping'.	Not clear/ likely not
Off-list cases		
Type 4	A claimant requests an off-list intervention that is safe and highly cost-effective according to the scientific consensus yet excluded from the government's list for no justified reason.	Clearly yes
Type 5a	A claimant requests an off-list intervention that is safe and effective according to the regulatory authorities yet has a therapeutic alternative that is less safe and/ or less effective, yet more cost-effective.	Not clear

Table 8.1 *(cont.)*

Type	Description	State failure?
Type 5b	A claimant requests an off-list intervention that is safe and effective according to the regulatory authorities, yet is extremely expensive and has *no* cheaper therapeutic alternative.	Not clear
Type 5c	A claimant requests an off-list intervention that is safe and effective according to the regulatory authorities yet is extremely expensive and *has* a safe and more cost-effective therapeutic alternative.	Clearly not
Type 6	A claimant requests an off-list intervention which has been duly assessed and rejected by the health authorities (i.e., failed the incorporation process), for unquestionably justified reasons such as lack of safety and ineffectiveness.	Clearly not

the previous sections is nonetheless useful, as I will try to show now, for us to draw some more robust (even if still tentative) conclusions than those currently available in the literature.

8.5 Assessing the Drivers and Social Impact of Health Litigation

When we look at the type of claims on which health litigation in Brazil has consistently focused, it is difficult not to conclude that its overall social impact is negative. Although exact numbers are hard to get, the increasing available data shows a large proportion of claims falling under those types in which, according to my proposed framework, the state should either clearly not provide health interventions (Types 5c and 6) or where there are plausible valid reasons that support that view (Types 5a and 5b). Claims involving interventions where it is questionable whether the state ought to provide or not (Types 2a, b and c, 3a and b) are also rather common. Claims that the state should provide but clearly fails to (Types 1 and 4) are much less frequent. This section develops these conclusions in more detail with support from the available empirical data.

Many of the medicines featuring recurrently in litigation across many states in Brazil and representing a large proportion of the costs of litigation fall into what I described as a Type 6 claim. To briefly recall, this type occurs when a claimant requests an *off-list* intervention that has been duly assessed and rejected by the health authorities (i.e., failed the incorporation process), for unquestionably justified reasons such as lack of safety and/or lack of effectiveness.

I have already mentioned what is perhaps the most glaring recent example, the so-called cancer pill (Phosphoethanolamine), which was granted in thousands of cases despite lack of approval by the regulatory authorities and lack of clinical trials to test its effectiveness and safety.[44] Given the commotion that a potential cure for cancer obviously caused, the Brazilian state ended up investing millions in rushed clinical trials with significant opportunity costs to the public system, which eventually demonstrated the ineffectiveness of the 'cancer pill'.[45]

The 'cancer pill' is far from an isolated case. Courts have been regularly granting several other interventions not approved by the Brazilian authorities and, sometimes, not approved anywhere in the world (i.e., experimental treatments).[46] Some studies have identified the percentage of medicines in their sample without approval from the National Sanitary Vigilance Agency (ANVISA) and, though not very high, they are far from negligible (see Figure 8.4).

Much more common are Type 5c claims, in which a claimant requests an intervention that is safe and effective according to the regulatory

[44] N. Pondé, et al., 'Phosphoethanolamine and the Danger of Unproven Drugs', (2016) 10 (681) *Ecancermedicalscience*, doi:10.3332/ecancer.2016.68. The pressure from civil society was so great to force the state to provide the 'cancer pill' that Congress passed Law 13.269/2016, authorising the production and use of the substance despite lack of sanitary approval. The Brazilian Medical Association challenged the constitutionality of the law in the Supreme Federal Tribunal (ADI 5501), and on 19 May 2016, the Tribunal suspended the effects of the law. See also Wang, Ferraz, 'Fosfoetanolamina – A Proteção Judicial à Medicina sem Base em Evidência'.

[45] See C. Dantas, 'Fosfoetanolamina: Instituto do Câncer suspende novos testes devido à 'ausência de benefício clínico significativo', G1, 31 March 2017, available at: https://g1.globo.com/bemestar/noticia/fosfoetanolamina-instituto-do-cancer-suspende-testes-devido-a-ausencia-de-beneficio-clinico-significativo.ghtml, accessed 23 June 2019.

[46] For an analysis of fourteen cases decided in the STJ from 2002 to 2011 requesting treatment abroad, most of them eye surgery in Cuba declared as ineffective by Brazilian authorities, see G. P. Machado, 'O Superior Tribunal de Justiça e os pedidos de custeio de tratamentos médicos no exterior', MPhil Dissertation, Universidade Federal Fluminense (2013).

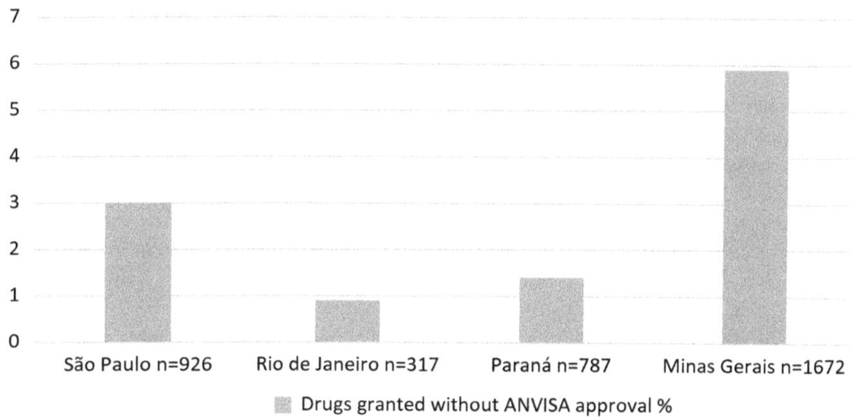

Figure 8.4 Drugs judicially granted without regulatory approval.
Source: Own formulation with data from several studies[47]

authorities yet is extremely expensive but has a safe and more cost-effective therapeutic alternative, that is, they offer no or little improvement compared to the therapeutic options already incorporated in the system yet cost much more. No rational administrator would incorporate such medicines, as the equity and economic impact would be obviously negative. If they did, the judiciary would be justified in quashing such a decision on quite traditional and uncontroversial administrative law grounds (irrationality or unreasonableness). Yet in Brazil, judges very often concede such claims, with a significant and growing impact on the health budget.

A current example that causes significant expenditure in several states is litigation involving a newer, more expensive type of insulin (so-called analogue insulin) than the standard treatment already offered by the state for the treatment of diabetes (so-called regular human or animal insulins). The World Health Organization's 18th Expert Committee on the Selection and Use of Essential Medicines had this to say in their *Review of*

[47] Chieffi, Barata, 'Judicialização da política pública de assistência farmacêutica e eqüidade'; Pepe et al., 'Characterization of Lawsuits for the Supply of "Essential" Medicines in the State of Rio de Janeiro, Brazil'; Pereira, Pepe, 'Acesso a medicamentos por via judicial no Paraná'; Machado et al., 'Judicialization of Access to Medicines in Minas Gerais State, Southeastern Brazil'.

the Evidence Comparing Insulin (Human or Animal) with Analogue Insulins:

> The new data did not alter the conclusions of the Singh et al. (2009) review, which indicated that analogue insulins had little advantage over conventional insulins in terms of glycaemic control or reduced hypoglycaemia. Statistically significant advantages associated with analogues are generally less than clinically important minimal differences, and advantages for occurrence of hypoglycaemia are not consistent across comparisons. Recent health technology assessments in the UK and Germany indicated no advantage for long-acting analogue insulins in Type 1 and 2 diabetes . . .. Reviews of analogue use and cancer risk indicate increased cancer risk in some analyses and no difference with human insulins in other analyses.[48]

CONITEC, the Brazilian agency linked to the Ministry of Health that assesses all new technologies and makes recommendations about their incorporation in the public health system (see Appendix), has carried out no less than four assessments in the past few years and recommended, in line with the international evidence, that analogue insulins should *not* be incorporated in the Brazilian system.[49] The estimated budgetary impact of potential incorporation was colossal (between R$242 million and R$404 million a year for the rarer Type 1 diabetes, regarded as conservative by CONITEC,[50] and a staggering R$3.6 billion to R$61.9 billion for the more common diabetes Type 2).[51] If we recall that the whole budget of the Ministry of Health approved for 2019 amounts to R$130 billion, it seems hard to conclude that forcing the Brazilian state to incorporate analogue insulins, especially for Type 2 diabetes, would be appropriate.

48 WHO, 'Evidence Comparing Insulin (Human or Animal) with Analogue Insulins 4', 18th Expert Comm. on the Selection & Use of Essential Medicines (2011), available at: www.who.int/selection_medicines/committees/expert/18/applications/Insulin_review.pdf, accessed 23 June 2019.

49 All recommendation reports issued by CONITEC are available on their official webpage 'Recomendações sobre as tecnologias avaliadas' ('Recommendations on Technologies Evaluated), http://conitec.gov.br/decisoes-sobre-incorporacoes. In 2017, and under unclear circumstances, CONITEC suddenly reversed its previous recommendations for Type 1 diabetes (the rarer type). It recently confirmed its recommendation for non-incorporation for Type 2 diabetes. For all the reports related to the treatment of Diabetes with analogue insulins see Reports 103/2014, 114/2014, 245/2017, 434/2019, 440/2019 and 489/2019.

50 CONITEC, Report 245/2017, 'Insulinas análogas de ação rápida para Diabetes Mellitus Tipo I', at 51.

51 CONITEC, Report 434/2019, 'Insulinas análogas de ação prolongada para Diabetes Mellitus Tipo II', at 7.

Yet courts of several states have been granting these drugs for over a decade now, with significant and increasingly higher costs to the system.[52]

The analogue insulin example, again, is far from an aberration. As we saw in Figure 8.1, in almost every state, a large proportion of claims are for off-list drugs. Not all of these claims, of course, are Type 5c cases, but there is a strong indication that a large proportion of them are. According to Machado et al.'s detailed study of health litigation in the state of Minas Gerais:

> Among the medicines not available in HD/MG [Health Department/ Minas Gerais] programs [off-list medicines], approximately 80% had a therapeutic alternative in the public care system, which is close to that found in a study in São Paulo where 73% had alternatives in the local list of essential medicines and in the SUS programs.[53]

Type 5c claims are not only very frequent but also among the ones that generate the highest costs to the state. In two recent studies of the most costly judicially granted drugs in cases against the federal government, it was found that a very limited number of off-list drugs with stratospheric price tags, many of them with dubious efficacy, generated approximately 85 per cent of the total costs of judicialisation (see Figures 8.5 and 8.6).[54]

These were all off-list drugs at the time of litigation and only five (out of twenty-two) have been incorporated in the meantime, always for very specific indications and under conditions of price reductions by the

[52] See, for a good analysis of diabetes litigation, the case study developed by Wang and colleagues for the FGV Law School Casoteca, an interesting database of cases for use in legal education. D. Wang, D. Franco, F. Terrazas, M. Vilella, N. Pires, 'Judiciário e fornecimento de insulinas análogas pelo sistema público de saúde: direitos, ciência e políticas públicas', Casoteca GV, no date, https://direitosp.fgv.br/casoteca/judiciario-fornecimento-de-insulinas-analogas-pelo-sistema-publico-de-saude-direitos-cienci, accessed 23 June 2019.

[53] Machado et al., 'Judicialization of Access to Medicines in Minas Gerais State, Southeastern Brazil'. However, it cannot be assumed that all patients would benefit from the alternatives available in the SUS. Each case would have to be evaluated based on the patient medical history and drug experience (treatment failure, allergies and adverse reactions). For the São Paulo study, see F. Vieira, P. Zucchi, 'Distorções causadas pelas ações judiciais à política de medicamentos no Brasil', (2007) 41(2) *Revista de Saúde Pública*, 214–222.

[54] For an excellent discussion of the judicialisation of some of these drugs, see Diniz et al., 'Consequências da judicialização das políticas de saúde'.

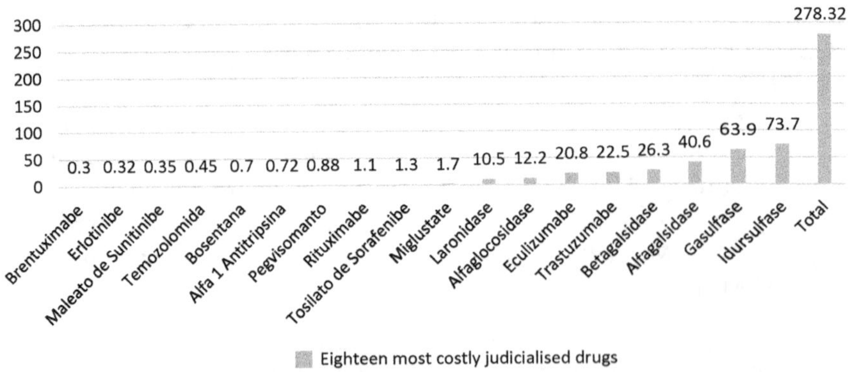

Figure 8.5 Eighteen most costly judicialised drugs, cases against federal government, 2012, in R$ millions.
Source: AGU, 2013

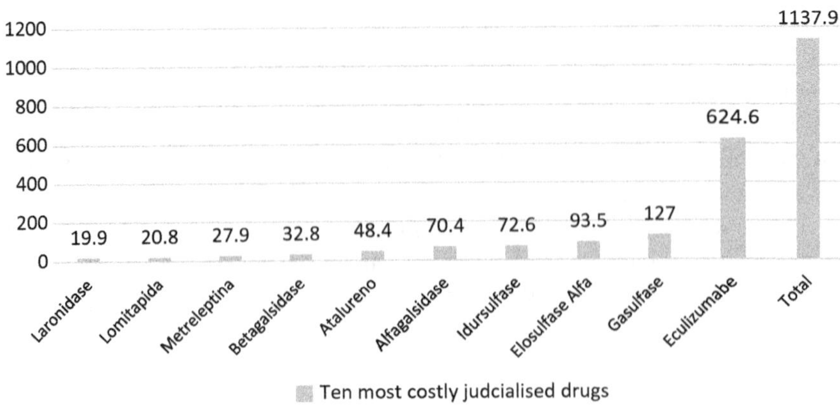

Figure 8.6 Ten most costly judicialised drugs, cases against federal government, 2016, in R$ millions.
Source: Xavier, 2018

manufacturers.[55] It is difficult to classify these cases definitively according the typology proposed here but it is possible to infer, from different sources, that many of them would fall into Type 5c cases. At

[55] This seems to contradict Brinks and Gauri's statement that all litigated drugs end up being incorporated in the Brazilian system. Many don't. See D. Brinks, V. Gauri, 'The Law's Majestic Equality? The Distributive Impact of Litigating Social and Economic Rights', Policy Research Working Paper 5999 (2012). Only five out of the twenty-two most costly litigated drugs have now been incorporated in the public system (three in

least nine of these medicines have been assessed by CONITEC and rejected for lack of evidence of therapeutic efficacy or superiority over the options available in the public system at much lower costs.[56] Lopes et al. reached similar conclusions in their study of litigation involving cancer drugs in São Paulo between 2006 and 2007. According to them, in that short period, the Health Secretariat of the State of São Paulo had to incur high costs to meet court orders for the supply of antineoplastic drugs for indications that were not supported by medical evidence.[57] Many of the drugs in his study are the same as those on the federal government's list (Bevacizumab, Capecitabine, Cetuximab, Erlotinib, Rituximab, Imatinib and Temozolomide). Temozolomide, although rejected as far back as 2014 by the CONITEC for 'lack of evidence of superiority' over the chemotherapy offered in the public system, continues to be granted via litigation and to generate significant expenses to the public system.[58]

This focus of litigation on newer and expensive medicines of debatable efficacy and priority and high budgetary impact is hardly a new and passing trend. It seems hardwired into litigation in Brazil for reasons I will return to in the conclusion of this chapter. In the early 2000s, when litigation was picking up as we saw in Chapter 5, one of the most litigated medicines in several states were those for rheumatoid arthritis, in particular, two so-called biological medicines: etanercept and adalimumab. According to public health experts, these drugs offered insufficient improvement in therapeutic terms to justify their much higher costs.[59] According to a study I conducted in co-authorship with Fabiola Sulpino

2013 and another two in 2018). None of these are included in the WHO's latest Essential Medicines List, available at: https://apps.who.int/iris/bitstream/handle/10665/273826/EML-20-eng.pdf?ua=1, accessed 28 March 2019.

56 All CONITEC reports are available on their website, http://conitec.gov.br/decisoes-sobre-incorporacoes.

57 L. C. Lopes et al., 'Rational Use of Anticancer Drugs and Patient Lawsuits in the State of São Paulo, Southeastern Brazil', (2010) 44(4) *Revista de Saúde Pública*, 620–628.

58 See, for CONITEC's report: http://conitec.gov.br/images/Artigos_Publicacoes/Temozolomida_FINAL.pdf, accessed 27 May 2019; for a recent Technical Note (Nota Técnica) of the Ministry of Health against a request for that drug, see: https://sei.saude.gov.br/sei/documento_consulta_externa.php?id_acesso_externo=26156&id_documento=4989465&infra_hash=12a0665b0cebac5816b23e017e810c1e, accessed 27 May 2019.

59 For Machado et al., 'Judicialization of Access to Medicines in Minas Gerais State, Southeastern Brazil', at 4, etanercept, though a therapeutic innovation, 'may not add much to therapeutic practice depending on the indication', whereas adalimumab was not even a therapeutic innovation and also 'does not bring significative contributions to therapy'. See also Campos Neto et al., 'Doctors, Lawyers and Pharmaceutical Industry

Vieira, a pharmacist and health economist with vast experience in health policy, if these new drugs were provided in the public system to all Brazilians that potentially qualified (about 620,000 individuals) the cost for the public system would be approximately R$83billion, that is, about 3.6 per cent of the GDP or roughly the same as the *total* expenditure of the public system in that year (2007)![60] Again, it is hard to conclude that the public health system should provide these drugs (even if they were affordable and proven to be much superior, in therapeutic terms, to the alternative treatments available, which they were not).

It is true that some of the drugs that feature in litigation end up being incorporated by the public system and could in principle fall into what I described as Type 4 claims above, that is, claims involving interventions that should clearly be provided by the health system but aren't. But further examination seems to indicate that this is not often the case. Of the five drugs incorporated out of the twenty-two listed in Figures 8.5 and 8.6, three (Idursulfase, Gasulfase and Laronidase) are extremely expensive medicines for rare diseases. They fall, thus, into Type 5b cases, which are in my view the hardest to decide whether the state should provide or not. The other two are medicines for cancer (Erlotinib and Trastuzumab) whose comparative efficacy is not beyond doubt and whose incorporation was perhaps the result of hard to resist pressure from patients and pharmaceutical companies and was conditioned on price negotiations with the suppliers.

Is it suggestive that none of these twenty-two medicines cited above is included in the core component of the WHO Essential Medicines list and that only two are part of the complementary component of that list.[61] Seven of these medicines, interestingly, are also commonly litigated in Costa Rica,

on Health Lawsuits in Minas Gerais, Southeastern Brazil', (2012) 46(5) *Revista de Saúde Pública*, 784–790, arguing that as many of these claims were initiated by a small group of prescribers and lawyers, they may 'suggest inappropriate relationships between these professionals and the pharmaceutical companies, mischaracterizing the guarantee to the right to health as the overriding motivation in these lawsuits'.

60 O. L. M. Ferraz, F. S. Vieira, 'Direito à saúde, recursos escassos e equidade: Os riscos da interpretação judicial dominante', (2009) 52(1) *Dados*, 223–251, at 237–238.

61 The core list presents a list of minimum medicine needs for a basic health-care system, listing the most efficacious, safe and cost-effective medicines for priority conditions. Priority conditions are selected on the basis of current and estimated future public health relevance and potential for safe and cost-effective treatment. The complementary list presents essential medicines for priority diseases, for which specialised diagnostic or monitoring facilities and/or specialist medical care and/or specialist training are needed. In case of doubt, medicines may also be listed as complementary on the basis of consistent higher costs or less attractive cost-effectiveness in a variety of settings. WHO, *Model List of Essential Medicines*, 20th ed. (WHO, 2017).

as we can learn from the excellent studies carried out by Ole Norheim, Bruce Wilson and colleagues in health litigation there. None of them can be classified as 'high priority' according to the well-established criteria of priority-setting they employ. One (Trastuzumab) is classified as 'medium priority', and the other six are classified as 'low priority'. It is regrettable that no similar comprehensive study has yet been conducted about litigation involving medicines in Brazil, but it would be surprising if the conclusions would be too different. According to them, only a very small minority (2.7 per cent) of health litigation involving medicines in Costa Rica focus on high priority drugs.[62]

***

The overall picture that emerges from the discussion in this section is one of health litigation focused by and large on interventions that the public system should either not provide (Types 5c and 6) or over which there is debate and reasonable doubt over whether it should (Types 5a and 5b) according to well-established safety, effectiveness and priority setting criteria.[63] Moreover, the opportunity costs of such litigation, as we have already seen in Chapter 5 (Section 5.5), are very high: the R$1.1 billion spent with the 10 most costly drugs in 2016 went to 995 patients, that is, approximately R$1.1 million in per capita terms (around US$300,000 at the time), 889 times more than the overall per capita expenditure of the public health system.[64]

62 O. R. Loaiza et al., 'Revisiting Health Rights Litigation and Access to Medications in Costa Rica: Preliminary Evidence from the Cochrane Collaboration Reform', (2018) 20(1) *Health and Human Rights*, 79–91. In their sample of cases in Costa Rica, they reached the conclusion that only 2.7 per cent of the medicines litigated could be classified as high priority according to standard fairness criteria from the public health and priority-setting literature; 27 per cent were classified as of medium priority, 48.6 per cent low and 21.6 per cent experimental. Only three of the drugs were already on the official WHO essential drugs list.

63 More examples could be cited but these seem sufficient to reaffirm the conclusions I reached above. For further examples involving the drugs Duloxetine, Glucosamine and Chondroitine, see Ministério da Saúde, *Nota Técnica No. 45/2012 Duloxetina* (Brasília: Ministério da Saúde, 2012) and J. M. Ucker et al., 'Perfil dos medicamentos fornecidos via processo judicial na assistência farmacêutica do município de Santa Rosa/RS', (2016) 10(1) *Tempus, Actas de Saúde Colet*, Brasília, at 134–135.

64 The exact amount was R$1,138,519,335.90; see C. A. Xavier, 'Judicialização da Saúde: Perspectiva Crítica sobre os Gastos da União para o Cumprimento das Ordens Judiciais', in CONASS (eds.), *Coletânea Direito à Saúde Dilemas do Fenômeno da Judicialização da Saúde*, 1st ed. (Brasília: Conselho Nacional de Secretários de Saúde – CONASS, 2018), at 56. For the historical exchange rates between the Brazilian Real, R$ and the US dollar, US$, I used www.x-rates.com/, accessed 1 April 2019. See also the report of the audit

I am not suggesting that health litigation in Brazil is never driven by state failure and genuine unattended medical need. There are well-known problems in the public health system, highlighted in Chapter 4, which could of course (and do to some extent) motivate litigation.[65] But the increasingly richer data emerging from the studies discussed in this chapter comprehensively refute the narrative that state failure is the main, or even one of the main drivers of litigation.

8.6 Who Really Benefits from Health Litigation?

As I explained in the introduction to this chapter, to reach a more robust and nuanced conclusion about the social impact of health litigation, that is, *whom* it really benefits, we had to explore in greater detail the objects of litigation, that is *what* is litigated. This was due to the potential

conducted by the Tribunal de Contas da Uniao (Federal Union Public Accounts Tribunal – TCU) 2015 (TC 009.253/2015-7), at para 7, stating: 'It was found that the judicialization of health caused the emergency reallocation of resources of the program, discontinued the treatment of regular patients of the program, threatened the managers for possible noncompliance with judicial decisions and enabled pharmaceutical laboratories to increase prices in the event of emergency procurement to comply with judicial decisions.' It also found medicines judicially granted and acquired but never collected, indicating significant waste of precious public resources, at para 8.

65 See Macedo et al., 'A Technical Analysis of Medicines Request-Related Decision Making in Brazilian Courts', at 5, listing cases in which state failure may lead to litigation, such as 'outdated clinical protocols, therapeutic approaches supported by sufficient scientific evidence but not yet incorporated into SUS programs and lack of medications in health facilities, due to problems with selecting, planning, purchasing, inventory control, storage, distribution, or the dispensation of medications by unqualified workers'. See Ucker et al., 'Perfil dos medicamentos fornecidos via processo judicial', at 136, arguing that the judicialisation of the medicine Formoterol 12 mcg for respiratory diseases in Rio Grande do Sul may have been caused by shortages in the public system. See also Gomes et al., 'Access to Medium and High-Complexity Procedures in the Brazilian Unified National Health System', at 39, arguing that difficult access to services of medium and high complexity may cause litigation; Conselho Nacional de Secretários de Saúde, *Assistência Farmacêutica: Medicamentos de dispensação em caráter excepcional*, 1st ed. (Brasília: CONASS, 2004); Conselho Nacional de Secretários de Saúde, *Nota técnica 19, de 15 de agosto de 2005* (Brasília: CONASS, 2005); Pepe et al., 'Characterization of Lawsuits for the Supply of "Essential" Medicines in the State of Rio de Janeiro, Brazil', at 469; Gomes, Amador, 'Studies Published in Indexed Journals on Lawsuits for Medicines in Brazil', at 10: 'When decisions are made to purchase a given drug without a prior analysis of the treatment alternatives that are already included in the SUS budget, health policy is being overlooked, with potential harm to both the user and the system as a whole. In addition, existing flaws in the organization of the country's pharmaceutical care can lead to shortages in the government pharmacies.'

so-called *indirect* effects of litigation. As Daniel Brinks and Varun Gauri have forcefully argued:

> The most obvious effect of a judicial decision, of course, is the direct effect of that decision on the litigants themselves, and therefore most studies of the effect of health rights litigation, for instance, have been limited to direct effects on litigants (Vieira and Zucchi 2007; Da Silva and Terrazas 2011; Ferraz 2011). But decisions can also have direct and indirect effects on nonlitigants, as when litigants sue for (de facto) non-excludable goods (e.g., higher quality care in a hospital, or a handicap access ramp in a school), or when decisions change public policies in some way. In such cases, the benefits are extended to all those who share a policy space with the litigants.[66]

Indirect effects materialise mainly, thus, when non-litigants benefit from changes in state behaviour (I will call these simply 'policies') prompted by litigation in which they have not participated as parties (individualised cases) or direct beneficiaries (collective cases or 'class actions').[67] As important as *who* litigates, thus, is *what* is litigated and what happens after litigation, that is, *if* and *how* it changes health policy.

As I argued in Section 8.1, the best possible scenario of positive indirect effects would be this: a large proportion of health litigation focusing on objects that (i) should be provided by the public health system but weren't and (ii) lead to effective policy changes making these health interventions available to everyone. The data presented and discussed in the previous chapters and sections of this chapter seem sufficient to show how far from that scenario health litigation in Brazil currently is.

The mere fact that health litigation concentrates almost exclusively on secondary and tertiary health care, that is, curative treatment – in particular, medicines – almost everywhere in Brazil (see Figure 5.6, Chapter 5) and not on primary care and public health measures, which

66 Brinks, Gauri, 'The Law's Majestic Equality?', at 15.

67 The literature uses different classifications in an attempt to capture different types of effects of litigation. Some talk about *material* and *symbolic* effects, others refer to *judicial* and *extra-judicial* effects and others to *direct* and *indirect* effects. See: G. Rosenberg, *The Hollow Hope: Can Courts Bring About Social Change?* (Chicago: University of Chicago Press, 1991), for judicial and extrajudicial effects; M. McCann, *Rights at Work: Pay Equity Reform and the Politics of Legal Mobilization* (Chicago: University of Chicago Press, 1994), for material and symbolic effects. I use here direct and indirect effects as used by V. Gauri, D. M. Brinks (eds.) *Courting Social Justice: Judicial Enforcement of Social and Economic Rights in the Developing World* (New York: Cambridge University Press, 2008).

are arguably the highest priorities for the population, in particular, for the most disadvantaged (see Chapter 4) – is in itself a stark signal of the limited progressive potential of judicialisation to indirectly benefit those excluded from that route, that is, the majority of the population (see Chapter 6). The fact that a large proportion of litigation, and the bulk of the expenditure it generates, concentrates on a very limited number of medicines of dubious (to say the least) priority, makes it even harder to envisage any potential positive indirect effects.

As we saw in Chapter 3, in the past two decades there has been an important and welcome shift of focus and priority in Brazil's health policies towards primary care (atenção básica) with a significant positive impact on the health of the most disadvantaged. Programmes such as the Family Health Strategy have been expanded with palpable effects on infant and child mortality, maternal health and general morbidity of the poor population (see Section 3.3 in Chapter 3).

Yet these policies, as we saw, are still far from reaching all of those who badly need them and are far from providing primary care of a very high quality for those who have gained access in the past few decades. There are still important deficiencies in facilities, shortage of doctors, nurses and other health professionals, equipment and materials throughout the public system, in particular, in the poorer regions of the North and Northeast (see Chapter 4).

It is doubtful whether litigation could be an appropriate vehicle to address these problems (I discuss this further in Chapter 9). But the fact that little (if any) litigation exists involving these high priority areas for the most disadvantaged signal strongly that its potential progressive effects (direct or indirect) are, at best, very limited. What does not exist can obviously not benefit anyone, directly or indirectly.

This mismatch between health litigation's focus and the priorities of the population is not surprising in the highly unequal context I have extensively described and discussed in this book. The concept of 'shared spaces', or 'shared policy environment' developed by Daniel Brinks and Varun Gauri in the article already cited above is helpful to illustrate this point. As they explain:

> One can enjoy the benefits of [litigation's] indirect effects without having the resources to litigate, *but only if one shares the same policy environment as the litigants*. Often that means geographic proximity, a similar social class, or both. So, if a wealthy family sues to secure a ramp to their daughter's elementary school or to improve services at a hospital, everyone who attends the school or uses the hospital enjoys the benefit. But one

> must share a school or a hospital with this wealthy family to benefit, and *the wealthy seldom share schools with the poor; they sometimes share public hospitals, but rarely primary care physicians with the poor*. In short, benefitting in this way requires a close identification with the issues involved in the original litigation, even if it does not depend on being able to litigate.[68] (my emphasis)

The likelihood of shared policy environments in such unequal and segregated countries like Brazil is rather small. As we saw in Chapters 4 and 6, the gap between different socioeconomic groups is still very large and, as a direct consequence, so are the health policies that each of these groups could benefit mostly from. As we saw, a large proportion of Brazilian households still lack basic sanitation, an important determinant of several serious health problems such as infant and child mortality and morbidity, to cite only a couple of important ones. We also saw that the extension and improvement of primary care policies such as the Family Health Strategy (ESF) have had a proven significant impact on child mortality but are far from being universalised. Here are, thus, two of the top undisputed priorities for the most disadvantaged to which the health system should clearly devote more attention and resources.

These are not, however, health interventions that could benefit the better off, as they already have reasonably good access to them. It is not surprising, thus, that health litigation involving basic sanitation is very low and health litigation involving the Family Health Strategy programme virtually non-existent, whereas claims for state-of-the-art medicines and more sophisticated hospital treatment, which cannot be described as a priority for the poor living in the remote rural areas of the country or in the favelas of the big cities, can be counted in the tens of thousands in many states.

The blunt reality is that, in highly unequal societies like Brazil, the rich and the poor will rarely share policy spaces and priorities. Brazil's pronounced inequalities determine not only *who* manages to reach the courts but also *what* gets litigated, limiting significantly, therefore, not only the *direct*, but also the *indirect* effects of litigation.

The limited progressive potential of litigation involving medicines is compounded in the Brazilian context by another conspicuous fact: the budget for medicines (pharmaceutical assistance in official idiom) has seen significant growth in absolute terms and as a percentage of total

[68] Brinks, Gauri, 'The Law's Majestic Equality?', at 15–16.

health expenditure in the past few decades. The amount of resources of the health budget devoted to medicines has jumped from 5.39 per cent in 2002, to 10.70 per cent in 2007, reaching 11 per cent in 2010 and 16 per cent in 2016.[69] In 2015, it achieved the significant amount of almost R$20 billion (a growth of 40 per cent from the already high levels of 2010). More and more resources are thus spent every year on medicines, with obvious opportunity costs for other areas. Even if all health litigation in Brazil involving medicines focused on drugs that the public system ought undoubtedly to provide under the right to health (Types 1 and 4 in the typology proposed earlier, Section 8.4 and Table 8.1), its potential progressive impact would be limited, as pharmaceutical assistance is a well-resourced area in the public health system in comparative terms. Health litigation would in the best possible scenario be adding more resources to an area that has hardly been neglected in the past few decades.[70] Given the profile of the medicines most claimed and their

[69] F. S. Vieira, 'Evolução do Gasto com Medicamentos do Sistema Único de Saúde no Período de 2010 a 2016', Texto para Discussão 2356, IPEA (2008).

[70] This empirically unsupported image of health litigation as a natural reaction to state failure seems to be in part a legacy of the early HIV-AIDS highly visible litigation of the 1990s. Hoffmann and Bentes, for instance, claim that 'the great majority of actions [health litigation] have concerned governmental failure to fulfil specific demands for medicines and treatment'. See F. Hoffmann, F. R. N. M. Bentes, 'Accountability for Social and Economic Rights in Brazil, in Gauri, V. and Brinks, D. M. (eds.), *Courting Social Justice: Judicial Enforcement of Social and Economic Rights in the Developing World* (New York: Cambridge University Press, 2008) 100–145, at 122. Back then, litigation was more clearly linked to the difficulties of the state to organise the efficient provision of medicines that were part of its own policies and lists. However, as Ana Messeder and colleagues argue in a detailed study of ten years of health litigation in Rio de Janeiro (from 1991 to 2001), since 1997, with the better structuring of the National Programme of Sexually Transmitted Diseases/AIDS, access to antiretrovirals have improved and lawsuits claiming these drugs started to significantly decrease. Messeder et al., 'Mandados judiciais como ferramenta para garantia do acesso a medicamentos no setor público', at 532. It is possible and likely, of course, that the same problems may repeat today in different areas. But as the discussion above has hopefully shown, the drivers of health litigation are much more complex, combining state failure, resource scarcity and what I call 'rights opportunism' from those who can use courts as a convenient channel to extract from the public health system resources that ought to be invested elsewhere, in part influenced by pharmaceutical companies' well-known strategies to promote their drugs among patients and doctors and by lawyers eager to profit from health litigation, a rather lucrative business. See J. Lexchin, 'What Big Pharma Pays Your Doctor', *The Conversation*, 5 July 2018, available at: https://theconversation.com/what-big-pharma-pays-your-doctor-99431, accessed 24 June 2019. See also the early important contribution by former editor-in-chief of the New England Journal of Medicine: M. Angell, *The Truth about the Drug Companies: How They Deceive Us and What to Do About It* (New York: Random House, 2005); J. P. Kassirer, *On the Take: How Medicine's Complicity with Big*

budgetary impact discussed earlier, it is difficult not to conclude that health litigation in Brazil is highly regressive, including in its indirect effects.[71]

8.7 Conclusion

This chapter concludes Part II of the book. As we have seen, health litigation in Brazil is not a homogenous phenomenon. It varies across the country in volume and characteristics. It is inappropriate, therefore, to talk of a *Brazilian model* in the strict sense of an identical or a very

Business Can Endanger Your Health (New York: Oxford University Press, 2005); R. Smith, *The Trouble with Medical Journals* (London: Royal Society of Medicine Press, 2006). Machado et al., 'Judicialization of Access to Medicines in Minas Gerais', at 4, raise this possibility in their study, as they found that a 'small number of private lawyers and doctors were involved in many lawsuits, mainly demanding etanercept and adalimumab'. See also: Neto et al., 'Doctors, Lawyers and Pharmaceutical Industry on Health Lawsuits in Minas Gerais'; A. L. Chieffi, R. B. Barata, 'Ações judiciais: Estratégia da indústria farmacêutica'; G. Carvalho, 'Saúde: O tudo para todos que sonhamos e o tudo que nos impingem os que lucram com ela', (2005) 69(29) *Rev Cent Bras Estud Sáude*, 99–104; C. C. F. Vidotti et al., 'New Drugs in Brazil: Do They Meet Brazilian Public Health Needs?', (2008) 24(1) *Rev Panam Salud Publica*, 36–45. See also: Messeder et al., 'Mandados judiciais como ferramenta para garantia do acesso a medicamentos no setor público', 530, showing that NGOs focusing on certain diseases are also an important driver of litigation, financing claims for their members. See also See also P. C. Gotzsche, *Medicamentos mortais e crime organizado: Como a indústria farmacêutica corrompeu a assistência médica*, trans. A. P. Farjado (Porto Alegre: Bookman, 2016), at 211–213, recounting the incorporation of Erlotinib in Denmark, unjustified in his view.

71 As Machado et al. plausibly state: 'The fact that alternative therapies are available shows that access to drugs has not been neglected by SUS managers and that SUS has implemented comprehensive public policies to cover several areas of health.' Machado et al., 'Judicialization of Access to Medicines in Minas Gerais State, Southeastern Brazil', at 5. As Menicucci et al. have noted, 'Regarding the medication requested by lawsuits, there is an interesting configuration of distinct profiles for the type of medication required by citizens in different risk categories. The non-standard and exceptional or high cost medicines are mostly requested by citizens living in areas of low risk (50% and 39% of requests, respectively). Strategic drugs, albeit with low frequency, were all requested by residents in high risk areas, while basic medicines were mostly requested by residents in areas of medium risk (54%).' T. M. G. Menicucci, J. A. Machado, 'Judicialization of Health Policy in the Definition of Access to Public Goods: Individual Rights versus Collective Rights', (2011) 5 *Brazilian Political Science Review*, 33–68, at 53. See Silva, Terrazas, 'Claiming the Right to Health in Brazilian Courts', finding a similar pattern in litigation for cancer drugs in Sao Paulo. See also Vieira, Zucchi, 'Distorções causadas pelas ações judiciais à política de medicamentos no Brasil'; Chieffi, Barata, 'Judicialização da política pública de assistência farmacêutica e eqüidade', at 1847.

similar manifestation everywhere in the country. There is a *model* of sorts, however, in the sense that, in the pockets where it occurs with more intensity, health litigation tends to display a set of similar characteristics. It is in this weaker but still relevant sense that I think that what I called the Brazilian model of right to health litigation in an earlier contribution to the debate can still be useful. As I argued then:

> The defining features of this 'Brazilian model' are related to the *profile of claims* (the litigator and the object of litigation) and the *outcome of litigation* (the rates of success and failure of litigation). As to the *profile of claims*, the vast majority of right-to-health cases in Brazil to date have been filed by individual claimants and have concerned the provision of curative medical treatment (mostly medicines) which can be enjoyed individually. As to the *outcome of litigation*, the Brazilian model is characterized by an extremely high success rate for claimants.[72]

Given such features, and the available evidence then that those reaching the courts were not the poorest in any plausible definition of the term, I suggested that health litigation in Brazil was most likely worsening health inequities 'although the extent to which this occur[ed was] difficult to determine with any precision without further research on the opportunity costs of such litigation'.[73] Two years later, with the improved data I was able to access in the Harvard-Bergen study cited in Chapter 5, I reached the same, but perhaps slightly stronger conclusion:

> The [Brazilian model of litigation's] overall social impact is negative. Rather than enhancing the provision of health benefits that are badly needed by the most disadvantaged – such as basic sanitation, reasonable access to primary health care, and vaccination programs – this model diverts essential resources of the health budget to the funding of mostly high-cost drugs claimed by individuals who are already privileged in terms of health conditions and services.[74]

The data and analysis presented in Chapters 5–7 have shown that the Brazilian model has not changed much, if at all, in the past decade. Under the still prevalent 'right to everything' conception of the right to health, most lawsuits are still individualised, successful and focused on curative medical treatment, in particular, medicines. What has changed

[72] O. L. M. Ferraz, 'The Right to Health in the Courts of Brazil: Worsening Health Inequities?', (2009) 11(2) *Health and Human Rights*, 33–45.
[73] Ferraz, 'Health Inequalities, Rights, and Courts'.
[74] Ibid.

significantly, as we saw, is the number of these lawsuits, now reaching between 120,000 to 220,000 a year according to more or less conservative estimates, and the corresponding costs to the health budget, which have also risen significantly (from US$1.5 to US$3.5 billion, or about 3 per cent of the total Health Budget of the whole country). There seems to be little reason, thus, and sadly, for a revision of that general conclusion. On the contrary, as the costs of judicialisation have become much higher, its regressive effects have also most likely increased. As long as the barriers to access to justice discussed in Chapter 6 don't diminish significantly and, most importantly, the Brazilian model of health litigation doesn't change, it is hard to see how health litigation can become, through direct or indirect effects, 'a grassroots instrument for the poor to hold the state accountable', that is, to '[address] a dysfunctional health system that fails to provide for their needs'.[75]

[75] J. Biehl et al., 'The Judicialization of Health and the Quest for State Accountability', at 218.

Appendix

The Regulatory Control and Approval of Health Interventions in Brazil

The initial step for any health intervention to be legally used in health systems, private or public, is regulatory approval as regards its quality (i.e., efficacy and effectiveness) and safety. This is a task usually carried out by the executive branch of government, often through specialised agencies whose remit is exclusively to assess and approve (or reject) health interventions that individuals or, most often, companies, want to introduce in the market. Perhaps the most famous and oldest such agency is the US Food and Drug Administration (FDA), created in 1906 through the 1906 Food and Drugs Act.[76] But the practice of regulatory control goes much further back. In the United Kingdom, for instance, it seems to date back to 1540, when the Apothecaries Wares, Drugs and Stuffs Act was passed.[77]

76 For the fascinating history of its creation and the immediate judicialisation of the issue, see Richard A. Merrill, 'Regulation of Drugs and Devices: An Evolution', (1994) 13(3) *Health Affairs*, at 48–49. As he explains, the Act 'gave the FDA the authority to interdict the marketing of drugs that were adulterated or misbranded. A misbranded drug was one whose label bore "any statement ... regarding such article, or the ingredients or substances contained therein which shall be false or misleading in any particular." The government argued in United States v. Johnson 221 U.S. 488 (1911), the first major test of the 1906 act, that the quoted language was meant to prohibit the marketing of a drug for which deceptive therapeutic claims were made. The Supreme Court, however, held that the statute was not aimed at "all possible false statements, but only at such as determine the identity of the article." Though describing a drug as containing an ingredient that it lacked constituted misbranding, it was not misbranding to claim, falsely, that it cured cancer.'

77 And the first four inspectors were appointed. See C. J. van Boxtel et al. (eds.), *Drug Benefits and Risks: International Textbook of Clinical Pharmacology*, rev. 2nd ed. (Amsterdam: IOS Press and Uppsala Monitoring Centre, 2001), at 65. Some form of light regulation dates even further back, to the thirteenth century, see ibid.: 'History of Pharmacopoeias, the official books of drug quality standards, probably dates back to one of the proclamations of the Salerno Medical Edict issued by Fredrick II of Sicily (1240), and ordered apothecaries to prepare remedies always in the same way – forma curiae.'

In Brazil, the task of controlling the quality and safety of health interventions is mainly entrusted to the Brazilian Health Regulatory Agency (ANVISA – Agência Nacional de Vigilância Sanitária), a financially and administratively autonomous agency linked to the Ministry of Health and part of the Brazilian National Health System (SUS). It coordinates the Brazilian Health Regulatory System (SNVS) and has a rather broad role: 'to promote the protection of the population's health by executing sanitary control of the production, marketing and use of products and services subject to health regulation, including related environments, processes, ingredients and technologies, as well as the control in ports, airports and borders'.[78]

For a health intervention to be legally used in Brazil, it needs to be 'registered' by ANVISA, that is, it needs to obtain registration, which is the positive culmination of the process of regulatory assessment, that is, approval.[79] Yet regulatory approval, by itself, is *not a sufficient condition* for a certain health intervention to be offered by a health system, be it private or public. All that regulatory approval does is to make legal the use of the approved health intervention within Brazil. Whether the health intervention will be used or not depends on other factors, including the *willingness* of potential users to do so (i.e., the existence of a demand for it) and, most importantly for our purposes, their *ability* to afford it.

Some individuals, that is, the richest in society, are able to make these decisions themselves, that is, individually, often of course with the aid of medical professionals. Most of us, however, depend either on private health insurance or a public health system. Neither, as explained in Section 8.2.2, are capable of offering the full list of health interventions that receive regulatory approval to everyone. Due to the inevitable fact of resource scarcity, they need to decide which health interventions among those with regulatory approval will be offered to all individuals within the system. This is often called the process of 'incorporation', which culminates with the elaboration of a package, or a list, also often called a formulary, of health interventions offered in a particular system. As defined in a recent report by the UK advice body on incorporation, the National Institute for Health and Care Excellence – NICE: a 'formulary is the output of processes to support the managed introduction,

[78] ANVISA was created by Federal Law no. 9.782, 26 January 1999, available at: http://portal.anvisa.gov.br/institucional, accessed 23 June 2019.

[79] Although, in recent years, both Parliament and the courts have been circumventing such rule, see: https://analisepoliticaemsaude.org/oaps/noticias/94ea6894d8ea35c9c88172df9c5c9c82/, any person can consult the status of a health intervention, or any other substance regulated by ANVISA on its website https://consultas.anvisa.gov.br/#/, accessed 23 June 2019.

utilisation or withdrawal of healthcare treatments within a health economy, service or organisation'.[80]

Incorporation[81]

Although, as noted above, incorporation is a necessary process in both private and public health systems, I will focus here on the latter due to our focus on the right to health and the corresponding duties of the *state* to guarantee that right. The process of incorporation of health interventions in a public system is even more complex and controversial than that of regulatory approval. It involves technically, politically and morally intractable decisions about how to allocate finite resources for health at several different levels of comprehensiveness. To simplify and facilitate understanding, I distinguish between four, ranging from the most to the least comprehensive level: the *super-macro*, the *macro*, the *meso* and the *micro* levels.[82]

The *super-macro* level relates to the amount of resources a government has available to spend in a certain fiscal year, captured in international human rights law instruments on social and economic rights and some constitutions by the phrase 'maximum available resources'. Such resources are made up by the revenue a state has managed to collect through taxes, fees, profits from companies it controls, loans, international aid, etc. It is often called 'general government revenue' in the specialised literature and can be consulted in the so-called national accounts in transparent countries. Decisions at the super-macro level determine the aggregate distribution of resources between government and society, that is, the proportion of resources that the state appropriates from society and the proportion it leaves in private hands.

Not surprisingly, countries vary significantly in their general government revenue since they also vary in their endowment of natural resources, level of economic development, fiscal, industrial and economic policies, etc., that is, in all variables that determine the general government revenue. To give a concrete example, France and Italy, two European countries with similar levels of economic development, differ significantly in general government revenues (in 2015, France had a total revenue of €1,166,276 billion and Italy €827,780 billion almost 25 per cent lower).[83] It is an interesting issue whether the phrase 'maximum available resources' should be interpreted as the resources a state

[80] NICE, 'Developing and Updating Local Formularies', at 14.

[81] This section draws on O. L. M. Ferraz, 'What Course without Evils?'.

[82] The public health literature tends to refer only to three levels: macro, meso and micro. See R. Klein et al., *Managing Scarcity* (Buckingham: Open University Press, 1996), at 7–10, as cited by K. Syrett, *Law, Legitimacy and the Rationing of Health Care* (New York: Cambridge University Press, 2007), at 21.

[83] OECD, *National Accounts of OECD Countries, General Government Accounts 2016* (OECD 2017), available at: dx.doi.org/10.1787/na_gga-2017-en, accessed 23 June 2019.

has actually available or ought to have available according to some normative paradigm. For the sake of simplicity, let us assume, here, that the macro-level, that is, 'maximum available resources', is whatever the particular state has available to spend in its budget in a particular year.[84]

In the most recent budget of the Brazilian Federal Union approved by Congress in 2018 for the year 2019, we see that the total revenue for that year is precisely R$3.262,209,303,823,[85] that is, just over R$3.2 trillion, the equivalent of US$830 billion. This is what we could say the Brazilian state has available to allocate among the myriad areas in which any modern state needs to invest resources. It is from this amount that a portion will be devoted to health and other large areas of government, such as social security, education, justice, environment, agriculture, security, sports, culture, etc. These allocations are often proposed by the executive and approved by the legislature in democratic countries, forming what is often called the government's budget. I call this the macro level of allocative decisions. In 2019, the Brazilian Congress approved the precise amount of R$129,816,331,109 for the Ministry of Health, that is, just below R$130 billion (the equivalent of US$34 billion).[86] This, despite being one of the highest amounts allocated to an area, represents just below 5 per cent of the total federal budget.[87]

Meso level decisions are those taken at the level of each department in the allocation of its budget among the several fixed expenses (capital and human resources), programmes and actions to be implemented in a given year. In health, that includes a complex array of decisions such as how much to spend in the recruitment and training of health personnel (doctors, nurses, technicians, etc.), in the acquisition of health equipment, in the implementation of health prevention programmes, in each of the broad areas of medicine (cardiovascular, oncology, infectious diseases, neurology, etc.), etc. In Brazil, the health budget is elaborated through a long and complex process, which begins in each municipality, state and in the Federal Union, through the elaboration of so-called health plans. Health plans are discussed, modified and transformed

[84] For a good discussion of this issue, see R. E. Robertson, 'Measuring State Compliance with the Obligation to Devote the "Maximum Available Resources" to Realizing Economic, Social, and Cultural Rights', (1994) 16(4) *Human Rights Quarterly*, 693–714; Bilchitz, *Poverty and Fundamental Rights*.

[85] Ministério do Planejamento, Desenvolvimento e Gestão, 'Texto do Projeto de Lei Quadros Orçamentários Consolidados Detalhamento da Receita Legislação da Receita e da Despesa', Brasilia (2018), www2.camara.leg.br/orcamento-da-uniao/leis-orcamentarias/loa/2019/tramitacao/texto-final, accessed 23 June 2019. This is just below 50 per cent of the GDP of 2018, R$6.8 trillion (US$1.8 trillion), see IBGE, www.ibge.gov.br/explica/pib.php, accessed 23 June 2019.

[86] These are rough estimates using the exchange rate of 26 March 2019.

[87] The highest expenditures seem to be with pensions and interests on public debt.

into budget proposals by the executive powers of each unit of the federation. They are then sent to the respective legislative powers that can again discuss and modify them before voting and approval, which generate the budgetary laws, within which the health budget is inserted. It is also important to remember that health proposals must adapt to the priorities set for the public administration as a whole and, in a way, compete for resources with other sectors of administration, such as education, security, culture, etc., although the Brazilian Constitution establishes minimum health expenditures (Article 198).[88]

Micro decisions are taken within each programme and action involving the distribution of services among individuals and groups. In health, for instance, think of the difficult decision faced by many health departments around the world about who, among several individuals with similar needs, should have priority in the access of a certain scarce health resource, such as, for instance, renal dialysis, hip replacement surgery, organ transplantation, hospital beds, etc.[89]

The following chart summarises the process just explained.

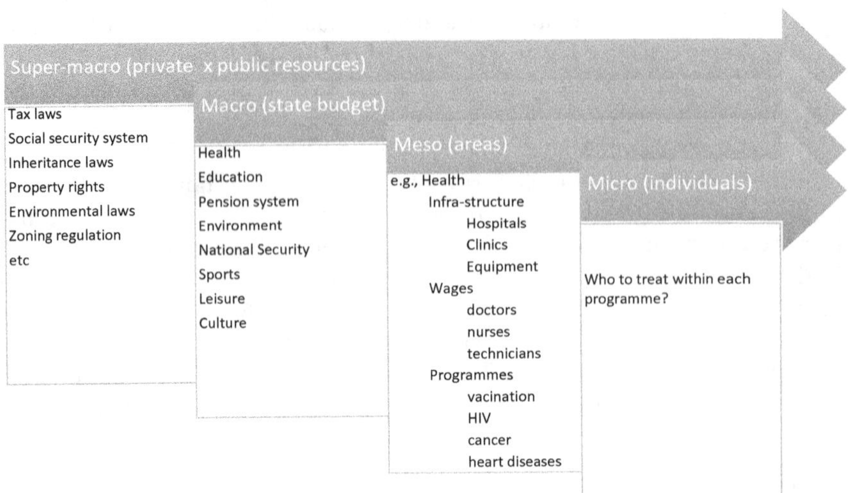

[88] For a comprehensive guide, see CONASS, O processo de planejamento e orçamento no SUS, www.conass.org.br/guiainformacao/planejamento-e-orcamento-no-sus/, accessed 23 June 2019.

[89] Recall that, Brazil being a federal union divided into 27 state units and 5,570 municipalities, the same process is followed in each of these units to reach the corresponding health budgets for each of them.

This necessarily overly simplified picture seems sufficient, however, to emphasise the complexity of the process of incorporation of health interventions in the public health system. What is ultimately included in the package (i.e., the lists, formularies) that the system will offer to everyone is the culmination of this long and complex technico-political process of resource allocation that starts at the super-macro level and ends at the hospital bed or the doctor's consultation room (micro level), passing by politicians in congress representing their constituents and public health administrators in the executive trying to put together the best package of health policies within the limited resources available, both under significant pressures from the public, patient organisations, corporate interests (pharmaceutical companies, healthcare providers, etc.).

In recent decades, the process of incorporation in Brazil has become more streamlined, transparent, participatory and influenced by scientific method through the creation of organs such as the CONITEC – Comissão Nacional de Incorporação de Tecnologia em Saúde (The National Commission for Health Technology Incorporation)[90] and the COMARE (The Technical and Multidisciplinary Commission for the Update of RENAME),[91] and the improvement of government formularies and lists, that is, the RENAME (National List of Essential Medicines)[92] and the RENASES (National List of Health Actions and Services).[93] The process of incorporation is of course far from perfect and free from undue influences, as the discussion in this chapter emphasised, but it exists, despite not being much known by many involved in the practice and debate of health litigation.

[90] Law no. 12.401, of 28 April 2011.

[91] Portaria no. 1, of 22 January 2008.

[92] Portaria GM no. 3.916, of 30 October 1998; Resolução CNS no. 338, of 6 May 2004.

[93] Portaria no. 841, of 2 May 2012.

PART III

What Role for Courts?

9

Conclusion

To Interfere or Not to Interfere? *The Court's Dilemma*[1]

> The democratic process is a gamble on the possibilities that a people, in acting autonomously, will learn how to act rightly.[2]
>
> Robert Dahl

> Courts are, at the end of the day, never an instrument of total societal revolution . . . never a substitute for direct political action.[3]
>
> Upendra Baxi

Can courts play a legitimate and competent role in the adjudication of the right to health? If so, what should this role be? These questions are of course not peculiar to the right to health. They are age-old ones that have been accompanying social and economic rights in general ever since the idea of such rights started to gain traction. The issue is often referred to as the question of social rights *justiciability*. Social rights are perceived by many to present atypical challenges for courts due to the complexity of the issues that their implementation involves, in particular, the requirement of wide-ranging decision-making on how to collect and allocate societal resources among a myriad of complex social policies.

The issue of social rights justiciability is far from academic, as it once was. As more and more constitutions now expressly recognise these rights, courts around the world are increasingly called to adjudicate concrete disputes arising under them, notably in Latin America but also

1 This chapter draws partly on a paper I presented at the XIII Conference of the Colombian Constitutional Jurisdiction (XIII Encuentro de la Jurisdicción Constitucional) in Bogota in January 2019. I am extremely grateful to Jeff King for detailed comments on an earlier version of that paper, which have been invaluable for the development of many of the ideas of this chapter.

2 R. Dahl, *Democracy and Its Critics* (New Haven: Yale University Press, 1989), at 192.

3 U. Baxi, 'The Avatars of Indian Judicial Activism', in Verma, S. K. and Kusum, S. K. (eds.), *Fifty Years of the Supreme Court of India: Its Grasp and Reach* (New Delhi: Oxford University Press, 2000), at 161.

increasingly elsewhere.[4] The difficulties that social rights' justiciability raises are becoming thus more evident and more urgent.[5] The judicialisation of health in Brazil discussed in great detail in Chapters 5–8 of this book is a good illustration (see Part II).

As I have argued in those chapters, Brazilian courts have not been doing a particularly good job of adjudicating the right to health in the past two decades. The model of health litigation prevalent so far (I call it the *Brazilian model*) has neither strengthened the accountability of the state nor brought more equity to health in Brazil. It has by and large served a sizeable minority of individuals (perhaps 1 per cent of the population), shifting resources towards expensive health technologies of dubious priority in a chronically underfunded health system that struggles to universalise even the basics to the whole population (see Chapter 4).

The Brazilian model provides support, thus, to those sceptical or cautious about social rights' justiciability. It illustrates rather well their legitimate concerns about the involvement of courts with social policies. If the Brazilian model were an inevitable corollary of courts' attempts to adjudicate social rights, then the case for nonjusticiability would be rather difficult to respond to.

As I argue in this final chapter of the book, the Brazilian model is *not* the only available one, though there seems to be a rather strong tendency for social rights' litigation and, in particular, health litigation, to conform to it (and not only in Brazil).[6] The challenge, thus, is to prevent that

[4] As David Landau notes, perhaps with some hyperbole: 'For all practical purposes, the debate about whether to include social rights in constitutions is over . . . there is now a "near consensus" (outside of the United States) that countries should include such rights in their constitutions. Moreover, there is an increasingly vibrant and varied jurisprudence on what these rights mean and how they should be enforced. Social rights are not mere paper rights; courts around the world are actively enforcing them.' D. Landau, 'The Reality of Social Rights Enforcement', (2012) 53(1) *Harvard International Law Journal*, 189–247, at 190.

[5] The involvement of courts with social policies and the debate it entails did not start, of course, with the constitutionalisation of social rights. Even in countries where most of these rights are not recognised in the federal constitution, courts have increasingly interfered with social policies and generated a heated debate on the appropriateness and impact of such involvement. For an early discussion in the context of the United States, see: D. Horowitz, *The Courts and Social Policy* (Washington, DC: Brookings Institution, 1977).

[6] As Mark Tushnet aptly notes, what he calls weak-form judicial review may escalate into strong-form review, see M. Tushnet, 'New Forms of Judicial Review and the Persistence of Rights- and Democracy-Based Worries', (2003) 38 *Wake Forest Law Review*, at 814–815.

model from taking root, and, where it already has, to replace it with a more positive model, that is, one that can actually promote state accountability and contribute to health equity. My aim is to suggest a different model of health litigation that harnesses courts' institutional competence towards those positive outcomes and avoids the pitfalls discussed at length in Part II.

But we should not have unrealistic hopes that, even in this changed and improved form, health litigation can play a major role in advancing the enjoyment of the right to health by the Brazilian population (and this may apply to other countries as well). As I hope is clear from the history of the right to health in Brazil recounted in Parts I and II of this book, it is through politics that the health of the population has experienced significant improvement in the past three decades, and there is reason to believe that this will continue to be the most effective tool of progress in the future. Lawyers and courts may, under favourable conditions, play an important but necessarily supporting (not leading) role in this effort, or so I argue in this final chapter.[7]

9.1 The Court's Dilemma

Recognising health (and other similar complex goods) as constitutional rights leads to the following dilemma: If health is a constitutional right, courts should hold the political branches accountable when they fail to respect, protect and fulfil it; yet, as the precise content of the right to health is not clearly established by the constitution, courts have no clear constitutional standard against which to hold the state accountable and little institutional competence to develop such standards. On the one hand, we want these rights to work as rights normally do, that is, to entail some form of strong judicial accountability on the political branches of

[7] I actually tend to agree with arguments such as Mark Tushnet's that the value of judicial review is often overrated and that a world without it may well be one in which rights are better and not less protected than one with it. As he persuasively argues, it is 'wildly unlikely that the courts can save us from ourselves'. And, later: 'We do not have to have a court that will strike down laws – a court with the power of judicial review – to have a vibrant language of fundamental rights available to us.' See M. Tushnet, *Taking the Constitution Away from the Courts* (Princeton: Princeton University Press, 1999), at 71 and 168. See also, for excellent discussions on this topic with detailed comparative analysis of several jurisdictions, R. Hirschl, *Towards Juristocracy* (New Haven: Yale University Press, 2004) and R. Hirschl, 'The Nordic Counternarrative: Democracy, Human Development, and Judicial Review', (2011) 9(2) *International Journal of Constitutional Law*, 449–469.

the state.[8] On the other hand, we fear that courts will get 'disastrously mixed up in matters beyond their province and their ken as judges of the law'.[9]

Legal scholar Frank Michelman has captured the dilemma most eloquently as one between abdication and usurpation, even if in a deliberately exaggerated formulation:

> By constitutionalizing social rights, the argument often has run, you force the judiciary to a hapless choice between usurpation and abdication, from which there is no escape without embarrassment or discredit. One way, it is said, lies the judicial choice to issue positive enforcement orders in a pretentious, inexpert, probably vain but nevertheless resented attempt to reshuffle the most basic resource-management priorities of the public house-hold against prevailing political will. The other way lies the judicial choice to debase dangerously the entire currency of rights and the rule of law by openly ceding to executive and parliamentary bodies an unreviewable privilege of indefinite postponement of a declared constitutional right.[10]

As Michelman himself affirms, the problem is overstated, as these two extreme positions (abdication or usurpation) are not the only available ones. I agree (and will discuss other options available to courts later). We should not underestimate, however, the magnitude of the challenge of finding a role for courts that is at the same time within the boundaries of their institutional competencies (i.e., legitimacy and expertise) *and* sufficiently meaningful to hold the political branches accountable.[11]

[8] As constitutional scholar Frank Michelman puts it, once social rights are constitutionalised, we tend to see them 'as laws to be enforced like other laws . . . no less intended to be obligatory upon those to whom it is addressed than are legal rights in general and no less intended to be subject to enforcement by some means from among those available for the effectuation of legal rights in general'. F. I. Michelman, 'The Constitution, Social Rights, and Liberal Political Justification', (2003) 1(1) *International Journal of Constitutional Law*, 13–34, at 14. See also Robert Alexy: 'This model is the expression of the idea . . . that the fundamental rights of the German Constitution are positions that, from the point of view of constitutional law, are so important that the decision to guarantee them or not cannot be simply left to parliamentarian majority.' (My translation). R. Alexy, *Teoria dos Direitos Fundamentais* (São Paulo: Malheiros Editores, 2008), at 511–512.

[9] Michelman, 'The Constitution, Social Rights, and Liberal Political Justification', at 15: 'Courts, they fear, will find themselves unable to make clear assessments of the government's compliance or noncompliance with social rights guarantees, or to fashion apt and pointed remedial orders in case of a finding of noncompliance, without getting themselves disastrously mixed up in matters beyond their province and their ken as judges of the law.'

[10] Ibid., at 16.

[11] As he immediately adds after the passage quoted: 'The objection quite obviously is overstated.' Ibid. Yet his dismissal of the conundrum as not as important as often thought to be seems to me too quick. His reasons are that 'social rights can sometimes be "negatively protected" by comfortably kosher forms of judicial intervention'. Ibid., at

Many academics and judges have been seriously grappling with this problem for some time now and have offered important contributions towards its better understanding and potential resolution. My aim in this chapter is to add to this effort using the rich experience of two decades of health litigation in Brazil. As I mentioned in the introduction, the debate on the appropriate role of courts in adjudicating social and economic rights is far from academic. Health litigation in Brazil and elsewhere is perhaps one of the most prominent examples, though far from unique.[12] We have therefore a growing body of experience on which to draw to assess potential responses to the quandary highlighted above.[13]

I will start by discussing what, in my view, are unsatisfactory responses from which we can nonetheless still learn a great deal. I will then move on to more appropriate ones which are still somewhat problematic. I will conclude with a suggestion about how we should deal with the seeming lack of a definitive solution to the conundrum.

9.2 Unsatisfactory Responses: Too Much and Too Little Judicial Interference

I see as inadequate the two following opposite responses to the dilemma. They fall chiefly under the descriptions of abdication and usurpation in the passage quoted earlier from Frank Michelman. They are both over-reactions to the conundrum. One simply evades it; the other simply ignores it.[14]

17. As I discuss in the text, these 'kosher' forms are seen by many as not strong enough to protect social rights. His example of the South African case of *Minister of Public Works* v. *Kyalami Ridge Association* is a good illustration.

[12] For discussions in the field of health in six different countries from Latin America, Africa and Asia, see: A. Yamin, S. Gloppen, (eds.), *Litigating Health Rights: Can Courts Bring More Justice to Health*? (Cambridge, MA: Harvard University Press, 2011); For education and health in four countries, see V. Gauri, D. M. Brinks (eds.), *Courting Social Justice: Judicial Enforcement of Social and Economic Rights in the Developing World* (New York: Cambridge University Press, 2008). For a broader discussion of social rights in the courts of new democracies, see R. Gargarella, et al., *Courts and Social Transformation in New Democracies: An Institutional Voice for the Poor?*, 1st ed. (London: Routledge, 2006).

[13] I have discussed some of this experience before, see O. L. M. Ferraz, 'Between Abdication and Usurpation: Social Rights in the Courts of Brazil, India and South Africa', in Vilhena, O., Baxi, U. and Viljoen, F. (eds.), *Transformative Constitutionalism: Comparing the Apex Courts of Brazil, India and South Africa* (Pretoria: Pretoria University Law Press, 2013).

[14] See also Rosalind Dixon: 'In cooperative constitutional understandings, majoritarian political processes are often subject to serious blockages, such that very strong judicial deference to the legislature (super-weak judicial review) – or pure legislative supremacy –

On the abdicative extreme, we have very deferential responses, in which it is argued that judges should *never* interfere with decisions made by the political branches regarding health policies and other social rights. Their limited institutional competence (legitimacy and expertise) is seen as an insuperable obstacle. Executive and parliamentary bodies are given an 'unreviewable privilege' to implement social rights as they see fit. The only mechanisms of accountability under this view are political, that is, elections, demonstrations, the press, etc.

Not many commentators or courts seem to hold this more extreme view any longer, especially not when countries recognise social rights in the constitution and do not expressly qualify them as unjusticiable directives of state policy.[15] But it was once more popular, including among Brazilian judges, who for a decade or so held the view that the social rights of the Brazilian Constitution were to be understood as so-called programmatic norms, that is, not to be directly enforced by courts but aimed exclusively at the legislature (see Chapter 6, Section 6.3.1 for a

will tend to produce results that fall far short of a fully inclusive and responsive constitutional ideal.' R. Dixon, 'Creating Dialogue about Socioeconomic Rights: Strong-Form versus Weak-Form Judicial Review Revisited', (2007) 5(3) *International Journal of Constitutional Law*, 391–418, at 402.

15 One possible prominent holder of this position in academia was Cass Sunstein, who argued against the constitutionalisation of social rights due to their unenforceability by courts: '*Many positive rights are unenforceable by courts.* Courts lack the tools of a bureaucracy. They cannot create government programs. They do not have a systematic overview of government policy. In these circumstances, it is unrealistic to expect courts to enforce many positive rights. Consider, for example, another provision in the Hungarian Constitution: 'People living within the territory of the Republic of Hungary have the right to the highest possible level of physical health.' How could courts enforce this right? The same problem appears for many (not all) of the positive rights, including the right to work, the right to a clean environment, and the right to training for the disabled.' See C. Sunstein, 'Against Positive Rights. Why Social and Economic Rights *Don't* Belong in the New Constitutions of Post-Communist Europe', (1993) 2(1) *E. Eur. Const. Rev.*, 35–38, at 37. But he expressly clarified that his argument was aimed exclusively at Eastern European countries coming out of communist regimes and he later applauded the less deferential reasonableness approach of the South African Constitutional Court, see C. R. Sunstein, 'Social and Economic Rights? Lessons from South Africa', (2001) 11(1) *Constitutional Forum*, 123–132. Moreover, his main concern was perhaps not with judicial overreach, but rather that the judiciary would simply not enforce these rights and, as a consequence, the constitution would be discredited as 'a mere piece of paper' and judges might even stop enforcing other rights as well. These concerns proved mistaken, at least in Hungary, Brazil and elsewhere in Latin America. For Hungary, see: A. Sajó, 'How the Rule of Law Killed Hungarian Welfare Reform', (1996) 5(1) *E. Eur. Const. Rev.*, 31–41.

more detailed discussion).[16] This 'super-deferential' stance is in my view unsatisfactory as it 'addresses' the conundrum by evading it. It eliminates from social rights any measure of legal accountability.[17]

At the opposite, usurpative extreme, is the view that constitutionalisation of social rights provides an automatic and sufficient mandate for judges to interfere strongly (i.e., impose strong remedies) with the decisions of the other branches whenever there is a violation of the right to health (as with any constitutional right). Little concern, if any, is expressed under this view about courts' lack of legitimacy or expertise. The conundrum is 'addressed', thus, by ignoring it, often under the problematic assumption that the constitution is clear about what needs to be done to implement the right to health and that courts are simply enforcing that right against recalcitrant legislative and executive bodies.

This view is rather popular among some human rights activists and academics,[18] and has also spread in the past two decades across courts in some countries, most notably in Brazil and other countries in Latin America.[19] It is the prevalent view among judges in Brazil in the field

[16] Another example is perhaps the Irish judiciary. In *D* v. *Minister for Education*, (2001) 4 I.R.259 (Ir S C), a case where the right to education, though included in the justiciable part of the Irish Constitution, was nonetheless deemed not to be subject to judicial enforcement beyond mere declaratory orders, as 'it is not the function of the court to make an assessment of the validity of the many competing claims on national resources', As cited by Tushnet, *Taking the Constitution Away from the Courts*, at 240. Note, however, that there is a difference between total non-justiciability and declaratory remedies.

[17] This 'super-deferential' approach might be appropriate if it becomes evident, empirically, that whenever courts try to interfere in certain areas, even when using very weak remedies, they end up making things much worse than they were before judicial interference. This empirically based determination of the role of courts is sometimes called an institutional approach. I have discussed this in more detail in a paper presented at the XIII Conference of the Colombian Constitutional Jurisdiction, on which parts of this chapter draw, see n. 1). See also: J. King, *Judging Social Rights*, 1st ed. (Cambridge: Cambridge University Press, 2012), ch. 5; J. King, 'Institutional Approaches to Judicial Restraint' (2008) 28 *Oxford Journal Of Legal Studies*, at 409.

[18] I believe this is the view of D. Bilchitz, 'Giving Socio-Economic Rights Teeth: The Minimum Core and Its Importance', (2002) 119 *South African Law Journal*, 484–501. See also D. Bilchitz, *Poverty and Fundamental Rights: The Justification and Enforcement of Socio-Economic Rights* (Oxford: Oxford Scholarship Online, 2007), at 183–196, and my review of it: O. L. M. Ferraz, 'Poverty and Human Rights', (2008) 28(3) *Oxford Journal Of Legal Studies*, 585–603.

[19] Courts in Colombia and Costa Rica seem to have also adopted this position at times, see A. Yamin, S. Gloppen (eds.), *Litigating the Right to Health: Can Courts Bring More Justice to Health Systems?* (Cambridge, MA: Harvard University Press, 2011). See also O. L. M. Ferraz et al., 'Judging the Price of Life: Cost Considerations in Right-to-Health

of health, as we saw in Part II (see Chapter 6, Section 6.3.1).[20] The following passage of a leading decision of the Brazilian Supreme Federal Tribunal in a right to health case summarises the approach:

> Between protecting the inviolability of the right to life and to health, an inalienable fundamental right guaranteed by the Constitution itself (Art. 6 and Art. 196) or ensuring, against this fundamental prerogative, a financial and secondary interest of the state, I believe – once this dilemma is established – ethical and legal reasons impose on the judge one single and possible option: unswerving respect for life and human health .... The interpretation of a programmatic norm cannot transform it into a toothless constitutional promise.[21]

As we saw in Part II, this interpretation of the right to health as virtually an absolute right (I call it a 'right to everything') is in great part responsible for the significant growth of health litigation in Brazil and the extremely high success rates in such litigation, forcing the state to provide virtually any health benefit that litigants claim (see Chapter 6, Section 6.3.1 and Chapter 8, Section 8.2.1). It should be clear by now why this complete disregard for the health policies of the state is deeply problematic. Firstly, it mistakes the nature of the constitutional obligations that flow from the right to health, taking for absolute and precise obligations what are in fact vague and qualified ones, that is, which are in need of specification involving complex decisions of resource allocation, policy design and implementation. Moreover, when courts simply substitute the political branches' decisions for their own in this peremptory manner, they are not simply overstepping the boundaries of their legitimacy, they are also potentially distorting social policies and worsening inequalities, that is, producing a negative impact rather than contributing to the

Litigation', in Aasen, H. S., Gloppen, S., Magnussen, A. and Nilssen, E. (eds.), *Juridification and Social Citizenship in the Welfare State* (Cheltenham: Edward Elgar Publishing, 2014), 121–145.

20 It is important to note though that this assertive approach has not been applied consistently by Brazilian courts across all social rights. In housing cases and minimum wage cases, for instance, the courts have been notably less assertive than in health and education. See O. L. M. Ferraz, 'Between Activism and Deference: Social Rights Adjudication in the Brazilian Supreme Federal Tribunal', in Garcia, H. A., Klare, K. and Williams, L. A. (eds.), *Social and Economic Rights in Theory and Practice: Critical Inquiries* (London: Routlegde, 2015).

21 Min. Celso de Mello decision on the ARE 730.741/SP, cited by Min. Ricardo Lewandowski in ARE 724.293 (Rio Grande do Sul, 19 March 2013). My translation from the Portuguese. Full text, in Portuguese, is available at the STF website: www.stf.jus.br/portal/processo/verProcessoPeca.asp?id=133345682&tipoApp=.pdf.

implementation of social rights.[22] As Part II of this book has shown, these negative effects are very real in the field of health litigation in Brazil.

***

The tendency for social rights adjudication to gravitate towards one of these two problematic extremes is not negligible and explains, in great part, the heated debates that social rights' justiciability arouses between sceptics and supporters. Those more concerned with the negative consequences of courts' overreach emphasise the perils of the usurpative tendencies of judges. Those more preoccupied with political neglect of rights stress the risks of abdication.

There is some exaggeration in both views, but we should not underestimate, I emphasise, the seriousness of either tendency. This is what makes the dilemma a real and important one. Let us look now into less extreme and more promising responses to the conundrum.

9.3 More Promising (Intermediate) Responses

Responses that have actually tried to address the justiciability conundrum, that is, to strike a balance between the extreme super-deferential and super-assertive positions rather than evade or ignore the conundrum, could perhaps be classified along a spectrum that goes from 'less interfering' to 'more interfering' forms of adjudication. I prefer to use these inelegant descriptors rather than say *weak* and *strong* forms of adjudication, or *procedural* and *substantive* forms of adjudication, because, as it will become clear in the discussion below, I don't think that these qualifiers map perfectly onto what I call less and more interfering modes of adjudication.[23]

[22] See also O. L. M. Ferraz, 'The Right to Health in the Courts of Brazil: Worsening Health Inequities?', (2009) 11(2) *Health and Human Rights, An International Journal*, 33–45; O. L. M. Ferraz, 'Health Inequalities, Rights and Courts: The Social Impact of the "Judicialization of Health" in Brazil', in Yamin, A. and Gloppen, S. (eds.), *Litigating the Right to Health: Can Courts Bring More Justice to Health Systems?* (Cambridge, MA: Harvard University Press, 2011).

[23] For a comprehensive treatment of the subject, see M. Tushnet, *Weak Courts, Strong Rights: Judicial Review and Social Welfare Rights in Comparative Constitutional Law* (Princeton: Princeton University Press, 2008). See also Tushnet, 'New Forms of Judicial Review and the Persistence of Rights- and Democracy-Based Worries' (2003) 38 Wake Forest L. Rev. 813 and M. Tushnet, 'Social Welfare Rights and the Forms of Judicial Review', (2004) 82 *Texas Law Review*, 1895.

9.3.1 *Less Interfering Forms of Adjudication*

Those more concerned with judicial overreach but still eager to find some meaningful role for courts tend to support forms of adjudication that fall under what I call the less interfering modes of adjudication (some might refer to them as *procedural*, or *weak* forms of adjudication). There are variants of these forms of adjudication, as we shall see, but they share the understanding that courts ought not to interfere with the *outcome* of decisions of the representative branches involving resource allocation and formulation of social policies simply because they think a better decision was available. But courts may still do quite a bit under these adjudication forms. At the less interfering end of the spectrum, they can review the *manner* in which legislative and executive bodies have reached those decisions to guarantee that they have followed *due process*. Perhaps the most detailed formulation and defence of such a role for courts can be found in Jeff King's *Judging Social Rights*. Here is how he describes the core of the approach:

> The special role of the court foreseen in contemporary constitutional adjudication and especially social rights adjudication is that it focuses on the process of decision-making in respect of the asserted human rights interest, rather than on the state's achievement of some particular state of affairs. It seeks to test the adequacy of the justification or reasoning underlying the public action or omission, the plausibility of its premises, and validity of its inferences, and at times the scope of participation afforded during that process, the availability of effective policy alternatives, and (where applicable) the compatibility of the resulting decision with the conceptual core of the asserted right. To prove that a right has been violated, it is not enough to show that someone has been incarcerated without a hearing, or evicted from a home despite substantial need, or was prevented from speaking at a political rally. We know only after assessing the state's justification, unless (in rare cases) the constitution states an absolute obligation that triggers an irresistible duty upon some conditions having been met.[24]

Due process is of course a broad term and, depending on how it is interpreted, will give courts more or less scope to interfere. The least interfering conception of due process involves the traditional grounds of rationality and non-discrimination present in the administrative law of many countries. A good example concerning the right to health is the

[24] King, *Judging Social Rights*, at 107.

famous UK case *Child B*. In this case, the claimant sought an order from the court to force the public health system (the NHS) to fund treatment that the health authority had decided not to fund within its budget, chiefly for priority-setting reasons. After stating that resources are not unlimited and must therefore be allocated in some way by the state, Lord Bingham, the leading judge in the case, concluded that courts should not interfere with such decisions unless there was a clear defect in the process, such as irrationality or discrimination:

> I have no doubt that in a perfect world any treatment which a patient, or a patient's family, sought would be provided if doctors were willing to give it, no matter how much it costs, particularly when a life was potentially at stake. It would however, in my view, be shutting one's eyes to the real world if the court were to proceed on the basis that we do live in such a world. It is common knowledge that health authorities of all kinds are constantly pressed to make ends meet. They cannot pay their nurses as much as they would like; they cannot provide all the treatments they would like; they cannot purchase all the extremely expensive medical equipment they would like; they cannot carry out all the research they would like; they cannot build all the hospitals and specialist units they would like. Difficult and agonising judgments have to be made as to how a limited budget is best allocated to the maximum advantage of the maximum number of patients. That is not a judgment which the court can make.[25]

In a very similar South African case also involving the right to health, the judges followed the same understanding when they refused to grant the claimant's request for renal dialysis treatment. The treatment had been refused on very similar grounds as in *Child B*, that is, for reasons of priority-setting in the context of scarce resources. Here is the court's conclusion:

> The provincial administration which is responsible for health services in KwaZulu-Natal has to make decisions about the funding that should be made available for health care and how such funds should be spent. These choices involve difficult decisions to be taken at the political level in fixing the health budget, and at the functional level in deciding upon the

[25] *R* v. *Cambridge Health Authority* (1995) 2 All ER 129, whose leading opinion was given by Tom Bingham, who went on to become Lord Chief Justice in 1996 and Senior Law Lord in 2000. The other judges in that case were Sir Stephen Brown P and Simon Brown LJ. For a good discussion of the changes in British jurisprudence, see: D. W. L. Wang, 'From Wednesbury Unreasonableness to Accountability for Reasonableness', (2017) 76(3) *The Cambridge Law Journal*, 642–670.

> priorities to be met. A court will be slow to interfere with rational decisions taken in good faith by the political organs and medical authorities whose responsibility it is to deal with such matters.[26]

More or less interfering modes of adjudication can be reached depending on how *rationality* is interpreted. As the development of British administrative law illustrates, rationality can be interpreted in a more restrictive manner, something close to madness ('so absurd or outrageous in their defiance of logic or morality that no reasonable person addressing the question would have come to the same conclusion', as in the classic *Wednesbury* case), but also in a more expansive manner, closer to proportionality.[27] The so-called reasonableness approach developed by the South African Constitutional Court after Soobramoney, in cases such as *Grootboom* and *TAC*, seems a good example of the latter.

The most thorough formulation of an expanded rationality approach to right to health adjudication, although not originally developed with courts in mind, is Norman Daniels' well received 'accountability for reasonableness' framework.[28] According to Daniels, a fair process of decision-making in the allocation of scarce health resources displays four main characteristics: it is based on evidence (i.e., reasons), it is transparent, it is participatory and it is subject to review.[29]

26 *Soobramoney* v. *Minister of Health (Kwazulu-Natal)* (CCT32/97) (1997) ZACC 17; 1998 (1) SA 765 (CC); 1997 (12) BCLR 1696 (27 November 1997).

27 D. W. L. Wang, 'From Wednesbury Unreasonableness to Accountability for Reasonableness'.

28 N. Daniels, *Just Health: Meeting Health Needs Fairly*, 1st ed. (New York: Cambridge University Press, 2008).

29 Ibid., at 300: 'It requires, at a minimum, "the careful collection of evidence for interventions, the thorough review of arguments for establishing particular priorities, the involvement of all relevant stakeholders in the process, and transparency for all aspects of the process, including the rationales for the priorities adopted." As he convincingly argues, given that reasonable disagreement about how to solve "conflicts among claimants within and across rights" is inevitable and requires, thus, a procedural rather than a substantive solution, i.e. a "systematic rationale" to address the underlying moral disagreements among reasonable people'. Daniels rather plausible point is that, since different reasonable principles of distributive justice will necessarily lead to different and reasonable conflicting answers, that is, people will reasonably disagree on what the correct one is, the solution can only be procedural. Ibid., at 328. I cannot engage here in a deep analysis of Daniels' rich and complex proposal and the criticisms it has attracted. For a good discussion, see A. Rid, 'Justice and Procedure: How Does "Accountability for Reasonableness" Result in Fair Limit-Setting Decisions?', (2009) 35(1) *Journal of Medical Ethics*, 12.

Daniel Wang argues persuasively that British courts have adopted such an 'accountability for reasonableness' approach since *Child B.*[30] Keith Syrett provides a detailed defence of this approach as the most appropriate response to what I call the justiciability dilemma.[31]

Such a procedural accountability role is neither trivial nor easy to perform, unlike some critics often assume. Done well, it could potentially contribute to the improvement of the quality of legislative and administrative decision-making on social policies in general and health policy in particular. As Wang shows in his detailed review of health litigation in the United Kingdom, 'by continuously requiring better reasons and procedural fairness ... [courts] have contributed to change the way in which the decisions about priority-setting in health care are made.[32]

Yet this approach, focused on so-called procedural fairness rather than the correct outcome of the decision, falls way short of what many people believe ought to be a strong protection of rights. For many, this model risks relegating social rights to a second-class position, rather different (i.e., weaker) from what is expected from genuine rights.[33] As much as the requirements of transparency, participation and rationality go some way beyond the extreme super-deferential end of the spectrum of social rights' adjudication, they do not guarantee any particular substantive and immediate benefit to the right-holder, as rights are supposed to do according to many.

[30] Daniels himself highlights this: 'Accountability for reasonableness provides a systematic rationale for key elements of fair process in what is commonly thought to be part of a rights based approach.' Ibid., at 328. See also Syrett, *Law, Legitimacy and the Rationing of Health Care: A Contextual and Comparative Perspective* (New York: Cambridge University Press, 2007), at 266.

[31] In his excellent book, Syrett provides a defence of accountability for reasonableness as a legitimate and robust framework for the involvement of courts in health allocation decisions. Syrett, *Law, Legitimacy and the Rationing of Health Care*. See also N. Daniels et al., 'Role of the Courts in the Progressive Realization of the Right to Health: Between the Threat and the Promise of Judicialization in Mexico', (2015) 1(3) *Health Systems & Reform*, at 233: 'The courts should, where they have the discretion, focus on promoting an equal right to health care for all, which requires a broad view of the entire health system and a focus on the fairness of allocation implications for different populations.'

[32] Wang, 'From Wednesbury Unreasonableness to Accountability for Reasonableness', at 668–669. But Wang is not unambiguously positive about such changes. He aptly cautions against potential negative effects of the 'judge over your shoulder': 'fear of litigation may lead to what decision-makers would see as second-best policies'. Ibid., at 670.

[33] See Bilchitz, 'Giving Socio-Economic Rights Teeth', at 119.

9.3.2 More Interfering Responses: The Minimum Core Approach

It is a desire to afford stronger protection to social rights that motivates what I call more interfering responses. Surely – one might claim – there is more that courts could do to protect these rights than ensuring transparency, participation and rationality in the decisions of the political branches.[34] Especially in less robust democracies, where the legislature and the executive are perceived to systematically fail to give due consideration to the social rights of the most vulnerable, courts ought to be able to force the state to respect, protect and fulfil the right to health (and other social rights) more strongly.

One of the main arguments of this book is that these claims are often overstated, both on the alleged delinquency of political branches and on the purported willingness and ability of courts to redress these failures (see Parts I and II). I will return to these important but often neglected issues later on in the conclusion of this chapter.[35] Here I want to explore this sort of claim (exaggerated but not fallacious) in more detail.

There is no doubt that, in an ideal scenario of legal accountability, it would be good if courts could legitimately and expertly provide stronger protection to the right to health and other social rights. It is beyond question, as we saw in Chapter 4, that Brazil (and many other countries) could guarantee better health to its population than it currently does. If courts could make legislative and executive bodies improve their record, this is what they ought to do as part of their duty to enforce rights recognised in the constitution.

When someone is found to have been arbitrarily imprisoned, we expect courts to order their immediate release; if someone is illegally prevented from registering to vote, we expect judges to issue a positive injunction ordering their prompt registration; if it is proven that a detainee has been tortured by the police, we expect the judiciary to condemn the official involved and make the state pay compensation to the victim. In none of these cases would we be contented with less than such substantive and immediate judicial responses.[36]

[34] See also King entertaining a similar potential challenge to his approach: 'a judge's job is to define [a substantive core of the right] and require the state to implement it'. King, *Judging Social Rights*, at 97.

[35] For a similar argument, see D. Wang, 'Social Rights Adjudication and the Nirvana Fallacy', (2018) July *Public Law*, 482–499.

[36] As Mary Ann Glendon puts it: 'The language of rights is the language of no compromise. The winner takes all and the loser has to get out of town. The conversation is over.' M. A.

Less interfering modes of adjudication such as the reasonableness approach raise the justified apprehension of being perhaps too weak to protect fundamental rights. If these are *real* rights, the argument goes, some stronger measure of protection from courts is expected.[37]

The trouble is to find a role for courts that is at the same time stronger than the reasonableness approach and does not overstretch courts' institutional competence, especially when complex rights such as the right to health are at stake. As Part II of this book highlights, the risk is not trivial and the consequences not negligible. Strong adjudication of the right to health in Brazil has meant, so far, two decades of reallocation of resources towards expensive health technologies of dubious priority in a chronically underfunded health system that struggles to universalise even the basics to the whole population. But perhaps the Brazilian model can be avoided. Perhaps there is a less deferential form of adjudication that conscientious judges may exercise without overstepping their legitimacy, overstretching their capacity and generating the pernicious effects of the Brazilian model.

The most plausible such model seems to be the so-called *minimum core approach*. The basic idea of this approach is rather intuitive. It starts by recognising that the social and economic rights to health, education, housing, etc. of international human rights instruments and national constitutions provide little specific guidance on what states are under a duty to do. These legal instruments often say little about the amount of resources that states should invest in each social right let alone on how these resources should be allocated within each social right among the myriad of available options.[38] This is of course not a failure of legal draftsmanship, but rather a necessary feature of these rights. It is precisely this indeterminacy, as we saw, that raises concerns about courts' institutional competence to hold legislative and executive bodies accountable to their social rights' constitutional duties and generates the justiciability dilemma. The minimum core provides an intuitive solution to the problem. If all courts had to work with were the vague statements that 'everyone has a right to the highest possible standard of

Glendon, *Rights Talk: The Impoverishment of Political Discourse* (New York: The Free Press, 1993), at 9.

37 As Rosalind Dixon notes: 'where a court order lacks any coercive dimension, it will have little direct impact on administrative inertia'. Dixon, 'Creating Dialogue about Socioeconomic Rights' at 412.

38 Although sometimes they do ring-fence resources for social rights, as we saw is the case of the Brazilian Constitution after Amendment 29, of 2000. See Chapter 4.

health, education, housing etc affordable within available resources', it would be hard to see anything they could do beyond the reasonableness review discussed earlier. If, however, one can carve a more precise sub-set out of each of these generically formulated rights and claim that states are under a more urgent duty to respect, protect and fulfil them than the 'rest' of the right, then courts (and international human rights adjudicative bodies) might exercise a stronger but still legitimate legal accountability role.

The *minimum core* is this sub-set of the right. If it 'exists', that is, if it can be plausibly justified and determined, it seems to strike a rather plausible golden mean between the extremes of deferential abdication and assertive usurpation. Given its purported *minimum* character, it seems to allow for just the right amount of tolerable interference by courts in the political process, leaving ample scope left for the political branches to go about their business of allocating scarce resources and designing and implementing social policy. Yet, as they need to observe at least the minimum core, they are also subject to a reasonably strong measure of legal accountability, which is, as we saw, what many believe is lacking in the less interfering forms of adjudication such as the reasonableness approach. As Kate Young notes in her insightful article on the topic: 'With the minimum core concept as its guide, economic and social rights are supposed to enter the hard work of hard law.'[39]

This intuitive appeal of the minimum core idea emerges clearly from its most well-known official formulation, issued by the UN Committee on Economic, Social and Cultural Rights in General Comment No. 3:

> 10. . . . the Committee is of the view that a minimum core obligation to ensure the satisfaction of, at the very least, minimum essential levels of each of the rights is incumbent upon every State party. Thus, for example, a State party in which any significant number of individuals is deprived of essential foodstuffs, of essential primary health care, of basic shelter and housing, or of the most basic forms of education is, prima facie, failing to discharge its obligations under the Covenant.[40]

[39] K. Young, 'The Minimum Core of Economic and Social Rights: A Concept in Search of Content', (2008) 33 *Yale International Law Journal*, 113–175, at 114.

[40] CESCR General Comment No. 3: The Nature of States Parties' Obligations (Art. 2, Paragraph 1, of the Covenant) Adopted at the Fifth Session of the Committee on Economic, Social and Cultural Rights, on 14 December 1990 (Contained in Document E/1991/23).

Although the Committee did not expressly mention that the minimum core should be justiciable, nor do all of its proponents advocate this position, my specific concern here is with the view that the minimum core may be an adequate response to what I am calling the justiciability dilemma.[41] For the idea of the minimum core to be operational within this particular purpose of adjudication, the content of the minimum core of the particular right in question must be either clear (or subject to legitimate and competent determination by courts) and amenable to effective judicial enforcement.

9.3.3 Defining the Minimum Core

Many have argued that defining the content of the minimum core is ridden with the exact same kind of complexity and contestation involved in the definition of 'full' social rights, that is, that it involves the same intractable decisions on resource allocation and policy formulation that makes us question the legitimacy and capacity of courts. If this is so, we are back to the exact problem that the minimum core was supposed to solve in the first place.[42] Is it so?

I believe it is, but not for the reasons nor to the extent often claimed by sceptics of the idea of the minimum core. Those who admit that defining the content of the minimum core presents important challenges often mention two main related difficulties: resource scarcity and the myriad of potential social policies available to advance essential levels of social rights and the likelihood of fierce disagreement about which ones should

[41] See J. Tasioulas, *Minimum Core Obligations: Human Rights in the Here and Now* (Washington, DC: World Bank, 2017), available at: https://openknowledge.worldbank.org/handle/10986/29144 and J. Tasioulas, *The Minimum Core of the Human Right to Health* (Washington, DC: World Bank, 2017), available at: http://documents.worldbank.org/curated/en/194751515587192833/The-minimum-core-of-the-human-right-to-health, both accessed 23 June 2019.

[42] Young, among others, also raises doubt about the usefulness of the minimum core: 'Without this clarity, the concept cannot supply a predetermined content to economic and social rights, rank the value of particular claims, or set the level and criteria of state justification required for a permissible infringement. Indeed, I suggest that it is unlikely that the concept will ever offer the relative determinacy required for these three tests. Yet it can assist as an object of interpretive agreement-or disagreement-around claims for socioeconomic protection.' Young, 'The Minimum Core of Economic and Social Rights', at 116. See also *Government of the Republic of South Africa* v. *Grootboom*, (2001) (1) SA 46 (CC), 32–33, rejecting a minimum core approach given the difficulties of establishing its content.

receive priority.[43] The argument goes along the following lines. Resources are so limited in many countries that not even a minimum core is affordable. The same intractable decisions about which social policies should be prioritised will therefore need to be made. How should a country prioritise its limited resources among several potential social policies, all equally essential? Should it universalise basic sanitation first or provide a minimum of clean water to everyone? Or should it put every child in primary school first? Or should it perhaps provide accommodation to the homeless as a top priority? The list could go on and on. Focusing on essential levels might diminish the scale of the task compared to considering the 'full' right, but not by much when resources are severely limited.

These challenges are real, but it is important not to misapprehend their actual nature, as is easily and often done in the literature, muddling somewhat the search for a solution. Resource scarcity, in most countries today, should not be understood as *absolute insufficiency* of resources. Very few countries in the world today can genuinely claim that they are so poor that it would be simply impossible for them to guarantee universal access to 'essential foodstuffs ... essential primary health care ... basic shelter and housing, or ... the most basic forms of education' to the whole population. This was certainly the case for many countries in the 1960s, when the idea of recognising social rights in international treaties was being fiercely debated.[44] It is certainly not the case now. To illustrate, even since the end of the Cold War, in the late

[43] Dixon, for instance, argues: 'It is quite possible, as an abstract theoretical matter, that there are answers to these questions that are both morally and constitutionally "right." However, as free and equal citizens, with extremely different life experiences and perspectives, it is also both likely and reasonable that South Africans should reach a variety of different answers to these questions. There is, thus, little chance of resolving these questions by reference either to collective South African understandings of the concrete content of sections 26 and 27, or agreed objective standards of constitutional or social morality in South Africa. Rather, rights-based controversies must be resolved in South Africa by more squarely democratic deliberative processes that attempt to give effect to constitutional understandings in the broader "constitutional culture".' Dixon, 'Creating Dialogue about Socioeconomic Rights', at 401. Jeremy Waldron has also argued, in turn, that there will be little basis for truly 'countermajoritarian' judicial enforcement of rights guarantees, since such enforcement would clearly fail to respect principles of equality among citizens in processes of democratic constitutional deliberation. J. Waldron, *Law and Disagreement* (Oxford: Oxford University Press, 1999), at 165–187.

[44] Back then, arguments that social rights were simply impossible to be implemented in most of the world (the infeasibility argument) were rather plausible. See M. Cranston, 'Are There Any Human Rights?', (1983) 112(4) *Daedalus*, 1–17.

1980s, world GDP has almost quadrupled from US$22.6 trillion to US$75 trillion while the world population grew at a much lower pace (42 per cent).[45] That resulted in substantial gains in GDP per capita, which more than doubled from US$4,275 in 1990 to US$10,748 in 2017.[46] If we go further back, to 1966, when the International Covenant on Economic, Social and Cultural Rights was adopted, world GDP was US$2.1 trillion, a per capita amount of a meagre US$628, that is, US$1.7 a day, or seventeen times lower than today.[47] As development economist Andy Sumner aptly puts it:

> Economic growth since the Cold War has expanded national resources in developing countries, and consequentially the causes of much global poverty have become less about the lack of resources and more about questions of national inequality, and issues of social policy ... the poor now live in countries that are substantially better-off countries than a generation ago. The majority of global poverty is now in countries that many foreign aid donors see as sufficiently well off to reduce or end development aid .... In other words the context for poverty reduction efforts is now one of poverty amid growth and new wealth rather than, as it was towards the end of the Cold War, poverty reduction amid stagnation and insufficient domestic resources to address absolute poverty.[48]

Most countries today are therefore economically capable, in principle, to afford a pretty robust set of those essential social policies that human beings require to lead minimally decent lives (basic sanitation, essential immunisation, clean water, sufficient food, basic primary education, basic shelter, etc.). There will always be disagreement, of course, about the exact levels of provision a country could guarantee access to (e.g., how many litres per day of clean water, what quality of primary education, accommodation, etc.). But this is not the main challenge against the minimum core approach.[49] We can all roughly agree on what an essential

[45] This data is available at: https://data.worldbank.org/indicator/ny.gdp.mktp.cd?end=2015&start=1990, accessed 23 June 2019. World population in 1990 was 5.288 billion and is now 7.53 billion, that is, a 42 per cent increase. See https://data.worldbank.org/indicator/SP.POP.TOTL?view=chart, accessed 23 June 2019.

[46] Also in current dollars, available at: https://data.worldbank.org/indicator/NY.GDP.PCAP.CD, accessed 23 June 2019.

[47] Ibid.

[48] See A. Sumner, *Global Poverty* (Oxford: Oxford University Press, 2016), at 1–3.

[49] For a definition of a minimum core in housing that no one would disagree with, see the decision of judge Davis on section 28(1)(c) of the South African Constitution, holding that it did impose an obligation on the state where parents were unable to provide a child with basic shelter, defined as, at a bare minimum, 'tents, portable latrines and a regular

basket of health, housing, education, food and water is required for a minimally decent life in the contexts of particular societies.[50] But the distribution of resources in most countries is such that a lot of people are still unable to enjoy these minimum social goods. Inequality, not insufficiency, is the main explanation for why so many people are still below the minimum core threshold.[51]

The right to health in Brazil discussed in this book provides a good illustration. Few people would reject that primary care for very young children and pregnant women should be part of the minimum core of the right to health anywhere, including in Brazil. If asked in a poll if such care should be one of the top priorities of the health system, I doubt that many people would say no. We have seen in Chapter 2 that great strides have been made in reducing child, infant and (less radically) maternal mortality in the past thirty years in Brazil, in no small part because the Brazilian state (i.e., the successive governments in power since the 1988 Constitution) has taken reasonably seriously the right to health included in Article 196 and have seen as part of its duties flowing from that right to implement policies, actions and services aimed at the reduction of infant, child and maternal mortality. It is also clear, however, that Brazil could and should do even better than it does in these areas given its level of economic development as an upper middle-income country. Costa Rica, a Latin American country with a similar GDP per capita to Brazil's,

supply of water (albeit transported)', 2000 (11) BCLR 1169 (CC) at paras. 25–26 (S. Afr.). As cited in Dixon, 'Creating Dialogue about Socioeconomic Rights', at 400.

50 The famous linen shirt passage in Adam Smith's *Wealth of Nation* provides a good illustration of the intuitive nature of the minimum core: 'By necessaries I understand, not only the commodities which are indispensably necessary for the support of life, but whatever the custom of the country renders it indecent for creditable people, even of the lowest order, to be without. A linen shirt, for example, is, strictly speaking, not a necessary of life .... But in the present times, through the greater part of Europe, a creditable day-labourer would be ashamed to appear in public without a linen shirt .... Custom, in the same manner, has rendered leather shoes a necessary of life in England. The poorest creditable person of either sex would be ashamed to appear in public without them .... Under necessaries, therefore, I comprehend, not only those things which nature, but those things which the established rules of decency have rendered necessary to the lowest rank of people.' A. Smith, *An Enquiry into the Nature and Causes of the Wealth of Nations* (1776), book 5, chapter 2.

51 A longer version of this argument can be found in O. L. M. Ferraz, 'Inequality, Not Insufficiency: Making Social Rights Real in a World of Plenty', (2014) 12(1) *The Equal Rights Review*, 77–94.

invests much more in public health and has much lower rates of infant, child and maternal mortality than Brazil.[52]

Once we understand that resource insufficiency is not any longer an unsurmountable obstacle in most countries of the world for the enjoyment of a minimum core by everyone, we must approach the challenges to the definition of the minimum core in a different way. Our premises change dramatically and so must our conclusions. When it is simply unfeasible, due to absolute poverty, to guarantee a minimum core of each social right to everyone in a certain country, it is virtually impossible to determine what and whose minimum core should receive priority. Should we invest more on childcare, maternal care or care for the elderly? Should we eliminate first hunger, homelessness or illiteracy? We are in deep 'tragic choices' realm.[53]

Under the much more favourable circumstances of relative resource abundance as the one in which most countries in the world currently find themselves, it is perfectly plausible to argue that the duties to respect, protect and fulfil the minimum core of rights x, y and z are being violated by a state that fails to guarantee such minimum levels to the whole of its population. To use the Brazilian example again, why not conclude that Brazil is in breach of its duty to guarantee the minimum core of the right to health to all infants, children and pregnant mothers when, despite being an upper middle-income country, its levels of infant, child and maternal mortality are so high by international standards?

But this empirical clarification of the (in principle) affordability of the minimum core does not in itself establish its justiciability. It is one thing to show that (i) what the minimum core requires is reasonably clear and (ii) that there are enough resources in most countries in the world to guarantee it to the whole population and another to say that courts are therefore perfectly legitimised and capable to enforce the minimum core.

To take that further step, we would need to establish, also, that courts can effectively enforce the minimum core. Can they?[54]

[52] Here are, to recall, the three rates in each country: infant mortality (Brazil: 13.3/1,000; Costa Rica: 5.7/1,000); child mortality (Brazil: 15.1/1,000; Costa Rica: 8.8/1,000); maternal mortality (Brazil: 44/100,000; Costa Rica: 25/100,000). World Health Statistics, WHO, available at: http://apps.who.int/gho/data/node.home, accessed 23 June 2019. For the full discussion see Chapter 4.

[53] G. Calabresi, P. Bobbit, *Tragic Choices* (New York: W.W. Norton & Company, 1978), at 18.

[54] My view seems to differ from Dixon's in that, unlike her, I believe that there is widespread consensus in most societies, and certainly in Brazil, about what the minimum core requires in terms of investment priority. The problem of justiciability, for me, is not therefore lack of societal consensus but rather potential lack of judicial competence to

The Brazilian example with the right to health is again useful in our inquiry. If my argument so far in this book is correct, we know that Brazil disrespects the minimum core of the right to health. This brief summary of the picture (explained in greater detail in Chapter 4) is sufficient to clarify the main causes of Brazil's failure to guarantee the minimum core: *insufficient and inequitably allocated resources for essential health actions and services.*[55] The crucial question is this. Can the minimum core be effectively used by Brazilian courts to address these causes?

9.3.4 Brazilian Courts and the Minimum Core

Whether courts should employ the stronger form of adjudication that the minimum core approach suggests hinges on their actual capacity to improve things and not on some theoretical idea of judges as 'guardians' of rights totally independent from what actually happens on the ground when they exercise that purported guardianship. Whether and how courts should enforce social rights (or interfere with any other matter) is much better seen as a dynamic and *empirical* question of comparative institutional performance (sometimes referred to as the 'institutional approach').[56] It depends, ultimately, on whether and how courts can do a good job or not vis-à-vis the institutional alternatives. As American political scientist Robert Dahl aptly notes when discussing judicial enforcement of rights in general:

> It is misleading to suggest that there is one universally best solution to the problem of how best to protect fundamental rights and interests in a polyarchy. Although American lawyers typically assume that the solution must include a supreme court with the authority to strike down national legislation that violates fundamental rights and interests, such a system of quasi guardianship is neither necessary nor, on American experience, sufficient. In the absence of a universally best solution, specific

enforce the minimum core. See Dixon, 'Creating Dialogue about Socioeconomic Rights', at 417

55 There are of course also problems of inefficiency and corruption, but these seem less significant in comparison with the lack of investment in public health according to studies discussed in Chapter 4.

56 See King, *Judging Social Rights*, in particular, chapter 5, for a discussion of 'institutional approaches'. See also his longer piece, J. A. King, 'Institutional Approaches to Judicial Restraint', (2008) 28 *Oxford Journal of Legal Studies*, 409–441.

> solutions need to be adapted to the historical conditions and experiences, political culture, and concrete political institutions of a particular country.[57]

Under such an institutional approach, if it is clear that the courts of a particular country make things worse when they adopt what I called a more interfering form of right to health adjudication, the appropriate conclusion has to be that they should refrain from doing it. To assess if the minimum core approach can be an appropriate form of adjudication of the right to health in Brazil, we need to look at the institutional capacity and performance of Brazilian courts.

The extended empirical analysis carried out in Part II of this book has done precisely that. As we saw, health litigation has not (with a few exceptions) focused on any of the main well-known minimum core deficiencies of the system discussed at length in Chapter 4 and summarised in Section 9.3.3. Whereas cases challenging the insufficiency and inequity of public health actions and primary care services in the poorest parts of Brazil are virtually non-existent, hundreds of thousands of cases come to the courts of the most developed cities every year (and mostly succeed) demanding more sophisticated and expensive secondary and tertiary care such as hospital treatments and medicines. As we also saw, this is hardly surprising given the significant inequalities in access to justice that prevail in Brazil (Chapter 6). Moreover, a large proportion of that litigation is made up of claims for new and expensive medicines that the public system has decided not to fund within its limited resources for perfectly valid reasons, such as lack of evidence of safety, effectiveness and/or cost-effectiveness. As shown in Chapter 8, a few of these drugs feature in thousands of claims and are responsible for a large part of the increasing costs of judicialisation which, according to estimates, could have reached about 3 per cent of the total health budget of the country and as much as 8 per cent of the budget of some states. The opportunity costs of such budgetary impact would be serious in any well-resourced health system. In a severely underfunded one like the Brazilian SUS, they are extremely concerning.

The type of health litigation currently prevalent in Brazil (the Brazilian Model) is clearly not capable, thus, to contribute to the improvement of the minimum core of the right to health of the Brazilian population.

[57] Dahl, *Democracy and Its Critics*, at 192. See also, for a similar view, W. Sadurski, 'Judicial Review and the Protection of Constitutional Rights', (2002) 22(2) *Oxford Journal of Legal Studies*, 275–299.

On the contrary, it exacerbates the system's equity problems by forcing the state at all administrative levels (federal, state and municipal) to spend an increasingly larger part of its limited resources on health benefits (medicines and hospital treatment) and for individuals (those with access to justice) who are comparatively much better off than the large numbers who still lack some essential health actions and services. It does the very opposite to what the minimum core approach requires.[58]

If my description of the Brazilian model of health litigation is accurate, we should be very sceptical of the minimum core approach as an effective form of right to health adjudication in Brazil. If the cases that tend to arrive at the courts are rarely minimum core ones, not even in principle could the minimum core approach represent the strong protection for the right to health that it is supposed to.

One may wonder if this problem could be addressed through improvements to access to justice. If the poorest could reach the courts in larger numbers than they currently do, their highest priorities (public health and primary care) would feature more often in health litigation and the impact of courts decisions would be more positive, as the state would be forced to invest more resources in those areas.

That would certainly represent a significant improvement on the current situation. But it is unlikely that it will happen anytime in the near future and, even if it did, it is doubtful that it would effectively address the problem. Here is why. As we saw in Chapter 6, it would represent a genuine revolution for the poor to reach the courts in great numbers in Brazil. With all the advances in access to justice since 1988, litigation is still a very distant possibility for large sections of the population, in particular, the most disadvantaged. Approximately 50 million Brazilians, by and large those at the bottom quintile of income, live in municipalities without state legal services, so even if they had the knowledge and financial resources that are necessary to make effective use of those services (also in very short supply as we saw), they are simply not available in sufficient numbers and physical proximity.

[58] This is where the otherwise accurate analysis of some commentators goes wrong, as I argued in Chapter 8. Whereas they make a correct diagnosis of the problems of the public health system (underfunding, inequitable priority-setting etc), they go on to assume, wrongly, that health litigation is a response to these problems, see: L. Buíssa, et al., 'Impactos Orçamentários da Judicialização das Políticas Públicas de Saúde', in CONASS (eds.), *Dilemas do Fenômeno da Judicialização da Saúde* (Brasília: CONASS, 2018), 26–51.

But let us assume, for the sake of the argument, that access to justice gradually improves in Brazil to the point that large numbers of people at the bottom quintiles of income start to reach the courts claiming the minimum core of their right to health, for example, basic medicines, access to primary care, access to basic sanitation, etc. As I said, this would certainly represent a significant improvement on the current inegalitarian model of litigation, but would it be an effective tool to guarantee the minimum core? Not necessarily, and perhaps unlikely.

Two important challenges would remain, both related to the issue of resource limitations discussed at length earlier and in Chapter 4. As we saw, the Brazilian public health system is severely underfunded. With resources of 3.8 per cent of GDP (less than US$600 per capita), there is little room in the budget for a radical extension of the provision of minimum core actions and services to the tens of millions of Brazilians who still lack it. For any improvements on the minimum core to take place via litigation either (or both) of the following two unlikely scenarios would need to obtain. (i) Minimum core litigation would need to entail an increase in the health budget of the exact (or larger amount) required to cover its costs; (ii) minimum core litigation would need to entail a reallocation of the health budget from non-core to core components of the right to health (e.g., from expensive non-essential drugs to primary care).

For either of these two scenarios to have any chances of materialising, a radical change would need to occur in the misguided interpretation of the right to health currently prevailing in Brazilian courts. As we saw, the right to health is seen today as entailing a virtually absolute obligation on the state to provide everyone with any health action or service they demand, so long as it is backed by a doctors' prescription (I call it the 'right to everything').

Until that interpretation changes, Brazilian courts will continue to concede right to health–based requests almost automatically, as it currently does, and a large proportion of these requests will continue to be made up of costly claims requesting the newest treatments, equipment and medicines that are not part of the minimum core and, as such, the public health system have valid reasons not to provide (at least not until the minimum core is universalised). No increases or reallocations of the health budget, even if likely, would suffice.

But even if (again not a very likely scenario) Brazilian courts could change their current problematic interpretation of the right to health and adopt an appropriate egalitarian (minimum core) one (see Chapter 8,

Section 8.2), there is no guarantee that their rulings would entail the necessary increase or reallocation of resources required for the minimum core to be effectively universalised to the whole population. A more likely scenario would be one in which those in the imagined new cohort of poor litigants would displace others who are even more disadvantaged and less capable of accessing the courts.

All in all, thus, the prospects for the protection of the right to health in Brazil through a more interfering form of adjudication based on the minimum core approach are not that encouraging. The experience with twenty years of health litigation discussed in detail in Part II of the book indicates that courts are neither willing nor capable of prodding the Brazilian state to improve the minimum core of the right to health.

9.4 Conclusion: Politics and Litigation in the Real World

The impatience that many instinctively experience to find a strong role for courts in the adjudication of social rights derives in great part from the suspicion that legislative and executive bodies are not to be trusted to fulfil their duties properly. Without a judge over their shoulder, politicians and administrators are sure to neglect the social rights recognised in the constitution, especially if we are talking about so-called developing countries. The following passage from David Landau's insightful piece, 'The Reality of Social Rights' Enforcement', is representative of what many intuitively believe:

> Systematic failures in both legislative and bureaucratic politics in developing countries make dialogic approaches unlikely to work in those countries – the intended recipient of the dialogue is unlikely to respond effectively ... there is a desperate need to innovate with aggressive remedies if social rights are to live up to their transformative promise.[59]

As this book has shown, this often-portrayed scenario, in which recalcitrant politicians and administrators can only be chastened by competent and stern judges, bears little resemblance to the reality on the ground, at least in the field of health in Brazil. According to this popular view, which I call the 'rights revolution narrative' in this book, health litigation in Brazil is a transformative tool, that is, an instrument used by the most

[59] Landau, 'The Reality of Social Rights Enforcement', at 192. See also, making a similar point, Rosalind Dixon 'where a court order lacks any coercive dimension, it will have little direct impact on administrative inertia'. Dixon, 'Creating Dialogue about Socioeconomic Rights', at 412.

neglected and disadvantaged as a legitimate and effective response to state failure. A very different picture emerges from the available empirical data of twenty years of health litigation in Brazil.

As demonstrated in Chapter 3, the political branches in Brazil have not been doing a bad job of their obligations under the 1988 Constitution, especially not in the field of health. In the past three decades, a wide set of policies have been implemented aimed at reducing 'the risk of illness and other hazards' and at providing 'universal and equal access to actions and services for [health] promotion, protection and recovery' to the Brazilian population, precisely as mandated in Art. 196 of the Constitution. Most prominent among these policies was the creation of a universal public health system, the SUS, which, as we saw in Chapter 3, gave access to health actions and services to tens of millions of Brazilians who, before the Constitution, were virtually (and very often literally) abandoned by the state. Public expenditure on health rose significantly in absolute and in per capita terms. There is widespread consensus among experts that such policies have played a crucial role in the significant improvements in the population's health, as discussed at length in Chapter 3.

The picture of systematic constitutional neglect by the political branches – often assumed as a premise with no need of demonstration in justiciability debates – simply does not match the Brazilian reality of the right to health.

Is everything thus absolutely fine with the right to health in Brazil? Of course not. As I argued in great detail in Chapter 4, despite the non-trivial increase in public investment and the redirection of resources to programmes that benefit the most disadvantaged after the Constitution, the public system is still palpably underfunded, inequitable in important ways and inefficient in many areas. As we saw, Brazil invests annually less than 4 per cent of its GDP in the public health system, which is supposed to look after its whole vast population of circa 210 million people. For comparison, the WHO recommends 6 per cent as a minimum benchmark; Costa Rica, with a similar GDP per capita, spends 6.2 per cent; countries that take public health more seriously tend to invest around 8 per cent or more. In per capita terms, the same is true. At US$594, Brazil's investment is much lower than it could be given its level of economic development. Costa Rica invests US$977, Argentina US$922, Chile US$1,156, Uruguay US$1,220.

Moreover, the limited resources of the public system are unequally distributed in per capita terms across regions, states and municipalities, very often in a regressive manner. As we saw in Chapter 4, many states of the North and Northeast (where a large part of the Brazilian population with the worse health conditions live), have the lowest per capita public expenditure on health in the country.

We have also seen that the priority-setting decisions about where the limited resources of the public system are invested are often questionable in terms of health equity. To illustrate, despite Brazil's still relatively high levels of infant, child and maternal mortality and other health problems that require investment on public health and primary care actions and services, a significant part of the public health budget goes to secondary and tertiary care, including highly sophisticated medical equipment, expensive procedures and medicines. Pharmaceutical assistance provides a good example. Whereas the public system is still unable to provide everyone with all *essential medicines*, which explains the high levels of so-called out of pocket expenditure by the Brazilian population (which of course affects disproportionately the poorer), increasingly larger proportions of the budget are spent with non-essential drugs (in some part due to litigation, as we saw in Chapter 8).

To compound the problem, the richest 20 to 25 per cent in Brazil are incentivised to desert the public system through generous income tax exemptions. That puts Brazil in the apparently unique (and highly inegalitarian) situation of being the only country in the world to recognise a universal right to health in the Constitution yet have higher private expenditure (5 per cent of GDP) than public (3.8 per cent). Rather than a universal and egalitarian system of the sort of the British NHS on which it was inspired, the Brazilian system resembles more closely the American highly unequal one, of a more basic Medicaid and Medicare for the poorer and private insurance for the wealthier.

It is not surprising, thus, that health inequalities in Brazil are still so high despite the improvements of the past thirty years. As we saw in Chapter 4, life expectancy can vary as much as twelve years across districts in the same city, infant mortality is almost three times higher in some states of the North and Northeast as in others of the South and Southeast and so on with virtually all health indicators (see Chapter 4 for a full picture).

It seems clear, thus, that not all is fine with the right to health in Brazil. Brazilian society has a long way still to go to fulfil the constitutional promise of a genuinely comprehensive, universal and egalitarian public health system. But that picture is very different from the one often assumed in justiciability debates, in which the state is painted as a total failure.

As to the judiciary – often seen as the obvious and effective remedy to this perceived state negligence – this book has shown how disconnected from the reality on the ground that picture can be. The available empirical data of two decades of health litigation in Brazil found nothing resembling the rights revolution narrative. Very few claims, if any, address the most pressing health priorities of the poor such as the public health actions and primary care services that we saw are still lacking for many (see Chapter 4). The vast majority of claims can be traced to a few comparatively more developed states, cities and even districts within cities in Brazil. Most focus on curative treatment, a large part on newly developed, expensive medicines of dubious priority, a far cry from any plausible conception of a minimum core. The costs of these claims keep growing every year, having achieved concerning levels in some states and municipalities and are estimated to consume currently around 3 per cent of the aggregate health budget of the country.

Once this more accurate picture of the comparative performance of the political and judicial branches is put together, our reaction to the justiciability dilemma changes. The less interfering forms of adjudication discussed above start to appear much more attractive than the more interfering ones. If politics is not that bad, and litigation is not that great, it seems inapposite to transfer powers of substantive decision-making from the former to the latter. As Neil Komesar aptly notes, 'tasks that strain the abilities of an institution may wisely be assigned to it anyway if the alternatives are even worse'.[60]

***

My motivation to study the judicialisation of health in Brazil in depth derived in great part from a strong belief in social and economic rights. As a graduate of the 1993 class of the University of São Paulo Law School (the first class to study the whole five years of the law degree under the then new 1988 Constitution), I thought that its generous list of social rights would help Brazil to address what in my view was and continues to be its most important problem: socioeconomic inequality. As perhaps expected from a then young lawyer, I thought lawyers like me and progressive judges across Brazil would be leading actors in this transformative egalitarian enterprise. The right to health, given its centrality to

[60] N. K. Komesar, *Imperfect Alternatives: Choosing Institutions in Law, Economics, and Public Policy* (Chicago: University of Chicago Press, 1994), at 6.

well-being and close connection to all other social rights, seemed a promising candidate for the type of transformative litigation I had in mind.

Two decades of health litigation have proven my expectations wrong. As this book has argued with the support of a wealth of empirical data, the right to health has indeed contributed to significant improvements in the well-being of the Brazilian population. Yet, unlike I expected back then (and many still seem to believe), the main driver of such improvements has not been litigation and its leading actors have not been lawyers and judges. Quite the opposite, most of the progress has been achieved through the implementation of policies by legislative and executive bodies, partly spontaneously (out of a sense of constitutional and moral duty), partly pressurised by civil society. Health litigation, with few exceptions, has mostly disrupted these efforts, forcing the public health system to provide health benefits of dubious justification and high opportunity costs to a minority of individuals who manage to reach the courts.

There seems to be no reason to believe that this scenario will or can change in the foreseeable future. Those of us who are interested in the further improvement of the right to health, in Brazil and elsewhere where similar conditions obtain, are well advised to look away from courts and focus our limited resources on the political sphere. The politics and judicialisation of health in Brazil provide a sobering but also inspiring illustration of how health as a human right works and doesn't.

BIBLIOGRAPHY

Albert, C. E., 'Análise: Sobre a Judicialização da Saúde nos Municípios', (2016) 101 *Revista Técnica CNM*, 151–175.

Albiston, C. R., Sandefur, R. L., 'Expanding the Empirical Study of Access to Justice', (2013) 101 *Wisconsin Law Review*, 101–120.

Alexy, R., *Teoria dos Direitos Fundamentais* (São Paulo: Malheiros Editores, 2008).

Alfradique, M. E., Bonolo, F., Dourado, I. et al., 'Ambulatory Care Sensitive Hospitalizations: Elaboration of Brazilian List As a Tool for Measuring Health System Performance (Project ICSAP – Brazil)', (2009) 25(6) *Cad Saúde Pública*, 1337–1349.

Almeida, P. R., 'O Brasil e o FMI desde Bretton Woods: 70 Anos de História', (2004) 10(2) *Revista Direito GV*, 469–496.

Alston, P., 'Phantom Rights: The Systemic Marginalization of Economic and Social Rights', Open Global Rights, 6 August 2016, www.openglobalrights.org/phantom-rights-systemic-marginalization-of-economic-and-social-rights/.

Andrade, E., Machado, C. D., Faleiros, D. R. et al., 'A judicialização da saúde e a política nacional de assistência farmacêutica no Brasil: Gestão da clínica e medicalização da justiça', (2008) 18(4) *Revista Médica de Minas Gerais*, 46–50.

Angell, M., *The Truth about the Drug Companies: How They Deceive Us and What to Do about It* (New York: Random House, 2005).

Anjos, R. S., 'Judicialização e eqüidade no tratamento da hepatite C: Estudo de caso sobre o tratamento com interferona alfa em um serviço de referência do SUS em Porto Alegre, RS', MPhil dissertation, Universidade Federal do Rio Grande do Sul (2009).

Aquino, L., 'O Território como Referência para (Re)pensar o Judiciário: O caso da Justiça da Infância e da Juventude', (2012) 2 *Bolteim de Análise Potítico-Institucional*, 61–67.

Arretche, M., 'Democracia e redução da desigualdade econômica no Brasil: A inclusão dos outsiders', (2018) 33(96) *Revista Brasileira de Ciências Sociais*, dx.doi.org/10.17666/339613/2018.

Backman, G., Hunt, P., Khosla, R. et al., 'Health Systems and the Right to Health: An Assessment of 194 Countries', (2008) 372 *Lancet*, 2047–2085.

Baldoni, A. O., 'Estudos de utilização de medicamentos em idosos atendidos pelo Sistema Único de Saúde', MPhil dissertation, Faculdade de Ciências Farmacêuticas de Ribeirão Preto, Universidade de São Paulo (2010).

Barcellos, A. P., 'Sanitation Rights, Public Law Litigation, and Inequality: A Case Study from Brazil', (2014) 16(2) *Health and Human Rights*, 35–46.

Barreto, M. L., Genser, B., Strina, A. et al., 'Effect of City-Wide Sanitation Programme on Reduction in Rate of Childhood Diarrhoea in Northeast Brazil: Assessment by Two Cohort Studies', (2007) 370(9599) *Lancet*, 1622–1628.

Barreto, M. L., Rasella, D., Machado, D. B. et al., 'Monitoring and Evaluating Progress towards Universal Health Coverage in Brazil', (2014) 11(9) *PLoS Medicine*, doi.org/10.1371/journal.pmed.1001692.

Barros, B. R., Henriques, R., Mendonça, R., 'Desigualdade e Pobreza no Brasil: Retrato de uma realidade inaceitável', (2000) 15(42) *Revista Brasileira de Ciências Sociais*, 123–142.

Barros, M. B., Francisco, P. M., Zanchetta, L. M., César, C. L., 'Trends in Social and Demographic Inequalities in the Prevalence of Chronic Diseases in Brazil. PNAD: 2003–2008', (2011) 16(9) *Cien Saúde Colet*, 3755–3768.

Barroso, L. R., 'Da falta de efetividade à judicialização excessiva: Direito à saúde, fornecimento gratuito de medicamentos e parâmetros para a atuação judicial', (2009) 60(188) *Revista Jurisprudência Mineira*, 29–60.

Bastos, M. L., Menzies, D., Hone, T. et al., 'The Impact of the Brazilian Family Health on Selected Primary Care Sensitive Conditions: A Systematic Review', (2017) 12 *PLoS One*, doi.org/10.1371/journal.pone.0182336.

Baxi, U., 'The Avatars of Indian Judicial Activism', in Verma, S. K. and Kusum, S. K. (eds.), *Fifty Years of the Supreme Court of India: Its Grasp and Reach* (New Delhi: Oxford University Press, 2000), 156–209.

Bertolozzi, M. R., Greco, R. M., 'Health Politics in Brasil: Historical Review and Perspectives', (1996) 30(3) *Rev. Esc. Enf. USP*, 380–398.

Bhutta, Z. A., Chopra, M., Axelson, H. et al., 'Countdown to 2015 Decade Report (2000–10): Taking Stock of Maternal, Newborn, and Child Survival', (2010) 376 *Lancet*, 2032–2044.

Biehl, J., Amon, J., Socal, M., 'Between the Court and the Clinic: Lawsuits for Medicines and the Right to Health in Brazil', (2012) 14(1) *Health and Human Rights*, 36–52.

'The Challenging Nature of Gathering Evidence and Analyzing the Judicialization of Health in Brazil', (2016) 32(6) *Cadernos de Saúde Pública*, doi.org/10.1590/0102-311x0086315.

'The Judicialization of Health and the Quest for State Accountability: Evidence from 1,262 Lawsuits for Access to Medicines in Southern Brazil', (2016) 18(1), *Health and Human Rights*, 209–220.

'On the Heterogeneity and Politics of the Judicialization of Health in Brazil', (2016) 18(2) *Health and Human Rights*, 269–271.

Bilchitz, D., 'Giving Socio-Economic Rights Teeth: The Minimum Core and Its Importance', (2002) 119 *South African Law Journal*, 484–501.

Poverty and Fundamental Rights: The Justification and Enforcement of Socio-Economic Rights (Oxford: Oxford University Press, 2007).

Bodstein, R., Souza, R. G., 'Relação Público e Privado no Setor Saúde: Tendências e perspectivas na década de 90', in Goldenberg, P., Marsiglia, R. M. G. and Gomes, M. H. A. (eds.), *O Clássico e o Novo: Tendências, objetos e abordagens em ciências sociais e saúde* (Rio de Janeiro: Editora Fiocruz, 2003).

Boing, A. C., Bloemer, N. S., Roesler, C. et al., 'The Judicialization of Access to Medicines in Santa Catarina State: A Challenge for the Management of the Health System', (2013) 14(1) *Revista de Direito Sanitário*, 82–97.

Borges, D. C. L., Ugá, M. A. D., 'Conflicts and Impasses in the Judicialization of the Supply of Medicines: Circuit Court Rulings on Claims Brought against the State of Rio de Janeiro, Brazil, in 2005', (2010) 26(1) *Cadernos de Saúde Pública*, 59–69.

Boxtel, C. J., Santoso, B., Edwards, I. R. (eds.), *Drug Benefits and Risks: International Textbook of Clinical Pharmacology*, rev. 2nd ed. (Amsterdam: IOS Press and Uppsala Monitoring Centre, 2001).

Bresser Pereira, L. C., 'Os limites da "abertura" e a sociedade civil', (1983) 23(4) *Revista de Administração de Empresas*, 5–14.

Brinks, D., Gauri, V., 'The Law's Majestic Equality? The Distributive Impact of Litigating Social and Economic Rights', Policy Research Working Paper 5999, World Bank, Washington, DC (2012).

Brundtland, G. H., 'Global Partnerships for Health', (1999) 13 *WHO Drug Information*, 61–64.

Buíssa, L., Bevilacqua, L., Moreira, F. H. B. B., 'Impactos Orçamentários da Judicialização das Políticas Públicas de Saúde', in *CONASS Dilemas do Fenômeno da Judicialização da Saúde* (Brasília: CONASS, 2018), 26–51.

Buss, P. M., 'A IX Conferência Nacional de Saúde', (1991) 7(3) *Cadernos de Saúde Pública*, 297–300.

Buss, P. M., Pellegrini Filho, A., 'Iniqüidades em saúde no Brasil, nossa mais grave doença: Comentários sobre o documento de referência e os trabalhos da Comissão Nacional sobre Determinantes Sociais da Saúde', (2006) 22(9) *Cad. Saúde Pública*, 2005–2008.

Calabresi, G., Bobbit, P., *Tragic Choices* (New York: W. W. Norton & Company, 1978).

Campbell, T., Ewing, K. D., Tomkins, A. (eds.), *The Legal Protection of Human Rights: Sceptical Essays* (Oxford: Oxford University Press, 2011).

Campos Neto, O. H., Acurio, F. A., Machado, M. A. V. et al., 'Doctors, Lawyers and Pharmaceutical Industry on Health Lawsuits in Minas Gerais', (2012) 46 *Revista de Saúde Pública*, 784–790.

Cardia, N., (ed.), *Pesquisa nacional, por amostragem domiciliar, sobre atitudes, normas culturais e valores em relação à violação de direitos humanos e violência: Um estudo em 11 capitais de estado* (São Paulo: Núcleo de Estudos da Violência da Universidade de São Paulo, 2012).

Carmo, G. M., Yen, C., Cortes, J. et al., 'Decline in Diarrhea Mortality and Admissions after Routine Childhood Rotavirus Immunization in Brazil: A Time-Series Analysis', (2011) 8(4) *PLoS Medicine*, doi:10.1371/journal.pmed.1001024.

Carvalho, G., 'Saúde: O tudo para todos que sonhamos e o tudo que nos impingem os que lucram com ela', (2005) 69(29) *Rev Cent Bras Estud Saúde*, 99–104.

'Financiamento da saúde pública no Brasil no pós-constitucional de 88', (2008) 2(1) *Tempus – Actas de Saúde Coletiva*, 39–51.

Carvalho, J. M., *Cidadania no Brasil: O Longo Caminho*, 7th ed. (Rio de Janeiro: Civilização Brasileira, 2005).

Pontos e bordados: Escritos de história e política (Belo Horizonte: Editora da UFMG, 2005).

Carvalho, R. A., Santos, V. S., Melo, C. M. et al., 'Inequalities in Health: Living Conditions and Infant Mortality in Northeastern Brazil', (2015) 49(5) *Rev Saúde Pública*, doi:10.1590/s0034-8910.2015049004794.

Charlton, V., Littlejohns, P., Kieslich, K. et al., 'Cost Effective but Unaffordable: An Emerging Challenge For Health Systems', (2017) 365 *BMJ*, doi:10.1136/bmj.j1402.

Chieffi, A. L., 'Análise das demandas judiciais de medicamentos junto a Secretaria de Estado da Saúde de São Paulo à luz da política de assistência farmacêutica', PhD thesis, Universidade de São Paulo, Faculdade de Medicina (2017).

Chieffi, A. L., Barata, R. B., 'Judicialização da política pública de assistência farmacêutica e eqüidade', (2009) 25(8) *Cadernos de Saúde Pública*, 1839–1849.

'Ações judiciais: Estratégia da indústria farmacêutica para introdução de novos medicamentos', (2010) 44(3) *Revista de Saúde Pública*, 421–429.

Chor, D., Ribeiro, A. L. P., Carvalho, M. S. et al., 'Prevalence, Awareness, Treatment and Influence of Socioeconomic Variables on Control of High Blood Pressure: Results of the ELSA-Brasil Study', (2015) 10(6) *PLoS One*, doi:10.1371/journal.pone.0127382.

Cobham, A., Sumner, A., 'Putting the Gini Back in the Bottle? "The Palma" As a Policy-Relevant Measure of Inequality', King's International Development Institute, King's College London (2013).

Conselho Nacional de Justiça, *Panorama do Acesso à Justiça no Brasil* (Brasilia: Conselho Nacional de Justiça, 2011).

Justiça Pesquisa: Judicialização da saúde no Brasil – dados e experiências (Brasília: CNJ, 2015).

Justiça em Números 2018 (Brasília: CNJ, 2018).

Judicialização da Saúde no Brasil: Perfil das Demandas, Causas e Propostas de Solução (São Paulo: Instituto de Ensino e Pesquisa – Insper, 2019).

Conselho Nacional de Secretários de Saúde, *Assistência Farmacêutica: Medicamentos de dispensação em caráter excepcional*, 1st ed. (Brasília: CONASS, 2004).

Nota técnica 19, de 15 de agosto de 2005 (Brasília: CONASS, 2005).

Conselho Nacional do Ministério Público, *Ministério Público, Um Retrato*, vol. 7 (Brasília: Conselho Nacional do Ministério Público, 2018).

Cordeiro, H., 'O Instituto de Medicina Social e a Luta pela Reforma Sanitária: Contribuição à História do SUS', (2004) 14(2) *Physis: Revista de Saúde Coletiva*, 343–362.

Costa, N. R., 'Inovação Política, Distributivismo e Crise: A Política de Saúde nos Anos 80 e 90', (1996) 39(3) *Dados*, doi.org/10.1590/S0011-52581996000300007.

Coutinho, D. R., Vojvodic, A. M. (eds.) *Jurisprudência Constitucional: Como decide o STF?* (São Paulo: Malheiros, 2009).

Coulter, A., Ham, C., *The Global Challenge of Healthcare Rationing* (Buckingham: Open University Press, 2000).

Cranston, M., 'Are There Any Human Rights?', (1983) 112(4) *Daedalus*, 1–17.

Dahl, R., *Democracy and Its Critics* (New Haven: Yale University Press, 1989).

Dain, S., 'Os vários mundos do financiamento da Saúde no Brasil: Uma tentativa de integração', (2007) 12 Suppl. *Ciência & Saúde Coletiva*, 1851–1864.

Daly, T., *The Alchemists: Questioning Our Faith in Courts As Democracy-Builders* (Cambridge: Cambridge University Press, 2017).

Daniels, N., *Just Health: Meeting Health Needs Fairly*, 1st ed. (New York: Cambridge University Press, 2008).

Daniels, N., Charvel, S., Gelpi, A. H. et al., 'Role of the Courts in the Progressive Realization of the Right to Health: Between the Threat and the Promise of Judicialization in Mexico', (2015) 1(3) *Health Systems & Reform*, 229–234.

Diniz, D., Medeiros, M., Schwartz, I. V. D., 'Consequências da judicialização das políticas de saúde: Custos de medicamentos para as mucopolissacaridoses', (2012) 28(3) *Cadernos de Saúde Pública*, 479–489.

Diniz, D., Machado, T. R. C., Penalva, J., 'A judicialização da saúde no Distrito Federal', (2014) 19(2) *Ciênc. Saúde Coletiva*, 591–598.

Dixon, R., 'Creating Dialogue about Socioeconomic Rights: Strong-Form versus Weak-Form Judicial Review Revisited', (2007) 5(3) *International Journal of Constitutional Law*, 391–418.

Dourado, I., Oliveira, V. B., Aquino, R. et al. 'Trends in Primary Health Care-Sensitive Donditions in Brazil: The Role of the Family Health Program', (2011) 49(6) *Med Care*, 577–584.

Drumond, M., Barros, M., 'Desigualdades socioespaciais na mortalidade do adulto no Município de São Paulo', (1999) 2(1–2) *Revista Brasileira de Epidemiologia*, 34–49.

Epp, C. R., *After the Rights Revolution: Lawyers, Activists and Supreme Court in Comparative Perspective* (Chicago: University of Chicago Press, 1998).

Escorel, S., *Reviravolta na saúde: Origem e articulação do movimento sanitário* (Rio de Janeiro: Editora FIOCRUZ, 1999).

Fagundes, M. J. D., Soares, M. G. A., Diniz, N. M. et al., 'Análise bioética da propaganda e publicidade de medicamentos,' (2007) 12 *Revista Ciência & Saúde Coletiva*, 221–229.

Falleiros, I., Lima, J. C. F., Matta, G. C. et al., 'Saúde Como Direito de Todos e Dever do Estado', in Ponte, C. F and Fallerios, I. (eds.), *A Constituinte e o Sistema Único de Saúde* (Rio de Janeiro: Fiocruz, 2014), 239–278.

Faria, R., Santana, P., 'Variações espaciais e desigualdades regionais no indicador de mortalidade infantil do estado de Minas Gerais, Brasil', (2016) 25(3) *Saúde Soc.*, 736–749.

Feeley, M. M., 'The Concept of Laws in Social Science: A Critique and Notes on an Expanded View', (1976) 10 *Law & Society Review*, 501.

Fernandes, R. C., Campolina, B., Silveira, F. G., 'The Distributive Impact of Income Taxes in Brazil', Working paper number 171, International Policy Centre for Inclusive Growth (IPC-IG) (2018).

Ferraz, L. S., 'Challenges and Limitations for Legal Empirical Research in Brazil: Exploring a Study on Itinerant Justice', (2017) 4(1) *Revista de Estudos Empíricos em Direito*, 37–56.

Ferraz, O. L. M., 'Poverty and Human Rights', (2008) 28(3) *Oxford Journal of Legal Studies*, 585–603.

'The Right to Health in the Courts of Brazil: Worsening Health Inequities?', (2009) 11(2) *Health and Human Rights: An International Journal*, 33.

'Health Inequalities, Rights and Courts: The Social Impact of the "Judicialization of Health" in Brazil', in Yamin, A. and Gloppen, S. (eds.), *Litigating the Right to Health: Can Courts Bring More Justice to Health Systems?* (Cambridge, MA: Harvard University Press, 2011).

'Between Abdication and Usurpation: Social Rights in the Courts of Brazil, India and South Africa', in Vilhena, O., Baxi, U. and Viljoen, F. (eds.), *Transformative Constitutionalism: Comparing the Apex Courts of Brazil, India and South Africa* (Pretoria: Pretoria University Law Press, 2013).

'Inequality, Not Insufficiency: Making Social Rights Real in a World of Plenty', (2014) 12(1) *The Equal Rights Review*, 77–94.

'Between Activism and Deference: Social Rights Adjudication in the Brazilian Supreme Federal Tribunal', in Garcia, H. A., Klare, K. and Williams, L. A. (eds.), *Social and Economic Rights in Theory and Practice: Critical Inquiries* (London: Routlegde, 2015).

'Where's the Evidence? Moving from Ideology to Data in Economic and Social Rights', OpenGlobalRights, 27 January 2015, www.openglobalrights.org/wheres-evidence-moving-from-ideology-to-data-in-economic/.

'Moving the Debate Forward in Right to Health Litigation', (2016) 18(2) *Health and Human Rights*, 265–268.

'Two Conceptions of Social and Economic Rights: Basic Needs versus Equality', in Campbell, T. and Bourne, K. (eds.), *Political and Legal Approaches to Human Rights* (Oxford: Routledge, 2017).

'Right to Health Litigation in Brazil: Are Collective Suits Harder to Enforce?', in Langford, M. and Rodriguez-Garavito, C. (eds.), *Making It Stick: Compliance with Social Rights Judgments in Comparative Perspective* (Cambridge: Cambridge University Press, 2018).

'Still the Country of the Future', (2018) 12(3) *Brazilian Political Science Review*, doi: 10.1590/1981-3821201800030009.

'What Course without Evils?: Rare Diseases, Children's Right to Health and the Sustainable Development Goals', in Fenton-Glynn, C. (ed.), *Children's Rights and Sustainable Development: Interpreting the UNCRC for Future Generations* (Cambridge: Cambridge University Press, 2019), 78–113.

Ferraz, O. L. M., Gloppen, S., Maestad, O. et al., 'Judging the Price of Life: Cost Considerations in Right to Health Litigation?', in Aasen, H. et al. (eds.), *Juridification and Social Citizenship* (Cheltenham: Edward Elgar, 2014).

Ferraz, O. L. M., Vieira, F. S., 'Direito à saúde, recursos escassos e equidade: Os riscos da interpretação judicial dominante', (2009) 52(1) *Dados*, 223–251.

Ferreira, M. G. M., 'Perfil das demandas judiciais para acesso a Medicamentos no Município de Itaperuna: Uma contribuição sobre novas perspectivas de acesso racional e igualitário', MPhil dissertation, Universidade Estácio de Sá (2007).

Figueiredo, T. A., 'Análise dos medicamentos fornecidos por mandado judicial na Comarca do Rio de Janeiro: A aplicação de evidências científicas no processo de tomada de decisão', MPhil dissertation, Escola Nacional de Saúde Pública (2010).

Figueiredo, T. A., Osorio-de-Castro, C. G., Pepe, V. L., 'Evidence-Based Process for Decision-Making in the Analysis of Legal Demands for Medicines in Brazil', (2013) 29(1) *Cadernos de Saúde Pública*, 159–166.

Fishlow, A., 'Brazil's Economic Miracle', (1973) 29(11)*The World Today*, 474–481.

Fleury, S., 'Brazilian Sanitary Reform: Dilemmas between the Instituing and the Institutionalized', (2009) 14(3) *Ciência & Saúde Coletiva*, 743–752.

'Revisitando a questão democrática na área da saúde: Quase 30 anos depois', (2009) 33 *Saúde em Debate*, 156–164.

Fonseca, J. E., Carneiro, M., Pena, J. L. et al., 'Reducing Occurrence of Giardia Duodenalis in Children Living in Semiarid Regions: Impact of a Large Scale Rainwater Harvesting Initiative', (2014) 8(6) *PLoS Neglected Tropical Diseases*, doi.org/10.1371/journal.pntd.0002943.

França, E. B., Passos, V. M. A., Malta, D. C. et al., 'Cause-Specific Mortality for 249 Causes in Brazil and States during 1990–2015: A Systematic Analysis for the Global Burden of Disease Study 2015', (2017) 15(1) *Population Health Metrics*, doi.10.1186/s12963-017-0156-y.

Fredman, S., *Human Rights Transformed, Positive Rights and Positive Duties* (Oxford: Oxford University Press, 2008).

Fundação Getúlio Vargas, *Índice de Confiança na Justiça – ICJ* (São Paulo: Fundação Getúlio Vargas, 2017).

Galanter, M., 'Why the Haves Come Out Ahead? Speculations on the Limits of Legal Change', (1974) 9(1) *Law & Society Review, Litigation and Dispute Processing: Part One*, 95–160.

Garcia, L. P., Ocké-Reis, C. O., Magalhães, L. C. G. et al., 'Gastos com planos de saúde das famílias brasileiras: Estudo descritivo com dados das Pesquisas de Orçamentos Familiares 2002–2003 e 2008–2009', (2015) 20(1) *Ciênc & Saúde Coletiva*, 1425–1434.

Gargarella, R., Roux, T., Domingo, P., *Courts and Social Transformation in New Democracies: An Institutional Voice for the Poor?*, 1st ed. (Oxford: Routledge, 2006).

Gauri, V., Brinks, D. M. (eds.), *Courting Social Justice: Judicial Enforcement of Social and Economic Rights in the Developing World* (Cambridge: Cambridge University Press, 2008).

Gauri, V., Brinks, D. M., 'Human Rights As Demands for Communicative Action', Policy Research Working Paper 5951 (2012).

Glendon, M. A., *Rights Talk: The Impoverishment of Political Discourse* (New York: The Free Press, 1993).

Gloppen, S., 'Courts and Social Transformation: An Analytical Framework', in Gargarella, R., Roux, R. and Domingo, P. (eds.), *Courts and Social Transformation in New Democracies: An Institutional Voice for the Poor?*, 1st ed. (Oxford: Routledge, 2006).

Gomes, F. F. C., Cherchiglia, M. L., Machado, C. D. et al., 'Access to Medium and High-Complexity Procedures in the Brazilian Unified National Health System: A Matter of Judicialization', (2014) 30(1) *Cadernos de Saúde Pública*, 31–43.

Gomes, V. S., Amador, T. A., 'Studies Published in Indexed Journals on Lawsuits for Medicines in Brazil: A Systematic Review', (2015) 31(3) *Caderno de Saúde Pública*, 1–12.

Gotzsche, P. C., *Medicamentos mortais e crime organizado: Como a indústria farmacêutica corrompeu a assistência médica*. Trans. A. P. Farjado (Porto Alegre: Bookman, 2016).

Gragnolati, M., Lindelow, M., Couttolenc, B., *Twenty Years of Health System Reform in Brazil: An Assessment of the Sistem Único de Saúde* (Washington, DC: World Bank, 2013).

Guran, M. (ed.), *O Processo Constituinte 1987–1988: Documentação fotográfica, A Nova Constituição* (Brasília: AGIL, 1988).

Hirschl, R., *Towards Juristocracy* (New Haven: Yale University Press, 2004).

'The Nordic Counternarrative: Democracy, Human Development, and Judicial Review', (2011) 9(2) *International Journal of Constitutional Law*, 449–469.

Hirschl, R., Rosevear, E., 'Constitutional Law Meets Comparative Politics: Socio-Economic Rights and Political Realities', in Campbell, T., Ewing, K. D. and Tomkins, A. (eds.), *The Legal Protection of Human Rights: Sceptical Essays* (Oxford: Oxford University Press, 2011).

Hoffmann, F., Bentes, F. R. N. M., 'Accountability for Social and Economic Rights in Brazil', in Gauri, V. and Brinks, D. M. (eds.), *Courting Social Justice: Judicial Enforcement of Social and Economic Rights in the Developing World* (New York: Cambridge University Press, 2008) 100–145.

Holland, A., *Forbearance As Redistribution: The Politics of Informal Welfare in Latin America* (Cambridge: Cambridge University Press, 2017).

Horowitz, D., *The Courts and Social Policy* (Washington, DC: Brookings Institution, 1977).

Hunt, P., *Reclaiming Social Rights: International and Comparative Perspectives* (Aldershot: Dartmouth, 1996).

Instituto Brasileiro de Geografia e Estatística - IBGE. *Um panorama da saúde no Brasil: Acesso e utilização dos serviços, condições de saúde e fatores de risco e proteção à saúde, 2008* (Rio de Janeiro: IBGE, 2010).

Instituto de Pesquisa Econômica Aplicada – IPEA, *Diagnóstico sobre os Juizados Especiais Cíveis* (Brasilia: IPEA, 2013).

Democratização do acesso à Justiça e efetivação de direitos: A Justiça Itinerante no Brasil (Brasília: IPEA, 2015).

Jowett, M., Brunal, M. P., Flores, G., Cylus, J., *Spending Targets for Health: No Magic Number* (Geneva: World Health Organization, 2016).

Kassirer, J. P., *On the Take: How Medicine's Complicity with Big Business Can Endanger Your Health* (New York: Oxford University Press, 2005).

Ke Xu, A. S., Kutzin, J., *Public Spending on Health: A Closer Look at Global Trends* (Geneva: WHO, 2018).

King, J., *Judging Social Rights* (Cambridge: Cambridge University Press, 2012).

Kinney, E. D., Clark, B. A., 'The Right to Health: Institutional Effects of Constitutional Provisions on Health Outcomes', (2004) 37(2) *Cornell International Law Journal*, 285–355.

Klein, R., Day, P., Redmayne, S., *Managing Scarcity* (Buckingham: Open University Press, 1996).

Komesar, N. K., *Imperfect Alternatives: Choosing Institutions in Law, Economics, and Public Policy* (Chicago: University of Chicago Press, 1994).

Kritzer, H. M., 'To Lawyer or Not to Lawyer: Is That the Question?', (2008) 5(4) *Journal of Empirical Legal Studies*, 875–906.

Landau, D., 'The Reality of Social Rights Enforcement', (2012) 53(1) *Harvard International Law Journal*, 189–247.

Lavinas, L., *The Takeover of Social Policy by Financialization: The Brazilian Paradox* (New York: Palgrave Macmillan, 2017).

Law, D. S., Versteeg, M., 'The Evolution and Ideology of Global Constitutionalism', (2011) 99 *California Law Review*, 1163.

Levy, D., de Almeida, L. M., Szklo, A., 'The Brazil SimSmoke Policy Simulation Model: The Effect of Strong Tobacco Control Policies on Smoking Prevalence and Smoking-Attributable Deaths in a Middle Income Nation', (2012) 9(11) *PLoS Medicine*, doi: 10.1371/journal.pmed.1001336.

Liebenberg, S., *Socio-Economic Rights: Adjudication under a Transformative Constitution* (Cape Town: Juta & Co, 2010).

Lima, A. L. G. S., Pinto, M. M. S., 'Fontes para a história dos 50 anos do Ministério da Saúde', (2003) 10(3) *História, Ciências, Saúde*, 1037–1051.

Lima, T. M., 'O direito à saúde revisitado: Entre os ideais da Constituição de 1988 e o drama jurídico atual', (2014) 51(202) *Revista de Informação Legislativa*, 181–201.

Lopes, L. C., Barberato-Filho, S., Costa, A. C., Osoriode-Castro, C. G. S., 'Rational Use of Anticancer Drugs and Patient Lawsuits in the State of São Paulo, Southeastern Brazil', (2010) 44(4) *Revista de Saúde Pública*, 620–628.

Lotufo, P. 'Coffee, Samba, Football and . . . Inequalities: Reflections on Mortality in São Paulo, Brazil', (2001) 119(3) *São Paulo Medical Journal*, 94–96.

Louvison, M. C., Lebrão, M. L., Duarte, Y. A. et al., 'Inequalities in Access to Health Care Services and Utilization for the Elderly in São Paulo, Brazil', (2008) 42(4) *Rev Saúde Pública*, 733–740.

Luiza, V. L., 'Acesso a medicamentos essenciais no Estado do Rio de Janeiro', PhD thesis, Escola Nacional de Saúde Pública (2003).

Machado, C. V., Salvador, F. G., O'Dwyer, G., 'Mobile Emergency Care Service: Analysis of Brazilian Policy', (2011) 45(3) *Rev Saúde Pública*, 519–528.

Machado, G. P., 'O Superior Tribunal de Justiça e os pedidos de custeio de tratamentos médicos no exterior', MPhil dissertation, Universidade Federal Fluminense (2013).

Machado, M. A. A., Acurcio, F. A., Brandão, C. M. R. et al., 'Judicialization of Access to Medicines in Minas Gerais State, Southeastern Brazil', (2011) 45(3) *Revista de Saúde Pública*, 590–598.

Macedo, E. I., Lopes, L. C., Barberato-Filho, S., 'A Technical Analysis of Medicines Request-Related Decision Making in Brazilian Courts', (2011) 45(4) *Revista de Saúde Pública*, 706–713.

Macinko, J., Guanais, F. C., de Fátima, M., de Souza, M., 'Evaluation of the Impact of the Family Health Program on Infant Mortality in Brazil, 1990–2002', (2006) 60(1) *Journal of Epidemiol Community Health*, 13–19.

Macinko, J., Harris, M. J., 'Brazil's Family Health Strategy – Delivering Community-Based Primary Care in a Universal Health System', (2015) 372/23 *New England Journal of Medicine*, 2177–2181.

Macinko, J., Szwarcwald, C., 'A Panorama of Health Inequities in Brazil', (2016) 15 *International Journal for Equity in Health*, www.biomedcentral.com/collections/HIB.

Maestad, O., Rakner, L., Ferraz, O. L. M., 'Assessing the Impact of Health Rights Litigation: A Comparative Study of Argentina, Colombia, Costa Rica, India and South Africa', in Yamin, A. and Gloppen, S. (eds.), *Litigating Health Rights: Can Courts Bring More Justice to Health?* (Cambridge, MA: Harvard University Press, 2011).

Malloy, J., *A Política de Previdência Social no Brasil* (Rio de Janeiro: Graal, 1985).

Mapelli, R., *Judicialização da Saúde – Regime Jurídico do SUS e Intervenção na Administração Pública* (São Paulo: Atheneu, 2017).

Marinho, F., Passos, V. M. A., Malta, D. C. et al., 'Burden of Disease in Brazil, 1990–2016: A Systematic Subnational Analysis for the Global Burden of Disease Study 2016', (2018) 392(10149) *The Lancet*, 760–775.

Marmot, M., 'Brazil: Rapid Progress and the Challenge of Inequality', (2016) 15(1) *International Journal for Equity in Health*, 177.

Marques, S. B., Dallari, S. G., 'Safeguarding of the Social Right to Pharmaceutical Assistance in the State of São Paulo', (2007) 41 *Revista de Saúde Pública*, 101–107.

Massuda, A., Hone, T., Leles, F. et al., 'The Brazilian Health System at Crossroads: Progress, Crisis and Resilience', (2018) 3(4) *BMJ Global Health*, doi:10.1136/bmjgh-2018-000829.

McCann, M., *Rights at Work: Pay Equity Reform and the Politics of Legal Mobilization* (Chicago: University of Chicago Press, 1994).

Medeiros, M., Souza, P. H. G. F., Castro, F. A., 'A estabilidade da desigualdade de renda no Brasil, 2006 a 2012: Estimativa com dados do imposto de renda e pesquisas domiciliares', (2015) 20(4) *Ciência Saúde Coletiva*, 971–986.

Mendes, E. V., '25 anos do Sistema Único de Saúde: Resultados e desafios', (2013) 27 *Estudos Avançados*, 78.

Menezes, T., Campolina, B., Silveira, F. G. et al. 'O gasto e a demanda das famílias em saúde: Uma análise a partir da POF de 2002–2003', in Silveira F. G., Servo, L. M. S. and Menezes, T. et al. (eds.), *Gasto e consumo das famílias brasileiras contemporâneas* (Brasília: IPEA, 2006), 313–344.

Menicucci, T. M. G., Machado, J. A., 'Judicialization of Health Policy in the Definition of Access to Public Goods: Individual Rights versus Collective Rights', (2011) 5 *Brazilian Political Science Review*, 33–68.

Merrill, A. R., 'Regulation of Drugs and Devices: An Evolution', (1994) 13(3) *Health Affairs*, 47–69.

Messeder, A. M., Osorio-de-Castro, C. G., Luiza, V. L., 'Mandados judiciais como ferramenta para garantia do acesso a medicamentos no setor público: A experiência do Estado do Rio de Janeiro', (2005) 21(2) *Cadernos de Saúde Pública*, 525–534.

Michelman, F. I., 'The Constitution, Social Rights, and Liberal Political Justification', (2003) 1(1) *International Journal of Constitutional Law*, 13–34.

Michiles, C., *Cidadão Constituinte: A saga das emendas populares* (Rio de Janeiro: Paz e Terra, 1989).

Ministério da Saúde, *Nota Técnica No. 45/2012 Duloxetina* (Brasília: Ministério da Saúde, 2012).

Ministério da Justiça, *Governo do Brasil, Atlas de Acesso à Justiça: Indicadores Nacionais de Acesso à Justiça* (Brasília: Ministério da Justiça, 2013).

IV Diagnóstico da Defensoria Pública no Brasil (Brasília: Ministério da Justiça, 2015).

Miquilin, I. O., Marín-León, L., Monteiro, M. I., Corrêa Filho, H. R., 'Inequalities in Health Services Access and Use among Formal, Informal, and Unemployed Workers, Based on Data from the Brazilian National Household Sample Survey, 2008', (2013) 29(7) *Cadernos de Saúde Pública*, 1392–1406.

Moore, J. C., Stinson, L. L., Welniak, E. J. Jr, 'Income Measure Error in Surveys: A Review', (2000) 16(4) *Journal of Official Statistics*, 331–361.

Mota, G. P., 'Judicialização do acesso a leitos de UTI no Distrito Federal: Dimensões clínica, ética e legal', MPhil dissertation, Univesrity of Brasilia (2017).

Moulin, S. R. A., Mendes, J. B. A., Pizetta, G. M., 'Judicialização do Acesso à Internação em UTI no SUS: Análise Concreta de Pacientes do Estado do Espírito Santo', in Gebran Neto, J. P. (ed.), *Direito da Saúde em Perspectiva. Judicialização, Gestão e Acesso*, vol. 2 (Vitória: Editora Abrages, 2017), 73–90.

Moyer, L. H., Fansler, N. E., Lee, M. A. et al., 'How Do People Answer Income Questions?', US Census Bureau (1997).

Moyn, S., *Not Enough: Human Rights in an Unequal World* (Cambridge, MA: Harvard University Press, 2018).

Neves, R. G., Flores, T. R., Duro, S. M. S. et al., 'Tendência temporal da cobertura da Estratégia Saúde da Família no Brasil, regiões e Unidades da Federação, 2006–2016', (2018) 27(3) *Epidemiologia e Serviços de Saúde*, doi.org/10.5123/s1679-49742018000300008.

Nisihara, R. M., Possebom, A. C., Borges, L. M. C. et al., 'Demanda judicial de medicamentos na Justiça Federal do Estado do Paraná', (2017) 15(1) *Einstein*, 85–91.

Norheim, O. F., Wilson, B. M., 'Health Rights Litigation and Access to Medicines: Priority Classification of Successful Cases from Costa Rica's Constitutional Chamber of the Supreme Court', (2014) 11(16) *Health and Human Rights*, 47–61.

Noronha, J. C. D., Levcovitz, E., 'AIS-SUDS-SUS: Os caminhos do direito à saúde', in Guimarães, R. and Tavares, R. (eds.), *Saúde e sociedade no Brasil – anos 80* (Rio de Janeiro: Relume do Mará, 1994), 73–111.

Nunes, B. P., Thumé, E., Tomasi, E. et al., 'Socioeconomic Inequalities in the Access to and Quality of Health Care Services', (2014) 48(6) *Rev Saúde Pública*, 968–976.

Nunes, C. F. O., Ramos Júnior, A. N., 'Judicialização do direito à saúde na região Nordeste, Brasil: Dimensões e desafios', (2016) 24(2) *Cadernos de Saúde Coletiva*, 192–199.

Ocké-Reis, C. O., Gama, F. N., *Radiografia do gasto tributário em saúde* (Brasília: IPEA, 2016).

OECD, *Government at a Glance 2017* (Paris: OECD Publishing, 2017), doi.org/10.1787/gov_glance-2017-en.

Oliveira, F. L., Cunha, L. G., 'Medindo o acesso à Justiça Cível no Brasil', (2016) 22(2) *Opinião Pública*, 318–349.

Oliveira, J. A., 'Reformas e reformismos: Para uma teoria política da reforma sanitária (ou, reflexões sobre a reforma sanitária de uma perspectiva popular)', in Costa, N. R., Minayo, C. S., Ramos, C. L. et al. (eds.), *Demandas populares, políticas públicas e saúde* (Petrópolis: Vozes, 1989).

Oliveira, M. S. C., 'Participação, Saúde e Direito na Assembléia Constituinte: Um Resgate do Debate' (no date), www.publicadireito.com.br/conpedi/manaus/arquivos/anais/XIVCongresso/093.pdf.

Ostry, D. J., Loungani, P., Furceri, D., 'Neoliberalism: Oversold?', (2016) 53(2) *Finance & Development*, 38–41.

Paim, J. S., *Reforma sanitária brasileira: Contribuição para a compreensão e crítica* (Salvador: Edufba; Rio de Janeiro: Editora Fiocruz, 2008).

'A Reforma Sanitária Brasileira e o Sistema Único de Saúde: Dialogando com hipóteses concorrentes', (2008) 18(4) *Physis Revista de Saúde Coletiva*, 625–644.

Paim, J. S., Travassos, C., Almeida, C. et al., 'The Brazilian Health System: History, Advances, and Challenges', (2011) 377(9779) *Lancet*, 1778–1797.

Paiva, C. H. A., Teixeira, L. A., 'Health Reform and the Creation of the Sistema Único de Saúde: Notes on Contexts and Authors', (2014) 21(1) *História, Ciências, Saúde – Manguinhos*, 15–36.

Palma, J. G., 'Homogeneous Middles vs. Heterogeneous Tails, and the End of the 'Inverted-U': The Share of the Rich Is What It's All About', Cambridge Working Papers in Economics (CWPE) 1111 (2011).

Paula, C. S., 'Uso Off Label de Medicamentos: Análise das Demandas Judiciais no CEMEPAR e Conduta dos Farmacêuticos no Paraná', MPhil dissertation, Universidade Federal do Paraná (2010).

Pepe, V. L. E., Ventura, M., Sant'ana, J. M. B. et al., 'Characterization of Lawsuits for the Supply of "Essential" Medicines in the State of Rio de Janeiro, Brazil', (2010) 26(3) *Cadernos de Saúde Pública*, 461–471.

Pereira, J. G., Pepe, V. L. E., 'Acesso a medicamentos por via judicial no Paraná: Aplicação de um modelo metodológico para análise e monitoramento das demandas judiciais', (2014) 15(2) *Revista de Direito Sanitário*, 31–45.

Pereira, J. R., Santos, R. I., Nascimento Junior, J. M. et al., 'Análise das demandas judiciais para o fornecimento de medicamentos pela Secretaria de Estado da Saúde de Santa Catarina nos anos de 2003 e 2004', (2010) 15(Suppl. 3) *Ciência & Saúde Coletiva*, 3551–3560.

Pessoa, N. T., 'Perfil das solicitações administrativas e judiciais de medicamentos impetradas contra a secretaria de saúde do estado do Ceará', MPhil dissertation, Universidade Federal do Ceará (2007).

Pierantoni, C. R., '20 anos do sistema de saúde brasileiro: O Sistema Único de Saúde', (2008) 18(4) *Physis: Revista de Saúde Coletiva*, 617–624.

Pierro, B., 'Demandas Crescentes', (2017) 252(18) *Pesquisa Fapesp*, 18–25.

Pilatti, A., *A Constituinte de 1987–1988: Progressistas, Conservadores, Ordem Econômica e Regras do Jogo* (Rio de Janeiro: Editora Lumen Juris, 2008).

Piola, S. F., França, J. R. M., Nunes, A., 'The Effects of Constitutional Amendment 29 on the Regional Allocation of Public Funds for the National Health Service in Brazil', (2016) 21(2) *Ciência & Saúde Coletiva*, 411–421.

Pizzarossa, L. B., Perehudoff, K., Forte, J. C., 'How the Uruguayan Judiciary Shapes Access to High-Priced Medicines: A Critique through the Right to Health Lens', (2018) 20(1) *Health and Human Rights*, 93–105.

Pondé, N., Azambuja, E., Ades, F., 'Phosphoethanolamine and the Danger of Unproven Drugs', (2016) 10(681) *Ecancermedicalscience*, doi:10.3332/ecancer.2016.681.

Provin, M. P., Leite, S. N., Amaral, R. G., 'Social Inequalities in Lawsuits for Drugs', (2013) 43(3) *Brazilian Journal of Pharmaceutical Sciences*, 465–474.

Rabe, H. D., 'Advocacia pro bono: Um estudo acerca de sua implementação no Brasil', LLB monograph, Pontifícia Universidade Católica do Rio de Janeiro (2016).

Ramseyer, J. M., Rasmusen, E. B., 'Comparative Litigation Rates', 681/11 Discussion Paper, John M. Olin Center for Law, Economics, and Business (2010).

Rasella, D., Aquino, R., Barreto, M. L., 'Reducing Childhood Mortality from Diarrhoea and Lower Respiratory Tract Infections in Brazil', (2010) 126(3) *Pediatrics*, doi:10.1542/peds.2009-3197.

'Impact of Income Inequality on Life Expectancy in a Highly Unequal Developing Country: The Case of Brazil', (2013) 67(8) *Journal of Epidemiology and Community Health*, 661–666.

Rasella, D., Harhay, M. O., Pamponet, M. L. et al., 'Impact of Primary Health Care on Mortality from Heart and Cerebrovascular Diseases in Brazil: A Nationwide Analysis of Longitudinal Data', (2014) 349 *BMJ*, doi.org/10.1136/bmj.g4014.

Rid, A., 'Justice and Procedure: How Does "Accountability for Reasonableness" Result in Fair Limit-Setting Decisions?', (2009) 35(1) *Journal of Medical Ethics*, 12.

Rodrigues, L. M., *Partidos, Ideologia e Composição Social:Um Estudo das Bancadas Partidárias na Câmara dos Deputados* (Rio de Janeiro: Centro Edelstein de Pesquisas Sociais, 2009).

Rodriguez-Garavito, C. and McAdams, S. L., 'A Human Rights Crisis? Unpacking the Debate on the Future of the Human Rights Field' (2016), https://papers.ssrn.com/sol3/papers.cfm?abstract_id=2919703.

Rodriguez Neto, E., *Saúde: Promessas e limites da constituição* (Rio de Janeiro: Fiocruz, 2003).

Romero, L. C., *Judicialização das políticas de assistência farmacêutica: O caso do Distrito Federal, Textos para Discussão 41.* (Brasília: Consultoria Legislativa do Senado Federal, 2008).

Ronsein, J. G., 'Análise do perfil das solicitações de medicamentos por demanda judicial no Estado de Santa Catarina no período de 2005 a 2008', MPhil dissertation, Universidade Federal de Santa Catarina (2010).

Rosenberg, G., *The Hollow Hope: Can Courts Bring About Social Change?* (Chicago: University of Chicago Press, 1991).

Sadek, M. T. A., 'Controle externo do Poder Judiciário', in Sadek, M. T. A. (ed.), *Reforma do Judiciário* (São Paulo: Fundação Konrad Adenauer, 2001).

'Acesso à Justiça: Um Direito e seus Obstáculos', (2014) 101 *Revista USP*, 55–66.

Sadurski, W., 'Judicial Review and the Protection of Constitutional Rights', (2002) 22(2) *Oxford Journal of Legal Studies*, 275–299.

Sampaio, P. A. 'Para Além da Ambiguidade: Uma Reflexão Histórica sobre a CF/1988', in Cardoso Junior, J. C. (ed.), *A Constituição brasileira de 1988 revisitada: Recuperação histórica e desafios atuais das políticas públicas nas áreas econômica e social* (Brasília: IPEA, 2009).

Sant'ana, J. M. B., 'Essencialidade e assistência farmacêutica: Um estudo exploratório das demandas judiciais individuais para acesso a medicamentos no Estado do Rio de Janeiro', MPhil dissertation, Escola Nacional de Saúde Pública, Fundação Oswaldo Cruz (2009).

Santos, B. S., 'The Law of the Oppressed: The Construction and Reproduction of Legality in Pasargada', (1977) 12(1) *Law and Society Review*, 5–126.

Santos, I. S., dos Santos, M. A. B., Borges, D. C. L., 'Mix público-privado no sistema de saúde brasileiro: Realidade e futuro do SUS', in *A Saúde no Brasil em 2030 – prospecção estratégica do sistema de saúde brasileiro: Estrutura do financiamento e do gasto setorial* (Rio de Janeiro: Fiocruz/IPEA/Ministério da Saúde/Secretaria de Assuntos Estratégicos da Presidência da República, 2013), vol. 4, 73–131.

Santosa, A., Stig, W., Fottrell, E. et al., 'The Development and Experience of Epidemiological Transition Theory over Four Decades: A Systematic Review', (2014) 15(7) *Global Health Action*, doi: 10.3402/gha.v7.23574.

Sartoni Junior, D., Leivas, P. G. C., Souza, M. V. et al., 'Judicialização do acesso ao tratamento de doenças genéticas raras: A doença de Fabry no Rio Grande do Sul', (2012) 17 *Ciências & Saúde Coletiva*, 2717–2728.

Scheffer, M., Salazar, A. L., Grou, K. B. (eds.), *O Remédio via Justiça: Um estudo sobre o acesso a novos medicamentos e exames em HIV/Aids no Brasil por meio de ações judiciais*, Série Legislação no. 3 (Brasília: Ministério da Saúde, 2005).

Scheingold, S., *The Politics of Rights: Lawyers, Public Policy and Political Change*, 2nd ed. (Ann Arbor: University of Michigan Press, 2004).

Secretaria de Políticas de Saúde, Departamento de Atenção Básica, 'Programa Saúde da Família', (2000) 34(3) *Rev. Saúde Pública*, 316–319.

Short, M. E., Goetzel, R. Z., Pei, X. et al., 'How Accurate Are Self-Reports? Analysis of Self-Reported Health Care Utilization and Absence When Compared with Administrative Data', (2009) 51(7) *Journal of Occupational and Environmental Medicine*, 786–796.

Sikkink, K., *Evidence for Hope, Making Human Rights Work in the Twenty-first Century* (Princeton: Princeton University Press, 2017).

Silva, A. R. H., Corte, E. D., 'Judicialização na Assistência Farmacêutica do Sistema Único de Saúde', (2011) 8(27) *Ciência em Movimento*, 19–25.

Silva, J. A., *Aplicabilidade das normas constitucionais* (São Paulo: Malheiros, 1999).

Poder Constituinte e Poder Popular: Estudos sobre a Constituição (São Paulo: Malheiros Editores, 2002).

Silva, P. L. B., Medici, A. C., 'Considerações sobre o Gasto em Saúde no Brasil: Dilemas até o Final do Século', (1988) 1(4) *Cadernos de Saúde Pública*, 88–105.

Silva, V. A., *The Constitution of Brazil: A Contextual Analysis* (Oxford: Hart Publishing, 2019).

Silva, V. A., Terrazas, F. V., 'Claiming the Right to Health in Brazilian Courts: The Exclusion of the Already Excluded', (2011) 36(4) *Law & Social Inquiry*, 825–853.

Smith, Adam., *An Enquiry into the Nature and Causes of the Wealth of Nations* (1776), http://files.libertyfund.org/files/220/0141-02_Bk.pdf.

Smith, R., *The Trouble with Medical Journals* (London: Royal Society of Medicine Press, 2006).

Soares, A., Santos, N. R., 'Financiamento do Sistema Único de Saúde nos governos FHC, Lula e Dilma', (2014) 38(100) *Saúde em Debate*, 18–25.

Sumner, A., *Global Poverty* (Oxford: Oxford University Press, 2016).

Sunstein, C., 'Against Positive Rights: Why Social and Economic Rights Don't Belong in the New Constitutions of Post-Communist Europe', (1993) 2(1) *Eastern European Constitutional Review*, 35–38.

'Social and Economic Rights? Lessons from South Africa', Coase-Snador Working Paper Series in Law and Economics (2001).

Syrett, K., *Law, Legitimacy and the Rationing of Health Care* (New York: Cambridge University Press, 2007).

Szwarcwald, C. L., Mota, J. C., Damacena, G. N., Pereira, T. G. S., 'Health Inequalities in Rio de Janeiro, Brazil: Lower Healthy Life Expectancy in Socioeconomically Disadvantaged Areas', (2011) 101(3) *American Journal of Public Health*, 517–523.

Szwarcwald, C. L., Souza Júnior, P. R. B., Marques, A. P. et al., 'Inequalities in Healthy Life Expectancy by Brazilian Geographic Regions: Findings from the National Health Survey, 2013', (2016) 15(1) *International Journal for Equity in Health*, 141.

Tate, C. N., Vallinder, T., *The Global Expansion of Judicial Power* (New York: New York University Press, 1997).

Tasioulas, J., *Minimum Core Obligations: Human Rights in the Here and Now* (Washington, DC: World Bank, 2017).

The Minimum Core of the Human Right to Health (Washington, DC: World Bank, 2017).

'Saving Human Rights from Human Rights Law', www.law.berkeley.edu/wp-content/uploads/2019/03/SAVING-HUMAN-RIGHTS-FROM-HUMAN-RIGHTS-LAW-Jan-16-2019.pdf.

Terrazas, F. V., 'O poder judiciário como voz institucional dos pobres: O caso das demandas judiciais por medicamentos', MPhil dissertation, University of São Paulo (2008).

'O poder Judiciário como voz institucional dos pobres: O caso das demandas judiciais de medicamentos', (2010) 253 *Revista de Direito Administrativo*, 79–115.

Tobin, J., *The Right to Health in International Law* (New York: Oxford University Press, 2012).

Torres, I., 'Judicialização do acesso a medicamentos no Brasil: Uma revisão sistemática', MPhil dissertation, Universidade Federal da Bahia: Instituto de Saúde Coletiva (2013).

Tushnet, M., *Taking the Constitution Away from the Courts* (Princeton: Princeton University Press, 1999).

Weak Courts, Strong Rights: Judicial Review and Social Welfare Rights in Comparative Constitutional Law (Princeton: Princeton University Press, 2008).

'New Forms of Judicial Review and the Persistence of Rights- and Democracy-Based Worries', (2003) 38 *Wake Forest Law Review*, 813.

'Social Welfare Rights and the Forms of Judicial Review', (2004) 82 *Texas Law Review*, 1895.

Ucker, J. M., Oliveira, K. R., Bandeira, V. A. C. et al., 'Perfil dos medicamentos fornecidos via processo judicial na assistência farmacêutica do município de Santa Rosa/RS', (2016) 10(1) *Tempus, Actas de Saúde Colet*, 127–149.

Valença, M. M., 'The Lost Decade and the Brazilian Government's Response in the 1990s', (1998) 33(1) *The Journal of Developing Areas*, 1–52.

Vanhala, L., 'Legal Opportunity Structures and the Paradox of Legal Mobilization by the Environmental Movement in the UK', (2012) 46(3) *Law & Society Review*, 523–556.

Ventura, M., Simas, L., Pepe, V. L. E., Schramm, F. R., 'Judicialização da saúde, acesso à justiça e à efetividade do direito à saúde', (2010) 20 *Physis* 77–100.

Vianna, L. W, Burgos, M. B., Salles, P. M., 'Dezessete anos de judicialização da política', (2007) 19(2) *Tempo Social, Revista de Sociologia da USP*, 39–85.

Vianna, L. W., Carvalho, M. A. R., Melo, M. P. C. et al., *A judicialização da política e das relações sociais no Brasil* (Rio de Janeiro: Revan, 1999).

Victora, C. G., Aquino, E. M., do Carmo Leal, M. et al., 'Maternal and Child Health in Brazil: Progress and Challenges', (2011) 377 *Lancet*, 1863–1876.

Vidotti, C. C. F., Castro, L. L. C., Calil, S. S., 'New Drugs in Brazil: Do They Meet Brazilian Public Health Needs?', (2008) 24(1) *Rev Panam Salud Pública*, 36–45.

Vieira, F. S., 'Evolução do Gasto com Medicamentos do Sistema Único de Saúde no Período de 2010 a 2016', Texto para Discussão 2356 (2008).

Vieira, F. S., Benevides, R. P. S., 'O Direito à Saúde no Brasil em Tempos de Crise Econômica, Ajuste Fiscal e Reforma Implícita do Estado', (2016) 10(3) *Revista de Estudos e Pesquisas sobre as Américas*, dx.doi.org/10.21057/repam.v10i3.21860.

Vieira, F. S., Zucchi, P., 'Distorções causadas pelas ações judiciais à política de medicamentos no Brasil', (2007) 41(2) *Revista de Saúde Pública*, 214–222.

Vilhena, O. V., *A Batalha dos Poderes* (São Paulo: Cia das Letras, 2019).

Da transição democrática ao mal-estar constitucional (São Paulo: Cia das Letras, 2018).

Vilhena, O. V., Baxi, U., Viljoen, F. (eds.), *Transformative Constitutionalism: Comparing the Apex Courts of Brazil, India and South Africa* (Pretoria: Pretoria University Law Press, 2013).

Xavier, C. A., 'Judicialização da Saúde: Perspectiva Crítica sobre os Gastos da União para o Cumprimento das Ordens Judiciais', in CONASS (eds.), *Coletânea Direito à Saúde Dilemas do Fenômeno da Judicialização da Saúde*, 1st ed. (Brasília: Conselho Nacional de Secretários de Saúde – CONASS, 2018).

Waldron, J., *Law and Disagreement* (Oxford: Clarendon Press, 1999).

Wang, D. W. L., 'From Wednesbury Unreasonableness to Accountability for Reasonableness', (2017) 76(3) *The Cambridge Law Journal*, 642–670.

'A fumaça do retrocesso', *F. de São Paulo*, 6 April 2019, www1.folha.uol.com.br/autores/daniel-wei-l-wang.shtml.

'Social Rights Adjudication and the Nirvana Fallacy', (2018) 3(July) *Public Law*, 482–499.

Wang, D. W. L., Ferraz, O. L. M., 'Reaching Out to the Needy? Access to Justice and Public Attorneys' Role in Right to Health Litigation in the City of São Paulo', (2013) 10(18) *SUR International Journal on Human Rights*, 159–179.

Pharmaceutical Companies vs. the State: Who Is Responsible for Post-Trial Provision of Drugs in Brazil? (2012) 40(2) *The Journal of Law, Medicine & Ethics*, 188–196.

Wang, D. W. L., Franco, D., Terrazas, F. et al., 'Judiciário e fornecimento de insulinas análogas pelo sistema público de saúde: Direitos, ciência e políticas públicas', Casoteca GV (no date), https://direitosp.fgv.br/casoteca/judiciario-fornecimento-de-insulinas-analogas-pelo-sistema-publico-de-saude-direitos-cienci.

Webber, G., Yowell, P., Ekins, R. et al., *Legislated Rights: Securing Human Rights through Legislation* (Cambridge: Cambridge University Press, 2018).

Westin, R., 'Por 100 anos, analfabeto foi proibido de votar no Brasil [For One Hundred Years the Illiterate was forbidden to vote in Brazil]', Senadonotícias, 4 November 2016.

Williamson, J., 'What Washington Means by Policy Reform', in Williamson, J. (ed.), *Latin American Adjustment: How Much Has Happened?*, https://piie.com/commentary/speeches-papers/what-washington-means-policy-reform.

Williamson, J., 'What Washington Means by Policy Reform', in Williamson, J. 'A Short History of the Washington Consensus' (2004), https://piie.com/publications/papers/williamson0904-2.pdf.

World Health Organization (WHO), *Model List of Essential Medicines*, 20th ed. (Geneva: WHO, 2017).

World Health Statistics 2017 (Geneva: WHO, 2017), 29–30, http://apps.who.int/iris/bitstream/10665/255336/1/9789241565486-eng.pdf?ua=1.

Yamin, A., 'Will We Take Suffering Seriously? Reflections on What Applying a Human Rights Framework to Health Means and Why We Should Care', (2008) 10(1) *Health and Human Rights*, 45–63.

Yamin, A. E., Gloppen, S. (eds.), *Litigation Health Rights* (Cambridge, MA: Harvard University Press, 2011).

Young, K., 'The Minimum Core of Economic and Social Rights: A Concept in Search of Content', (2008) 33 *Yale International Law Journal* 113–175.

Zaffalon, L., Cardoso, L. Z. L., *A Política da Justiça: Blindar as Elites, Criminalizar os Pobres* (São Paulo: Hucitec, 2018).

INDEX

Books in the Series

Diseases of the Will: Alcohol and the Dilemmas of Freedom Mariana Valverde

The Politics of Truth and Reconciliation in South Africa: Legitimizing the Post-Apartheid State Richard A. Wilson

Modernism and the Grounds of Law Peter Fitzpatrick

Unemployment and Government: Genealogies of the Social William Walters

Autonomy and Ethnicity: Negotiating Competing Claims in Multi-Ethnic States Yash Ghai

Constituting Democracy: Law, Globalism and South Africa's Political Reconstruction Heinz Klug

The Ritual of Rights in Japan: Law, Society, and Health Policy Eric A. Feldman

Governing Morals: A Social History of Moral Regulation Alan Hunt

The Colonies of Law: Colonialism, Zionism and Law in Early Mandate Palestine Ronen Shamir

Law and Nature David Delaney

Social Citizenship and Workfare in the United States and Western Europe: The Paradox of Inclusion Joel F. Handler

Law, Anthropology, and the Constitution of the Social: Making Persons and Things Edited by Alain Pottage and Martha Mundy

Judicial Review and Bureaucratic Impact: International and Interdisciplinary Perspectives Edited by Marc Hertogh and Simon Halliday

Immigrants at the Margins: Law, Race, and Exclusion in Southern Europe Kitty Calavita

Lawyers and Regulation: The Politics of the Administrative Process Patrick Schmidt

Law and Globalization from Below: Toward a Cosmopolitan Legality Edited by Boaventura de Sousa Santos and Cesar A. Rodriguez-Garavito

Public Accountability: Designs, Dilemmas and Experiences Edited by Michael W. Dowdle

Law, Violence and Sovereignty among West Bank Palestinians Tobias Kelly

Legal Reform and Administrative Detention Powers in China Sarah Biddulph

The Practice of Human Rights: Tracking Law between the Global and the Local Edited by Mark Goodale and Sally Engle Merry

Judges beyond Politics in Democracy and Dictatorship: Lessons from Chile Lisa Hilbink

Paths to International Justice: Social and Legal Perspectives Edited by Marie-Bénédicte Dembour and Tobias Kelly

Law and Society in Vietnam: The Transition from Socialism in Comparative Perspective Mark Sidel

Constitutionalizing Economic Globalization: Investment Rules and Democracy's Promise David Schneiderman

The New World Trade Organization Knowledge Agreements: 2nd Edition Christopher Arup

Justice and Reconciliation in Post-Apartheid South Africa Edited by François du Bois and Antje du Bois-Pedain

Militarization and Violence against Women in Conflict Zones in the Middle East: A Palestinian Case-Study Nadera Shalhoub-Kevorkian

Child Pornography and Sexual Grooming: Legal and Societal Responses Suzanne Ost

Darfur and the Crime of Genocide John Hagan and Wenona Rymond-Richmond

Fictions of Justice: The International Criminal Court and the Challenge of Legal Pluralism in Sub-Saharan Africa Kamari Maxine Clarke

Conducting Law and Society Research: Reflections on Methods and Practices Simon Halliday and Patrick Schmidt

Planted Flags: Trees, Land, and Law in Israel/Palestine Irus Braverman

Culture under Cross-Examination: International Justice and the Special Court for Sierra Leone Tim Kelsall

Cultures of Legality: Judicialization and Political Activism in Latin America Javier Couso, Alexandra Huneeus, and Rachel Sieder

Courting Democracy in Bosnia and Herzegovina: The Hague Tribunal's Impact in a Postwar State Lara J. Nettelfield

The Gacaca Courts, Post-Genocide Justice and Reconciliation in Rwanda: Justice without Lawyers Phil Clark

Law, Society, and History: Themes in the Legal Sociology and Legal History of Lawrence M. Friedman Edited by Robert W. Gordon and Morton J. Horwitz

After Abu Ghraib: Exploring Human Rights in America and the Middle East Shadi Mokhtari

Adjudication in Religious Family Laws: Cultural Accommodation, Legal Pluralism, and Gender Equality in India Gopika Solanki

Water on Tap: Rights and Regulation in the Transnational Governance of Urban Water Services Bronwen Morgan

Elements of Moral Cognition: Rawls' Linguistic Analogy and the Cognitive Science of Moral and Legal Judgment John Mikhail

Mitigation and Aggravation at Sentencing Edited by Julian V. Roberts

Institutional Inequality and the Mobilization of the Family and Medical Leave Act: Rights on Leave Catherine R. Albiston

Authoritarian Rule of Law: Legislation, Discourse and Legitimacy in Singapore Jothie Rajah

Law and Development and the Global Discourses of Legal Transfers Edited by John Gillespie and Pip Nicholson

Law against the State: Ethnographic Forays into Law's Transformations Edited by Julia Eckert, Brian Donahoe, Christian Strümpell and Zerrin Özlem Biner

Transnational Legal Ordering and State Change Edited by Gregory C. Shaffer

Legal Mobilization under Authoritarianism: The Case of Post-Colonial Hong Kong Waikeung Tam

Complementarity in the Line of Fire: The Catalysing Effect of the International Criminal Court in Uganda and Sudan Sarah M. H. Nouwen

Political and Legal Transformations of an Indonesian Polity: The Nagari from Colonisation to Decentralisation Franz von Benda-Beckmann and Keebet von Benda-Beckmann

Pakistan's Experience with Formal Law: An Alien Justice Osama Siddique

Human Rights under State-Enforced Religious Family Laws in Israel, Egypt, and India Yüksel Sezgin

Why Prison? Edited by David Scott

Law's Fragile State: Colonial, Authoritarian, and Humanitarian Legacies in Sudan Mark Fathi Massoud

Rights for Others: The Slow Home-Coming of Human Rights in the Netherlands Barbara Oomen

European States and Their Muslim Citizens: The Impact of Institutions on Perceptions and Boundaries Edited by John R. Bowen, Christophe Bertossi, Jan Willem Duyvendak, and Mona Lena Krook

Environmental Litigation in China: A Study in Political Ambivalence Rachel E. Stern

Indigeneity and Legal Pluralism in India: Claims, Histories, Meanings Pooja Parmar

Paper Tiger: Law, Bureaucracy and the Developmental State in Himalayan India Nayanika Mathur

Religion, Law and Society Russell Sandberg

The Experiences of Face Veil Wearers in Europe and the Law Edited by Eva Brems

The Contentious History of the International Bill of Human Rights Christopher N. J. Roberts

Transnational Legal Orders Edited by Terence C. Halliday and Gregory Shaffer

Lost in China? Law, Culture and Society in Post-1997 Hong Kong Carol A. G. Jones

Security Theology, Surveillance and the Politics of Fear Nadera Shalhoub-Kevorkian

Opposing the Rule of Law: How Myanmar's Courts Make Law and Order Nick Cheesman

The Ironies of Colonial Governance: Law, Custom and Justice in Colonial India James Jaffe

The Clinic and the Court: Law, Medicine and Anthropology Edited by Ian Harper, Tobias Kelly, and Akshay Khanna

A World of Indicators: The Making of Government Knowledge through Quantification Edited by Richard Rottenburg, Sally Engle Merry, Sung-Joon Park, and Johanna Mugler

Contesting Immigration Policy in Court: Legal Activism and Its Radiating Effects in the United States and France Leila Kawar

The Quiet Power of Indicators: Measuring Governance, Corruption, and Rule of Law Edited by Sally Engle Merry, Kevin Davis, and Benedict Kingsbury

Investing in Authoritarian Rule: Punishment and Patronage in Rwanda's Gacaca Courts for Genocide Crimes Anuradha Chakravarty

Contractual Knowledge: One Hundred Years of Legal Experimentation in Global Markets Edited by Grégoire Mallard and Jérôme Sgard

Iraq and the Crimes of Aggressive War: The Legal Cynicism of Criminal Militarism John Hagan, Joshua Kaiser, and Anna Hanson

Culture in the Domains of Law Edited by René Provost

China and Islam: The Prophet, the Party, and Law Matthew S. Erie

Diversity in Practice: Race, Gender, and Class in Legal and Professional Careers Edited by Spencer Headworth and Robert Nelson

A Sociology of Constitutions: Constitutions and State Legitimacy in Historical-Sociological Perspective Chris Thornhill

A Sociology of Transnational Constitutions: Social Foundations of the Post-National Legal Structure Chris Thornhill

Shifting Legal Visions: Judicial Change and Human Rights Trials in Latin America Ezequiel A. González Ocantos

The Demographic Transformations of Citizenship Heli Askola

Criminal Defense in China: The Politics of Lawyers at Work Sida Liu and Terence C. Halliday

Contesting Economic and Social Rights in Ireland: Constitution, State and Society, 1848–2016 Thomas Murray

Buried in the Heart: Women, Complex Victimhood and the War in Northern Uganda Erin Baines

Palaces of Hope: The Anthropology of Global Organizations Edited by Ronald Niezen and Maria Sapignoli

The Politics of Bureaucratic Corruption in Post-Transitional Eastern Europe Marina Zaloznaya

Revisiting the Law and Governance of Trafficking, Forced Labor and Modern Slavery Edited by Prabha Kotiswaran

Incitement on Trial: Prosecuting International Speech Crimes Richard Ashby Wilson

Criminalizing Children: Welfare and the State in Australia David McCallum

Global Lawmakers: International Organizations in the Crafting of World Markets Susan Block-Lieb and Terence C. Halliday

Duties to Care: Dementia, Relationality and Law Rosie Harding

Insiders, Outsiders, Injuries, and Law: Revisiting "The Oven Bird's Song" Edited by Mary Nell Trautner

Hunting Justice: Displacement, Law, and Activism in the Kalahari Maria Sapignoli

Injury and Injustice: The Cultural Politics of Harm and Redress Edited by Anne Bloom, David M. Engel, and Michael McCann

Ruling Before the Law: The Politics of Legal Regimes in China and Indonesia William Hurst

The Powers of Law: A Comparative Analysis of Sociopolitical Legal Studies Mauricio García-Villegas

A Sociology of Justice in Russia Edited by Marina Kurkchiyan and Agnieszka Kubal

Constituting Religion: Islam, Liberal Rights, and the Malaysian State Tamir Moustafa

The Invention of the Passport: Surveillance, Citizenship and the State, Second Edition John C. Torpey

Law's Trials: The Performance of Legal Institutions in the US "War on Terror" Richard L. Abel

Law's Wars: The Fate of the Rule of Law in the US "War on Terror" Richard L. Abel

Transforming Gender Citizenship: The Irresistible Rise of Gender Quotas in Europe Edited by Eléonore Lépinard and Ruth Rubio-Marín

Muslim Women's Quest for Justice: Gender, Law and Activism in India Mengia Hong Tschalaer

Children as 'Risk': Sexual Exploitation and Abuse by Children and Young People Anne-Marie McAlinden

The Legal Process and the Promise of Justice: Studies Inspired by the Work of Malcolm Feeley Jonathan Simon, Rosann Greenspan, Hadar Aviram

Sovereign Exchanges: Gifts, Trusts, Reparations, and Other Fetishes of International Solidarity Grégoire Mallard

Measuring Justice: Quantitative Accountability and the National Prosecuting Authority in South Africa Johanna Mugler

Negotiating the Power of NGOs: Women's Legal Rights in South Africa Reem Wael

Indigenous Water Rights in Law and Regulation: Lessons from Comparative Experience Elizabeth Jane Macpherson

The Edge of Law: Legal Geographies of a War Crimes Court Alex Jeffrey

Everyday Justice: Law, Ethnography, and Injustice Sandra Brunnegger

The Uncounted: Politics of Data in Global Health Sara L. M. Davis

Transnational Legal Ordering of Criminal Justice Gregory Shaffer and Ely Aaronson

Health as a Human Right: The Politics and Judicialisation of Health in Brazil Octávio Luiz Motta Ferraz

For EU product safety concerns, contact us at Calle de José Abascal, 56–1°, 28003 Madrid, Spain or eugpsr@cambridge.org.

www.ingramcontent.com/pod-product-compliance
Lightning Source LLC
LaVergne TN
LVHW052031200926
848481LV00005B/1643
* 9 7 8 1 1 0 8 7 2 9 0 1 7 *